MATERIALS in TODAY'S WORLD
third edition

Peter Thrower
Pennsylvania State University

Thomas Mason
Northwestern University

 **Learning Solutions**

Boston   Burr Ridge, IL   Dubuque, IA   New York   San Francisco   St. Louis
Bangkok   Bogotá   Caracas   Lisbon   London   Madrid
Mexico City   Milan   New Delhi   Seoul   Singapore   Sydney   Taipei   Toronto

Materials in Today's World, Third Edition

1 2 3 4 5 6 7 8 9 0 BLA BLA 0 9 8

ISBN-13: 978-0-07-340882-8
ISBN-10: 0-07-340882-4

*Cover Photo: Atomic force microscopy image of a DNA-encapsulated single-walled carbon
nanotube. The periodic modulation in height along the length of the nanotube is consistent
with the proposed helical wrapping of DNA around single-walled carbon nanotubes. Image
size = 80 nm x 80 nm. Courtesy of the Hersam Research Group, Northwestern University.*

Learning Solutions Specialist: Thomas Weitz
Production Editor: Nicole Baumgartner
Printer/Binder: Perfect Printing

ABOUT THE AUTHORS

Peter A. Thrower is professor emeritus of materials science in the Materials Science and Engineering Department of the Pennsylvania State University in State College, Pennsylvania. He received a B.A. degree in physics from Cambridge University and was later awarded a Ph.D. degree by the same university. Dr. Thrower was a teacher of graduate and undergraduate courses in materials science, with particular interest in making the subject interesting to students entering the major, and to those who have no leaning towards things scientific whatsoever. His own research interests are concerned with carbon materials, and he has been Editor-in-Chief of the international scientific journal *Carbon* since 1983.

Thomas O. Mason is professor of Materials Science and Engineering at Northwestern University in Evanston, Illinois. He received a B.S. degree in ceramic science from the Pennsylvania State University and a Ph.D. degree in materials science and engineering from the Massachusetts Institute of Technology. Dr. Mason teaches undergraduate and graduate courses in materials science, with a special interest in "introductory" courses for majors (e.g., thermodynamics) and non-majors (e.g., the subject of this book). His own research involves the study of electronically and ionically conductive electroceramics, with a more recent interest in the learning and teaching of nanoscience/nanotechnology.

This book is dedicated to our wives who, as daughters of Sarah,
"do well, and are not afraid..." (I Peter 3 v. 6)

CONTENTS

Preface   vii

1. INTRODUCTION   1

2. WHAT IS MATERIALS SCIENCE AND ENGINEERING?   5

3. THE MATERIALS SCIENCE AND ENGINEERING PARADIGM   9

4. MATERIALS PROPERTIES   21

5. BONDING   25

QUESTIONS: CHAPTERS 1–5   36

6. CRYSTAL STRUCTURES   39

7. AMORPHOUS MATERIALS   51

8. DEFECTS IN SOLIDS   55

QUESTIONS: CHAPTERS 6–8   66

9. WHAT DO WE MEAN BY 'STRONG'?   69

QUESTIONS: CHAPTER 9   76

10. MAKING METALS STRONGER
      or HOW TO STOP THOSE DISLOCATIONS MOVING   77

11. CASE STUDY: ALUMINUM-LITHIUM ALLOYS FOR AEROSPACE   85

12. CASE STUDY: MAGNESIUM ALLOYS, POTENTIAL
      LIGHTWEIGHT AEROSPACE MATERIALS   93

13. CASE STUDY: HSLA STEELS FOR CAR BODIES   95

QUESTIONS: CHAPTERS 10–13   101

14. POLYMERS ARE NOT JUST PLASTIC   103

15. POLYETHYLENE: THE MOST COMMON POLYMER   111

16. CASE STUDY: FROM RUBBER TO HIPS TO ABS   119

17. POLYMER RECYCLING   125

QUESTIONS: CHAPTERS 14–17   128

18. HOW HEAT AFFECTS MATERIALS   131

19. CERAMICS: DO THEY HAVE TO BE BRITTLE?   137

20. CASE STUDY: GLASS-CERAMICS FOR COOKWARE   143

21. CAN CERAMICS BE TOUGH? THE ZIRCONIA STORY   149

QUESTIONS: CHAPTERS 18–21   153

22. COMPOSITE MATERIALS—GETTING THE BEST OF TWO (OR MORE) WORLDS   157

23. CASE STUDY: CARBON/CARBON COMPOSITES   161

QUESTIONS: CHAPTERS 22–23   170

24. ELECTRONS IN MATERIALS   173

25. ELECTRON INTERACTIONS WITH LIGHT or SOME CAUSES OF COLOR   183

QUESTIONS: CHAPTERS 24–25   191

26. ELECTRONS IN SEMICONDUCTORS   193

27. SEMICONDUCTOR DEVICES   199

28. CHANGING THE CONDUCTIVITY OF MATERIALS   207

QUESTIONS: CHAPTERS 26–28   211

29. THE OPTICAL BEHAVIOR OF MATERIALS   215

30. CASE STUDY: OPTICAL FIBERS FOR TELECOMMUNICATIONS   223

QUESTIONS: CHAPTERS 29–30   231

31. MAGNETIC MATERIALS   233

QUESTIONS: CHAPTER 31   242

32. NANOMATERIALS   245

33. CASE STUDY: NANOELECTRONICS   253

34. BIOMATERIALS   257

QUESTIONS: CHAPTERS 32–34   261

SUMMARY QUESTIONS   263

GLOSSARY   267

SOLUTIONS TO QUESTIONS   285

INDEX   289

Preface to the third edition

It seems impossible that it is now thirteen years since the second edition of this book was written. I (PAT) had written the first edition for a general education course I was teaching at The Pennsylvania State University. It was written in the space of six weeks of intense activity in the Spring of 1990 so that it could be available for the upcoming semester. Even now I find this difficult to believe! The need for a second edition was prompted by a course enrolment that had grown to a thousand each semester, and by the need to add new material. At that time (1995) I had already planned to retire in three years and the thought of a third edition never entered my mind. It was therefore a great surprise and pleasure to be approached by Tom Mason with a suggestion that we collaborate on this new edition.

Tom had been an undergraduate student at Penn State during my early years there and we had stayed in contact during his career. I knew that he had been using the book for a course he teaches at Northwestern University and my immediate reaction was therefore positive.

In the preface to the second edition I wrote: "I never cease to wonder at the materials developments of the last few decades, which have had such an amazing influence on so much of what we do. As a skier I am aware of the tremendous differences in equipment that have occurred in the last thirty years. Composites and polymers have created boots and skis that were but a dream when I made my first 'run'. The same can probably be said of other sporting activities. When I was a student we did not have portable cassette players and pocket calculators; they are the result of quite recent materials' developments. Advances in semiconductors, electronics and computers are still continuing at a tremendous pace, and the revolution promised by optical fiber communication is perhaps one development we can realistically anticipate in the lifetimes of today's students."

Preparing this third edition has forced us to consider changes that have occurred in the last decade. In the extract from the preface to the second edition I mentioned "cassette players", but they are already a thing of the past. Magnetic recording tape for domestic applications has almost disappeared. Audio cassette players in automobiles were once standard but are now replaced by CD players and iPods. A few camcorders still use a magnetic tape cassette but hard drives are taking over. On the recent need to replace a small TV, I was amazed to find that the local stores sold nothing but TVs with flat panel screens. The old vacuum tube sets with a screen of phosphor dots had disappeared! Video cassette recorders and VHS tapes have also disappeared from the scene.

We cannot pretend to have addressed all such changes in this book and the near future will undoubtedly bring others that we have not anticipated. The original aim of the book remains "to better prepare today's students for the exciting materials developments that await them in future years, and provide some understanding of the new materials that are already affecting our daily lives."

There are always many people to thank during the writing of any book and support from colleagues and students is gratefully acknowledged. In particular PAT would like to recognise his former department head, Dr. Richard Tressler, who sadly died recently. Dick recognised the value of the course to the Department of Materials Science and Engineering at Penn State, from both prestige and financial aspects. TOM would like to similarly thank current and former department chairmen, Peter Voorhees and Kathy Faber for their support of the "Modern Materials & Society" course at Northwestern. He would also like to thank the many former and current TAs, who have helped run the many exhibits and demos for this course over the years, but the list is prohibitively long. You know who you are, and you have my heartfelt thanks!

In the second edition, PAT wrote "Last, but by no means least, I must thank my wife Carol for her patience and encouragement during the writing of this revision." That is equally true for this 2nd revision, to which TOM "seconds the motion" by expressing his "thanks to my wife Gayle for her wonderful support and encouragement throughout the process."

Peter A. Thrower   *June, 2008*
Thomas O. Mason

Acknowledgments:

We are grateful to Tom Ruznak, Pat Winand and Paul Howell for help with some of the photographs taken for this book. We are also grateful to Kendra Erk, Zack Feinberg, Danny Jorgensen, Eugene Pushuck, Nicola Perry, Cynthia Pierre, and Michelle Seitz for their help in finding all our mistakes.

1. INTRODUCTION

Materials have always played a major role in man's development. Indeed archaeology recognizes this by the names assigned to stages in this development. For example, the stone, bronze and iron ages are named according to the then best available materials for implements and/or weapons.

During these early times man became aware of the ability to change the nature and properties of the materials available. To heat a paste of clay and water and produce a pot resembling stone must have given early man a sense of achievement and control over the matter around him, which was totally new. By 4000 B.C. man had learned to use metals, with naturally occurring (native) copper being shaped for both ornament and implement. At this stage it was learned that heat helped to soften the metal and hence aided the forming process. There then followed (3000–1000 B.C.) the importance of bronze, a metal formed by mixing molten copper and tin. This is perhaps the first man-made **alloy**, a mixture of metals.

Of course at the same time there were many elaborate techniques developed for forming gold and silver into beautiful jewelry. Many of these manufacturing methods have had to be rediscovered in recent years. It may be hard to believe that such arts could be lost, but it is a fact that many of the techniques used to make jewelry found in the ancient tombs of the middle east had to be reinvented.

The iron age followed, but there were no facilities to produce pure metal and it was only iron which contained large amounts of carbon which could be melted and cast into shapes, hence the term **cast iron**. The crude iron which was formed and shaped by hammering always contained large inclusions and lots of impurities which weakened the material.

Iron ore obtained from the earth, mostly in the form of iron oxides, was heated in a charcoal hearth. The carbon in the charcoal reacted with the iron oxide to produce carbon dioxide and iron, the former escaping as a gas and leaving iron behind as a spongy mass which could be formed by hammering, etc., as already mentioned. Continued heating caused some of the carbon atoms to move into the iron producing what we now know as steel. Eventually the iron would take up enough carbon to form cast iron, which is quite brittle.

We should note here that there were quite drastic changes occurring in the iron during all this, but the metal workers were totally unaware of them. In fact some of their conclusions were the opposite of the truth. Fire was known to have a purifying influence. In biblical times the concept of "refined by fire" was well established. It was therefore natural to assume that the harder, stronger and more brittle material was the result of purification, whereas it was the dissolving of carbon in the iron, which was producing the effect. Nowadays we are well aware that impurities can have a dramatic effect on the properties of materials, sometimes bad and sometimes beneficial, but the ancient blacksmiths were unaware of these facts. In fact, we shall see that defects and impurities in a material are what largely dictate its properties.

Many materials that have been made in man's history were developed by empirical, or we could even say accidental, techniques. The manufacturing methods worked! The steel in some old Japanese swords is a good example of this. The reason for the remarkable properties of this material was not known until relatively recently, and the manufacturing techniques had to be rediscovered.

During the following years it is obvious that a large body of knowledge was developed, which was purely empirical, meaning that it was known that a certain treatment, heating, alloying, hammering, etc., produced a certain effect on the metal's properties, but the reasons given were either completely unknown or wrong. The sixteenth century saw the publication of the first three books which catalogued this knowledge, the most famous of which is probably *De Re Metallica* by Georgius Agricola, the title of which means 'about metallic things.'

During the eighteenth and nineteenth centuries iron and steel became cheaper and their properties, mainly strength, improved. However, little was yet known about their structure. In 1864 an Englishman called Henry Sorby was responsible for a major breakthrough. He developed a technique for chemically removing, or etching, the surface layer of a polished metal specimen and then examining it in a microscope under reflected light. For the first time it was possible to see that the material consisted of a number of small interlocking **grains** or **crystals**. Different grains appeared to have a different brightness in the reflected light microscope he used. For the first time the **microstructure** of a material was revealed, i.e., metals are typically made of a large number of crystals oriented in different directions, and fitted together and joined along special boundaries called **grain boundaries**.

This first view of microstructure was very revealing, but it was not until the twentieth century that one can say that materials science truly developed. The question of "how" materials behaved was transformed to the question of "why" they behaved as they did. Modern techniques such as x-ray diffraction, electron microscopy, etc., have enabled us probe the structures of materials and understand what makes them behave the way they do (**materials science**). More recently, we have been able, as a result of this understanding, to design new ways of intentionally altering the microstructure of materials, thereby improving their properties (**materials engineering**).

The first Departments of Materials Science at universities were established in the 1950's and 1960's. Many of these were based on existing Departments of Metallurgy, because metals were then the materials about which most was known. Some universities also had Ceramic Science departments, and these too were incorporated into the new departments. Along the way, polymer science (the science of plastics) became an equal partner with metals and ceramics. Today there are Departments of Materials Science and Engineering at most major universities worldwide. With the increased importance of electronic and photonic (light-related) applications for high speed information processing and communications, electronic materials (semiconductors) are now an important component in most Departments of Materials Science and Engineering.

Throughout man's history, materials have been "enablers" of technological innovation. As the new century/millennium opens, this continues to be the case. For example, there is a limit to how far we can downsize the dimensions of microelectronic integrated chips or IC's with the current approach. This downsizing determines the speed and memory capacity of such devices. To go further, we will need a nanoelectronic revolution, and the new field of **nanomaterials** will lead the way. (A nanometer is a thousand times small than a micrometer, which is a hundred times smaller than the period at the end of this sentence.) Another emerging area involves **biomaterials**, where a materials science approach (see the next chapter) is brought to bear in assembling new tissues and structures of interest to biology. Such materials hold the prospect for greatly improving the quality of human life!

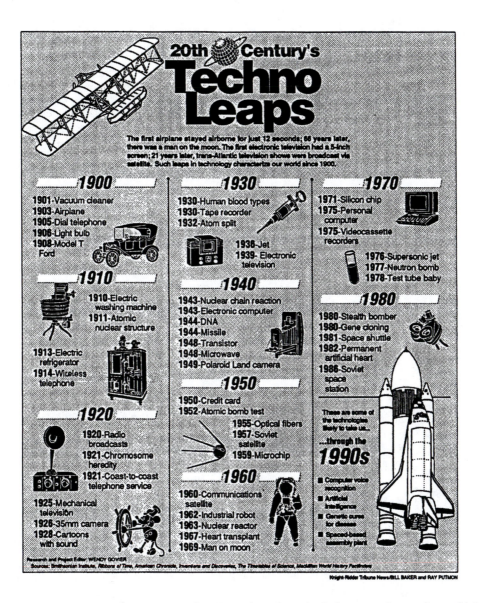

20th Century's Techno Leaps

The first airplane stayed airborne for just 12 seconds; 66 years later, there was a man on the moon. The first electronic television had a 5-inch screen; 21 years later, trans-Atlantic television shows were broadcast via satellite. Such leaps in technology characterize our world since 1900.

1900
- 1901-Vacuum cleaner
- 1903-Airplane
- 1905-Dial telephone
- 1906-Light bulb
- 1908-Model T Ford

1910
- 1910-Electric washing machine
- 1911-Atomic nuclear structure
- 1913-Electric refrigerator
- 1914-Wireless telephone

1920
- 1920-Radio broadcasts
- 1921-Chromosome heredity
- 1921-Coast-to-coast telephone service
- 1925-Mechanical television
- 1926-35mm camera
- 1928-Cartoons with sound

1930
- 1930-Human blood types
- 1930-Tape recorder
- 1932-Atom split
- 1938-Jet
- 1939-Electronic television

1940
- 1943-Nuclear chain reaction
- 1943-Electronic computer
- 1944-DNA
- 1944-Missile
- 1948-Transistor
- 1948-Microwave
- 1949-Polaroid Land camera

1950
- 1950-Credit card
- 1952-Atomic bomb test
- 1955-Optical fibers
- 1957-Soviet satellite
- 1959-Microchip

1960
- 1960-Communications satellite
- 1962-Industrial robot
- 1963-Nuclear reactor
- 1967-Heart transplant
- 1969-Man on moon

1970
- 1971-Silicon chip
- 1975-Personal computer
- 1975-Videocassette recorders
- 1976-Supersonic jet
- 1977-Neutron bomb
- 1978-Test tube baby

1980
- 1980-Stealth bomber
- 1980-Gene cloning
- 1981-Space shuttle
- 1982-Permanent artificial heart
- 1986-Soviet space station

These are some of the technologies likely to take us...

...through the **1990s**
- Computer voice recognition
- Artificial intelligence
- Genetic cures for disease
- Space-based assembly plant

Research and Project Editor: WENDY GOVIER
Sources: Smithsonian Institute, Ribbons of Time, American Chronicle, Inventors and Discoveries, The Timetable of Science, MacMillan World History Factfinder

Knight-Ridder Tribune News/BILL BAKER and RAY PUTMON

The tabulation of '20th Century Techno Leaps' as above includes many innovations which were the result of new materials developments—the development of synthetic polymers, the invention of stainless steel, fine particle magnets for magnetic tape in both audio and video tape recording, optical fibers for high speed communications and medical instrumentation, lightweight materials for avionics and space travel, pure silicon for microelectronics and the proliferation of personal computers, etc.—all can be traced to the development of new materials.

And when future generations read the history books (or investigate our garbage dumps), what will they call our current age? Several possibilities come to mind: the uranium age, or the age of plastics, or the silicon age. Others may occur to you.

This book is designed to give some insight into why materials behave as they do and how their properties can be changed and improved, hopefully to the benefit of society. Some of today's newer materials are highlighted in more detail as specific examples of our recent accomplishments. Here are **science** and **engineering** as they affect our everyday lives! It is hoped that the concepts presented can be appreciated with very little scientific and mathematical background. It is also hoped that the material and its presentation will be interesting and informative. We begin by considering science and engineering, and more specifically, materials science (why materials behave the way they do) and materials engineering (how we can control the structure and properties of materials through careful processing).

2. WHAT IS MATERIALS SCIENCE AND ENGINEERING?

Before we answer this question, it will help to understand the processes of "science" vs. "engineering." The scientific method has three important steps: observation, hypothesis, and experimentation. Scientists make observations and form hypotheses. They then carry out experiments to confirm their hypotheses. For example, in the 16th century Copernicus made observations of the motions of the stars and the phases of the moon and hypothesized that smaller heavenly bodies (satellites) orbited around larger heavenly bodies (including the earth around the sun). It was not until a century later, however, that Galileo, employing the latest in modern technology (a telescope copied from a Dutch design), viewed the four principal moons orbiting the planet Jupiter. Copernicus' hypothesis had been confirmed. It is only when other scientists are able to repeat one's experiments with the same outcome that a confirmed hypothesis becomes "scientific fact."

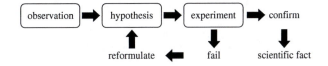

Schematic of the scientific method.

The process of engineering design is somewhat different. If scientists are explorers, engineers are problem-solvers. The stages of engineering design are: analysis (of a problem), design (of a solution), and fabrication or implementation. Keep in mind that some engineers make "things," e.g., an electrical engineer fabricating a microelectronic circuit or a civil engineer overseeing construction of a bridge. Other engineers might make software programs to solve problems, like how best to do word processing on a personal computer (e.g., Microsoft). An important part of the design process is "prototyping" (e.g., making a sample product, or "beta" version if software), which can be tested to see if it delivers the prescribed solution to the original problem.

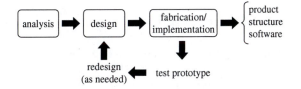

Schematic of the engineering design process.

So where does materials science and engineering fit in? Materials science is the study of processing-structure and structure-property relationships in materials of various kinds. Think of these relationships as links in a chain. The first chain link is between processing and structure. Processing is how a given material is fabricated. Structure refers to the internal architecture of the resulting material, and will be more fully described in the next chapter. The next link is between structure and properties. This link is very important, since it determines the usefulness of the resulting material. For example, the fibrous/highly porous structure of a ceramic tile on the space shuttle protects the hull from heat (or does not, if damaged!). Materials scientists study the relationships between processing and structure and between structure and properties (top-down). Materials engineers exploit these relationships to fabricate materials with designed properties (bottom-up).

How does this differ from what other engineers do? Well, the properties resulting from the materials science and engineering paradigm become the "materials" from which other engineers make their products/structures, whether micro-electronic circuits or bridges. The key outcome of such engineering is "performance," whether one is talking about load-bearing capacity (as in a bridge) or processing speed (as in a computer). Ultimately, performance is intimately linked with the properties of the materials used to make those products/structures. So materials scientists discover and materials engineers design the materials needed by other engineers to make the "stuff" on which much of our modern society is based.

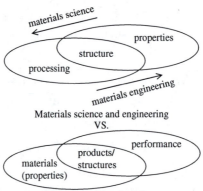

Materials science and engineering
VS.

Other engineering disciplines.

Comparison of materials science and engineering with other engineering disciplines.

Materials scientists and engineers are always going about the process of discovering/developing new materials. New materials may be roughly divided into two types: (a) those that are made by combining **elements** which have not been previously combined, and (b) those that are made by modifying existing materials.

We have just used the term "element". A chemical element is essentially a basic building block for materials. It is "a substance which cannot be resolved by chemical means into simpler substances". We are all familiar with the elements oxygen, iron, copper, carbon, aluminum, hydrogen, nitrogen. . . . We may be less familiar with germanium, nickel, boron, titanium, tungsten . . . We may have never heard of, and will probably never see a clump of gadolinium, dysprosium, holmium. . . . There are about a hundred elements which are arranged by scientists into an array known as the Periodic Table (shown in next page). The number given to the element denotes the number of electrons and protons it contains. Elements in the same column have somewhat similar properties. You may know that silicon (Si) and germanium (Ge) are semiconductors, and that neon (Ne) and argon (Ar) are inert gases, and by the end of this book you should be aware of some other similarities such as carbon (C) and silicon (Si), and oxygen (O) and sulfur (S). Note that the great majority of elements are metals and that nearly all the non-metals are in the upper right corner of the table.

Many scientists memorize at least the first fifty or so elements in the periodic table, but there is no need for you to do so. When one of the authors was in high school he remembers a chemistry teacher

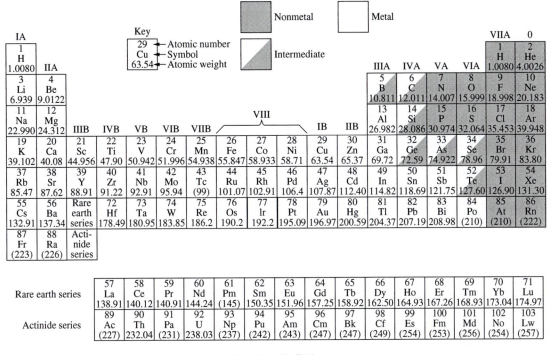

The Periodic Table

(W. D. Callister, Jr., *Materials Science and Engineering*, John Wiley, New York, 1985. Fig. 2.6)

Note: Elements with atomic numbers of 104 and higher are omitted since they are rarely used by materials scientists.

saying, "**H**e **L**ikes **B**eef **B**ut **C**an **N**ot **O**btain **F**ood", and this little memory aid for the first row of the periodic table has never been forgotten. Perhaps you too will find it useful.

An example of new materials resulting from combining elements which had not previously been combined are the so-called ceramic **superconductors**. Superconductors are remarkable materials that lose all resistance to the passage of an electric current below a superconducting transition temperature. Prior to 1986, only metals tended to show this behavior, and at very low temperatures (<25 degrees Kelvin). Then in 1986/1987 scientists discovered new ceramic compounds involving lanthanum, strontium, copper and oxygen or yttrium, barium, copper and oxygen, which became superconductors at much higher temperatures (40K, 90K). Prior to these discoveries, nobody would have guessed that such combinations of elements would produce electrical conductors let alone superconductors. Now scientists continue the search for new materials with improved properties by studying the dizzying array of combinations of elements, a process sometimes referred to as combinatorial synthesis.

We mentioned earlier that there are really two types of new materials. Most of these are of the second type, i.e., they are made by modifying existing materials. Sometimes this means just purifying them, the outstanding example of which is silicon. We shall have much more to say about this element later, but for the time being it is sufficient to say that the element commonly exists combined with oxygen in the form of sand (SiO_2—known as silica). We can extract the silicon from sand but the material produced is not very useful because of impurities. We shall later see that regular window glass has a blue/green tinge (look at it through the edge) because of the iron present in the silica.

The development of silicon fit for semiconductor use required the production of a very high purity form of the element (99.9999999% pure) which then needed to have small amounts of a specific impurity element (e.g. boron, phosphorus) added. We call this intentional addition of impurity "**doping**" and it is a vital part of the production of silicon for the electronic components in your personal electronic equipment, MP3 players, hi-fi equipment, personal computers, cars, etc. The development of silicon for transistors required a modification of the available material, involving purification and doping. At the beginning of the 1960's there was barely a mention of these so-called 'solid-state electronics' in undergraduate physics curricula. Perhaps these materials would one day prove valuable! Just look how far we have come in the last 45 years as a result of this major materials development. We shall look at uses of doped silicon in our case studies.

In another of our case studies we shall discuss the new High Strength Low Alloy Steels (HSLA Steels). Steels have been made and used for well over a century, but these are steels, which are modified so that they are made of very small crystals, which increases strength. This is another example of a new material made by modifying an existing one. In this case it is the change in the processing of the material that is mainly responsible for its different properties.

Corning Ware® is a material that is found in most households. It too is a relatively new material, which is formed by modifying a glass. There are even some stories that it was discovered by accident, something scientists call 'serendipity' and which happens more often than we like to admit! We shall look at what it is that makes this material withstand extreme temperature variations, enabling you to take it straight from freezer to burner.

Another example of a new material which, incidentally is still the subject of considerable research, is the group of metal alloys (metal mixtures) made by combining aluminum (Al) and lithium (Li). This new group of materials is both lighter and stronger than aluminum alone, and has obvious uses in modern aircraft. Any weight saving is important in an aircraft wherever obtained. We shall discuss these materials later in a case study.

We began by defining materials science and engineering as understanding and exploiting processing-structure-property relationships in materials. Let's begin by talking about structure.

3. THE MATERIALS SCIENCE AND ENGINEERING PARADIGM

As we learned in the last chapter, materials science investigates and materials engineering exploits the relationships between processing, microstructure, and properties to arrive at materials with useful properties for other engineers to employ. Just as a material's properties depend upon its microstructure, so its microstructure depends upon how it is fabricated or manufactured. If we want to change a property by changing the structure, how do we go about it? The answer is that we have to do it by processing, i.e., the ways we treat the material during manufacture.

Processing

Here again we have a topic, which has so many aspects. Perhaps an analogy will help. Most people have baked a cake or something similar. The recipe usually starts with the list of ingredients, which is important. But what follows is perhaps even more important, instructions on how to combine them and treat them. Which ingredients do you blend first? Do you first mix the flour and sugar and then add the eggs, or should the order be different? Do you just throw the eggs in the bowl straight from the shell, or do you beat them first? Do you bake in a shallow or a deep pan? Do you bake for ten minutes at 450°F or forty minutes at 350°F? All these actions are part of the processing, and variations will result in different products. There may also be some art (experience) involved. How many times has one followed another person's recipe to the letter, only to find that the product turned out to be completely different!

The processing of materials is in many ways analogous to baking a cake. The ingredients are important—materials engineers refer to them by the term, "**composition**"—but how we treat them is just as important, if not more so. Sometimes traditional procedures are more of an art than a science! Here are some general questions the materials scientist has to answer:

Metals are usually formed from a melt. How fast do we cool them? Do we stop the cooling at any point and hold the temperature there? If so, for how long? What happens if we plunge our red hot metal into ice water?

Ceramics are usually formed from powders. How fine should the powder be? What liquid should we mix it with to make a formable paste? What temperature should we fire it to in the **kiln**? (**Ceramists** usually call their furnaces kilns.) For how long? Does it matter how we cool it?

We have already mentioned other aspects of processing for specific materials: e.g.,

We insert impurity atoms into silicon, changing the atomic structure.

We add TiO_2 to glass to promote fine scale crystal formation, and thus produce a glass ceramic, changing both atomic and microstructure.

The following diagram, much like a recipe for baking a cake (ingredients   mixing   baking) captures the essence of materials processing. And just as with baked products, which can be "formed" pre-baking (cutout cookies), during baking (angel food cake), or after baking (bread slicing), materials can be formed before, during, or after firing.

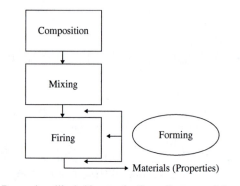

Materials Processing: like baking a cake (ingredients   mixing   baking)

Structure

Structure concerns a wide spectrum of sizes, from the structure of the individual atoms, which make up the solid to the design and shape of the part being produced. We shall define five different scales of structure: electron(ic), atom(ic), crystal, micro and macro, in increasing size order.

To further explain what we mean by structure we shall look at what is certainly the element demonstrating the widest range of structures known to us. That element is carbon.

Carbon

Diamond and graphite

If you look at the periodic table on page 7 you will find carbon designated by its chemical symbol C. Above the C is the number 6, while underneath is the number 12.011. The first is what we know as the **atomic number**. All atoms are made up of a nucleus of positively charged particles called protons and neutral (no charge) particles called neutrons. This nucleus is surrounded by negatively charged particles called electrons, which move around the nucleus in a manner similar to the way the planets move around the sun. The atomic number simply tells us the number of electrons belonging to one atom. We shall discuss this subject in more detail in Chapter 5 when we consider chemical bonding.

The second number is the **atomic weight** or relative mass of a single atom, and is given in what are known as atomic mass units (amu). While there is perhaps no need to remember the exact figures for this study, we should note that the atomic weight tells us that 6.02×10^{23} carbon atoms weigh 12.011 grams.

These units (amu) are therefore very, very small. (In case you are unfamiliar with this notation, 6.02×10^{23} means 6.02 multiplied by ten twenty three times, i.e. 602,000,000,000,000,000,000,000.)

As mentioned above, the carbon atom has six electrons and, as we shall see in Chapter 5, four of these electrons, called the **valence** electrons, are available to form linkages or bonds to other atoms. How these electrons are used to form bonds relates to the **electron(ic) structure** of the material.

There are two common different forms of carbon with which you are probably familiar, and several other related forms. The two familiar forms are diamond and graphite; two more different materials you could hardly imagine!

Diamond is a transparent, colorless, crystalline material, which is very hard (scratches glass). It is an electrical insulator but a good conductor of heat. It is also rare and very expensive. The only place we are likely to see it is in jewelry, although small and imperfect crystals are used in glass-cutters and on cutting and grinding wheels. Scientists and engineers are hard at work growing thin films of diamond for a variety of purposes—for example as wear-resistant coatings and to help remove the heat from our increasingly hot microelectronic circuits. (For example, your laptop produces a lot of heat after just a short while on your lap!)

Graphite is an opaque, black, crystalline material, which is very soft and slippery, but is very strong and stiff in one plane. It also conducts heat and electricity pretty well. It is quite cheap, costing around a dollar a pound. We encounter it in the black lead pencils we still use. It also is used as a lubricant and as an electrode in the small A-, C- and D-cell batteries we use to power our portable electronics.

We should first state that both materials have the same **atomic structure**, meaning that they are both made up of the same carbon atoms. Every material, however pure, contains some impurity atoms, which alter the atomic structure or make-up of the material, but we shall ignore this for now. The main difference between these two materials lies in their **electronic structures** (bonding arrangements), which in turn give rise to different **crystal structures** (arrangements of atoms in space).

In diamond each carbon atom uses all four electrons to form equal linkages, or bonds, with four surrounding carbon atoms on the corners of a tetrahedron. This produces a three-dimensional network of atoms with strong bonds going in all directions. (A tetrahedron is a four-sided pyramid, each side of which is an equilateral triangle. The easiest way of drawing a tetrahedron is to place a carbon atom at the center of a cube and place other carbon atoms on alternate corners of the cube, as illustrated in the following diagram.)

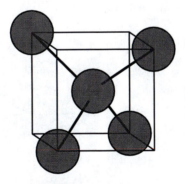

A carbon atom bonded to four others on the corners of a tetrahedron.

In graphite each carbon atom uses only three valence electrons to form bonds with three other carbon atoms in what we call a layer plane, and the fourth electron is released by the atom and allowed to move freely between these layer planes. This produces a two-dimensional planar hexagonal arrangement of atoms with strong bonds being confined to the planes. The graphite crystal is formed by stacking these planes on top of each other in an alternating sequence, as shown in the following diagram. Because the layer planes of carbon atoms in graphite are held together very weakly they can slide over each other easily and hence give graphite its lubricating property. This property also allows a pencil to write. Indeed the word graphite comes from the Greek word for writing. We shall later see that it is the fourth "free" electron, which causes graphite to conduct heat and electricity and be opaque.

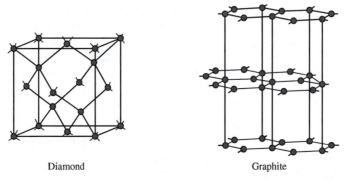

Diamond   Graphite

(R. Cotterill, *The Cambridge Guide to the Material World*, Cambridge University Press, 1985, p. 54)

This leaves us with microstructure and macrostructure to talk about. We mentioned **microstructure** in Chapter 1 in reference to the first microscopic observation of crystals in metals. We now know that all metallic materials consist of an assembly of crystals. Microstructure is a term used to describe the characteristics of these small crystals. How big are they? What shape are they? How are they arranged? We therefore say that microstructure defines the size, shape and orientation of the crystals.

The following two photographs of polycrystalline silicon carbide were taken in an electron microscope, where we are actually looking through a very thin piece of material. Each area of approximately the same shade is a little crystal or grain (we often use the term **crystallite** in referring to such small crystals, about a micron (μm) or two in *size* (a micron is a millionth of a meter). You can also see that the crystallites are about the same size in all directions, something we call an **equiaxed** microstructure (crystals whose three axes are about the same), referring to the *shape* of the crystallites. For truly equiaxed crystallites there is no *orientation* to consider.

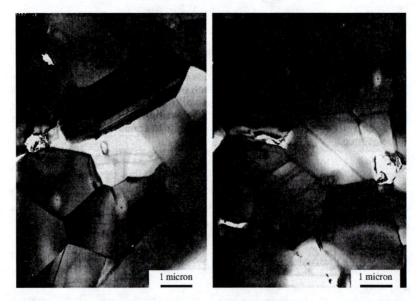

Two photographs of polycrystalline silicon carbide taken in an electron microscope. The grains are about one micron (μm) across. Note that many of the angles at the corners of grains are approximately 120°.

Now let's look at how this relates to graphite. Graphite crystals such as found in the electrode of a D-cell battery, tend to be flake-like (referred to as "lamellar" or "tabular"), a result of the layered crystal structure. They may be a micron or so wide but are not nearly as thick. In this material, therefore, the crystallites tend to lie parallel to each other as will a pack of cards if thrown onto a table. All we have said here describes the microstructure, the size (~1μm), the shape (tabular), and the orientation (parallel) of the crystals. Such a microstructure is typical of all graphites, although the crystallite sizes may differ.

If you go to buy a diamond, as many of you will, you may be advised to look at the four C's— color, clarity, cut and carat. We shall later look at some of the causes of color (Chapter 25), especially as it occurs in gemstones. At this point it is sufficient to state that color is often produced by impurities. We have already mentioned (Page 7) that small amounts of iron impurity in window glass give it a blue/green tinge, and we shall later discuss the importance of impurities in optical fibers.

The lack of any free electrons in diamond (they are all used to form bonds with other carbon atoms) allows light to pass right through it, i.e., the material is transparent. The addition of a few boron atoms to diamond (changing the **atomic structure**) gives it a blue tinge, whereas the addition of a few nitrogen atoms turns it slightly yellow. This occurs naturally in nature and is the reason for the slight color of some diamonds. Strangely enough, a slightly yellow tinge makes a diamond less valuable, whereas a blue diamond is more valuable. By the way, look at the periodic table and note that boron and nitrogen lie to either side of carbon and so, respectively, have one fewer and one more electron than carbon.

Many diamonds contain flaws, which are features of the **microstructure**. Flaws are usually in the form of small black inclusions, which are not really impurities because they are microscopic regions where the carbon atoms have decided to arrange themselves in the graphite crystal structure rather than that of diamond. There may also be some planar flaws, which are essentially places where two crystals join. These you certainly want to avoid. Your diamond should be a single crystal rather than polycrystalline. Polycrystalline diamonds are best crushed and used as abrasives in drill bits or cutting wheels. There is considerable research interest nowadays in the laboratory production of polycrystalline diamond films for electronics, and we shall see why there is this interest when we consider semiconductors (Chapter 26).

The value of a diamond can be greatly enhanced by expert cutting. Today's solitaire diamonds have what is known as a 'brilliant' cut in which the angles between the facets have been carefully calculated to produce the maximum fire and sparkle in the stone. Years ago diamonds were usually cut to conserve the maximum volume of the stone whereas today we sacrifice some of the stone for extra brilliance. A gem cutter will often spend weeks studying a large rough stone, usually costing millions of dollars, before making the first cut (what a responsibility!). This is because larger diamonds are proportionally more valuable than smaller ones. On the other hand cutting into smaller stones is often necessary to eliminate some major flaws. The shape (cut) and size of the diamond are descriptions of its **macrostructure**.

Other forms of carbon

In the last few years there has been considerable excitement about a new form of carbon called **fullerene** or C-60. A fullerene molecule consists of sixty carbon atoms arranged in a sphere as they would be if one were placed on each corner of the panels in a soccer ball, which has 20 hexagons (6-sided panels) and 12 pentagons (five-sided panels). The name reflects the fact that the atoms are arranged in the form of the geodesic domes created by Buckminster Fuller. In a crystal these spheres stack together in the same way that you would arrange balls for the break on a pool table. At the moment these 'buckyballs' are expensive and are not yet widely used. However, there are emerging applications, for example to aid more efficient electron harvesting in solar cells made from organic molecules.

A C-60 fullerene "buckyball".

Soot is very impure carbon, which has no crystal structure. It may contain some small regions in which there are very small graphite layers, but these layers are not arranged in any ordered manner. We therefore say that the material has short-range order, but no long-range order. Such materials are called **amorphous**, the atoms have no regular arrangement. Soot is a messy material, which has more uses than we probably realize. We know it as something which periodically has to be swept from chimneys, and in industrial areas it is a nuisance as it soils our clothes and laundry.

However we probably do not realize that it is essentially purified soot which is used as a colorant for inks, cosmetics (mascara) and candy (licorice) and as an important reinforcing agent in car tires, where it also serves to keep sunlight from penetrating and degrading the rubber. This material, known as **carbon black**, is produced under very carefully controlled conditions in special furnaces, and different processing enables the production of different microstructures. The microstructure of carbon black is usually similar to a string of malted milk balls melted together. The outer layer is somewhat crystalline (this is where there are rather imperfect graphite layer planes present) while the centers are totally amorphous, without even any short-range atomic order. Some of these materials are called "black pearls" to reflect the structure shown below. The microstructure is quite complex, and the sizes of the spheres and the lengths of the strands vary depending on the method of manufacture.

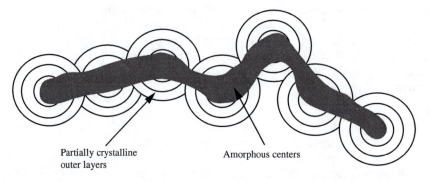

Partially crystalline
outer layers

Amorphous centers

Diagram illustrating the microstructure a carbon black particle.

Carbon fibers are another form of carbon, which you have probably encountered. They are nowadays quite common in tennis and squash rackets, skis, golf clubs and other sporting goods. If you have ever used such an article you will know that it combines light weight with a high stiffness, properties which are also desirable for aircraft frames, etc. The bonds between the carbon atoms in the graphite layers are very strong, and render them both very strong and rigid. In carbon fibers these layers are arranged to lie along the fiber length so that when you pull on the fiber you are pulling along these layers and hence pulling on the strong bonds between the atoms in the layers. This is an excellent example of how structure affects properties. We shall discuss carbon fibers and their use in composites in chapter 23.

Activated carbons are porous carbons used, for example, in filters for water purification. This carbon usually comes in the form of granules, which are enclosed in a cartridge that we attach to the faucet. (There are also some cigarettes that use activated carbon filters, but we trust our readers are smart enough to recognize the dangers of tobacco, even with such filters in place!). Similarly, there are numerous industrial applications. The structure of activated carbon is very complex. **Glassy carbon** is a hard brittle material in which graphite-like ribbons are all tangled up. It leaves no mark on paper as a result. Its only current use is as crucibles in chemical laboratories. We merely mention these two materials as further illustrations of the wide variety of carbon materials available.

Finally, we would be remiss not to mention the most recently discovered form of carbon—**nanotubes**. Imagine taking a graphite sheet from the graphite structure and rolling it up, much as one

Representation of a single-walled carbon nanotube.

does tobacco leaves to make a cigar. But carbon nanotubes are different in at least two ways. First, there is no overlapping of a given sheet upon itself—the carbon atoms at the leading edge of a given sheet are directly bonded to those of its trailing edge. Second, nanotubes have dramatically larger "aspect ratios" of length divided by diameter. For example, individual tubes can be a thousand times longer (micrometers) than they are wide (on the order of nanometers). Sometimes nanotubes consist of tubes inside other tubes, so-called multi-walled nanotubes. The excitement about carbon nanotubes is twofold. They are exceptionally deformable and strong, for potential use in composites. And if rolled properly, they can be conducting or semiconducting, for potential use in "nanoelectronics," to be discussed in Chapter 33.

All the materials mentioned so far are simply carbon and hence have the same atomic structures. Although there are certainly small amounts of impurities present, as is true of all materials, this is of no consequence here except as mentioned for diamonds. Diamond and graphite have different electron and crystal structures. All the materials mentioned can have a variety of micro- and macrostructures.

Silicon

As a further example we take a material, or element, which can be said to have exerted the greatest influence on society during the recent decades. Silicon is the basis of almost all electronics, and in today's world is involved in so many of our activities, both work and leisure. It has produced revolutions in the availability of personal electronics in the form of personal CD and MP3 players, the ignition system and instrumentation in our automobiles, household electronics such as security systems, microwaves, DVD players, etc. In the areas of computers and video games the advances can still be seen in the rapid rate of obsolescence.

It is perhaps difficult to believe that when Hewlett-Packard introduced their first portable calculator some 35 years ago it cost $395 and you had to wait six months to get one! In today's dollars this would be more than $2100. Today we can buy a much smaller unit with far more capabilities for under $10! The changes brought about by the silicon 'chips' which control the plethora of electronic devices around us are truly tremendous.

Silicon comprises about 25% of the earth's surface. It commonly exists in nature in the form of sand—silicon oxide (SiO_2). We shall later (Chapter 8) discuss one of the ways super-pure silicon can be obtained for use in a wide variety of electronic components, but here we simply want to ask what it is that makes this material a semiconductor. The answer lies in the way the electrons are arranged and held in the solid, in other words the **electronic structure**.

If you look once more at the periodic table you will see that silicon lies immediately under carbon, and we have already noted (Page 6) that "elements in the same column have somewhat similar properties." Like carbon, silicon has four outer or valence electrons and is also able to form bonds with four surrounding silicon atoms. In fact it does so in an identical manner such that the **crystal structure** of silicon is identical to that of diamond. Each silicon atom is again bonded to four other silicon atoms, which lie at the corners of a tetrahedron. There is therefore no need to show an illustration of the crystal structure of silicon because the diagram would be identical to that given earlier for diamond (Page 12). There is no form of silicon with the crystal structure of graphite.

Although carbon (diamond) and silicon have identical crystal structures and the *atoms* have similar electronic structures, the materials are quite different. Whereas pure diamond is transparent and colorless, silicon is opaque and has a shiny metallic luster. Why? The reason lies in the fact that the bonds between atoms in silicon are not nearly as strong as those in diamond. The electrons doing the bonding are somewhat loose and some of them occasionally break free to act much the same way as that they do in metals. In other words the electronic structures in the two *solids* are quite different. We shall explore this in more detail in chapter 26.

We saw earlier in this chapter that adding the impurity atoms boron and nitrogen to diamond changes the color. These elements are situated either side of carbon in the periodic table (Page 7). If we do the same thing with silicon, where the corresponding elements are aluminum and phosphorus, we change the electrical properties tremendously and open this material to a host of new applications. The impurities in diamond are added in nature, but in semiconductors we intentionally add the required impurities, a process called **doping**. In fact we can add different impurities to different areas of our silicon and hence produce the 'chips' which we hear so much about nowadays. In the doping process we change the atoms—the **atomic structure** of the material.

As already mentioned, there is only one possible crystal structure for silicon, and it is perhaps worth noting that crystal structure is usually the one level of structure which we have no control over. We cannot just go into a material and arrange the atoms to suit. However, we can sometimes make a material amorphous, with the atoms randomly arranged, i.e., no crystal structure. Amorphous silicon has been of interest for use in solar cells (Chapter 27).

Silicon Oxide

There is one example in nature of a material that has a large number of crystal structures. This is silicon oxide (SiO_2). In this material the silicon atom again forms four bonds, but this time with oxygen atoms. These oxygen atoms are also situated on the corners of a tetrahedron. To visualize it, all you have to do is look at the tetrahedron of carbon atoms shown earlier in this chapter and imagine that the central atom is silicon and the outer four are oxygens. (Notice how many similarities in structure we have encountered in looking at carbon, silicon and silicon oxide—three quite different materials).

Oxygen is an atom that has two valence electrons available to form bonds, and so wants to join up with two silicon atoms. The natural result of this is that the corners of one tetrahedron are shared with others, i.e., each oxygen atom can be considered to sit on the corners of two tetrahedra at the same time. This is what happens in the crystal structure illustrated below. Thus the four oxygen atoms are each shared between two tetrahedra, and in essence only two (four halves) oxygen atoms belong to the silicon atom. This gives us the chemical formula SiO_2. Note that this structure is what would be obtained by placing an oxygen midway between the silicon atoms in the structure of silicon just examined. This material is known as cristobalite.

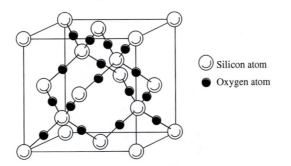

The crystal structure of cristobalite (SiO_2).

(W. F. Smith, *Principles of Materials Science and Engineering*, McGraw Hill, New York, 1986. Fig. 10.22. Reproduced with permission of the publisher)

There are two other arrangements of these tetrahedra for which all the corners are shared. They are more complicated than in cristobalite and there is no need to go into details. These two other forms are known as tridymite and quartz. Of these three possible arrangements of the tetrahedra, quartz is probably the only one you have heard of. It is a clear, colorless crystal, which is sometimes used as a (poor) fake diamond. It is also the crystal in quartz watches. If we make the crystals very small and embed them in glass, the material becomes opaque and white and is very strong. More importantly, the resulting microstructure can resist thermal shock (the shock resulting from sudden temperature changes). We commonly encounter this material as Corning Ware®. We call this material a glass ceramic because it starts life as glass, more than 90% of which is then changed to a crystalline ceramic by 'seeding' it with very small crystals of titanium oxide, which cause SiO_2 crystals to form from the glass. It is also sometimes called **pyroceram** (because it is a ceramic which tolerates large sudden changes in temperature: pyro = heat). We shall discuss this further in Chapter 20.

SiO_2 can also be made into an amorphous glass, sometimes referred to as fused quartz. It has the same SiO_4 tetrahedra arranged in a random manner. It is another example of a material in which the atoms have short-range order (tetrahedra) but have no long-range order. The following diagram of the atomic arrangement in glass portrays it as a distorted cube of cristobalite, but most glasses are far more complex because they have had other atoms added to modify the properties. Sometimes these impurities come between the tetrahedra producing weaker connections, thus making a glass that softens at a lower temperature (see Chapter 7).

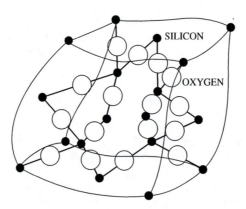

The random three-dimensional network of a silica glass (SiO_2)
(K. Easterling, *Tomorrow's Materials*, The Institute of Metals, London, U.K., 1988. Fig.5)

In nature the tetrahedra can also be arranged in a number of other ways. In one they are linked together in sheets as shown in the following diagram. (You are looking down on tetrahedra sitting on a flat sheet, so that they share the three corners on the base.) These sheets stack as shown in the side view with other atoms between their peaks. This material is called **talc**—the slippery mineral found in talcum powder. The other atoms hold the sheets of tetrahedra together very weakly so that they can slide over each other producing a slippery material.

This arrangement (talc) is one example of how the tetrahedra share three corners, with other atoms between the unshared corners. There are other arrangements where either three or two corners are shared. One of the latter is the rare and valuable gemstone known as emerald. All these materials have different **crystal structures** (arrangements of the atoms) and different **atomic structures** (other

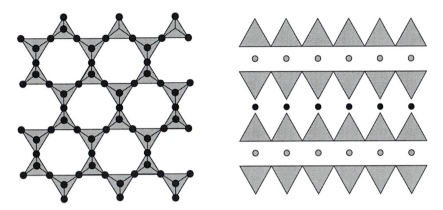

In the left hand diagram you are looking down on a sheet of silica tetrahedra. The right hand diagram shows how these sheets stack together to form talc. Potassium atoms ◎; Magnesium atom ●

atoms connected to the unshared corners of the tetrahedra.) This whole range of materials is known collectively as the silicate minerals.

In the above discussion we mentioned Corning Ware®, which is found in the form of cooking pans in most kitchens. These give an excellent example of the importance of the **macrostructure** of materials. You will see that the corners are rounded. Not only does this make the article easier to clean, but more importantly it reduces the chances of breakage. Sharp corners are places where breakage is likely to occur, or to use the technical jargon, fracture can be initiated. This is somewhat like making a sharp fold in a piece of paper before tearing it so that the tear goes (maybe) where you want it to.

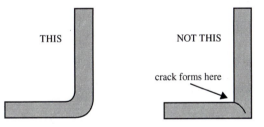

Diagram illustrating how a sharp corner acts as a place
where breakage starts, or fracture initiates.

So we have covered two of the three key elements of the materials science and engineering paradigm—processing and structure. But what about properties? That is the subject of the next chapter.

4. MATERIALS PROPERTIES

So far we have looked briefly at the processing of materials (how they are made) and quite extensively at their structure (their internal architecture) on all levels—from the electronic structure to atomic structure to crystal structure to microstructure, and finally to macrostructure. But what enables materials to be utilized by other engineers in applications ranging from the silicon in the latest microelectronic circuits to the lightweight, high-strength alloys in advanced aircraft is their unique properties.

Materials scientists classify materials based upon similarities of properties, i.e., how they behave optically, mechanically, electrically, magnetically, etc. We will see in the next chapter how these differences can be related to the different kinds of bonds associated with each class of materials. But long before scientists understood the differences in their bonding, artisans and engineers could identify the different classes of materials according to their physical properties.

The widely recognized major classes of materials are **metals**, **ceramics** (including glasses), **polymers**, and **semiconductors**. More recently **biomaterials** have been added as a separate class of materials. **Composites** combine two (or more) types of materials, often from separate classes, into a hybrid material, thereby making use of the best properties of both materials. Keep in mind that although most materials within a category behave similarly, there are always exceptions to the rule, which we talk about at the end of this chapter.

Let's start with **METALS**—What do we know about them?

They are usually recognizable because they are opaque and have a shine or luster. If they are dull it is usually because the surface has been oxidized by contact and reaction with the air. If we scratch them we remove this oxide layer and reveal new shiny metal. You may want to try this with a piece of aluminum, where the surface is a thin layer of aluminum oxide.

Most metals are quite ductile. We can bend a copper wire into any shape. We form body panels of cars from steels by placing them in a press with a mold of the part to be formed. Then we depend upon "crumple zones" in the body panels of vehicles to absorb energy in case of violent collisions. On the other hand, we are also aware that if we keep bending a metal (e.g., a paper clip), it becomes hard and brittle so that it eventually breaks.

Steels are quite strong and are used as I (eye) beams in constructing large buildings. Here we have metals that don't bend easily (they don't sag) and carry a lot of weight. Steel is the traditional strong metal. We can therefore immediately appreciate that there are considerable differences between the strengths and stiffnesses of metals.

There are only three common metals (iron, nickel and cobalt) that are magnetic, but there are some circumstances in which even these are not magnetic. Note that most metals, including many steels (e.g., stainless steel), are not magnetic.

Metals usually conduct heat and electricity well, although we know from cooking pans that copper and iron conduct heat better than stainless steel, which is usually given an aluminum or copper base to overcome this deficiency. We do not usually make seats of bare metal because they conduct the heat away from our bodies rather quickly and hence feel cold to our touch. Electrical wiring in our houses is usually copper. We never think of using stainless steel wires to conduct electricity.

Most metals are elements and vice versa. (Consider how many of the elements in the periodic table on page 7 are metals.) There are some common traditional metals such as aluminum, copper, iron, gold, silver, etc. There are also some rather rare metals such as gadolinium, osmium, ruthenium and holmium.

Many metals we encounter in today's world are mixtures (alloys). The gold wedding band is a copper-gold alloy, and different colors of gold are produced by mixing different metals with the gold. Stainless steel is a mixture of iron, chromium and nickel, with a little carbon for good measure. Some magnets are mixtures of iron, aluminum, nickel and cobalt. There is no end to the number of metal alloys we can make. Not only do we have a choice of eighty metallic elements but we also have a choice of the proportions we mix them in. This truly provides an infinite number of possibilities.

Except when produced under very special circumstances, metals are crystalline. The crystallite size is controlled by changing the way the material is cooled from the melt, a process called 'heat treating.'

CERAMICS are non-metallic materials, but are typically compounds of metals. For example, reacting silicon with oxygen produces the ceramic, silica (SiO_2). Similarly, reacting aluminum with oxygen produces the ceramic, alumina (Al_2O_3). The name "ceramic" comes from the Greek for "burnt earth"—because when you burn something it combines with the oxygen in the air. Other modern ceramics result from reacting metals with boron (borides), carbon (carbides) and nitrogen (nitrides). However, you will probably not find these around the home except in small, specialized applications such as coatings on sand paper and drill bits. They are expensive and are mainly used in military and aerospace applications, but their special properties are finding more and more applications in automobiles, for example.

Traditional ceramics are often based on clay, which is an alumino-silicate mineral (Chapter 3), i.e., based upon alumina and silica. We see these traditional materials in porcelain and stoneware plates, bathroom fixtures, and bricks and pipes for building materials.

Because glass (e.g., window glass, container glass) is also alumino-silicate based and shares many of the same physical properties with crystalline ceramics (e.g., brittleness) it is classified as a ceramic material.

Ceramics are usually thought of as brittle and not easily bent. Compare the dropping of a pewter beer tankard vs. a porcelain or glass beer tankard! The metal tankard will do no more than dent, while the ceramic articles will almost certainly break catastrophically (shatter).

Ceramics do not conduct heat very well and can withstand high temperatures. They are used as thermal insulators in fireplaces (firebricks) and in insulation for houses (fiberglass). Large industrial furnaces used for steel manufacture, ceramic firing (called "kilns"), and glass manufacture (called "tanks") are lined with ceramic bricks because they can stand up to the high temperatures and are also insulating. Such ceramics are referred to as "refractories," after the French word for "high-melting." Their refractory character derives from their high bond strengths, as we will see in the next chapter.

Another consequence of high bond strength is high hardness. Ceramics like diamond are the hardest materials known to man. They are routinely used as abrasives in sand papers and grinding wheels, e.g., silicon carbide (SiC) on carborundum paper.

Ceramics usually don't conduct electricity. We see them used as electrical insulators on high voltage electrical transmission lines and in spark plugs in car engines. There are exceptions, however, which we mention at the end of this chapter.

Some ceramics are magnetic, i.e., those containing the same magnetic elements as in magnetic metals (e.g., cobalt, nickel, iron). Ceramics are used for the little magnets that hold notes to refrigerator doors, and the door seals consist of ceramic magnet powders mixed into a plastic. Ceramic magnets are also used extensively in TV sets and other electrical components. Their advantages over metal magnets are that they do not conduct electricity and do not rust.

Ceramics are usually crystalline, and like metals, their grain sizes can be controlled during the processing of the material, but in this case it is usually a result of the grain size of the ground powder used—finer powders give smaller grain sizes.

Glass and many other ceramics are transparent. We shall see that transparency is due to purity and that some materials are not as pure as we may think.

POLYMERS (from the Greek, poly—many; meros—part, many parts) are modern materials, although many naturally occurring materials (wool, cotton, skin, rubber, etc.) are polymeric. They are usually based on long chains or backbones of carbon atoms. Different polymers have different things attached to their backbones (a much simplified description as we shall later see).

You most likely have examples of transparent polymers in your kitchen cabinet, along with other polymers that are white. We will show that this is related to whether the polymer is amorphous and transparent or partially crystalline (which causes the scattering of light). Of course, polymers can be rendered just about any color by adding pigments.

Most polymers are **plastic**, meaning that they can be easily bent into a different shape, hence the more common term—but some can be brittle. Polymers are usually considered to be either **thermoplastics**, meaning that they become more flexible when heated, or **thermosets**, meaning that heat causes them to set hard and rigid (e.g., epoxy glue).

Polymers are usually thermal and electrical insulators. They are used for thermal insulation in houses and for insulation in electrical wiring and junction boxes etc.

Polymers are not magnetic.

Today we see polymers all around us—acrylic and nylon clothing, polycarbonate football helmets and protective lenses, polyurethane coverings for chairs, polystyrene food and beverage containers (styrofoam), polyethylene dishpans, polyvinyl chloride pipes, etc. Every year sees the development of hundreds of new polymers.

SEMICONDUCTORS are a special class of materials.

Silicon and germanium are the elements that most readily come to mind. They have similar electronic structures and the same crystal structures.

Semiconductors are true to their descriptive title—they conduct electricity much better than insulating ceramics, but not nearly as well as metals. Therefore, they are midway between insulators and conductors, hence they are "semi" conductors.

They also exhibit big changes in conductivity with doping, and can be doped with impurities to produce electrons (n-type for "negative" charge carriers) or to produce something referred to as "electron holes" (p-type for "positive" charge carriers). Our ability to control doping is what enables semiconductor devices (e.g., transistors) to be fabricated. Junctions are made between n-type and p-type regions on silicon at an extremely fine size scale. We discuss this further in Chapter 26.

Semiconductors can be black and shiny like metals (e.g., silicon) or they can be colored (e.g., cadmium sufide, CdS, is orange in color). We discuss the origin of color in semiconductors in Chapter 25.

Gallium arsenide (GaAs) is a newer semiconductor of which you may have heard. We shall see (Chapter 28) that it has many of the same structural characteristics of silicon and germanium. Its importance for the future is that electrons can travel faster in it than in the conventional semiconductors. Since these electrons are what carry the information in a computer, one can see that GaAs holds a possible key to even faster computers.

Most semiconductors are not magnetic, although new "alloys" are being investigated in an attempt to combine magnetism with semiconductor behavior.

BIOMATERIALS Some would argue that biomaterials do not deserve to be a separate materials category. In fact, humans carry examples of each of the abovementioned materials classes in their bodies. For example, caries (or cavities) in our teeth can be filled with metal amalgams (alloys) or with ceramic onlays. Metal springs called "stents" are used to prop open blocked coronary arteries. Or how about titanium-based metals in joint replacements or "hydroxylapatite" ceramics (hydroxylapatite is a crystalline calcium phosphate ceramic that is especially compatible with human bone tissue) in "bony defect repair" or polymers in bone cement, to mention a few examples. If we add the microelectronics employed in heart pacemakers and defibrillators, all the materials classes are accounted for.

But what sets biomaterials apart is their biocompatibility, i.e., how compatible they are with the human body. The subfield of biomaterials is at the intersection of materials science with biology and with medicine. We discuss biomaterials further in Chapter 34.

COMPOSITES Composites combine two (or more) materials, usually from different materials classes, into a hybrid structure in order to capitalize upon the best properties of both materials. For example, in fiberglass composites stiff/strong glass fibers are combined with a tough polymer (epoxy) matrix to produce a strong and tough composite. Modern golf clubs and tennis racquets are made from lightweight graphite fiber composites. And recently, aircraft are being made from lightweight (but stiff and strong) fiber-reinforced composites.

And what about **nanomaterials**? Again, all the abovementioned materials classes can be produced with nanometer scale dimensions, i.e., nanometals, nanoceramics, nanopolymers, nanosemiconductors, even composites with nanoparticles or nanofibers. As we will see in Chapter 32, properties change dramatically when one or more of a material's dimensions is reduced to the nanometer scale.

5. BONDING

We can better understand the differences between the various classes of materials by considering the subject of bonding, which is fundamental to understanding the structure-property relationships of all materials.

The Structure of Atoms

Atoms have a nucleus composed of two types of particles, neutrons which have no electrical charge and are therefore neutral, and protons which have a positive electrical charge. This nucleus is surrounded by electrons, which have a negative electrical charge. The number of surrounding electrons is equal to the number of protons in the nucleus so that the atom is electrically *neutral* because it contains equal numbers of electrons and protons.

A simple model of an atom compares it to the solar system. Electrons go round the nucleus in fixed orbits, just as the planets orbit the sun. These orbits give rise to **electron shells**. The further away from the nucleus, the larger the shell and the larger the number of electrons that can be accommodated in it.

The first shell can contain 2 electrons, corresponding to the two lightest elements, hydrogen and helium.

H   He

The second shell can contain 8 electrons, giving the elements lithium, beryllium, boron, carbon, nitrogen, oxygen, fluorine and neon.

Li   Be   B   C   N   O   F   Ne

The third shell can contain 18 electrons. Elements corresponding to the filling of this shell can be seen on the Periodic Table (Page 7).

The maximum number of electrons that can be accommodated in a shell is $2n^2$, where n in the number of the shell, so the fourth shell could contain a maximum of 32 electrons. However, nature keeps things simple—the first 8 electrons (e^-'s) in the shell are what make an atom stable. Look at the periodic table and you will see that the right-hand column contains what we call the **inert gases**. These are gases that tend not to react with other elements to form compounds. With the exception of helium, which can only have a maximum of two electrons in its one and only shell, they all have eight electrons in their outer shell. As an example the electron structure of neon is shown.

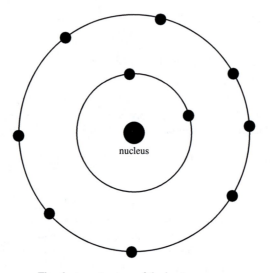

The electron structure of the inert gas neon.

Some of these inert gases may be familiar to you. Radon is something we have heard about recently in houses as a radioactive hazard. Xenon is sometimes found in photo flash tubes, and everyone has heard of neon lights.

Helium	2 e⁻'s in	1st shell
Neon	8 -----	2nd ----
Argon	8 -----	3rd ----
Krypton	8 -----	4th ----
Xenon	8 -----	5th ----
Radon	8 -----	6th ----

Atoms which have eight electrons in their outer shell are very stable and all atoms strive to achieve this state. In many respects it is the desire to have an outer shell of 8 electrons, sometimes called an "octet", which is responsible for chemical bonding. The different types of bonds that exist between atoms are often due to the different ways the atoms decide to redistribute their electrons to achieve the desired eight. Just think what people could do if everybody wanted to have only eight dollars. Some would just let their excess cash go to a pool (maybe to pay off the national debt!). Others with, for example four and four, would get together and share. Yet others, for example seven and nine, could engage in a give-and-take arrangement (the one with 9 "transfers" his extra dollar with his one-short friend). This example, however silly, is illustrative of the three major ways atoms use their electrons to form bonds with each other.

There are five main types of bond—three "primary" and two "secondary," and they are very instrumental in determining the properties of materials, although sometimes their role is minor. We shall therefore spend some time describing them and some of their major characteristics, which affect the properties of materials.

The Primary Bond Types

Metallic bonds

About eighty of the hundred or so elements are metals. What makes these elements metals? It is simply the way the electrons hold the atoms together. Naturally we call the bonds that hold these atoms together **metallic bonds**.

Metals are elements that have a tendency to release their electrons. In a pure metal the outer or valence electrons are not tightly bound and can be easily released, leaving behind a positively-charged ion core, often referred to as a **cation**.

From a variety of experiments, which are outside the scope of this discussion, we know that, on average, each atom releases approximately one electron. A simple model of the metallic solid is therefore of a number of singly-charged cations surrounded by a pool of **free electrons**. One of the fundamentals of physics with which you are probably familiar is that like charges (positive-positive and negative-negative) repel each other, whereas unlike charges (positive-negative) attract each other. Of course, the cations are positively charged and the electrons are negatively charged, which means that there is an attraction between them. It is this attraction which holds the atoms together. This **electrostatic attraction** between the cations and the pool of electrons has certain characteristics, which are important in determining the properties of metals.

The bond produced is quite strong. We cannot be too precise on this point because there are large variations. The bond between the atoms in mercury (Hg) is quite weak, a fact that is demonstrated by the fact that mercury is a liquid at room temperature. Similarly, lead (Pb) is a soft, easily deformable solid. When materials are heated the energy goes into making the atoms vibrate, and eventually this vibration energy is enough to break the bonds and the material melts. At room temperature the bonds between the mercury atoms have already been broken. On the other hand, the bonds in tungsten (W) are very strong. We use tungsten filaments in light bulbs and the tungsten does not melt! In fact tungsten does not melt until its temperature reaches 3400°C (6150°F).

The electrons in a metal are instantaneously moving in all directions at the same time. It is important to realize that they are free of the atoms, or cations, even though they are what is holding the material together. We some times refer to them as a **sea of electrons** or an **electron glue**. When we put a voltage across a piece of metal we put a force on the electrons, which forces them to travel preferentially in one direction. We call this an **electric current**. This explains why metals are electrical conductors.

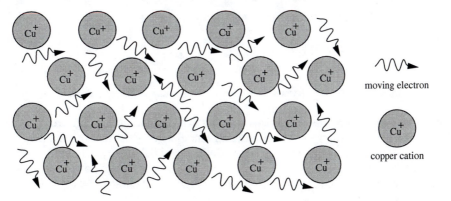

Illustration of how free electrons move randomly between the cations and form a metallic bond.

Metallic bonds have **no directionality**. This is a really important concept that requires amplification. Because the electrons act as a sort of glue, the metal atoms can arrange themselves in almost any way they want to. The bonds do not point in any direction. Think of the atoms being held together as if they were wooden balls held together by a glue that never really dries, rather than by nails. Nails would be directed and fix the balls in position, whereas the glue that never sets would allow the balls to be moved around. There are several consequences of this glue concept. The two most important are:

(i)   The atoms can pack closely; there is nothing to stop them from getting as close as possible, which is something they want to do. As a consequence metals are quite heavy or dense.

(ii)   The atoms can move over each other and change positions relatively easily. This is the basic reason why metals can be formed by pressing, hammering, etc.

We shall later see that there is much more to these two concepts, but it is true to say that they are due to the non-directionality of the metallic bonds.

Covalent bonds

While metal atoms pool their electrons throughout the piece of metal, there are some elements in which atoms share electrons with specific nearby atoms in order to achieve the stable octet (8) they wish to attain. The best way to understand this is to look at a specific example. We have spent some time talking about carbon materials (Page 10). The carbon atom is element number 6, which means it has six electrons, two in the first shell and four in the second. These four outer electrons are the **valence electrons**. In diamond a carbon atom gets its octet by sharing these four electrons with four neighboring atoms as shown in the following diagram. Each pair of shared electrons between adjacent atoms constitutes what we call a **covalent bond** (co- meaning 'together'). At least part of the time, each carbon atom has a share of eight valence electrons—four of its own, and four from the surrounding atoms. You can think of this like time-sharing a rental property—each carbon atom possesses both electrons in the bond half the time (with its neighbor).

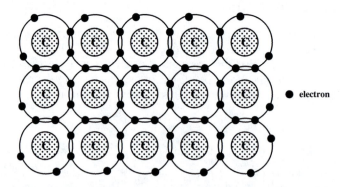

Illustration of how carbon atoms in diamond share electrons so that each has eight.

Notice that each atom has four bonds, each of which contains two electrons (electron pairs). Electrons are all negatively charged and therefore all four electron pairs repel each other. The bonds are pushed as far away from each other as possible, with the result that there is an angle of 109.5° between them. This is what causes the four surrounding carbon atoms to be situated on the corners of a tetrahedron with the other atom at the center. The following diagram of the diamond crystal structure specifically illustrates this point.

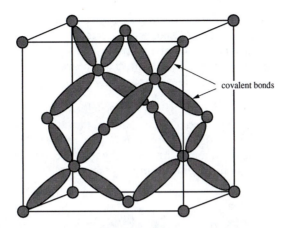

The crystal structure of diamond.
(W. F. Smith, *Principles of Materials Science and Engineering,* McGraw Hill, New York, 1986. Fig. 2.19.
Reproduced with permission of the publisher)

From the above discussion you can see that covalent bonds are **directional**, i.e., they place the surrounding atoms in fixed positions, as nails would fix wooden balls in position, as mentioned earlier. As a consequence, the atoms in solids that are held together by covalent bonds cannot pack as closely together as they do in metals, and the resulting materials are usually not as dense. Another result of this directional bonding is that it is difficult for the atoms to move past each other, and the materials do not deform as easily as do metals. Since there are no free electrons, materials with covalent bonds do not conduct electricity.

Finally we must note that covalent bonds are very strong, in fact the strongest bonds known in nature are covalent. Diamond is well recognized as one of the strongest/hardest materials, and the strength of the covalent bond in graphite is taken advantage of in carbon/graphite fibers. Silicon and germanium also have four outer electrons, and in the solid have the same atom arrangement (crystal structure) as do the carbon atoms in diamond, but the bonds are longer and not as strong as they are in diamond.

Covalent bonds are what hold the two atoms together in a molecule of oxygen (O_2) or a molecule of nitrogen (N_2). They are also important in many ceramic materials, and are what hold the carbon atoms together in long-chain polymer molecules. This is one reason why polymers are tough materials: the chains are difficult to break because of the very strong covalent bonds between the carbon atoms forming them.

Ionic bonds

Another way of achieving an octet of electrons in the outer electron shell is for atoms to exchange electrons among themselves. The most often used, and most simple, example is that of sodium chloride or common salt (NaCl).

Sodium (element number 11) has just one outer electron, while chlorine (element number 17) has seven outer electrons. If the chlorine takes one electron from the sodium they then both have an outer shell of eight electrons. (There are 8 electrons in the shell immediately below the one valence electron in sodium.)

Now the Na has lost an electron, it has one more positive charge on the nucleus than the number of electrons. This atomic entity is an ion (Na$^+$) and, because it is positively charged, it is called a **cation.** The chlorine has one more electron than the number of positive charges on the nucleus, which produces an **anion** (Cl$^-$) which is negatively charged. These positive and negative charges attract each other (**electrostatic attraction**) and hence produce an ionic bond.

In some respects the bond produced is similar to a metallic bond. The ions can attract each other in *any* direction. The electrons are in spherical shells around the atoms and there is therefore no preferred bonding direction. The **ions** can therefore pack as closely as possible and they do. However, for electrostatic reasons, positive ions want to be surrounded by negative ions, and vice versa. The following diagram illustrates this situation for sodium chloride (common salt).

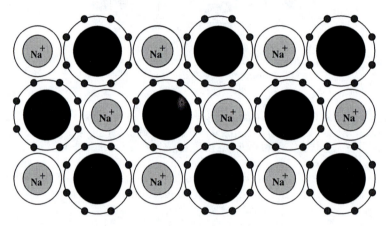

The packing of ions in sodium chloride.

Note that the cation is usually smaller than the corresponding neutral atom because the larger positive charge on the nucleus pulls the surrounding electrons in more. For similar reasons the anion is larger than the corresponding neutral atom. We therefore are now concerned with the packing of two different sizes of ions and the way the ions pack depends on their relative sizes. In general they pack as efficiently as possible as illustrated in the following diagram.

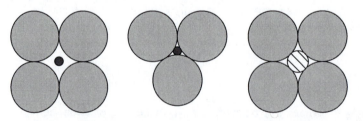

The small cation will not pack as shown on the left, but will be surrounded by three anions as shown in the center. However a larger cation (right) will be surrounded by four anions.

Ionic bonds are typically very strong and are important in many ceramics.

The three bond types considered so far—**covalent, ionic, metallic**—are known as the three **primary bonds**. They are the strongest bonds and one or more of them is involved in holding together the atoms in any useful solid material.

Before we go on let's summarize some of their important differences and characteristics.

- ionic bonds involve the transfer of electrons; covalent and metallic bonds involve the sharing or pooling of electrons.
- covalent bonds are directional; ionic and metallic bonds are non-directional.
- metallic bonds involve attraction between cations and a sea of electrons; ionic bonds involve attraction between cations and anions. Covalent bonds do not involve electrostatic attraction.

Secondary bonds

In addition to these three bonds, there are some much weaker bonds between atoms and molecules and these sometimes dictate the properties of a material, especially the strength. After all, a chain is only as strong as its weakest link. These other bonds, which we call **secondary bonds**, are often the weak points in materials.

Hydrogen bonds

This secondary bond is the one with which we are probably most familiar. It is the bond that holds water molecules together in ice.

Water consists of molecules of H_2O. The molecule is angular (not straight) with the hydrogens making an angle of 105° with the oxygen atom (the three atoms form an isosceles triangle). The hydrogen atoms are *covalently* bonded to the oxygen atoms but the electrons in the bonds are shifted somewhat towards the oxygen. Or to look at it another way, they spend more time with the oxygen atom than they do with the hydrogen atoms. This makes the molecule more negative at the oxygen atom and more positive at the hydrogen atoms.

This situation produces what we call a **polar molecule**. Just as a magnet has magnetic poles, north and south, with the north having an attraction for the south, a polar molecule has electrical poles, positive and negative, with there being an attraction between unlike poles in the same way that there is an attraction between positive cations and negative anions in an ionic bond.

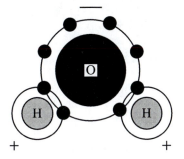

Diagram of a polar water molecule with covalent bonds between the atoms.

This imbalance in charges is a permanent feature of the molecule, i.e., it is like a triangle with a positive charge on two corners and a negative charge on the other. This charge is much smaller than the single electron charge such as there would be on a chlorine anion or a sodium cation, because the electron is not totally displaced as is the case in an ionic bond. The small charge results from the fact that the electron favors the oxygen rather than the hydrogen.

When two molecules of water come together at a low enough temperature the positively charged ends of the molecule are attracted by the negative end of an adjacent molecule with the formation of a bond between them. Just like the ionic bond, this **hydrogen bond** is the result of electrostatic attraction. However, it is much weaker because the charges involved are much smaller. This is why solid ice melts at quite a low temperature. The bonds between the molecules are quite weak.

We should also note another difference between ionic and hydrogen bonds. Ionic bonds hold ions together; hydrogen bonds hold molecules together.

We already mentioned that the water molecule contains an angle of 105°. This is not much different from the angle between the corners of a hexagon (120°). It is therefore perhaps not surprising that when these water molecules are joined together by hydrogen bonds to form ice, these angles are slightly stretched to 120° so that the molecules arrange themselves into hexagons as shown below.

This arrangement gives the ice crystals a **hexagonal symmetry** and accounts for the shape of snowflakes. You are probably aware that each snowflake is unique and has the form of a complex six-pointed star.

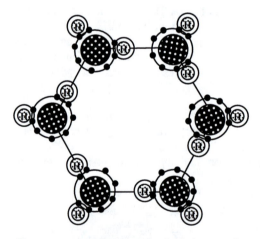

The arrangement of water molecules in ice crystals.

Another interesting fact about ice, which we can explain from what we know about the bonding between water molecules, has to do with density. The hydrogen bonds are **directional** bonds in the sense that they point in the direction of the hydrogen atoms in the molecule. This forces the adjacent molecules into the arrangement shown above, a hexagon with a large space in the middle. As a result, the density is low and solid ice is lighter than water. In the liquid the molecules can pack more closely together. Think about it! Nearly all liquids become denser when they freeze and the solid sinks to the bottom. This is not the case with water, which is why ice forms on the top of a pond rather than sinks to the bottom, or ice floats in your soft drink.

Hydrogen bonds are common between molecules that contain hydrogen. They are often important bonds between long chain polymer molecules. While they are not as strong as the primary bonds, they are somewhat stronger than the bonds (van der Waals) which usually exist between polymer molecules. The introduction of hydrogen bonding is therefore one possible way of strengthening the polymer.

Van der Waals bonds

Van der Waals bonds are the weakest of all chemical bonds. The only materials that have only van der Waals bonds are the solid inert gases. They melt at very low temperatures and cannot be considered useful materials.

Van der Waals bonds are more difficult to understand than are hydrogen bonds. They are also the result of electrostatic attraction between polar molecules, but in this case the polarity of the molecules is not permanent or fixed in direction as it is in water. It is always changing or fluctuating. Take the example of neon, an inert gas with 10 electrons (1st shell, 2; 2nd shell, 8), shown below. At any instant there may be 4 electrons on one side of the atom and 6 on the other. A fraction of a second later the situation may be reversed. This imbalance in the electron distribution gives rise to a **dipole** because the centers of the positive charge in the nucleus and the negative charge of the surrounding electrons do not coincide. However, the dipole is fluctuating. Two adjacent temporary dipoles of opposite sign attract each other.

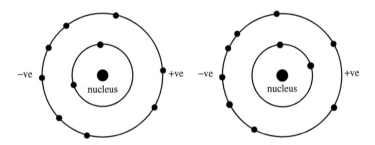

Van der Waals bond formed between two fluctuating dipoles in neon atoms.

These fluctuating dipoles, though weak and temporary, still allow for bonding between atoms or molecules. The bond is non-directional. How could it be anything else, when the dipole is itself always changing direction? Van der Waals bonds are important in polymers and in graphite.

In closing this discussion of the chemical bonding, which holds materials together, we shall make a few general important points.

- bonds other than covalent are really caused by positive and negative charges attracting each other.
- only covalent and hydrogen bonds are directional.
- no important engineering material has only hydrogen or van der Waals bonds. Such a material would be too weak to be of use.

These two bond types—**hydrogen** and **van der Waals**—are known as the **secondary bonds**. They are important in materials because, when present, they are often the weak links in an otherwise strong material.

Materials with both primary and secondary bonds

There are many important engineering materials that contain both primary *and* secondary bonds. For example graphite contains both covalent and van der Waals bonds. As mentioned earlier (Page 11), it consists of layers of carbon atoms held together by strong covalent bonds in a hexagonal 'chicken-wire' arrangement; these layer planes are held together by weak van der Waals bonds. The weak bonds between the layers allow them to slide over each other easily, hence the lubricating property of graphite.

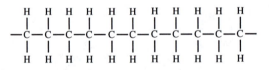

Types of bonding in a graphite crystal.

Polymers are materials that are based on chains of carbon atoms with strong covalent bonds between the carbon atoms in the chain, but there are usually weak secondary bonds between adjacent chains. For example, polyethylene has the chain shown in the following figure.

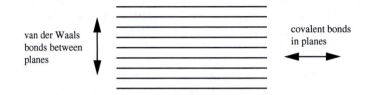

A portion of a polyethylene chain molecule.

A piece of solid polyethylene consists of millions of these chains of different lengths, each possibly containing thousands of carbon atoms, held together by weak secondary bonds. In general they are not aligned as shown in the following diagram, but are more convoluted and tangled, however the intention here is to indicate where the two types of bonds are situated.

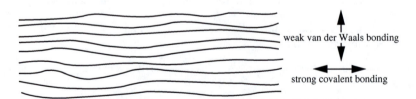

Illustration of a number of polymer chains with covalent bonds along the chains and van der Waals bonds between them.

The following diagram shows what the internal structure of a piece of solid polyethylene may really look like. Sometimes it is likened to a tangled mass of cooked spaghetti. The strands in the spaghetti (polymer chains) are relatively strong, while the bonds between them are quite weak, allowing the strands to slide over each other easily. This easy movement of the chains is what causes many polymers to be plastic, or easily deformed. We shall be reminded several times in this book that deformation of

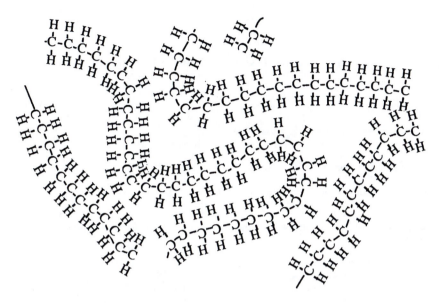

Diagram of how molecular chains may exist in a piece of polyethylene.

a material involves the motion of atoms. Here this occurs by the sliding of these molecular chains over each other.

Before we finish this section, we should remind ourselves that we have already mentioned another material, not as important as a structural solid, which contains two different types of bonds. Ice contains covalent bonds within a molecule and hydrogen bonds between molecules. In a similar manner, dry ice, solid CO_2, also has covalent bonds between the carbon and oxygen atoms in the carbon dioxide molecule, but van der Waals bonds between the molecules. There are many instances where a solid contains two different bonds. We have only mentioned the most important ones.

QUESTIONS: Chapters 1–5

1. Which of the following is not part of the scientific method?
   (a) fabrication   (b) experiment   (c) hypothesis   (d) observation

2. Which of the following is not part of engineering design?
   (a) fabrication   (b) analysis   (c) design   (d) hypothesis

3. Materials science and engineering is the study and control of processing-_____-properties relationships in materials.
   (a) design   (b) implementation   (c) structure   (d) temperature

4. New materials are made by new _____ of elements or by _____ existing materials.
   (a) isotopes, modifying   (b) combinations, modifying   (c) combinations, heating
   (d) isotopes, heating

5. Which of the following is not part of materials processing?
   (a) estimation   (b) firing   (c) composition   (d) mixing   (e) forming

6. Which of the following is the largest in terms of scale of structure?
   (a) electronic   (b) macro   (c) atomic   (d) crystal   (e) micro

7. Which of the following is not an amorphous form of carbon?
   (a) soot   (b) carbon black   (c) carbon nanotube   (d) glassy carbon   (e) none of the above

8. Which of the following is not one of the recognized classes of materials?
   (a) biomaterials   (b) semiconductors   (c) metals   (d) ceramics   (e) none of the above

9. Materials that are physical combinations of two or more materials from the same class or different classes are called?
   (a) composites   (b) nanomaterials   (c) metals   (d) ceramics   (e) all of the above

10. Which of the following is true for metallic bonding?
    (a) directional   (b) transfer of electrons   (c) attraction between cation and anion
    (d) allows for close packing of atoms   (e) both c and d

11. Metallic and ionic bonds are similar in what way(s)?
    (a) directional   (b) transfer of electrons   (c) close packing of ions   (d) both a and b
    (e) both a and c

12. Which of the following is not true of ionic bonding?
    (a) non-directional   (b) allows for close packing of ions   (c) strong
    (d) bonded atoms share an octet (8) of electrons

13. Graphite and diamond both have the same _____ structure.
    (a) atomic   (b) electron   (c) crystal   (d) micro   (e) macro

14. A good example of a material that has two different types of bonds is _____.
    (a) diamond   (b) silicon   (c) sodium chloride   (d) iron   (e) ice

15. The maximum number of electrons in the 3rd shell of an atom is _____.
    (a) 8   (b) 10   (c) 18   (d) 28   (e) none of these

16. The secondary bonds are _____.
    (a) covalent & hydrogen   (b) metallic & ionic   (c) hydrogen & ionic
    (d) hydrogen & van der Waals   (e) covalent and ionic

17. When buying a diamond, you should look at the "cut", "clarity", "carat", and "color". Which level of structure does "cut" relate to?
    (a) electron   (b) crystal   (c) micro   (d) macro   (e) electron

18. Graphite has secondary bonds in _____ dimension(s) which makes it a good _____.
    (a) two; conductor   (b) one; lubricant   (c) three; semiconductor   (d) two; superconductor

19. The addition of a small amount of nitrogen to diamond makes it _____.
    (a) brittle   (b) yellow   (c) stronger   (d) blue   (e) none of the above

20. The element sulfur has 16 electrons. How many are in its outermost shell?
    (a) 0   (b) 2   (c) 4   (d) 6   (e) 8

21. In diamond, all four valence electrons of a carbon atom are bonded to other carbon atoms with _____ bonds.
    (a) covalent   (b) ionic   (c) metallic   (d) van der Waals   (e) hydrogen

22. Which is not a primary bond?
    (a) covalent   (b) hydrogen   (c) ionic   (d) metallic

23. Carbon black is important in car tires because it _____.
    (a) reinforces   (b) repels water   (c) keeps light out   (d) both a and b   (e) both a and c

24. Which is true of a polymeric material?
    (a) only made from synthetic materials   (b) magnetic   (c) based on chains of argon atoms
    (d) usually thermal and electrical insulators   (e) usually brittle

25. In which of the following would you probably not find the element silicon?
    (a) sand   (b) semiconductors   (c) glass   (d) plastic

26. The intentional addition of foreign atoms to a material is called _____.
    (a) doping   (b) smelting   (c) refining   (d) etching   (e) forging

27. An alloy is a mixture of two or more _____.
    (a) ceramics   (b) metals   (c) polymers   (d) metals and ceramics   (e) ceramics and polymers

28. Elements desire to have _____ electrons in their outermost shell.
    (a) 0   (b) 4   (c) 6   (d) 8   (e) as many as possible

29. The outermost electrons surrounding an atom are called the _____ electrons.
    (a) orbiting   (b) inert   (c) free   (d) valence   (e) none of the above

30. When atoms release electrons they have a net positive charge and are called _____.
    (a) isotopes   (b) cations   (c) anions   (d) inert   (e) amorphous

31. Which of the following is not true of covalent bonding?
    (a) directional   (b) easy for atoms to move past each other   (c) strong
    (d) bonded atoms share an octet (8) of electrons

32. Which of the following is not an inert gas?
    (a) Hydrogen   (b) Neon   (c) Xenon   (d) Argon   (e) Helium

33. Van der Waals bonds are due to a(n) _____ imbalance.
    (a) atom   (b) anion   (c) cation   (d) electron

34. Which is the only bond not caused by the attraction of positive and negative charges?
    (a) metallic   (b) ionic   (c) covalent   (d) hydrogen   (e) van der Waals

35. Window glass has a slight green tint due to _____ impurities.
    (a) iron   (b) carbon   (c) sodium   (d) aluminum   (e) there are no impurities

36. Materials which lack a crystal structure are called _____.
    (a) amorphous   (b) crystalline   (c) anisotropic   (d) nanophasic   (e) none of these

37. The majority of elements in the periodic table are _____.
    (a) metals   (b) non-metals   (c) ceramics   (d) semiconductors   (e) superconductors

38. An anion is _____.
    (a) an atom which has gained an electron   (b) an atom which has lost a proton
    (c) an atom which has lost an electron   (d) an atom which has gained a proton   (e) charge neutral

39. Which is the incorrect statement?
    (a) some metals are non-magnetic   (b) most metals are ductile
    (c) no metals are liquid at room temperature   (d) most metals can be easily deformed
    (e) all these are correct

40. The following two bond types lead to close-packed structures.
    (a) covalent, metal   (b) covalent, ionic   (c) ionic, metallic
    (d) Van der Waals, covalent   (e) hydrogen, ionic

41. After the composition has been selected, changes in the processing of a material may affect the material's _____.
    (a) atomic structure   (b) microstructure   (c) properties   (d) both a and c   (e) both b and c

42. Van der Waals bonds are found in _____.
    (a) ceramic materials   (b) hydrogen atoms   (c) water   (d) inert gases   (e) semiconductors

43. Which of the following pairs of bonds is directional?
    (a) covalent, ionic   (b) ionic, metallic   (c) metallic, hydrogen   (d) hydrogen, van der Waals
    (e) none of these combinations is correct

44. Which of the following is not true for most metals?
    (a) they are ductile   (b) they are opaque   (c) they cannot be oxidized
    (d) they are not magnetic   (e) they conduct electricity

6. CRYSTAL STRUCTURES

Close-Packed Structures

To a large extent the bonding determines the way the atoms pack together in solids. We have already mentioned that the atoms in materials with non-directional bonds can pack more closely than those held together with directed bonds. This means that the easiest to consider are the pure metals (metallic bonding) and solid inert gases (van der Waals bonding). In these cases the atoms are all the same size and the bonds are non-directional so that the atoms can stack very close and efficiently in the same way that the balls are racked up on a pool table for the break.

We call the way they stack **close packing**. A plane of close-packed atoms is shown very simply in the following diagram.

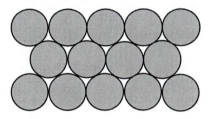

A close-packed plane of atoms in a metal.

Notice that where atoms touch each other there is a sort of triangular hole or depression into which another atom, placed on top of this plane, will naturally fall and rest. If we were to place another atom there it would form a tetrahedron with the three atoms it touches. We can continue to place atoms in these triangular depressions and so build up a second close-packed atom plane. Notice that this second plane can stack on the first plane in one of two positions. It is physically impossible to place atoms in both positions at the same time.

If the first layer is designated A, then the two possibilities for the second layer are B and C, shown by the medium and dark circles in the following diagram. The diagram also illustrates the impossibility of filling both sites at the same time.

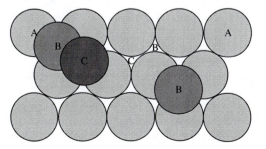

Stacking of two close-packed planes in a metal crystal. Note that it is impossible to have atoms in both B and C positions in the same plane.

If we now take a stack of two layers, AB, and build up a third layer, it too can occupy one of two positions on top of the B layer. One is directly on top of the original A layer and the other is in the C positions.

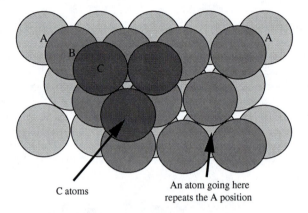

C atoms

An atom going here
repeats the A position

Stacking of three close-packed planes in the ABC sequence in a metal crystal.

These two stacking sequences, AB and ABC, form the basis of the crystal structures of many of the metals and all the solid inert gases. The latter are of no practical importance to us so we shall be mainly concerned with the metals.

A repetition of the AB sequence produces what we call the **hexagonal close-packed (HCP)** arrangement of atoms, whereas by repeating the ABC sequence we produce a **cubic close-packed (CCP)** arrangement.

ABABABABABABA -- is hexagonal close-packed (HCP)

ABCABCABCABCA -- is cubic close-packed (CCP)

These arrangements are exhibited by the following solid inert gases and metals. The list is not complete.

HCP—Helium, cadmium, titanium, magnesium, zinc, cobalt, zirconium

CCP—Argon, neon, gold, silver, copper, aluminum, iron, nickel

These crystal structures are close-packed in that there is no more efficient way to pack like-sized spheres. If one packs like-sized marbles into HCP or CCP structures, the marbles will occupy 74% of the available space. Materials scientists refer to this as the atomic packing factor, which is 0.74 for HCP and CCP.

One way to help visualize these two structures is to look for signature motifs. In the case of the CCP structure, the signature motif is a triangle. In the case of HCP, the signature motif is a hexagon. You can find both motifs on the following close-packed plane.

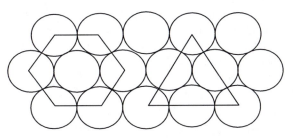

A close-packed plane of atoms showing the signature motifs of the HCP (hexagon) and CCP (triangle) structures.

When we stack atoms in the --ABCABCABCA-- sequence we say that we form a **cubic close-packed** structure. Why cubic? Simply because when stacking this way we form a cube. It is not easy to see that this is the case unless one has a three-dimensional model, but the following diagram may be a help. Note that the atoms in a close-packed plane touch each other as shown in earlier diagrams, but for the three dimensional diagram it is easier to use an 'exploded' view. Remember that the atoms are really in contact as discussed earlier. Observe the triangles, the signature motif of the CCP structure.

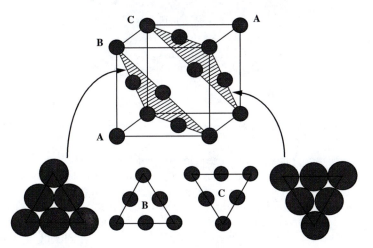

'Exploded' view of a cubic close-packed (CCP) crystal showing the close-packed planes.

This structure is very important in metals because it is these close-packed planes of atoms which slide over each other and allow metals to deform easily. The following diagram illustrates the effect of plane sliding. It is just like shearing a pack of cards.

Sliding of close-packed planes to produce shear in a crystal.

When this happens between two close-packed planes the atoms in one plane sort of zigzag across the adjacent plane as shown in the following diagram. The wavy grooves indicated are the directions in which the atoms can move relatively easily, because they are the directions in which there is the least up and down motion of one plane over the other.

There are three directions in which this slippage can occur and of course it can occur both backwards or forwards.

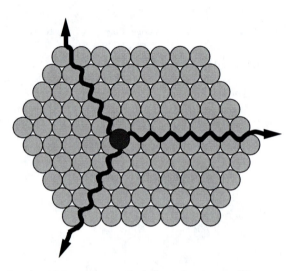

Directions in which one close-packed plane of atoms can slide over another.

If you can see that the packing of close-packed planes in the ABC sequence produces a cube, you should also be able to see that there are four close-packed planes in this crystal structure which are equivalent, and slip is just as likely to occur on any or all of them. Notice that in the diagram of the cube the close-packed plane is drawn by joining three corners of the cube to produce a diagonal plane. If you hold the cube (Page 41) by the corners marked A so that these corners are vertically over each other, the close-packed planes are horizontal. We could also hold the cube by any of the other three pairs of opposite corners and the arrangement would be identical. These four possibilities correspond to the four close-packed planes (**slip planes**), which exist in a CCP crystal and are illustrated below.

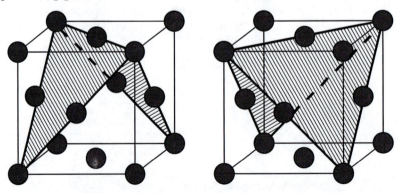

Diagrams illustrating the four completely different non-parallel close-packed planes.
Slipping can occur on any diagonal plane cutting through three corners of the cube.

Since there are **4** different non-parallel slip planes and each can slide along **3** directions, there are therefore **twelve** (4 × 3) ways close-packed planes can slide over each other. When we pull a crystal we are never far from one of these slipping possibilities (called **slip systems**) and the metal deforms.

Imagine that you are looking at a CCP metal single crystal along the diagonal of the top face as shown in the following diagram. The two shaded planes are two planes on which slip can occur and they are both parallel to your viewing direction. Now imagine you pull the crystal in the direction indicated. Slip can take place on these two planes, and the crystal elongates by a combination of these two slip motions as illustrated.

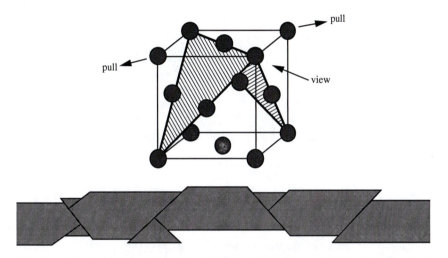

The upper diagram shows a cubic close-packed crystal with the two possible slip planes for the direction of pull. The lower diagram illustrates how deformation (stretch) may occur.

This is obviously a much simplified illustration, but it does indicate possibilities which do not exist in HCP metals which have ABABAB stacking. (As we mentioned previously, it's called HCP because the plane contains hexagons as indicated in the next diagram.) In the HCP structure, there are no close-packed planes other than this plane. Hence, slip can only occur on the parallel stacked close-packed planes. This means that HCP metals have only three slip systems and are hence not as ductile.

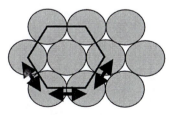

The hexagon in a close-packed plane of atoms. When the layers are stacked in the ABABA sequence no new close-packed planes are formed and slip can only occur on this one plane.

If we pull a single crystal of an HCP metal we get slip only on the parallel close-packed planes as illustrated in the following figure. The crystal shears like a stack of coins. This might be typical of a zinc crystal, shown in the photograph.

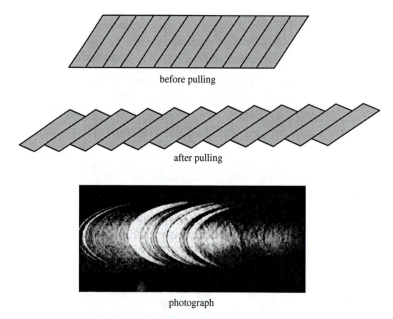

before pulling

after pulling

photograph

Diagrams and photograph of slip in a zinc crystal (HCP), which can only slip on one plane.
(Photo courtesy of Professor Earl Parker, Univ. of California at Berkeley)

Structures of some other Crystals

Some metals are what we call **body centered cubic (BCC)**. They also have atoms on the corners of a cube. But there is an additional one in the center of the cube rather than one on the center of each face. These atoms are not 'close-packed' although they are close to being so. The atoms in this arrangement occupy 68% of the total volume, compared to 74% for CCP and HCP crystals.

The following diagram shows a BCC crystal. It contains more open space than does CCP, but there is one very important difference, the open space in BCC may be more in total volume, but it is divided up into much smaller holes (**interstices**). Of course there are many more interstices in BCC crystals than in CCP to give the larger total empty volume, but the fact that the interstices are smaller gives the two structures very different properties.

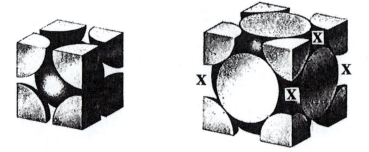

The left diagram shows a BCC crystal while the right is CCP. Note that the atoms are the same size and are in contact in both diagrams. This makes the CCP cell larger than the BCC. It is clear that the interstices at the edges of the CCP cell (X) are larger than any in the BCC cell.

BCC metals can also slip on planes in the crystals, and there are in fact just as many possibilities for slip as there are in CCP crystals. This makes BCC metals as **ductile** as the CCP metals, hence most metals are considered ductile. It is the HCP metals that are somewhat brittle. The following diagram shows one of the planes in the BCC crystal on which slip occurs. Any plane produced by making a diagonal cut perpendicular to a cube face will have the same arrangement of atoms. There are therefore five other identical planes in the crystal on which slip can occur, giving a total of six **slip planes**. See if you can find them.

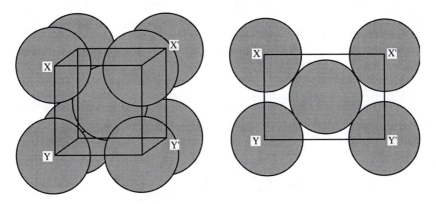

One of the six possible slip planes in a BCC crystal.

Each of the six slip planes in this BCC crystal has two directions in which an atom on an adjacent plane can move, as illustrated below, so that there are again twelve slip systems (**6 planes × 2** directions), which is the same number as in CCP crystals. We should therefore not be surprised to find that BCC metals are as ductile as are CCP metals.

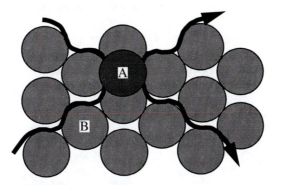

A close-packed plane of atoms in a BCC crystal (B) showing
the two directions in which an atom in an adjacent plane (A) can move.

Notes

1. Up to this point we have referred to the crystal illustrated on page 41 as CCP, cubic close-packed. Look at the figure again. You will see that there is an atom on each corner of the cube and one on the center of each cube face. For this reason we usually refer to this arrangement of atoms as face

centered cubic (FCC). However, note that FCC merely refers to the *arrangement* of the atoms. It does not indicate that they are in contact with each other, i.e. close-packed. Atoms in an FCC arrangement need not be close-packed, and are therefore not necessarily CCP. Atoms which are CCP are always FCC, but FCC crystals need not be CCP, and in fact are usually not.

2. The larger CCP (FCC) cube contains 4 atoms and the smaller BCC cube only two atoms. Count the various parts in the diagrams on page 44. The eight corners each have an eighth of an atom and there are halves of atoms on the six faces of the FCC cell. Of course we can't split atoms this way, we are simply showing that an atom is shared between between two or more cubes, or cells.

   Silicon & Diamond have their atoms bound together by covalent bonds. We have already discussed their crystal structure in chapter 3 but mention it here again to point out that it is in fact an FCC crystal. Remember that each atom forms covalent bonds with four other atoms on the corners of a tetrahedron.

   The diagram shows one tetrahedron, and also how several of these units are arranged to form an FCC crystal. Notice that this structure is more complicated than what we have seen so far because there are four extra atoms in the cell.

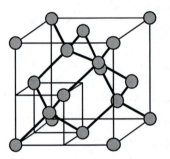

The crystal structure of diamond and silicon. Note the FCC arrangement.

   Notice also that these four extra atoms, shown darker in the following diagram, form their own FCC arrangement. We find that this is typical of all complex crystal structures. It's like having two interwoven cubes, both of which are face centered cubic. Perhaps the following diagram will help you see this. Remember that the darker atoms are the same type as the others.

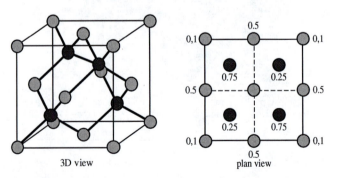

The crystal structure of diamond and silicon, showing the two different
FCC arrangements it contains (numbers give heights in the cube).

Silicon and diamond are examples of crystals which are FCC but are not CCP, i.e., the atoms are not touching.

Graphite has another crystal structure (Page 12), which we have already discussed. Each carbon atom uses three valence electrons to form covalent bonds in a plane while the fourth electron is allowed to move freely through the crystal between the planes. Note that this electron cannot move across the planes, which gives graphite the property of being able to conduct electricity along its layer planes but not across them. It is therefore an electrical conductor in the planes but an electrical insulator in the perpendicular direction. A material which shows different properties in different directions is called **anisotropic**.

Note that the planes in graphite also stack ABABAB, just as they do in HCP crystals, but there is no atom in the center of the hexagons.

Ceramic materials exhibit similar crystal structures to metals, but with an important difference. Ionic ceramics involve positively-charged 'cations' (e.g., Na^+ or Cs^+ or Mg^{2+}) and negatively-charged 'anions' (e.g., Cl^- or O^{2-}) These structures arrange themselves such that cations are surrounded by anions and vice versa, to neutralize charge.

Sodium Chloride has ionic bonds that are non-directed. However in this case it is not simply a matter of stacking atoms of the same size together, as is the case in pure metals, but two sizes of ions are involved. The ions stack as closely as possible, as shown in the following diagram.

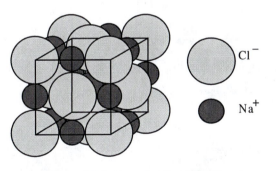

The crystal structure of sodium chloride.

Note that this is also a face centered cubic crystal. There is an FCC arrangement of Na^+ intertwined with an FCC arrangement of Cl^-.

As mentioned in the previous chapter, the packing arrangement of ions depends on their relative sizes, which gives rise to different crystal structures. In sodium chloride each sodium cation is surrounded by six chlorine anions, whereas in **cesium chloride** on the next page, eight chlorine anions can pack around the larger cesium cation. The arrangement of the ions in cesium chloride is shown below. Notice that it is similar to the BCC atom arrangement in some metals (Page 44). However here the atom in the center of the cube is of a different type and size.

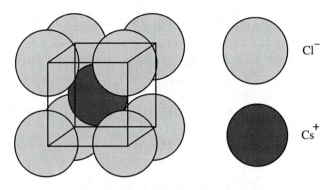

The crystal structure of cesium chloride.

Polymers are not often thought of as being crystalline. The long spaghetti-like molecules do not easily lend themselves to the neat orderly arrangements we have come to expect in crystals. However, there are many polymers that contain at least some crystalline regions. The most easily crystallized polymer is **polyethylene** (Page 34), which consists of a chain of carbon atoms with two hydrogen atoms on each carbon atom in the chain. These hydrogen atoms are very small, after all hydrogen is the smallest and lightest atom found in the universe. The 'straight' polyethylene chain actually zigzags as shown in the following diagram. If you can imagine looking at the chain from one end you would see something which could fit fairly well inside a rectangular beam, something like a two-by-four. (See also photos on page 104.)

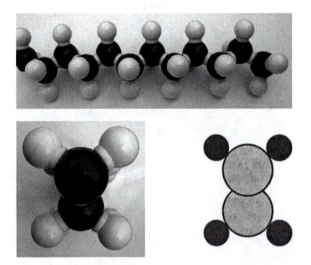

Photographs of a model of a polyethylene chain seen from the side (above) showing the zigzag backbone, and from the end (below) together with the diagram used on the next page.

Now, continuing to look at the chains from their ends, we can see how they stack when the material is crystalline. Their arrangement is more like a herringbone pattern. Adjacent chains are at an angle to each rather than being stacked parallel as you might usually see two-by-fours stacked in a lumber yard.

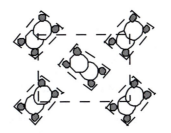

Stacking of polyethylene chains to form a crystal.

Note: Polyethylene is the simplest polymer. It only has small hydrogen atoms attached to the carbon chain, and these don't get in each other's way when the chains try to stack together in an ordered manner, i.e., crystallize. Other polymers do not crystallize so easily because the carbon chains have much larger and more irregular shaped chemical groups attached to them, which tend to get in each other's way when the chains try to stack together in a neat arrangement. We call this effect **steric hindrance** because in three dimensions (stereo) these large groups hinder the neat stacking of the chains.

However, even polyethylene never exists in a totally crystalline form. It usually contains both crystalline and amorphous regions. The reason for this is illustrated in the following diagram. A chain folds back on itself repeatedly to form a single crystal so that the 'surfaces' of the crystal are really amorphous because here the chains are not arranged in an ordered parallel manner.

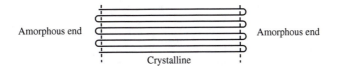

Chain folding to produce a 'single' crystal of polyethylene.

Another model for a polymer material is shown below. Many chains are wandering almost randomly but are occasionally parallel and form crystals. This produces crystalline regions in an amorphous surrounding or matrix.

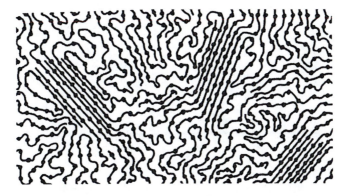

Formation of small polymer crystals in an amorphous matrix.
(K. Easterling, *Tomorrow's Materials*, The Institute of Metals, London, U.K., 1988. Fig. 2)

We shall later see (Page 106) that one way of stiffening a polymer is to increase the fraction of the total volume that is crystalline. This structural feature is therefore an important factor in determining properties.

Apart from glasses and most polymers, materials are generally crystalline. In museums and art galleries you will often see a display of crystals that are found in natural mineral deposits. These are rare and unusually large. Sometimes you can see the crystals in old brass door knobs and handles. This is because acids from hands have etched the material over the years and light reflects differently from adjacent crystals, as already mentioned in the Introduction to this book. These crystals are often several mm in size. In most materials, however, the crystals are too small to be seen by the naked eye, and in some special materials the crystals may only contain a few thousand atoms. This is very small indeed. (Note that a crystal cube with 20 atoms along the edge will contain 8000 atoms.) In fact there is a general rule which we shall later encounter which says that the smaller the crystals in a material, the stronger it is.

In all these materials the regular repetitive arrangement of atoms into crystals has a major effect on the properties. We shall encounter a major effect of different crystal structures when we consider metals in Chapter 10.

7. AMORPHOUS MATERIALS

When a crystalline material is heated, energy is being given to the atoms and they begin to vibrate. The crystal arrangements we have discussed in Chapter 6 represent the mean position of the atoms. In reality the atoms are vibrating around this position and as the material becomes hotter the atom motion becomes more energetic. Eventually this vibration becomes so energetic that the atoms are

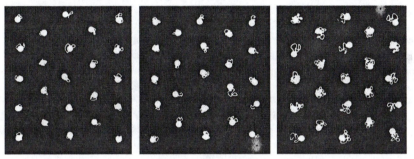

increasing temperature →

Illustration of how atoms move around their mean positions as temperature is increased.
(R. Cotterill, *The Cambridge Guide to the Material World*, Cambridge University Press, 1985. p. 41)

able to break the bonds which hold them together and the material melts. In this liquid form the atoms (or molecules, as in water) are moving quite freely and are usually arranged quite randomly, i.e., the material is **amorphous**. The word amorphous means that there is no **long range order** to the atoms or molecules. There may be a few clusters of atoms which have an ordered arrangement, called **short range order**, but on the whole there is no order over any longer distance.

Glass

In today's world we are quite familiar with the amorphous material glass, but we have a need for other materials in an amorphous state, especially metals. The problem is how to make them. As soon as we begin to cool the liquid, the atoms start to move back into their crystal positions. The only way to stop them is to remove their energy so quickly that they have no time to return to their crystalline arrangement. As a result we can understand that any material can be produced in an amorphous solid state as long as we can cool the liquid quickly enough. This rapid cooling is what we call **quenching**.

The question that we must answer is "how fast is quickly enough?" and this is a very difficult question to answer. It all depends on the speed at which the atoms are moving in the liquid. If the liquid contains very large molecules, especially of an irregular shape, they tend to move sluggishly with the result that the liquid is very **viscous**. If the liquid contains only small spherical atoms they tend to move easily and rapidly.

A good example of the former is sugar (sucrose). When we buy it, it consists of small crystals. If we heat it carefully until it melts and then cool it by dropping it in cold water we can produce a brittle hard candy, essentially a sugar glass. The large sucrose molecules find it impossible to return to the ordered crystalline state during the cooling process. Different cooling processes can be used to produce toffee and fudge. By warming the toffee we allow the molecules to move around more so that they form very small crystals, i.e., fudge. The technical term for this process is **devitrification** (vitreous means glassy), removing the glassy state.

We do something similar when we make Corning Ware® (Chapter 20), starting with a glass object and then causing some small crystals to form within it. The SiO_2 tetrahedra in glass are quite large and angular and therefore not particularly mobile. The liquid glass is very viscous immediately before it solidifies and therefore an amorphous solid is produced. In fact we can cool glass very, very slowly (1°C per million seconds) and it still remains amorphous. The enormous glass mirrors for some astronomical telescopes had to be cooled very slowly in order to avoid cracking. In Corning Ware® we add some very small nuclei to initiate the forming of crystals. These somehow persuade the SiO_2 tetrahedra to organize into very, very small crystals, i.e., the material devitrifies.

In regular glass, the SiO_2 tetrahedra link up to form a complex random three-dimensional network as shown schematically in the following figure. Note that the SiO_2 tetrahedra (only three of the four oxygen atoms are shown) are an example of short range order, but there is no long range order.

We can replace some of these strong covalent bonds with weaker ionic bonds by the addition of **fluxing ions** such as sodium to the molten glass. Some of the oxygen atoms are now only bonded to one silicon atom and have weaker bonds with the sodium atoms. These weaker bonds are of course broken more easily than the stronger covalent bonds with the result that the glass softens at a lower temperature.

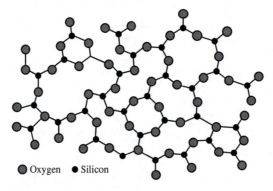

Oxygen   ● Silicon

Diagram illustrating the arrangement of silica (SiO_2) tetrahedra in glass.

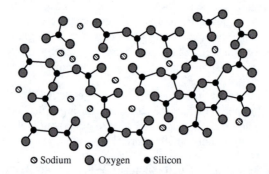

Sodium   Oxygen   ● Silicon

Arrangement of silica (SiO_2) tetrahedra in a sodium glass. The sodium atoms come between the tetrahedra linking them with ionic bonds rather than covalent.

Amorphous Metals

The uses of amorphous glass are well known, but why would we want to make amorphous metals? Remember that the atoms are randomly arranged. There are no planes of atoms to slip over each other so an amorphous metal would be very strong, but brittle. You should also be able to see that it would be less dense. However, it is the amorphous magnetic metals which are of special interest. The following illustrations represent the difference between crystalline and amorphous metals. In the latter there are some regions with short-range order—look for the hexagonal signature motif, i.e., a hexagon of atoms in alignment around a given atom—but there are no extensive three-dimensional arrangements. There are therefore no crystals and no atom planes.

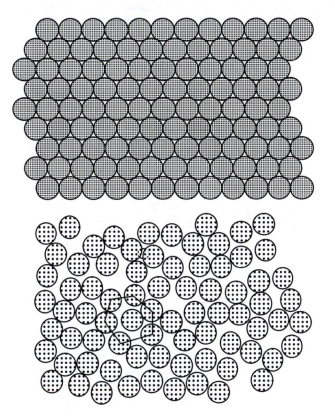

The different arrangements of atoms in crystalline (above) and amorphous metals (below).

Metals like to magnetize in certain directions in the crystal, as a result it is often difficult to change the direction in which a metal is magnetized. Amorphous metals have no crystals and therefore no crystal directions. They can therefore be magnetized equally easily in all directions and the direction of magnetization can be easily changed. This is just what we need to do in an electrical power transformer where we reverse the magnetization direction sixty times in one second. Amorphous magnetic metals have an important application here and are of tremendous interest in today's world.

Now comes the difficult part - cooling the metal quickly enough. The small spherical atoms move very quickly in the liquid and in order to keep them in this amorphous state they must cooled very,

very rapidly, as fast as a million degrees a second. This means that if the molten metal is at 1000°C it must be cooled to room temperature in a thousandth of a second. This is a real problem.

If you take a cake from the oven, it can cool so that the outside is cold, but when you cut into it the center is still hot. If you imagine this happening in a metal it means that the center has time to crystallize, something we don't want. To cool something very quickly all the way through it must be very thin. It is impossible to produce amorphous metals except in the form of relatively thin sheets, because it is only then that we can get the heat out quickly enough. In thick pieces there is no way to stop the atoms in the center from crystallizing.

The following diagram shows one method of doing this. A rapidly rotating copper (good conductor of heat) wheel is chilled with an internal coolant and a stream of molten metal is poured onto it. When the molten metal hits the wheel it is immediately quenched and thrown out into a very thin ribbon. Tens of meters of the thin amorphous metal ribbon are produced in one second!

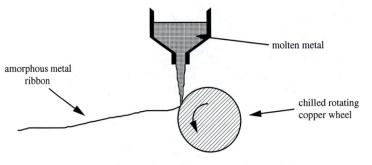

Process for making an amorphous metal.

Conclusion

Amorphous materials that we encounter in today's world are usually glasses and polymers. Metals are notoriously difficult to obtain in an amorphous state because the bonding allows for easy atom movement. Recent techniques are allowing us to produce amorphous metals, but only in very thin sheets. They are expensive to produce and their major application is in electrical transformers. We shall discuss some of their implications in the chapter on magnetic materials.

8. DEFECTS IN SOLIDS

Properties are determined by structure. The crystal and electron structures of graphite make it a good electrical conductor in one direction and an insulator in another. The stacking of atoms in metals (crystal structure) affects their ability to move and hence the deformability and ductility of the material. But what more often determines properties are the **imperfections** materials contain.

We have already mentioned that steel is strong because of carbon atoms being dissolved in it during heating, that diamonds are colored by impurities and that the doping of semiconductors with impurity atoms enables us to tailor their electrical properties to our needs. When the transatlantic telephone cable was laid in 1857, it was found that its electrical conduction was only 14% of that of the best copper available. We now know that this difference was caused by the presence of impurities. The fact that modern stainless steel cookware does not conduct heat as well as the old cast iron pots is due to the presence of the impurities we add to the iron to make it stainless. We shall later come to understand these different phenomena, but our immediate purpose is to understand something about these defects themselves.

We start with a different type of defect from those we have just mentioned. In our discussion of metal crystal structures, it was pointed out that metals deform by the closest packed planes of atoms sliding over each other. Early in the 1900's, physicists were able to calculate the force needed to slide these planes of atoms over each other and were puzzled to find that their calculations (theory) gave a value that was one thousand times greater than the measured force (experiment) to deform a metal.

If we find that our theory and experimental results differ by a factor of 2 or 3, we are usually content to think that we have come close to understanding what is going on in our experiments, and we then try to adjust the theory to get better agreement. In fact, in many phenomena we are quite happy to have a theory that agrees so closely with our measurements. However, an error, or discrepancy, of a thousand fold is too large to be due to calculation errors. There must be something wrong with the model, or something that we have overlooked. In this case it turns out that we have overlooked a defect, which we call a **dislocation**.

Dislocations

When the scientists formulated their theory of the slip of atom planes over each other in metals they assumed that when two planes slide over each other, **all** atoms on the planes are sliding at the same time. It turns out that this does not happen. To make things easier, the atoms move a row at a time. This is made possible by the presence of defects known as **dislocations**.

What is a dislocation? The easiest way to think of it is to take a book and imagine the pages to be the planes of atoms in the crystal. Now take a sheet of the same paper and place it between two pages of the book but only half way into the book. You have now inserted an extra 'half-plane' of atoms. Actually it's part of a plane, not precisely half a plane. This kind of dislocation is referred to as an **edge dislocation**, and the termination of the half-plane is a line and is called a **dislocation line**.

The diagram below shows what we have been talking about. The extra partial plane finishes at the line D, which we call the dislocation line. This is the defect. Notice that there is nothing we can call a defect if we go away from this line. Do the book experiment! Just by looking at the edges of the pages you will see nothing wrong or unusual except where the extra page terminates. A quarter of an inch away from this position in any direction and you can see no disturbance. Indeed the disturbance is confined to the region where the extra page, or in our case the extra atom plane, terminates. Observe that the bonds are stretched in the vicinity of the dislocation line—look at the bonds immediately to the right and left of 'D' in the diagram. It would be quite easy to break the bond, e.g., to the right of 'D', and reconnect the column of atoms beneath to the extra half-plane. In this way, the extra half-plane will have moved one step to the right. This is what causes plane A to slip over plane B a thousand times easier than it could slip without the defect. It does so because it introduces a mechanism for the planes to slide a little at a time.

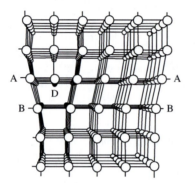

When plane A slides over plane B it uses the dislocation to move gradually— a little at a time.

Three dimensional diagram of a dislocation in a simple crystal.
(W. F. Smith, *Principles of Materials Science and Engineering*, McGraw Hill, New York, 1986. Fig. 4.18. Reproduced with permission of the publisher)

There are two analogies in your experience that may help you to understand what is happening. One is illustrated on the next page.

Remember how a caterpillar moves by using one pair of legs at a time rather than by moving them all at the same time. In the same way the crystal slips its atoms one row at a time, rather than moving all the atoms in a plane simultaneously (Page 57). This means that the force required at any one instant is less.

When the top part of the crystal wants to slide over the bottom part, it first moves the first atom plane, thus bunching up the next plane and producing a dislocation. In the same way a caterpillar moves its rear legs and produces a small kink or fold in its body; this fold is analogous to the dislocation. It then moves this fold along the body putting down the feet at the rear of the fold and lifting up those at the front.

In the same way the extra plane of atoms links up with a plane in the lower part of the crystal, forcing the next plane in the top part of the crystal to be the one producing the dislocation. This continues until it reaches the other side.

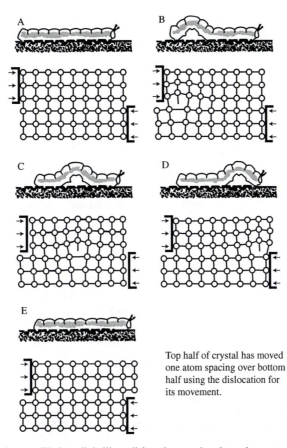

Top half of crystal has moved one atom spacing over bottom half using the dislocation for its movement.

A caterpillar's walk is like a dislocation moving through a crystal.
(R. Cotterill, *The Cambridge Guide to the Material World*, Cambridge University Press, 1985. p.70)

The previous diagram shows that a dislocation is created by forcing a few planes in the top of the crystal together. The dislocation can then move through the crystal, and when it reaches the other end the result is that one half of the crystal has slipped over the other half by **one** atom spacing. In the same way, the caterpillar has progressed one step as a result of the sequence of its leg movements.

The above concept is one we are all familiar with. Moving one item at a time is easier than trying to carry everything at once. Just think how you would transport a pile of bricks!

The second analogy is that of sliding a large carpet over a floor. To move the whole carpet involves overcoming the friction between it and the floor, and this might be too much for you to manage. A way of accomplishing the same thing is to put a wrinkle in the carpet and push this wrinkle across the floor (Page 58). The end result is that the whole carpet moves a distance equal to the length of material used to make the wrinkle you introduced. The force required is much less because you are only having to overcome the friction between a small strip of carpet and the floor at any instant.

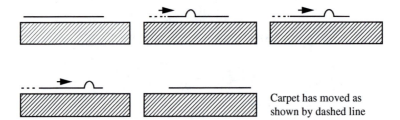

Carpet has moved as
shown by dashed line

It is easier to move a carpet on a floor by putting a wrinkle in it and pushing that along.

Now just consider the implications of what we have discussed. A dislocation is a defect that allows atoms to slide over each other, but it only produces a net movement of **one atom spacing**. When it exits the material at the far side, it is gone. We know of course that we can easily make metals move much more than one atom spacing. If you bend a paper clip, the atoms on the outside of the bend must have traveled large distances to produce the effect. If this movement is produced by dislocations, each moving the atoms by only one atom spacing, there must be millions of these dislocations to produce the large deformations we have just mentioned.

This is in fact the case. In a one pound block of highly deformed aluminum there are enough dislocations to circle the equator of the earth over **one thousand times** if they were all straightened out and placed end to end. This may be difficult to imagine, but it is true. We can see these defects in the electron microscope and measure their total length, and these are the values we obtain.

Summary

Dislocations make it a thousand times easier for the planes of atoms in a crystal to slide over each other than would be the case if they were to slide over each other as complete perfect entities. There are hundreds of miles of dislocations in even a very small piece of metal such as a deformed paper clip.

What's more, we saw (Page 42) that in cubic close packed crystals there are four different non-parallel planes that can slide over each other, i.e., there can be dislocations moving on many different planes at the same time. As already mentioned, the four planes, with each able to slip in three directions, produce a system of slip possibilities such that whatever way you apply a force to the crystal, it will never be far from one of them. The dislocations simply make such slip one thousand times easier. That's why metals usually deform easily.

Just think for a moment why it is the close packed planes of atoms that slide over each other. Are these the only planes that slip? The answer is 'yes' most of the time, and for our purposes we can assume that it is always the case. The reason is not really difficult to understand. In any given crystal there is a fixed number of atoms in a given volume. We can think of these atoms as lying on planes as shown in the following diagram. There are many possible planes, just as there are many different ways of seeing rows of trees in an orchard. As you walk among the trees you can align them in many different ways. In the same way we can look at atoms in a crystal.

Notice from the diagram that different planes have different atom densities (different numbers of atoms per unit area). The closer to each other the atoms are on a plane, the greater the distance to the next plane. If you think about it, this statement is a logical necessity. In a given volume there will be a certain number of parallel planes, and the number of atoms in this volume is given by multiplying the number of atoms on one plane by the number of planes. If we choose a different plane with fewer atoms on it then there must be more of these planes in the volume because the number of atoms in the volume has not changed. Also, if there are more of these new planes they must be closer together. This is also clear in the following diagram.

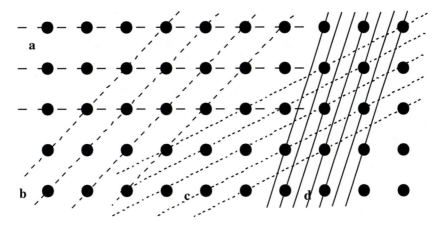

As you go from planes a to d, the planes get closer together and the atoms in the planes become further apart.

It should be easy to see that the planes with the highest atom density are those that are the furthest apart and thus are most easily able to move over each other. This is why the planes that have the largest number of atoms per unit area are the ones that slip. In the CCP crystal, these planes are, of course, the close packed planes. It's just impossible to have a higher atom density than they have. In the BCC crystal, the plane with the highest density of atoms is the one shown in the diagram on page 45. This is the plane on which slip occurs in metals with this crystal structure, and there are six identical non-parallel planes on which such slip can occur.

Another way of thinking of this fact is to consider the smoothness of two planes with different atom densities. The plane with the higher atom density is 'smoother' than the other, and it is therefore easier for an atom to move on this plane than on any other. This is illustrated in the following diagram.

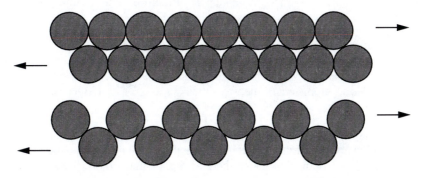

In the upper diagram the planes are smoother (closer packed) and an atom makes less up-and-down movement as it moves across, so that less force is required to move it.
In the lower diagram the atoms make much more vertical movement requiring a much larger force for their movement.

One final note on dislocations. Once a dislocation has moved in one direction, it would require an equal and opposite force to move it back. The atoms do not return to their original positions when the force is removed. Dislocations are therefore responsible for **plastic deformation** in a material.

Let's pause and consider what we mean by this. The easiest model is to once again consider an atom moving over a plane of atoms as shown in the previous diagram. In order to move, the atom has to climb over the atom in the plane underneath. If pushed hard enough it will go all the way over and fall down the other side. The atom will then stay there when the force is removed. The motion is permanent until a force is applied in the opposite direction. This is what we mean by plastic deformation. A force deforms a material and the material stays deformed when the force is removed. We say that the deformation is permanent (**plastic deformation**). However, if the force is less, and the atom is only pushed part way over the underlying atom (or part way up the hill), there is a deformation as a result of the atom displacement, but the atom returns to its original position when the force is removed. We call this **elastic deformation**. Just like a piece of elastic, the atoms and the material return to their original state when the force is removed.

Point Defects

Because dislocations are essentially **lines** that wander through the crystal, we call them **line** defects. Other major defects are **point** defects—they typically involve a single atom. Point defects are relatively simple to understand. They are often divided into two categories; those which come from the material itself (**intrinsic** defects) and those which come from outside impurities (**extrinsic**).

As far as we are concerned there are two extrinsic and two intrinsic point defects of importance.

Intrinsic point defects

Just as we have seen that there can be some imperfections in the way planes are arranged (thus forming dislocations) there can be imperfections in the way the atoms are arranged in the planes. The two common ones that occur in pure crystals are the **vacancy** and the **interstitial**.

A **vacancy** is quite simply a missing atom or group of two or three atoms. It is important because it produces a distortion in the neat orderly arrangement of the surrounding atoms, which move slightly to partially fill the hole left by the missing atom.

An intrinsic **interstitial** is a defect caused by an extra atom pushing its way into the sites between the atoms in the ordered arrangement. These normally unoccupied sites are referred to as **interstices**. If the extra atom is of the same type, and hence the same size, as the rest of the atoms in the crystal, it must elbow the surrounding atoms out of the way to make room for itself. Once again there is a distortion (strain) around the defect.

Because it takes a lot of energy to push atoms apart to allow an extra atom to enter the arrangement, there are usually very few of these "self" interstitial defects; they are not energetically favorable compared to vacancies, for instance, of which there tend to be many more. These vacancies are really important, as we will see.

The number of vacancies increases with temperature until, at the melting point, about 0.01% of the atoms are missing. This means that one out of every 10,000 atom places in the crystal is vacant.

(Note: they have not evaporated, they have just gone to positions on the edges of the crystals. This causes a measurable expansion of the material as it reaches the melting point).

Why are these defects so important? For two reasons. First, as already mentioned, they distort the arrangement of the atoms (the lattice). This makes it more difficult for electrons and dislocations to move around. Second, these defects provide a mechanism for atoms to move around in the crystal.

Also, atoms move in a crystal by means of these point defects. The most usual means is by using the vacancies because there are many more of them than there are interstitials. The situation is similar to moving tiles in the 4 × 4 arrangement shown below. We can rearrange the tiles in any way we wish because one tile (the vacancy) is missing. If there were no vacancy the only way to rearrange things would be to take everything apart. We do the latter in materials when we melt them and resolidify them, but vacancies allow materials to rearrange their atoms while still in the solid state. This means that we can consolidate particles together while they are still solid. When we fire (bake) a ceramic made by compacting tiny crystal particles, the crystals join (**sinter** is the technical term) because the vacancies allow the atoms to move around. Remember, there are more vacancies at higher temperatures, and that's why we apply heat. Not only does this give the atoms more energy but it also creates more vacancies for them to move through.

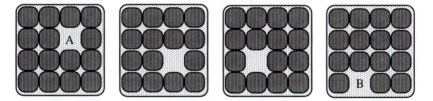

Arrangement of tiles as in the common game. Because they are all identical, there are many ways of going from the situation shown on the left to the one on the right. It would be impossible to say which tiles had moved—only that the hole had gone from A to B.

The empty space allows the tiles to move around in the same way that atom vacancies allow atoms to move around and rearrange themselves in a crystal. By following the sequence of diagrams you can tell which tile has been moved in each case. However if you compare the first and last diagrams you cannot tell which tiles have been moved to achieve the new arrangement. All you can say is that the empty space has moved from one position to another. The same thing happens in crystals, we can only tell that the vacancy has moved from one position to another. We therefore say that the rearrangement has occurred by **vacancy motion**.

Extrinsic point defects

The two defects in this category are both related to impurities. When an atom of an impurity is added to a material it can enter the atomic arrangement in two different positions, **interstitial** or **substitutional**. It is difficult to predict which one will occur, but it usually depends on the size of the impurity atom.

An extrinsic **interstitial** impurity atom sits in the spaces (**interstices**) between the original atoms. Because of this it is usually quite a small atom (carbon, nitrogen, boron). Even though there is a space between the atoms, there is almost never quite enough room for the impurity atom, so that once again there is a distortion as the surrounding atoms are pushed back. This also squeezes the surrounding intersticies so that they cannot accommodate an impurity atom. As a result there is a limit to the number of interstitial impurity atoms we can put into the crystal without them forming their own little crystals or precipitates.

Iron can exist in two crystal forms, CCP (FCC) and BCC. Note that the diagrams shown on page 44 indicate that even though the BCC arrangement has more empty space within it, it cannot accept as much interstitial carbon as can the FCC form because the space is divided up more, i.e., the empty space is split into a much larger number of smaller interstices.

A **substitutional** impurity atom is usually about the same size as the atoms of the host material. The foreign atom simply replaces one of the original atoms of the pure material. However even in this case there is always a distortion of the surrounding lattice because the impurity atom is never exactly the same size as the atom it replaces.

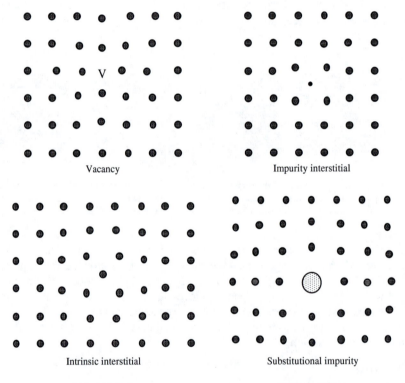

Illustrations of the four most common point defects in materials. In the vacancy (upper left) the atoms tend to collapse into the space left by the missing atom. A much smaller impurity atom (upper right) tends to push its way into an interstice, while a larger impurity atom (lower right) will substitute for one of the original atoms. Sometimes an extra atom of the original material forces itself into an interstitial position (lower left), but this is a highly unlikely occurrence.

In some cases the distortion produced by the impurity atoms is so small that we can replace the original atoms *ad infinitum* until we have only atoms of what was the original impurity, but such cases are not common. When this occurs we say that the two materials are completely soluble in each other—or that they show complete mutual **solid solubility**.

If we try to put more impurity in the material than it can accept, the impurity forms its own little crystals within the host material. In this case we say that we have formed precipitates of the impurity within the original material. We shall see an important example of substitutional impurity atoms and the formation of precipitates in the case of aluminum-lithium alloys in one of our case studies.

Note: Impurity atoms change the atomic structure of the material; precipitates change the microstructure of the material.

The previous diagrams illustrate these common point defects in materials. The strains (distortions) produced will depend on the relative sizes of the atoms involved.

How to Purify Materials

While we have seen that impurities can be added to change the atomic structure (doping) and hence the properties of materials, we are often faced with the problem of getting them out. Such was the problem with obtaining useful silicon for semiconductors. We needed to get unwanted impurities out before adding the ones we wanted.

As you may imagine, it is far more difficult to get impurities out than it is to add them, and the methods for removing impurities are difficult to explain at this level. It should be obvious that it is impossible to remove impurities from a solid. You can't just pluck them out with fine tweezers! There really is no way to do it. We therefore have to have our material in either a liquid or a vapor state. We shall discuss one example of each possibility, the former being used for silicon and the latter for chromium.

Note: Before we begin our discussion it is worth pointing out a sometimes confusing language problem. We often refer to purifying as 'refining'. A place where gasoline is produced from crude oil is called a refinery, and we earlier referred to the expression "refined by fire." We also use the word 'fine' to denote good or all right. On the other hand we use 'fine' to describe a powder or a cloth, i.e., the opposite of 'coarse'. In this sense the word 'refining' means making smaller. We shall now use the word in its first meaning, while later in the book when talking about HSLA steels and making grains smaller, we shall use it in its second meaning.

Zone refining

The technique known as **zone refining** was once the most common way to purify silicon and took advantage of the fact that one can dissolve more impurity in a liquid than in a solid. It turns out that by melting a solid and re-solidifying it one can reduce its impurity content, and by repeating the process several times one can obtain very pure materials.

The name zone refining comes from the practical way this is accomplished (see following diagram). A rod of the impure material is held in a container, which will not react with, or dissolve in, the silicon. A small furnace is placed around the bottom of the rod, which is slowly passed through

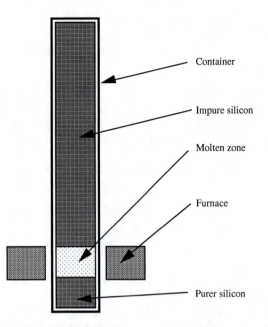

The zone refining of silicon. By repeating the process several times one can obtain very pure silicon at the bottom of the rod, which is cut off and used.

it. The material entering the furnace at the top is melted and the liquid leaving the furnace at the bottom solidifies. At this stage the impurities in the liquid have a choice of staying in the liquid or going into the solid that is formed. Because they prefer to stay in the liquid, the newly formed solid material is purer than the material that was originally melted. Most of the impurities remain in the liquid. As the "molten zone" moves up the rod, it acts as a vacuum cleaner to collect the impurities and move them to the top of the rod. By repeating the process the impurities are pushed more and more to the top end and eventually the bottom of the rod is pure enough to be useful.

Chemical vapor deposition

More recently a second technique has been employed to purify materials. It's called chemical vapor deposition or CVD. This technique takes advantage of the fact that it is quite easy to separate a mixture of liquids using a process called fractionation or distillation. If we boil a mixture of liquids by gradually increasing the temperature, we find that each liquid boils and evaporates at a different temperature. The process is used in the distillation of whiskey and brandy.

We'll illustrate the process with CVD purification of chromium, but CVD is also used to purify a wide range of materials, including semiconductor grade silicon. In this case we start with impure chromium metal and react it with iodine to form metal iodides. The chromium becomes chromium iodide, any nickel impurity becomes nickel iodide, etc. Metal iodides can often be easily melted and boiled, so the mixture of metal iodides is gradually heated until something begins to evaporate. Each metal iodide boils at a different temperature, and we know what this temperature is for chromium iodide. So as soon this temperature is reached we begin to collect what is evaporating, i.e., pure chromium iodide vapor.

The vapor is then passed through a furnace at a much higher temperature where it decomposes into pure chromium and iodine. The chromium metal, which is a solid at this temperature, falls from the decomposing vapor and deposits in the container in which it is heated, while the iodine vapor passes through the furnace and is collected for reuse. The pure chromium produced in this way is important for electrical contacts in modern semiconductor microchip technology.

Note that we have had to take a rather roundabout route to accomplish our goal of purifying the chromium. First we made another compound (the iodide), purified that, and then re-formed the solid chromium.

The CVD process of producing pure solids by decomposing a pure gas is one we shall encounter in our case study of optical fibers. A chemical vapor of the desired material is decomposed by heat so that the solid deposits in the furnace.

Impurities are still there!

Silicon has an atomic weight of 28.09, which means that this is the weight in grams of 6.02×10^{23} atoms (see Page 10). To put it another way, 28 grams of silicon, which incidentally is almost exactly an ounce, contain 6.02×10^{23} atoms. If we manage to obtain silicon that is 99.9999999% pure by zone refining or CVD, the purity level typically achieved, this means one impurity atom for every ten billion (10^{10}) silicon atoms; the ounce of silicon will still contain around 10^{13} (ten million million) impurity atoms!

The point to be made is that there are still many impurity atoms present. Whether they are important is a question we will address later.

Important Note

In most of the diagrams shown in this and all other books about materials there are three important differences between diagrams involving atom arrangements and the real situation.

1. Atom arrangements are three-dimensional. This is illustrated in the figure on page 56. The dislocation line extends into the page and out from the page, indefinitely (as far as we know). This is also true of other diagrams, but trying to show three dimensions makes things confusing.

2. The defects involve many more atoms than shown. On page 81 we show a dislocation stopping three atoms short of a precipitate. In reality, the dislocation would be stopped tens of atoms short of the precipitate, perhaps even hundreds. The diagrams of a dislocation on pages 56–57 use around a hundred atoms. A real dislocation involves many more atoms than this. The stacking of atoms is not back to normal just five or six atoms away from the dislocation. You would need to go at least a hundred atoms for this to happen. This is why metal whiskers (Page 78) cannot contain dislocations; they are not thick enough to have hundreds of atoms running from side to side.

3. Atoms are close-packed, as in CCP, or quite close to it, as in BCC. They are not separated as illustrated in this chapter, but are much like those shown on page 44. This means that interstices, for example, are not as large as you might expect from the diagrams on page 62.

QUESTIONS: Chapters 6–8

1. Carbon in iron is an example of _____.
   - (a) a point defect
   - (b) a substitutional impurity atom
   - (c) an interstitial impurity atom
   - (d) both a and b
   - (e) both a and c

2. In order to form amorphous metals, we have to cool liquid metals at a rate of _____.
   - (a) 100°C per second
   - (b) 1,000,000°C per hour
   - (c) 10,000°C per second
   - (d) 1,000,000°C per second

3. Zinc has a _____ crystal structure.
   - (a) hexagonal close packed
   - (b) cubic close packed
   - (c) body centered cubic
   - (d) face centered cubic
   - (e) both b and d

4. The main defects responsible for plastic deformation in a metal are _____.
   - (a) dislocations
   - (b) vacancies
   - (c) extrinsic interstitials
   - (d) substitutional atoms

5. The defect associated with a dislocation is a(n) _____ atom(s) which disturbs the perfect crystalline order.
   - (a) cluster of
   - (b) extra half plane of
   - (c) single
   - (d) tetrahedron of
   - (e) crystal of

6. A small space which exists between atoms in a perfect crystal is a(n) _____.
   - (a) vacancy
   - (b) hole
   - (c) interstice
   - (d) mer
   - (e) interstitial

7. When atoms in a material are arranged in a regular repeating order the material is _____.
   - (a) amorphous
   - (b) anisotropic
   - (c) crystalline
   - (d) glassy

8. Crystalline silicon and diamond both have the same _____ structure.
   - (a) atomic
   - (b) electron
   - (c) crystal
   - (d) micro
   - (e) macro

9. Which of the following does not describe an interstitial?
   - (a) a point defect
   - (b) occurs between lattice sites
   - (c) intrinsic or extrinsic
   - (d) a missing atom
   - (e) takes more energy to produce than a vacancy

10. In a cubic close packed (CCP) crystal there are ___ equivalent slip planes.
    - (a) 1
    - (b) 2
    - (c) 3
    - (d) 4
    - (e) none of these

11. A repetition of the AB sequence of planes in metals is called _____.
    - (a) HCP
    - (b) CCP
    - (c) FCC
    - (d) BCC

12. A material which shows different properties in different directions is called _____.
    - (a) anisotropic
    - (b) amorphous
    - (c) crystalline
    - (d) annealed
    - (e) inert

13. At the melting point of a material there are approximately _____% of the atoms missing due to vacancies.
    - (a) 0.01
    - (b) 0.1
    - (c) 1
    - (d) 10
    - (e) 100

14. A process used to purify silicon is called _____.
    - (a) grain refining
    - (b) precipitation hardening
    - (c) chemical vapor deposition
    - (d) zone refining
    - (e) c and d

15. Face centered cubic (FCC) crystals are _____ cubic close packed (CCP).
    - (a) always
    - (b) sometimes
    - (c) never

16. Dislocations allow planes of atoms to move approximately _____ times easier than in a perfect crystal.
    - (a) 0
    - (b) 10
    - (c) 100
    - (d) 1000
    - (e) none of these

17. Select the false statement from the following:
    (a) FCC and BCC metals both have twelve ways for close-packed planes to slip
    (b) HCP metals have a more efficient atom packing than do BCC metals
    (c) there are four different non-parallel slip planes in FCC metal crystals
    (d) BCC metals are more ductile than FCC metals
    (e) all CCP metals are also FCC

18. Dislocations in a solid are responsible for _____.
    (a) thermal conduction   (b) electrical conduction   (c) color
    (d) elastic deformation   (e) none of these

19. Amorphous materials lack _____.
    (a) long range order   (b) strong bonding   (c) molecules   (d) short range order   (e) stiffness

20. The addition of sodium to silica glass replaces some of the ___ bonds with ___ bonds.
    (a) covalent; ionic   (b) covalent; metallic   (c) ionic; covalent
    (d) metallic; hydrogen   (e) ionic; metallic

21. The planar stacking sequence ABCABC is found in _____ materials.
    (a) BCC   (b) HCP   (c) CCP   (d) all   (e) both a and b

22. Close packed planes in crystals _____.
    (a) are planes which are closest to each other   (b) are planes which are farthest apart
    (c) cannot slip over each other   (d) are imperfections   (e) none of these is correct

23. Which of these materials is the easiest to deform?
    (a) silicon   (b) silica   (c) aluminum   (d) diamond   (e) glass

24–26. The process during which molten metal iodides with different boiling points are separated is known
    as ___24___. This process is used to purify ___25___ for electronic applications. The pure ___25___ iodide gas is then
    reduced to a pure metal by a process known as ___26___.

    24. (a) distillation   (b) chemical vapor deposition   (c) zone refining   (d) vitrification
        (e) sintering
    25. (a) iron   (b) gold   (c) chromium   (d) nickel   (e) aluminum
    26. (a) distillation   (b) chemical vapor deposition   (c) zone refining   (d) vitrification
        (e) sintering

9. WHAT DO WE MEAN BY 'STRONG'?

Strength and Stress

'Strong' is a word we use frequently without stopping to ask ourselves what it really means. The dictionary defines it as meaning "having power of resistance, not easily broken or torn, or worn, firm, solid." Quite often we use the word 'strong' when we really mean 'rigid' and as we shall see, they are not the same. From a scientific standpoint, none of these definitions is really satisfactory. It's one of those words that you would probably define by using the well-worn phrase, "you know what I mean", meaning that you really are not sure! Even scientists sometimes use the word rather loosely because there is no single meaning for the term.

If you were given a piece of blackboard chalk and asked to break it you would almost certainly do so by bending it between your two thumbs and two forefingers. From a scientific standpoint you would be performing a four-point bend test. The following diagram illustrates what happens. At the center you push up, usually with your thumbs, while at the ends you press down with your fingers. In the laboratory this would be one way of measuring the strength of a material. This is called the **bend strength**.

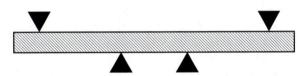

The four point bend test for a material. There are two central
points where a force is applied upwards, and two end points
where the force is downwards.

You could also hold one end of the chalk tightly in your fist while grabbing the other end and twisting it. If you try it, you will find that this method of breaking is more difficult, although you will probably succeed. You should also notice that fracture has occurred at an oblique angle to the length of the chalk rather than almost perpendicular to the chalk as was the case with the bend test.

In this case you will have tested the **shear strength** of the material. Shear strength is important for rods of material, which are rotating. You may have been driving a screw into a hard material only to have it break, or shear off. This is because you have exceeded the shear strength. Rotating axles in machinery sometime fail in this way.

If we take the piece of chalk and hold one end while pulling on the other until it breaks we are testing its **tensile strength**. If we hang a weight on a wire we are putting it into tension. The same occurs when we stretch a guitar string to tune the instrument. Too much tension and it breaks. We apply what we call a **tensile load** to the material; we are pulling it. As we increase the load the string stretches and then breaks. The same happens with our piece of chalk although we need special equipment to see the stretch because it is so small.

Materials such as the piece of chalk, notably ceramics, break in a brittle manner, showing very little stretch before they fail. Others, such as some plastics and rubber, will stretch to several times their original length before they break. When the material breaks we say that is has reached its breaking strength, or to use the correct scientific jargon, it has reached its **ultimate tensile strength (UTS)**. This is the maximum load the material can carry without breaking.

The following diagram illustrates a simple way of measuring the UTS. A rod of material is held tightly at one end while a weight, or load, is applied to the other. The weight is increased until the material can take no more and breaks.

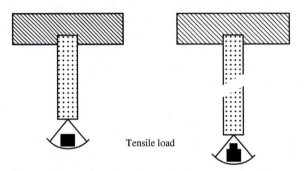

A material breaks in tension when its tensile strength is exceeded.

If we are building something, be it a building or a piece of equipment, we are always aware that we don't want components to break. If we think this may happen we have two alternatives: either use a stronger material or use a thicker piece of the same material, something we sometimes call "beefing it up." We are all aware that thicker things are more difficult to break. The simple reason in that there are more bonds to break. Never lose sight of the fact that in nearly all cases, breaking a material means breaking bonds between atoms.

Now while it may be good to know how much weight a material can bear before breaking, we are often not interested in approaching this value. What is of more concern, especially for a metal, is how much weight it can bear before it really begins to stretch. This means that the dislocations are now beginning to move freely in the material so that there is a lot of movement of **slip planes** over each other. But there is no definite point at which we can say this motion starts to be important so we need a more precise criterion. For engineering design we arbitrarily adopt the criterion of the material having permanently stretched by 0.2 percent of its original length. This means that a 100 cm long rod of the material is loaded so that it has a permanent stretch of 0.2% when the load is taken off. The rod has therefore been permanently lengthened to 100.2 cm. As you can well imagine, ceramics do not usually stretch by these amounts.

The load required to permanently stretch the rod by this amount is known as the **yield strength (YS)**. We say that the rod has suffered a 0.2% **plastic strain** deformation. As far as we are concerned we shall loosely say that the yield strength defines when the metal material begins to deform permanently. We shall come back to a definition of strain later.

For ceramic materials especially, we define a fifth strength, called the **compressive strength**. If we take a short thick rod of this material, place one end on a rigid, strong surface and pile weights on top, the material will again eventually fail. The weight required to produce this break defines the compressive strength of the material. For ceramics the compressive strength is much larger than the tensile strength and bend strength. This is why we can use concrete foundations to support large buildings. We shall later see why this is, and how we can use it to make ceramics more serviceable. Just try crushing a stick of chalk between your hand and a table: you will probably hurt your hand before the chalk breaks.

The following diagram illustrates how we measure the compressive strength of a material. Here again, fracture occurs at an oblique angle to the length of the piece although it is unlikely to be as clean a break as is depicted. Because we are really crushing the material there will usually be several pieces resulting from this test rather than just the two pieces shown.

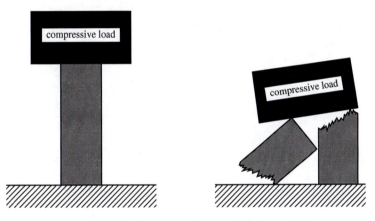

Testing the compressive strength of a material.

In the following discussion we shall only consider tensile, yield and compressive strengths, but do not forget that the others are very important.

We measure ultimate tensile strength using units of **pounds per square inch (psi)**. If our rod has a rectangular cross section one inch by two inches (1" × 2") the cross section area is two (1 × 2) square inches. If the rod breaks when a load of seventy pounds is hung on it, its ultimate tensile strength is 35 psi (70 pounds/2 square inches). The strength is therefore obtained by dividing the weight or load by the cross sectional area.

$$\textbf{UTS (psi)} = \frac{\text{weight at which rod breaks (pounds)}}{\text{cross sectional area (square inces)}}$$

You should now be able to see that by making our rod twice as thick (2" × 2") it can withstand twice the load without breaking (i.e. 140 pounds)

When we put a load on a material we rarely talk about the weight in pounds, we refer to the number of pounds per square inch applied to the material, a quantity we call the **stress**. Stresses can be tensile or compressive. When pulled, a material breaks at a constant stress, which is what we call its ultimate tensile strength, or quite often just 'strength'. The load can vary depending on the size of the rod but the stress (UTS) at which it breaks is constant.

We similarly measure **yield strength** in terms of a stress and for a metal it is usually much less than the UTS.

$$\textbf{Stress (psi)} = \frac{\text{Force or Load (pounds)}}{\text{Area (square inches)}}$$

Note: Today's scientists refer to strength and stress using units known as Pascals. We shall not use these units because you are more familiar with a pound and a square inch. If you ever come across them you will need to know that **one** psi is equal to 6895 Pascals.

Examples

1. A person weighs 170 pounds and wears a size 8 shoe with an area of 35 square inches per shoe sole, he/she exerts a compressive stress on the floor of:

$$\frac{170 \text{ pounds}}{2(\text{shoes}) \times 35 \text{ sq. in.}} = 2.43 \text{ psi}$$

when standing on both feet. When standing on one foot the stress is doubled.

2. A metal rod with a square cross section 0.5×0.5 inches bears a tensile load, which is increased until the rod breaks with a load of 350 pounds. The ultimate tensile stress is given by:

$$\text{UTS (psi)} = \frac{350 \text{ pounds}}{0.5 \times 0.5 \text{ square inches}} = 1400 \text{ psi}$$

3. What size rod of this last material is needed to support a one ton (2000 pounds) weight? Since the UTS is a constant, we can set:

$$1400 \text{ psi} = \frac{2000 \text{ pounds}}{\text{cross sectional area (square inches)}}$$

so the required area of rod $= 2000 \text{ pounds}/1400 \text{ psi} = 1.43 \text{ square inches}$

Thus a rod 1 inch by 1.5 inches (1.5 square inches) would be adequate, although you would probably make it larger to give a safety margin. We also haven't considered whether it will stretch too much to serve its purpose.

Strain

This quantity has a very simple definition for our purposes. It is the extension (or contraction) of a material divided by its original length. Because it is the ratio of two lengths it has no units—we say it is a **dimensionless quantity**. We can therefore measure lengths in inches, centimeters, yards, etc. as long as both original length and amount of stretch, or contraction, are in the same units. We usually express it as a percentage, and therefore multiply the fraction by one hundred.

Strain = Extension/Original length   OR   Extension/Original length × 100%

Examples

1. The yield strength occurs at a strain of 0.2% so:

    Strain = 0.2% = Extension/Original length × 100%

    Hence: Extension = 0.002 × Original length

    Therefore, if we started with a piece of wire 12 feet long (144 inches), it will now have stretched by 144 × 0.002 inches, i.e. 0.288 inches, or a little over a quarter of an inch.

2. If we take a rubber band and stretch it to three times its original length, the extension is 2 lengths, the original length is 1 length and the strain is therefore 200% or 2. Notice here that we haven't even said how long the elastic band was originally. A strain of two means that the length has been tripled.

It is worth pointing out as a follow-up to the previous example that a strain of 'one' means that the length has doubled. A strain of 'six' means that the band is seven times its original length.

Of course, your experience tells you that there are few materials that can exhibit such large strains. One class of materials is polymers called elastomers, and rubber is a well-known example.

Stiffness

Stiffness is what we often refer to in normal speech when we use the word 'strong'. If you ask many people whether a piece of plastic film is strong, they will say "no". They see it as not being stiff, which often implies weakness. In fact the film is quite strong. Try breaking a piece by pulling it in tension. It is not easy to do. Boxes of plastic film usually come with a cutting edge.

If we compare two materials by putting the same tensile stress on them, the stiffer of the two will stretch less. In any application we usually wish to know what strain (stretch) will be produced by a certain stress (force/area) and it is the stiffness which tells us this. We define stiffness using a quantity known as **Young's Modulus (YM),** which is defined by:

Young's Modulus = Stress applied/Strain it produces

(Note: strain is **not** a percentage here)

This equation satisfies the requirement that the smaller the strain (amount of stretch) for a given load, the greater the stiffness. You may also notice that if the strain is 'one' the Young's modulus is equal to the stress, in other words you can think of the Young's modulus as the stress required to double the length of the material.

The Young's modulus is also measured in psi, and values are typically around a million (1,000,000 or 10^6) psi.

Examples

1. If a piece of wire, 50 inches long, is pulled with a tensile stress of 2000 psi and stretches to 50.1 inches, the stiffness (Young's modulus) is calculated as follows:

   Strain = 0.1 inches (extension)/50 inches (original length) = 0.002

   so Young's Modulus = 2000 psi (stress)/0.002 (strain)

   = 1,000,000 psi

2. If we have a three feet long metal rod with a Young's modulus of 6×10^6 psi and apply a tensile stress of 5,000 psi we can calculate the strain as follows:

   $$YM = 6 \times 10^6 \text{ psi} = \frac{\text{stress}}{\text{strain}} = \frac{5000 \text{ psi}}{\text{strain}}$$

   $$\text{so strain} = \frac{5000 \text{ psi}}{6 \times 10^6 \text{ psi}} = 0.00083 \text{ or } 0.083\%$$

   $$\text{now strain} = \frac{\text{extension}}{\text{length}} = \frac{\text{extension}}{36 \text{ inches}}$$

   $$\text{therefore extension} = 0.00083 \times 36 \text{ inches} = 0.03 \text{ inches}$$

   This means that if we hang a weight of 5000 pounds (two and a half tons) on a rod which is three feet long and has a cross section of 1" × 1", it will stretch only 0.03 inches (three hundredths of an inch).

3. If a 3 feet long plastic rod has a Young's modulus of 5×10^4 psi, what stress is needed to stretch it one inch?

   the strain is 1 inch/36 inches = 0.028

   stress = YM × strain = $5 \times 10^4 \times 0.028 = 1389$ psi

   If this material were a 3 feet long circular filament, a tenth of an inch in diameter (radius = 0.05 inches), what weight would you need to hang on it to produce the one inch stretch?

   cross section area of filament = $\pi r^2 = \pi \times 0.05^2$ square inches

   = 0.0079 square inches (in^2)

   weight required = 0.0079 in^2 × 1389 psi = 10.97 pounds

4. If you pull a 50 inch piece of material with a UTS of 5000 psi and a YM of 5×10^6 psi, how much will it have stretched when it breaks?

Using YM = stress/strain, we have 5×10^6 psi = 5000 psi/strain
which gives a strain of $5000/5 \times 10^6 = 0.001$

The extension (stretch) is therefore 50 inches $\times 0.001 = 0.05$ inches, or a twentieth of an inch.

Remember that the larger the Young's modulus the stiffer the material. Here are some typical values:

ceramics have high values	-	100 million psi	$(100 \times 10^6 \text{ psi})$
metals have medium values	-	10 million psi	$(10 \times 10^6 \text{ psi})$
polymers have low values	-	100 thousand psi	$(0.1 \times 10^6 \text{ psi})$

But there are many exceptions to this trend.

If two materials have the same strengths (UTS), but different stiffnesses, it means that they will both break under the same load but the one with the lower Young's modulus will stretch more than the other. Some plastics are very strong (high UTS) but we would not use them for an aircraft wing because they lack rigidity (stiffness), i.e., have a low Young's modulus.

We are now in a position to more intelligently examine some of the mechanical properties of materials. Remember the definitions! We shall use them later, especially in our case studies.

Materials and Human Psychology

It is intriguing how scientific/technological terminology pervades our everyday speech. For example, we often refer to ourselves being "stressed out" or being under a lot of "strain." As materials experts, you are now in the position to use such terms correctly. One can be "under a lot of stress," but never "under a lot of strain." Strain is how you (the test specimen) respond to the external forces applying stress to your life!

QUESTIONS: Chapter 9

1. The Young's Modulus is also known as the _____.
   (a) strength   (b) stiffness   (c) stress   (d) strain   (e) extension

2. A ceramic usually is strongest in _____.
   (a) tension   (b) shear   (c) bending   (d) compression

3. If a 50 foot long piece of fishing line extends 6 inches then the strain is _____.
   (a) 6/50 inches   (b) 6/600 inches   (c) 1%   (d) 10%   (e) 0.1

4. If a 1000 pound weight is suspended from an iron bar of cross-section 2 inches by 5 inches the stress on the rod is:
   (a) 1000 p.s.i.   (b) 10 pounds   (c) 10 p.s.i.   (d) 100 p.s.i.   (e) 100 pounds

5–9. A bar of material is 100 inches long and has an cross sectional area of 50 square inches. If a weight of 50,000 pounds is placed on the rod it will feel a stress of __5__. If under this weight the rod extends 0.001 inches then the rod is experiencing a strain of __6__. Therefore, the Young's modulus of the rod is __7__. This value for Young's modulus would most likely correspond to a __8__. If we keep adding weight to the rod until at 1,000,000 pounds the bar finally breaks its ultimate tensile stress will be __9__.

   5. (a) 10 psi   (b) 100 psi   (c) 100 pounds   (d) 1,000 psi   (e) 10,000 psi
   6. (a) 0.1 %   (b) 0.001 %   (c) 0.001   (d) 10 %   (e) 10,000,000 %
   7. (a) 10,000 psi   (b) 100,000 psi   (c) 1,000,000 pounds   (d) 1,000,000 psi
      (e) 100,000,000 psi
   8. (a) polymer   (b) metal   (c) ceramic   (d) semiconductor   (e) not enough information
   9. (a) 20 psi   (b) 5,000 psi   (c) 20,000 psi   (d) 200,000 psi   (e) 5,000,000 psi

10. What type of material would likely have a Young's Modulus of 100,000 psi?
    (a) metal   (b) ceramic   (c) polymer   (d) semiconductor   (e) not enough information given

11. If a weight of 800 pounds is hung from the end of a 30 inch long rectangular bar of material (4 inches by 2 inches) the bar extends by 0.03 inches.
    Calculate the (a) stress,   (b) strain (in percentage) and   (c) Young's Modulus of the bar.
    We continue to add weight to the bar until at a total weight of 2400 pounds the bar breaks.
    (d) What is the ultimate tensile strength of this material?
    (e) Knowing this, could a bar of the same material with sides 2 inches by 2 inch hold the original weight of 800 pounds?

10. MAKING METALS STRONGER
or
HOW TO STOP THOSE DISLOCATIONS MOVING

We have now learned that metals deform by the movement of the closest packed planes of atoms in the structure as they slide over each other. We have also seen how dislocations facilitate this movement, making it a thousand times easier than would be the case if the planes slipped as complete entities. The dislocations allow these planes to slide one row of atoms at a time, which is much easier.

The idea of dislocations started as just that, an idea or theory. Nowadays we have millions of pictures of the defects taken with an electron microscope. For reasons that are too complex to go into here, the dislocation line (termination of the extra partial plane, see Page 56) shows up in these photos as continuous or spotty black lines. You must appreciate that in an electron microscope we are looking *through* the sample, just as you might be looking through a piece of glass. In the photograph on the next page the slip planes are at an angle to the specimen surface as shown below. The dislocations are effectively lines on these planes and they therefore appear as short line segments, one end of which intersects the top of the specimen and the other the bottom. The following diagram attempts to illustrate this.

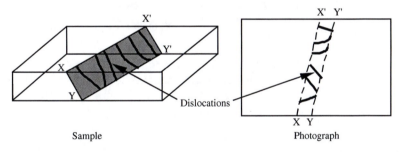

The diagram on the left shows a thin piece of metal (specimen) containing one slip plane XX'YY' on which there are six dislocations. When viewed from above, as in an electron microscope, one sees the dislocations as shown in the diagram on the right. Note that the lines XX' and YY' are not seen in the photograph.

In the photograph shown on the next page you can see dislocations on seven different parallel slip planes. You can also see that there are sometimes as many as ten dislocations in one micron (10^{-6} meters or 10^{-4} cm) so that they are as close as ten millionths of a centimeter (10^{-5} cm) to each other. This means that there are only around 500 atom spacings between dislocations. This should not be surprising bearing in mind that each only produces a movement of one atom spacing, and we need millions of these movements to produce something we can see with the naked eye.

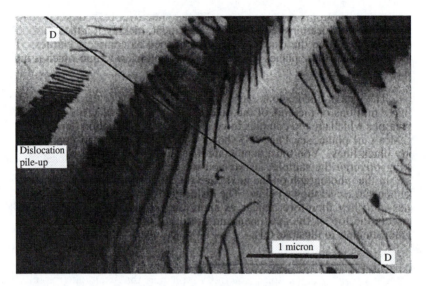

Photograph showing seven parallel slip planes in a metal crystal. The dislocations appear to lie and move on 'tram lines' which would be parallel and all the same width if the specimen were uniformly thick. This is obviously not the case.

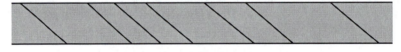

The seven parallel slip planes in section DD of the above photograph.

If indeed dislocations are the points of weakness in a metal, allowing it to deform at much lower stresses, to strengthen and stiffen the material we must either eliminate the dislocations or stop them from moving. There is only one way to accomplish the former and several approaches to the latter.

Metal Whiskers

Although we have talked of dislocations as lines, and a line has length but no other dimensions, the dislocations do have a width. They affect atoms for quite a distance away. The diagram on page 56 is really showing only maybe one atom in fifty. You must imagine that there are fifty atom planes for every one shown. If we were to show every atom, the diagram would fill a room rather than a page in a book! The reason for mentioning this is that dislocations affect quite a large volume of material as far as atomic dimensions are concerned. If there is not enough room it is impossible to form dislocations.

We find that this is the case with a class of materials known as metal whiskers, which have strengths close to the theoretical value (i.e., 1000X larger than the corresponding conventional metals). These whiskers are no more than a thousandth of a millimeter wide and a few millimeters long. Their narrow widths do not allow the hundreds of atoms (or more!) necessary to support the existence of dislocations. They are of theoretical interest but are not really of much practical value, owing to their relatively large cost. We want to use metals in the form of steel girders, not in such small entities. These are the only metals known not to contain dislocations. It is therefore logical that our only approach to strengthening metals is to stop the dislocations moving, or **pin** them.

Work Hardening

One method you should already be aware of for stopping dislocations, although you may not have understood what you were doing, or what the effect is called, is **work hardening**.

In a CCP (FCC) metal there are four possible non-parallel slip planes, and in a BCC metal there are six. Dislocations can move on many of these at once and of course the planes on which they are moving will often intersect each other, as shown below.

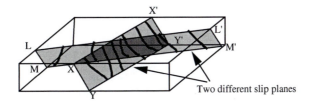

Diagram showing the previous XX'YY' slip plane together with another non-parallel
slip plane, LL'MM'. When two moving dislocations intersect they pin each other.

It is easy to think of a dislocation line (the termination of the extra partial plane) as a short length of twine. When two are moving on different non-parallel planes, as shown in the previous diagram, and meet, they form a kind of dislocation knot at the intersection. As the metal is deformed more, there are more and more of these knots or tangles formed and the dislocations are eventually unable to move. Here again we turn to the electron microscope to support this. The left hand photograph of the sequence shown below is just one mess of dislocation tangles. The metal (aluminum) has been deformed a great deal and the tangles are the result. Now that the dislocations are immobile, the material is quite brittle. We call this method of strengthening **work hardening**.

Annealing sequence showing loss of dislocation tangles.

You have probably taken advantage of this phenomenon when trying to break a piece of wire. If you bend a piece of wire or paper clip back and forth until it breaks you are creating so many dislocations that they literally lock each other in knots so that no further yielding is possible and the material becomes brittle and breaks. This is usually not a very practical way of hardening a material but it is used in some cases. A metalsmith may sometimes decorate the surface of an article by using a ball peen hammer, one which has a ball-like hitting surface on one end. Not only does this produce a decorative finish but it also hardens the surface of the metal. Sometimes we shoot small hard metal shot at the surface of a metal specimen in a process called shot-peening. Railroad lines are often shaped by passing through rollers when cold. The deformation produces a multitude of dislocations, which become tangled and the metal is hardened.

When a metalsmith forms a piece of metal by hammering or bending, it becomes hard and brittle and has to be periodically **annealed**. To anneal a material means to heat it, but there is more to it than that. Dislocations move atoms in certain directions on slip planes, and dislocation tangles are regions where the atoms have been forced in two or more directions at the same time and are therefore not in their correct positions in the crystals. The material therefore has to be made hot enough for the atoms to become very mobile, which needs vacancies, so that they can rearrange themselves into more perfect crystals with fewer of these defects. The temperature needed depends on the metal being used.

Sometimes an "up" edge dislocation and a "down" edge dislocation can annihilate one another, as in the following figure. Whereas two "up" dislocations will repel each other (as will two "down" dislocations), dislocations of opposite "sign" will attract. If their terminations are on the same plane, they can come together and annihilate one another, i.e., the two partial planes join into a complete plane of atoms, as shown. Heating a sample allows dislocations to become mobile. And if their terminations are not precisely on the same plane, vacancies can move atoms around to make it so.

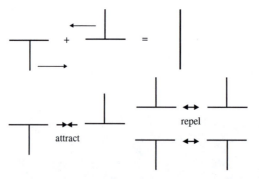

Schematic of edge dislocations attracting or repelling one another, and their annihilation.

The previous sequence of photos shows how annealing removes the dislocation tangles in aluminum. If the metalsmith fails to notice that the metal is getting hard and continues to beat it, the result is the formation of cracks and the piece is ruined.

Precipitation hardening and solid solution hardening

The method that is perhaps most frequently used for strengthening metals is to introduce something in the material which blocks the movement of the dislocations, and the most usual way of doing this is to somehow treat the material so that small precipitates of a different substance are produced within it. When we discussed point defects (Page 63) we mentioned that if we add too much impurity to a material there is a chance of producing small precipitates, and it is these precipitates that can pin the dislocations.

The reason for this effect is not difficult to understand. Remember that a dislocation moves along between the two planes that are slipping over each other (Pages 56–57). The planes slip one row

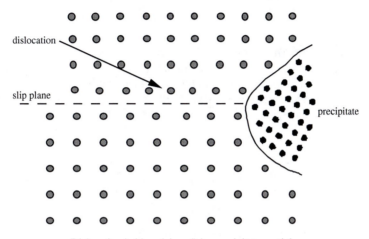

Dislocation held up (pinned) by precipitate particle.

of atoms at a time. If the precipitate cannot slip or get out of the way of the advancing row of atoms, it presents an obstacle to their motion.

Often the atoms in the precipitate are of a different type and of a different crystal structure, i.e., they are arranged quite differently. They may also be held together with different kinds of bonds, either covalent or ionic bonds. The dislocation can only proceed if the precipitate gives way and allows the dislocation to pass through to the main body of the material (usually referred to as the **matrix**). Refer to the diagram on page 57 and you can see that the top half of the crystal moves out one atom spacing because there is no obstacle to its motion; the precipitate provides such an obstacle. Precipitates in steels are usually combinations of carbon with some of the metal elements (iron or one of the alloying elements). These carbides are not bonded by metallic bonds and therefore do not slip as do pure metals.

Because there are millions of dislocations in the material what we really need are millions of very, very small precipitates rather than a few large ones so that there is always likely to be a precipitate in the way of the moving dislocations. This is where Materials Science comes in, providing the information of which atoms to introduce to form the precipitates, and how to process the metal by heating, cooling, etc., to produce the required precipitate distribution. This phenomenon is known as **precipitation hardening**.

In the following case study we shall discuss how this is done in aluminum-lithium alloys. Lithium is the lightest metal, so that not only does it make the aluminum stronger, it also makes the aluminum even lighter than it already is. Such a material is of great importance in aircraft manufacture where lighter, stronger materials reduce the operating costs of the planes.

Sometimes the precipitates take a long time to form in the metal, just as sugar precipitates may form in a bottle of syrup or honey, or tartrate crystals in a bottle of wine over a period of months or years. A good example of this is seen in sterling silver, which is an alloy of 92.5% silver, 7.5% copper. When left at room temperature for long periods of time the metal hardens because the copper forms precipitates. If a silversmith leaves a piece unfinished for a few weeks, the metal first has to be annealed to cause these precipitates to redissolve in the metal so that the dislocations can continue to move, and the metal may be worked to its desired shape. This is in addition to the periodic annealing necessary to eliminate the dislocation tangles produced by the hammering of the material, which we have already mentioned (Page 79).

Just having isolated impurity atoms in the metal can also produce some inhibition of dislocation motion. Look at the diagram below. Where the extra half plane of atoms finishes there is a quite large interstice. It is natural that an impurity atom should lodge there and when it does so, it makes it more difficult for the surrounding atoms to move as they do during dislocation movement. The dislocation is effectively pinned. This hardening mechanism is referred to as **solid solution hardening**.

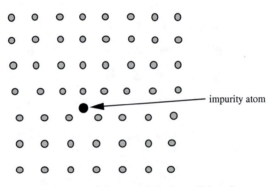

Impurity atom sitting at and pinning a dislocation.

Grain refining

One final way of strengthening a metal is to make the grains, or crystallites, smaller. In this case we are not concerned about dislocations being stopped by small crystals of a different material (precipitates) but by another crystal of the same material. However, the next crystal will have a different orientation and the plane on which the dislocation is moving does not continue across the boundary. The dislocation stops moving when it is close to the boundary because if it were to go right through the crystal it would create an atomic ledge (see diagram on page 57). There is no room for this unless the next crystal also slips and so the dislocation stops. The next dislocation stops behind the first, etc. and soon a sort of traffic jam is produced. We call this a **pile-up** (one is visible in the photo on page 78). The consequence is that dislocation motion is limited. Obviously the smaller the grain size, the more closely spaced are these barriers to dislocation motion. As a result, there is improvement in the material's strength.

You may well be asking why the next crystal, which is of the same material and can obviously also slip, does not just allow deformation to proceed? We shall leave this question until we discuss HSLA steels, which provide us with a practical application of this strengthening method in our second case study. These materials are used in automobile bodies where their higher strength allows thinner metal to be used. This reduces weight and improves fuel efficiency. Of course this is one reason why modern cars sometimes appear flimsy compared to the tank-like vehicles produced 35 to 40 years ago.

Although grain boundaries are barriers to dislocation motion, they are not absolute barriers. Otherwise, polycrystalline metals (most metals are "many-grained") would never be ductile! The blacksmith's experience tells us that this is *not* the case. But ductile metals are typically BCC or CCP in structure and have 12 slip systems, as we have shown. Years ago the **von Mises criterion** was developed. It says that for a polycrystalline metal to be ductile, it must possess five or more slip systems. This is why BCC and CCP metals, with their 12 slip systems, are ductile as polycrystalline materials; it is relatively easy to find another slip system in the grain across the boundary on which a dislocation can continue to move. In contrast, the HCP metals have only three slip systems; it is hard to find another slip system in the grain across the boundary on which a dislocation can continue to move. Therefore, polycrystalline metals such as titanium, with the HCP crystal structure, are notoriously brittle.

Conclusion

To summarize: the weaknesses in a metal are the dislocations. They allow the closest packed planes to slide over each other 1000X more easily than if there were no dislocations. Because of the dislocations the atoms move a row at a time. To strengthen the material we have two options:

eliminate dislocations: only possible if crystals are so small (whiskers) that they cannot accommodate a dislocation: this is not really a practical method.

pin dislocations: four possibilities

work harden—much deformation causes dislocation tangles so that the dislocations effectively pin each other.

precipitation harden—introduce small impurity precipitates to hinder dislocation motion.

solid solution harden—use impurities to pin dislocations, thereby hindering motion.

grain refining—dislocation motion is limited; dislocation pile-ups are produced at crystal boundaries.

11. CASE STUDY: ALUMINUM-LITHIUM ALLOYS FOR AEROSPACE

A Brief History

Today aircraft are so much a part of our everyday lives that we scarcely give a thought to the materials which go into them, but the fact that they fly should tell us that the lighter we can build them, the better. Every aircraft has a maximum takeoff weight, which depends on air temperature, weather, the altitude of the airport, etc. The lighter the aircraft itself, the greater the weight of passengers and freight that can be carried, hence the greater the potential for profits.

Early aircraft had their frames made of wood and their wings covered with fabric. Indeed wood has much to commend it for its combination of lightness and strength. However, it is clear that light-weight metals would be more durable. The first world war (1914–18) saw the development of all-metal aircraft, with the German Dornier RS1 flying boat being the first example. In 1930 lightweight aluminum alloys became the major structural materials used in airframes. Replacing steel with aluminum alloys produced tremendous weight savings*.

The theoretical weight saving of around 65% assumes that a given volume of steel would be replaced by the same volume of aluminum. Even if the aluminum struts in the airframe needed to be 25% thicker, the weight savings would still exceed 50%.

In today's aircraft, aluminum is still the major material for the main body and airframe, although specialty steels are used for the landing gear which suffers severe stresses during take-off and especially on landing. However in some aircraft, mostly military, aluminum is being replaced by even lighter composite materials based, for example, upon carbon fibers. These are also used extensively on the executive Learjets and are being introduced into some larger commercial passenger aircraft. The pie charts shown on the next page indicate the percentages of different materials used in two current aircraft, one a commercial passenger plane and the other a military fighter plane. Notice that both planes contain over 70% aluminum.

---

* **Note**: The density of a material is a measure of the weight of a certain volume. Scientists usually use the weight in grams (gm) of one cubic centimeter (cm^3) of material, i.e., a cube with an edge-length of one centimeter. By comparing densities we are looking at the relative weights of the same volume of material. Whereas iron-based materials (steels) have a density of around 7.8 gm/cm^3, aluminum-based materials have a density of around 2.8 gm/cm^3, so that if the same volume of material were used, the weight saving would be around 65% [(7.8 − 2.8)/7.8 × 100% = 500/7.8% = 64.1%]

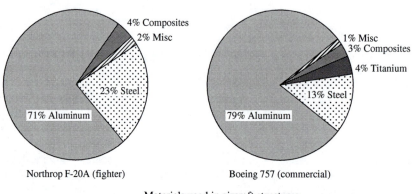

Northrop F-20A (fighter)   Boeing 757 (commercial)

Materials used in aircraft structures.

The reason for making the airframes lighter lies in the statement made earlier. The less the weight of the plane, the more cargo weight that can be carried. The following pie chart shows the weight distribution for a typical passenger aircraft about to take off on a 1,000 mile journey.

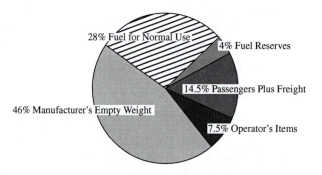

Various contributions to an aircraft's take-off weight.

Notice that the manufactured empty plane accounts for only 46% of the total weight and the passengers and freight for only 14.5%. Now if we could reduce the weight of the empty plane by one tenth (10% or 0.1) and keep the take-off weight the same, we could transfer 4.6% of the total weight (46% × 0.1) to passengers & freight. The load carried would increase from 14.5% of total weight to 19.1%. This means that the weight carried for profit (passengers & cargo) has gone up by nearly a third. Such a substantial increase is well worth striving for!

Another way of taking advantage of this weight saving is to reduce the take-off weight which in turn saves fuel, just as reducing the weight of an automobile increases miles per gallon. The lower fuel requirements also reduce take-off weight and the much lighter plane now needs less engine power so that the engines can also be made smaller and lighter. What started out as a reduction in the airframe weight has resulted in other weight savings, which add up to be far more significant.

One way of producing these significant weight savings, as already mentioned, is to replace metals with composite materials made of carbon fibers in an epoxy resin matrix. These materials have a density of less than 1.8 gm/cm³, more than 30% less than aluminum. They are also very stiff and quite strong, so could well replace much of the aluminum which is currently used in airframes and other aerospace vehicles.

Healthy Competition: Composites

The threat to the aluminum industry of being replaced by lightweight composite materials spurred scientists into a search for newer lightweight alloys of aluminum. This is where lithium comes in. Look at your periodic table (Page 7) and you will see that lithium is element number 3. It is a metal that is the lightest existing solid element at room temperature. If we can replace some of the aluminum atoms with lithium, we can obviously produce a weight saving. It turns out that by suitable manufacturing processes we can also increase strength and stiffness. This leads to even further weight savings because the load-bearing parts can also be reduced in size.

The Metallurgy of Aluminum-Lithium Alloys

We have earlier mentioned (Page 61) that impurities (extrinsic defects) can occupy one of two different positions in a metal, interstitial or substitutional. At that time we said that smaller atoms were likely to be interstitial and atoms of comparable size to be substitutional. As an example of the former we mentioned interstitial carbon (atomic number 6) in FCC iron (atomic number 26). Here we are thinking of putting lithium (atomic number 3) into aluminum (atomic number 13), which is also FCC. If you note that these numbers are in the same ratios you might expect lithium to be an interstitial impurity in aluminum. Fortunately you would be wrong!

If we add an extra atom in an interstitial position we are obviously adding more weight, and the material will be denser. If we replace an atom with a lighter one the density is decreased.

Aluminum is one of the many metals that have the cubic close packed (CCP) crystal structure, which results in a cube with atoms on the corners of the cube and in the centers of the cube faces. When we add lithium to the aluminum in the molten state, when the mix solidifies, the lithium atoms

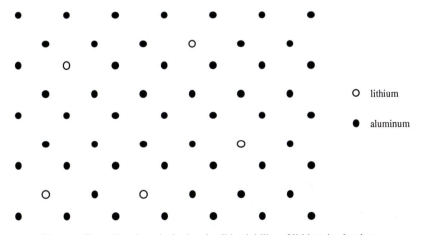

Diagram illustrating the substitutional solid solubility of lithium in aluminum.

are found to have replaced some of the aluminum atoms in this CCP arrangement. The lithium atoms are what we have previously called substitutional impurity atoms. They occupy the positions normally occupied by the aluminum atoms and form what we call a **substitutional solid solution**. In the previous two-dimensional diagram there are 59 atoms, 5 of which are lithium, i.e., there is an atom concentration of 5/59 × 100%, or 8.47%, of lithium in the aluminum.

When we make solutions of, for example, salt in water, we know that we can dissolve only a certain amount. If we put too much salt in the water, some will refuse to dissolve. If we heat the water we can dissolve more salt but when we allow it to cool, the salt precipitates out from the solution again. The maximum amount that can be dissolved is called the **solubility limit**. In reality, what we have is a saturated salt solution (brine) and also some precipitated salt crystals, which in fact contain some water, i.e., we have salt in the water and water in the salt. We call this a **two-phase mixture**. The word **phase** is scientific jargon and is a word that is difficult for even scientists to define. For our purposes we shall define it as meaning a distinguishable portion of matter. Fruit in jello would be a good example. The jello would be one phase, the pineapple chunks another, the bananas yet another, etc. In the case of salt in water we can distinguish the liquid (brine) from the solid (salt containing water). The solid is one phase and the liquid is the other.

When we add lithium to aluminum there is also a solubility limit and we take advantage of this fact. For some metal mixtures (e.g. copper and nickel) there is no solubility limit so that you can keep replacing the copper atoms with nickel atoms until you have 100% nickel. For lithium-aluminum this is not the case. If we add lithium so that we exceed the solubility limit we produce two phases, but in this case they are both solid. On the one hand we have an aluminum-lithium solid solution as described earlier and on the other we have precipitates of lithium that contain aluminum (we must be careful here because these precipitates really contain more aluminum than lithium).

These precipitates are rather unusual. They have a face centered cubic atom arrangement with lithium atoms on the corners of the cube, but with aluminum atoms at the face centers. If you carefully count the numbers of atoms in this arrangement, you will see that a precipitate has the chemical formula Al_3Li (remember that only an eighth of each corner atom is in the cube, and only half of each atom on the faces). Metallurgists designate this precipitate phase as **delta prime** ('). Don't ask why!

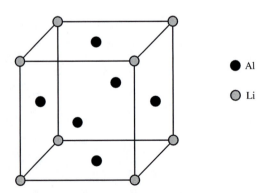

● Al

○ Li

The crystal structure of Al_3Li precipitates (').

Note that we cannot control whether or not one thing is soluble in another, neither can we control the amount that is soluble. In this case we know that there is a solubility limit (the solid aluminum will only accept so many lithium atoms) and that if we add too much there will be delta-prime precipitates (regions containing 25% lithium atoms) formed. What we can do by suitable processing (controlling cooling rates, heating treatments, etc.) is to ensure that we get a lot of small precipitates rather than a few large ones. Knowing what we can and cannot control in a material is perhaps the most important aspect of Materials Science.

The following photograph is taken in an electron microscope. It is a view through a sample about 3000 Å (300 nm) thick. The bright regions are discrete spheres of ' and the black background is the aluminum-rich Al/Li solid solution (meaning that this solid solution is mostly aluminum). Notice that the small ' precipitates are only around 200 Å in diameter (200 Å = 20 nm = 20×10^{-9} meters), i.e., about 100 atoms across. This is about a tenth of the specimen thickness.

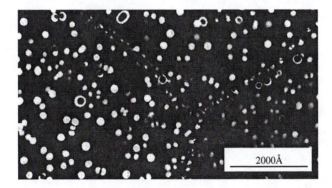

Photograph of an aluminum-lithium alloy taken in an electron microscope. Remember that you are looking through a thin piece of material and precipitates, the small white regions which are adjacent in the photograph, may be far apart in the material—one at the top and the other at the bottom.

This microstructure is just what we need for precipitation hardening. Lots of small precipitates will pin dislocations wherever they are moving. Just imagine these obstacles to dislocation motion dispersed throughout the specimen, each one being about a tenth of the specimen thickness. The next diagram may help you to visualize that the dislocation has NO chance of moving more than half a micron (5000 Å) before it encounters an obstacle! Remember the precipitates you see in the previous photograph are distributed throughout a three-dimensional sample.

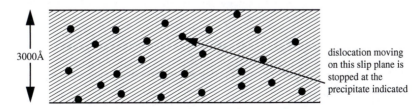

Side view of the specimen in the previous photograph.

The one remaining question is how we manage to get such a distribution of precipitates. How can we ensure that we don't just get a few large precipitates? For the moment we shall defer the answer while we consider how ineffective a few large precipitates would be. Imagine that all precipitates in the above diagram were combined to form one large precipitate. Only a few dislocations would have their motion stopped. If we now form two smaller precipitates of the same size from this large one (remember that they would have the same volume), each would have a diameter about 80% of the large single precipitate. Placing these two side by side produces a barrier that is 1.6 times taller than the one large precipitate and 0.8 times the width. The obstacles are now 1.6 × 0.8 = 1.28 of the original area. These two smaller precipitates can therefore stop the motion of more dislocations than could the single one. The following illustrations may help to explain this.

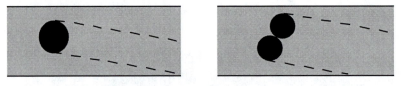

In the left diagram there is one large precipitate which can block the motion of dislocations moving on slip planes between the two shown by the dashed lines. The second diagram shows two precipitates with the same combined volume. They can block dislocations moving in a larger fraction of the crystal, again on all slip planes between the two indicated.

For the mathematically inclined, this is a consequence of the fact that volume is proportional to the cube of the linear dimension. For each precipitate to have half the volume of the original it must have a diameter equal to:

(the cube root of 0.5) × the diameter of the original.

The cube root of 0.5 is almost exactly 0.8.

Returning to the original question about the formation of many small precipitates, it is helpful to use an analogy. Imagine a large number of people moving around randomly in a big hall. On command they are to form themselves into large groups, but they only have a fixed time to do it in. Of course the less time they have, the smaller will be the groups they can form.

A metal alloy such as aluminum-lithium is formed by melting the elements together and making sure they are well mixed, then solidifying by cooling. In the molten state the atoms are all moving around freely and randomly but we have intentionally added so much lithium that the solubility limit at room temperature is exceeded. We therefore know that Al_3Li precipitates will form, and we can even tell how much. By controlling the cooling we can ensure that the atoms don't have enough time to form large clusters, or precipitates. In other words we want to cool quickly rather than slowly. We saw earlier that atoms have less mobility at lower temperatures.

The necessary cooling procedures have to be determined in the laboratory and can be quite complex, possibly involving letting the material sit at certain intermediate temperatures for some time

What is the Effect on Properties?

Stopping dislocation motion by precipitates is what we call **precipitation hardening**. The aluminum has been stiffened by precipitates produced by the addition of lighter lithium atoms. Every 1% of the original weight replaced by lithium produces about a 3.5% decrease in density. The table shows some of the property changes produced by adding about 3% lithium to aluminum. You can see that we have made a material that is lighter, stiffer and stronger.

Property	Conventional Aluminum Alloys	Al-Li Alloys	Change
Density (g/cm^3)	2.8	2.52	10% lighter
Young's Modulus (psi)	11x10^6	12x10^6	9% stiffer
*Ultimate Tensile Strength (psi)	77x10^3	80x10^3	4% stronger
*Yield Strength (psi)	62x10^3	67x10^3	8% stronger

*Yield strength**—the stress at which a material begins to deform permanently.
Ultimate tensile strength—the stress at which a material fails or breaks.

A good example of precipitation hardening was the development of an aluminum-lithium alloy by Alcoa for use in the vertical stabilizer and tailplanes of the Boeing 777 and Airbus A330/340. Tests show that it produces a weight savings of 650 pounds over conventional aluminum alloys at a cost of about $220 per pound of weight saved. Thus the cost is a one-time expense of under $150,000. If 650 pounds translates into three extra passengers with luggage, the cost is therefore around $50,000 per passenger. Using a conservative average ticket price of $250 and two flights a day, you should be able to appreciate that the investment is repaid in just 100 days. Not bad!

Aluminum-lithium alloys are therefore one answer the metallurgist has to the competition from composite materials. They are new materials, which have resulted from learning about how properties can be changed by modifying the structure.

Conclusion

In closing, let's give some thought to how science has aided in the development of this material.

First, consider that there are two facts that we have learned, but over which we really have no control. We cannot control whether lithium is a substitutional or interstitial impurity in aluminum, and we cannot control the solubility limit beyond which precipitates will form. What is important is that, armed with these facts, we can design a materials system that can be precipitation-hardened and also be of lighter weight.

Second, our control comes in (a) choosing a composition which is above the solid solubility limit, thus ensuring that precipitates form, and (b) making sure the material's cooling pattern produces a large number of small precipitates.

12. CASE STUDY: MAGNESIUM ALLOYS, POTENTIAL LIGHTWEIGHT AEROSPACE MATERIALS

Many people's memories of high school chemistry classes may include the time a piece of magnesium ribbon was held in a pair of tongs and then placed in a flame. The spectacular immediate combustion that ensued, in the form of a dazzling white flame, almost certainly gave the impression that here is a metal we want to avoid using. This is perhaps an example of a case where first impressions can be misleading.

Magnesium is the eighth most abundant element in the earth's crust, although it is not known to occur in a metallic state. Magnesite and dolomite are minerals from which it can be obtained, although it is more common to obtain it from salt water, which contains magnesium chloride in addition to sodium chloride. This, in itself, is attractive because it does not leave behind large holes in the ground or slag heaps.

This short chapter should make you aware of some exciting new developments in the metallurgy of magnesium. Before we do this we must dispel the fire hazard myth. It is true that thin ribbons and fine powders of magnesium burn vigorously in air, but larger pieces do not burn, mainly because magnesium is such a good conductor of heat that it is difficult to heat one spot so that it bursts into flames. The heat flows away from the spot so that it never reaches a high enough temperature.

Magnesium's principal attraction is its low density, which at 1.74 gm/cm^3 is considerably lower than that of aluminum (2.7 gm/cm^3). This means that changing from aluminum to pure magnesium would result in a weight savings of a third. As in the case of most metals, however, an alloy is used rather than the pure form. Magnesium alloys have been used extensively in car wheels ('mag wheels'), frames for soft-sided luggage, lawnmower housings, and in many items of machinery, where low weight is a priority. Volkswagen used quite a lot of magnesium on the 'Beetle', and some Mercedes sports cars have had magnesium seat frames. Chevrolet even experimented with the possibility of a magnesium engine block for the Corvette, which would be more than 100 pounds lighter than the cast-iron one typically used.

The Metallurgy of Magnesium and its Alloys

We mentioned earlier (Chapter 6) that magnesium has a hexagonal close packed crystal structure. Because of this there is only one possible slip plane, and deformation is limited in the same way as mentioned earlier for zinc (Page 44). Atoms have three directions of easy motion on this one slip plane but that is all. As a consequence, magnesium does not satisfy the von Mises criterion of five or more slip planes to be a ductile polycrystalline metal; it is quite brittle. In the uses mentioned earlier the items are not hammered or pressed into shape, but are formed by melting the magnesium alloy and pouring it into a mold of the required part, a process we call **casting**. Molten magnesium is very runny (has a low viscosity) and therefore can flow into even very small and complex areas of the mold. It is this property that allowed Audi to use magnesium for a complex dashboard support, which is only a millimeter thick in places.

How then can we make magnesium ductile? An answer was provided by some Japanese researchers—mix it with lithium to form a solid solution, just as we did with lithium and aluminum in the previous chapter. What happens is something which is probably most unexpected, adding lithium to magnesium changes the crystal structure from hexagonal close packed to body centered cubic (BCC), and we have already pointed out that BCC metals have six possible non-parallel slip panes with two slip directions in each, giving them twelve slip systems. Von Mises' criterion is satisfied and the material becomes ductile in polycrystalline form.

This change in crystal structure makes a dramatic change in the properties. An alloy of 57.4% magnesium, 37.6% lithium and 5% aluminum can be stretched 100% (a strain of 1), while another alloy of 56.5% magnesium, 38.5% lithium and 5% zinc can be stretched more than 200% (a strain greater than 2).

The fact that these alloys can be deformed so much should lead you to expect two things about the structure of the alloy. (Yes, you now have the necessary background to anticipate this!) The lithium causes no precipitation hardening, and it also is a substitutional impurity. If these were not true it would be extremely difficult to achieve the dislocation motion necessary for ductility, because interstitial atoms and precipitates impede dislocation motion.

Greatly increased ductility is not the only benefit, however. The density of pure lithium is just a little over half that of water, and as in the case of aluminum-lithium alloys we would expect its presence as a substitutional impurity in magnesium to produce a density reduction. This actually happens and the two alloys mentioned above are even lighter than water, with densities around 0.95 gm/cm^3. Applications for such materials in the aerospace industry are obvious.

Because magnesium and lithium powders and their molten liquids have to be handled very carefully, special care is needed in the manufacture of these alloys. This involves making sure that they do not come into contact with air (which contains oxygen), and the melting and mixing has to be performed in an inert atmosphere of argon. Manufacturing and handling costs will therefore be quite high such that these alloys will not be used in everyday articles. The economics of use in aerospace applications are quite different, as we mentioned in the previous chapter.

Conclusion

While much of what we have said above is reminiscent of aluminum alloys, there is an important difference, namely the crystal structure change induced by adding lithium. This is again something we have no control over, but once we discover that it happens we can turn it to tremendous advantage.

13. CASE STUDY: HSLA STEELS FOR CAR BODIES

Background

Steel is the traditional material of choice for car bodies, but, as we have seen in our earlier discussion of aluminum-lithium alloys, steels are quite heavy. Replacing them with aluminum and eventually by aluminum-lithium alloys is all very good where the economics can justify it, as in aircraft, but for an automobile body this is not the case. However, there is an incentive to reduce car body weight because of government regulations (requiring manufacturers to meet a minimum corporate fleet average fuel economy) and the volatile cost of petroleum. Another approach to the problem is to produce a steel that is stronger than traditional materials so that less is required. This is the thrust of the research, which led to the development of **high-strength low-alloy steels (HSLA steels)**.

During the two decades from 1975 to 1995 the weight of the typical U.S. passenger car was reduced by about 600 pounds, much of this as a result of the use of these high strength steels. At the same time a cost savings (owing to the use of less steel) amounted to around $40 was achieved. To accomplish the same weight savings using aluminum would have added approximately $460 to the cost.

The term 'high-strength' is well understood, but 'low-alloy' needs a little explanation because once again we are confronted with some metallurgical jargon. We call an impurity atom that we add intentionally to the steel an **alloying element**, and a steel with a *small* amount of these impurities is called **low-alloy**. In this chapter we shall discuss one of many high-strength low-alloy steels, which has niobium as one of the important alloying elements. The niobium forms niobium carbide precipitates, but unlike aluminum-lithium alloys where precipitates form within the crystallites to pin dislocations, these precipitates are formed at grain boundaries, i.e., between the crystallites, and it is these boundaries whose motion they stop.

The Metallurgy of HSLA Steels

We know that metals deform by the motion of dislocations that move on specific planes (close-packed planes) in the crystal. We call these planes **slip planes**. One of the major advantages of most metals is that they are ductile, i.e., they can be quite easily shaped to whatever object we require. On the other hand there are cases (bridges, buildings, etc.) when we want them to be stiff and able to carry large loads without yielding. We know that the way to accomplish this is by stopping dislocation motion. In aluminum-lithium alloys we have seen how we do this by precipitation hardening. HSLA steels are an example of another way of impeding dislocation motion.

When a metal solidifies it produces a polycrystalline structure, unless cooled very, very rapidly. A metal or alloy is therefore composed of many crystals or grains which can be several millimeters across or as small as 0.1 μm (1 μm = 10^{-6} meters or a millionth of a meter), corresponding to only about 500 atoms across. Two adjacent grains meet at a grain boundary, a planar defect, which can impede the passage of dislocations.

As we just mentioned, the dislocations move on specific slip planes in a crystal. However there is very little chance that this plane will continue across the grain boundary because the crystals on either side of the boundary have different orientations. Thus when the dislocation comes up to, and pushes on a grain boundary, the boundary stays put.

Notice that the dislocation is effectively pushing on the boundary. It wants to shift those atoms that are in front of it, but can only do so if the atoms across the boundary move also. The dislocation cannot therefore readily cross the boundary. A second dislocation comes along and stops behind the first, etc. However as more dislocations move along the slip plane and approach the boundary they add their force to that of the first dislocation and eventually the dislocation will find another slip plane in the opposing grain (albeit at a different angle). Once moving along a slip plane in the adjacent grain, dislocation move until they are stopped by the next grain boundary, where there will be another dislocation pile-up and the process repeats until eventually the whole material may deform.

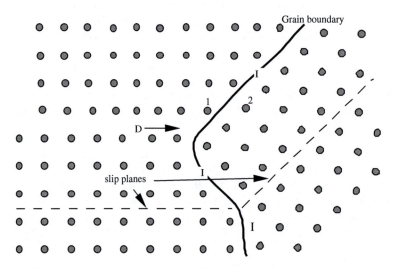

Illustration of a dislocation, moving in the direction of the arrow, stopped at a grain boundary. For further movement, atom 1 would have to move to the right where it is blocked by atom 2. Atom 2 has its slip plane going upward as shown (parallel to dashed line), and there is not enough force to move it in that direction. Also note that there are interstices (I) along the boundaries where impurity atoms could rest, precipitates start to form, or where atoms could start to rearrange into new crystals.

When the dislocations come to a boundary and are stopped they produce what we call a **pile-up**, a kind of traffic jam for dislocations (one was visible in the electron microscope photograph shown on page 78). In the following diagram of a pile-up, a dislocation is represented by the symbol ⊥. The accompanying photograph shows such a pile-up in a thin (1000 Å) sample of stainless steel when viewed in a transmission electron microscope. Remember that you are effectively looking through the sample and the slip plane is at an angle to the sample surface, as was the case when we looked at the photograph on page 78. The dislocations appear as dark spotty lines with one end at the top surface of the specimen and the other at the bottom.

Each dislocation is pushing on the grain boundary and the more dislocations the greater the combined force they exert. Think of the following analogy. People are lined up behind each other in single file trying to push down the dividing partition between two rooms. The more people pushing, the

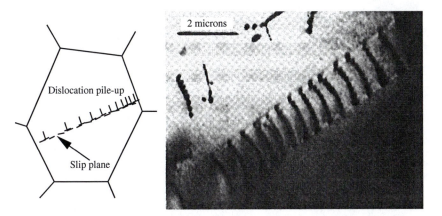

Diagram (left) and photograph (right) of a dislocation pile-up at a crystal boundary.

larger the force and the greater the chance of the partition collapsing (forget about the poor person in front getting crushed—it's only an analogy!). Now make the room smaller so that we can only line up three or four people behind each other. The chances of their being able to push the wall down are much reduced. The same thing happens in metal crystals. If we can make the grains so small that only a few dislocations can pile up in the grain, there is little likelihood that the grain boundary will move. Hence there is little overall deformation of the piece. Remember that even though each additional dislocation makes a smaller contribution to the total force, every little bit helps. The fewer dislocations there are, the greater the chance of the crystallite boundary holding and keeping the dislocations from advancing.

This gives us the clue to one further method of making a metal stronger: limit the dislocation motion by making the grains small. We call this process **grain-refining**. Note that by **refining** we here mean making finer or smaller. When we refine precious metals we usually mean that we are making them purer.

The main question now is how can we do it, i.e., refine the grains? The answer lies in taking advantage of the fact that iron changes from a BCC crystal to an FCC crystal when heated above 912 °C and reverses the change when cooled again below this temperature. The temperature is somewhat different for a steel (alloyed iron) but the principal is the same.

We first take a bar of the BCC iron, or in this case steel (something metallurgists call **ferrite**, or the **alpha phase**), and heat it so that it changes, or transforms, to the FCC form (**austenite**, or the **gamma phase**). After this change in crystal structure has been achieved, the steel is hot-rolled, meaning that it is rolled while still hot, or in the gamma form.[*]

This hot rolling has an effect on two structure levels, both of which are illustrated on the next page. First, and obvious, the steel bar is made longer and thinner, i.e., the **macrostructure** has changed. Second, and less obvious, the grains have also been flattened, something we sometimes call "pancaking".

---

[*]**Note:** Steels can also be cold-rolled, which strengthens them by work hardening. We mentioned the possible use of this for producing railroad lines (Page 80). In this case the material needs to be annealed between every few passes through the rolling mill to keep it soft enough to continue rolling. The reason for this is identical to that which we mentioned for a silversmith or blacksmith (Page 80).

The original **equiaxed microstructure**, which means that the grains are approximately the same size in all directions, has been changed into a **pancaked microstructure**.

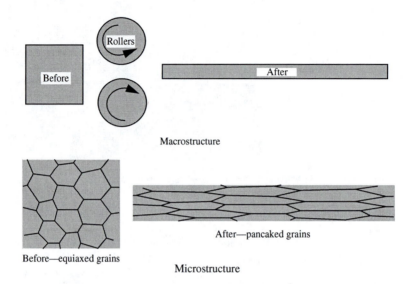

Illustration of the effect of hot rolling on macrostructure (above) and microstructure (below).

During the pancaking the grains have suffered gross deformation, something we know is produced by the motion of millions of dislocations. After the rolling the metal crystals are literally full of dislocations and under normal circumstances at these temperatures the atoms are very mobile and would move around to try to restore the original non-dislocated order, forming new crystals in a process we call **recrystallization**. In addition the crystals prefer to be equiaxed rather than pancaked, so this too incites the boundaries to move.

Here is where our materials science knowledge becomes useful. We know that by adding the alloying element niobium to the steel we can form very small precipitates (50 atoms across) of niobium carbide (NbC) (something which is done when the steel is first formed). These small precipitates stop recrystallization because they form on the grain boundaries and stop their motion. Because of this, the pancaked grain structure is retained.

The hot-rolled steel sheets are then allowed to cool, and below about 900°C the atoms do everything possible to change back to the BCC arrangement. To change their arrangement the atoms have to have some space to move around and the place where this can occur most easily is at the grain boundaries. If you look at the diagram of the grain boundary on Page 96 you will see that there are some large interstices between the two crystallites which give the atoms just enough space to start to rearrange themselves.

In other words the new BCC crystals start to form along the grain boundaries, which are pinned in position by the niobium carbide precipitates. These new BCC crystals grow until they bump into each other with the result that new grain boundaries are formed between them.

Now think what happens. In the direction in which the rolling force was applied, the original grain boundaries in the hot-rolled steel are very close together. As shown in the next diagram, the

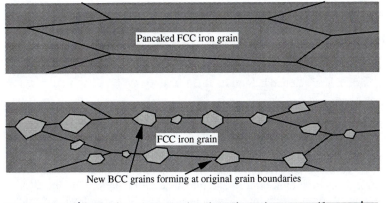

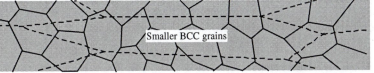

New BCC grains forming at original grain boundaries

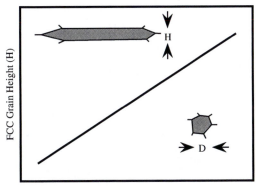

Illustration of what happens when a hot-rolled HSLA steel cools. The upper diagram shows the pancaked FCC grains. During cooling the atoms rearrange themselves to the BCC crystal structure, and find the space to do this at numerous points along the grain boundaries (center diagram). These nuclei continue to grow until the crystallites meet each other. Because opposing boundaries in the rolled material are very close, the crystallites do not grow much before this happens.

new crystals grow at many locations along these boundaries and they cannot grow any larger than the small dimension of the original pancaked grains because they meet each other approximately half way across the original grains. The material is now fully BCC and there is no need for further change. The consequence is that a very fine grain size has been produced. It is this fine ferrite grain structure (new microstructure) that produces the high strength in these steels.

Notice that the size of the final BCC grain depends on the height of the pancaked FCC grains as shown in the following graph. The more the rolling, the smaller the grain size and the less dislocation motion is possible.

The final BCC grain size depends on the height of the pancaked FCC grains.

In addition, experiments show that the smaller the grain size, the larger the **yield strength**. You can see below from the table of properties that the change is quite dramatic. Notice that the Young's modulus has not been changed.

Finally, let's consider how this new material has been developed by using some of the principles we have learned earlier. The science behind its manufacture involves two major factors:

- a phase transformation occurs (FCC to BCC) when steel is cooled below around 900°C.
- small precipitates of NbC can be formed at the grain boundaries and they stop the boundaries from moving.

Note that we cannot control the phase transformation. We take advantage of it during the processing. We control the rolling temperature and make sure it is higher than the BCC to FCC transition temperature. We control composition by adding an impurity (Nb), which we have determined will form precipitates along the grain boundaries. We can also control cooling rates to optimize desired properties, but discussion of this aspect is beyond the scope of this chapter.

What is the Effect on Properties?

Notice that in these materials we have not stopped the dislocations from moving as in work hardening and precipitation hardening. Instead, we have made it more difficult for dislocations to pass from one grain to another (at a greatly increased number of grain boundaries), hence the increase in yield strength as seen in the table below. These new materials are stronger than conventional sheet steels and the table shows some of these differences. You can see that both ultimate tensile strength and yield strength have increased quite remarkably, but that the stiffness, or Young's modulus is unchanged. The fact that the steel can take nearly three times the force without beginning to show a permanent deformation is what allows us to use thinner sheet metal in our autos. Some car manufacturers have reported decreased warranty claims for body dents as a result of using these steels.

Property	Conventional Steel	Comparable HSLA Steel	Change
Young's Modulus (psi)	30×10^6	30×10^6	no change
*Ultimate Tensile Strength (psi)	43×10^3	80×10^3	85% stronger
*Yield Strength (psi)	24×10^3	70×10^3	190% stronger

The thinner HSLA steel used for automobile bodies saves weight and consequently improves fuel economy. We may think today's cars are "tinny," but they do stand up to the rigors of everyday use. Unfortunately, our reaction is more psychological than scientific!

---

*Yield strength—the stress at which a material begins to deform permanently.
Ultimate tensile strength—the stress at which a material fails or breaks.

QUESTIONS: Chapters 10–13

1. Adding lithium to magnesium changes the crystal structure from _____.
   (a) BCC to FCC   (b) FCC to HCP   (c) HCP to FCC   (d) HCP to BCC   (e) HCP to CCP.

2. Which of the following structures would give the most brittle metal?
   (a) FCC   (b) BCC   (c) HCP   (d) CCP   (e) amorphous

3. Aluminum-lithium alloys are very strong because of _____.
   (a) work hardening   (b) precipitation hardening   (c) grain refining   (d) zone refining
   (e) chain stiffening

4. The magnesium-lithium alloys mentioned are _____ than pure magnesium.
   (a) lighter   (b) more conductive   (c) more ductile   (d) both a and c   (e) all of these

5. The hot rolling process used in the manufacture of steels changes which structure level(s)?
   (a) microstructure   (b) atomic structure   (c) macrostructure   (d) both a and b   (e) both a and c

6. When we anneal a work hardened material we reduce the number of _____.
   (a) vacancies   (b) dislocations   (c) interstitials   (d) planes   (e) impurity atoms

7. The term grain refining means _____.
   (a) purifying the grains   (b) changing crystals into grains   (c) changing the macrostructure without
   changing the microstructure   (d) decreasing the grain size   (e) none of these

8. Which of the following is in order of increasing ductility?
   (a) gold, zinc, amorphous iron   (b) amorphous iron, zinc, gold   (c) gold, amorphous iron, zinc
   (d) zinc, gold, amorphous iron   (e) none of these is in the correct order

9–13. When we make HSLA steels we hot roll the material. This changes the __9i__ structure and the __9ii__ structure. The grain boundaries are pinned by __10__ so that the grains remain __11__. When the material cools there is a change in __12__ structure from FCC to BCC. The end result is that we have __13__.

   9. (a) crystal, macro   (b) atomic, micro   (c) crystal, micro   (d) micro, macro
      (e) crystal, atomic
   10. (a) dislocations   (b) nickel carbide precipitates   (c) niobium carbide precipitates
       (d) vacancies   (e) substitutional impurities
   11. (a) pancaked   (b) needle-like   (c) amorphous   (d) rigid   (e) irregular
   12. (a) crystal   (b) macro   (c) atomic   (d) electron   (e) micro
   13. (a) purified the grains   (b) enlarged the material   (c) produced a denser material
       (d) refined the grains   (e) eliminated dislocations

14. Fine grained metals are stronger because there are more _____ to stop dislocation motion.
   (a) slip planes   (b) grain boundaries   (c) dislocation tangles   (d) vacancies
   (e) point defects

15. Which of the following is not true of HSLA steels compared with regular steels?
   (a) lighter   (b) stronger   (c) stiffer   (d) both a and b   (e) both a and c

16. For HSLA steels, the _____ the grain size, the _____ the yield strength.
   (a) larger, larger   (b) smaller, smaller   (c) smaller, larger
   (d) there is no connection between the two   (e) none of these is correct

17–28. HSLA steels and Aluminum-Lithium (Al-Li) are both __17__, which indicates that they both involve __18__. The alloying element of importance in HSLA steels is __19__, whereas in Al-Li it is the lithium which is added to the aluminum. In both cases there is only a small amount of the alloying element added, in fact only about __20__ lithium is added to aluminum to produce a 10% __21__. In both these materials the alloying element produces __22__ but their positions in the crystals and their functions are quite different. In HSLA steels the __22__ are formed __23__, while in Al-Li they are formed __24__. The purpose of __22__ in HSLA steels is to __25__. In Al-Li their purpose is to __26__. The strengthening mechanism used in HSLA steels is __27__, while in Al-Li it is __28__.

17. (a) cermets   (b) alloys   (c) semiconductors   (d) composites   (e) insulators
18. (a) electron/hole pairs   (b) a ceramic-metal mix   (c) fibers   (d) a mixture of metals
    (e) no free electrons
19. (a) europium   (b) silicon   (c) titanium   (d) chromium   (e) niobium
20. (a) 1%   (b) 3%   (c) 5%   (d) 7%   (e) 10%
21. (a) volume increase   (b) volume decrease   (c) density decrease   (d) strength increase
    (e) increase in electrical conduction
22. (a) dislocations   (b) activators   (c) a matrix   (d) precipitates   (e) cracks
23. (a) at the surface of the material   (b) at grain boundaries   (c) throughout the material
    (d) on dislocations   (e) at no particular location.
24. (a) at the surface of the material   (b) at grain boundaries   (c) throughout the material
    (d) on dislocations   (e) none of these
25. (a) decrease conductivity   (b) increase ductility   (c) pin dislocations
    (d) reduce corrosion   (e) pin grain boundaries
26. (a) decrease conductivity   (b) increase ductility   (c) pin dislocations   (d) reduce corrosion
    (e) pin grain boundaries
27. (a) grain refining   (b) work hardening   (c) crosslinking   (d) precipitation hardening
    (e) crystallization
28. (a) grain refining   (b) work hardening   (c) crosslinking   (d) precipitation hardening
    (e) crystallization

29–38. Aluminum-lithium alloys are the aluminum industry's answer to the threat posed by __29__ to replace aluminum in aircraft. Each __30__ (by weight) addition of lithium reduces the density of aluminum by 3.5%. Lithium in aluminum is a(n) __31__ impurity. Below the __32__, it is dissolved in the aluminum. Above the __32__ a two-phase mixture occurs. This two phase mixture takes the form of delta prime precipitates in an aluminum-lithium __33__. The precipitates form __34__. In order to effectively __35__ the material there must be __36__ precipitates to __37__. Al_3Li is the formula for the precipitates. This is known as a(n) __38__.

29. (a) HSLA steel   (b) carbon fiber composites   (c) titanium   (d) polymers   (e) ceramics
30. (a) 10%   (b) 3.5%   (c) 1%   (d) 7%   (e) 1.75%
31. (a) substitutional   (b) intrinsic   (c) activator   (d) ordered   (e) interstitial
32. (a) melting point   (b) precipitation hardening point   (c) solubility limit   (d) refining limit
    (e) recrystallization point
33. (a) composite   (b) melt   (c) steel   (d) laminate   (e) solid solution
34. (a) at grain boundaries   (b) near the surfaces of the piece   (c) randomly   (d) in rows
    (e) both a and d
35. (a) strengthen   (b) stiffen   (c) alloy   (d) both a and b   (e) all of these
36. (a) many small   (b) few small   (c) many large   (d) few large   (e) either a or d
37. (a) pin dislocations   (b) blunt cracks   (c) destroy dislocations   (d) absorb defects
    (e) heal cracks
38. (a) alloy   (b) ceramic   (c) composite   (d) intermetallic compound   (e) solid solution

14. POLYMERS ARE NOT JUST PLASTIC

Plastics, or what to a materials scientist are known as polymers, pervade every aspect of our lives. In addition to the natural polymers which account for much of our bodies and most living things around us, there are now thousands of man-made polymers which we use for clothing, household items, automobiles, furniture, appliances, electrical and thermal insulation, etc. Polyethylene, PVC, Teflon®, nylon, polypropylene, polyester, acrylic, and polycarbonate, among many others, are words which appear frequently in advertisements and are used more and more in our everyday language. Many people are unaware that paints and adhesives are also plastics nowadays, and much of the improvement in these materials is the result of plastics technology, or Materials Science.

It may be surprising to many that the first man-made polymers were not discovered until the start of the 20th century, and many of those were accidents. While some of these new discoveries were used during the second world war, notably nylon for parachutes, polyethylene for electrical insulation in radar installations, and Teflon in the atomic bomb, it was not until afterwards that certain polymers began to be available for public use. GI's enjoyed bartering power in England after the war as a result of their access to 'nylons', which at that time was an accepted synonym for ladies' hose.

There are three main types of polymer. Rubber is an **elastomer**: it can be stretched by large amounts and returns to its original length when the stress is removed. Polyethylene is a **thermoplastic**: it becomes soft when heated so that it can be shaped, and then becomes rigid again when cooled. Epoxy resins are **thermosets**: they become more rigid when heated because the chains become crosslinked with covalent bonds—more about that later.

As we have already seen (Page 34), polymers are based on a chain of carbon atoms, which are held together by very strong covalent bonds. However, if these bonds are so strong, why is it that these materials are often very flexible, sometimes elastic and often plastic? We don't see this behavior in diamond and other covalently bonded solids.

The reason is twofold. The first lies in the fact that in most polymers the atoms are not bonded in a three dimensional network but in a linear chain. We saw that the 'straight' polyethylene chain is kinked (Page 48), zigzagging back and forth along its length. This is a consequence of the directionality of these covalent bonds. The following photographs of a model of a polyethylene chain may help you to visualize this.

However, in a linear chain the bond only has a reference to the adjacent bond in the chain, which means that it can rotate around a cone, as illustrated in the following diagram, and still maintain the desired angle with the previous bond. As a consequence the bonds in the chain are able to wiggle around in all directions. In a polymer this can happen because of the rotational ability of the bonds.

The second reason for flexibility is that there are only secondary bonds between chains and these are too weak to prevent this bond rotation and the chains from sliding over each other. This is quite different from the rigid 3D network of covalent bonds, which exists in diamond or silicon, for example.

The following photographs of polyethylene chains illustrate how these chains can twist and turn in all directions. Model kits for organic chemistry such as used for these photographs, are available in many academic bookstores, and it may be helpful to obtain one to convince yourself of what we are illustrating.

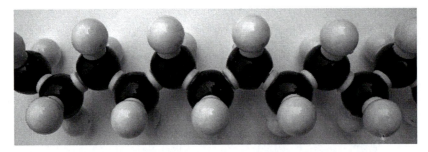

'Side' view of polyethylene chain model (compare to diagram on page 48),
showing the zigzag nature of a straight chain.

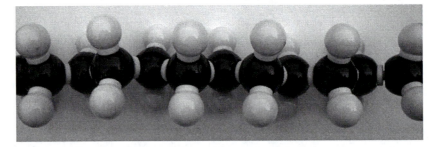

'Top' view of above model.

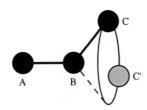

Using atoms A and B as
reference atom C can lie
anywhere on the rim of the
indicated cone, i.e. could be
in the C' position. The three
atoms will always have the
same angle between them.

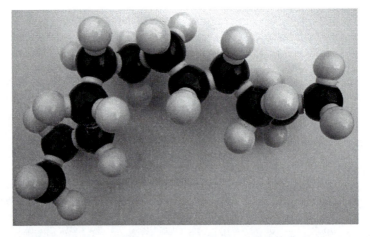

Photograph of convoluted polyethylene chain. Note that any three
consecutive (black) carbon atoms have the same angle between them.

The weakness in polymers is therefore this weak van der Waals bond between the chains. What we have to do to strengthen the material is to somehow stop these chains from moving easily over each other.

Here again there are several methods we can use, but there are three common approaches: crosslinking of chains, chain stiffening, and chain crystallization. In the first approach the chains are linked together with covalent bonds, in the second method some large atom groups are attached to the chains to inhibit their bending and movement, and in the third approach the chains lie straight and parallel to each other to maximize the van der Waals attraction.

Chain Crosslinking

This is perhaps the easiest of the three to understand. The carbon chains are usually separate and can therefore easily move over each other. If we can insert some permanent links between adjacent chains we can restrict their relative movement. To do this we need an atom that can form covalent bonds between two carbon atoms on different sections of a given chain or on different chains altogether, thereby producing a three-dimensional covalently bonded network of atoms. Charles Goodyear was the one who discovered how to do this in rubber by adding sulfur, a process known as **vulcanization**, to cross-link the rubber chains and thus stiffen the material. Natural rubber flows easily and is of little practical use. The sulfur atom (atomic number 16) needs two electrons to complete its octet, and gets these by sharing electrons (bonding covalently) with two of the carbon atoms in nearby chains. This prevents the chains from unfolding and moving past each other. Eventually, if we add enough sulfur, the rubber becomes a rigid black solid called **ebonite**, which for many years was used for bowling balls, musical instruments (clarinets), and the cover plates of electrical outlets and switches.

A rubber band placed in the window for a few weeks will become brittle because oxygen, with the help of the sunlight, not only produces some crosslinking, but also some chain rupture. Now you can see why carbon black in car tires is added to keep light out. It stops the rubber from becoming brittle.

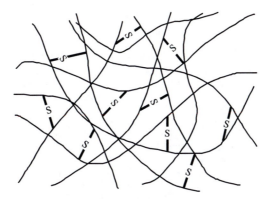

Sulfur atoms form two covalent bonds with polymer chains to produce crosslinking.

Chain Stiffening

The second, and perhaps most successful method of making polymers stronger is to make it more difficult for the chains to move to new configurations and also to move past each other. The secret to this process is to replace some of the small hydrogen atoms on the polyethylene chain with large groups of atoms such as benzene rings (C_6H_6), which produces polystyrene, but even single large atoms help. Now when the carbon atoms try to rotate their bonds around the cone they cannot do so because the large groups get in each other's way; there is a sort of atom group repulsion, something known as **steric hindrance**. The large groups therefore stop the chains from being flexible by simply getting in the way of bond rotation.

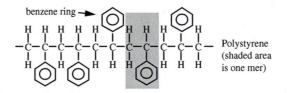

In addition, the large groups on the chain produce an effective roughening so that adjacent chains do not slide past each other so easily. It's like putting grains of sand on paper. Two sheets of sand paper do not slide over each other as easily as do two sheets of regular writing paper.

The chain stiffening produced by the benzene rings in polystyrene is enough to make it a hard plastic with a softening temperature above the boiling point of water, which is a good thing since one use of polystyrene is in disposable coffee cups. A similar effect is produced in Plexiglas® (polymethyl methacrylate) using (CH_3) and ($COOCH_3$) groups. It is also a hard, stiff plastic.

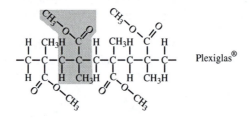

In today's world one of the strongest polymers is polycarbonate. It is used for lenses in protective eyewear, football helmets, car headlamp lenses, and for many household articles such as toilet tanks. It is extremely stiff and strong and gets this property from the large bulky atom groups both in and on the carbon chain. The atomic arrangement in the polymer is shown below.

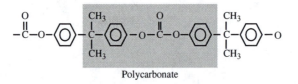

Polycarbonate

Chain Crystallization

The third approach is to crystallize the polymer. This involves packing the chains in a parallel closely packed arrangement as discussed earlier for polyethylene. Indeed polyethylene is the most crystallizable polymer available because the chains can be 'straightened' as shown earlier (Page 48) and there are only small hydrogen atoms on the chains which do not get in each others' way, i.e., they produce no steric hindrance. The van der Waals bonds are quite weak, but as shown in the diagram on page 35, the chains only come close to each other on a few occasions. When the carbon chains are far apart the bonds are very weak. When the chains are crystallized, i.e., they are arranged in a tight parallel configuration, the bonds are naturally stronger and there are more of them. The chains therefore do not move as easily and the material is stiffer, or stronger. The principle is exactly the same as that used by a carpenter in joining two long pieces of wood. They are first planed to be very straight and smooth so that they make contact over their whole length. The glue then makes a strong bond. If they only made passing contact every few inches the bond between them would be much weaker, and of course the finished article would look peculiar!

In addition to polyethylene we can also produce crystals of polyvinylidene chloride (Saran® wrap) and polypropylene. Another polymer with which you are familiar is Teflon®, simply polyethylene with all the hydrogen atoms replaced with fluorine atoms. In all these the atom groups attached to the main carbon chain are small.

Polypropylene

Polyvinylidene chloride

Polytetrafluoroethylene (Teflon®)

We have introduced quite a few new polymers in this chapter, along with the **mers** from which they are built, i.e., the shaded unit along each chain in the preceding diagrams. Here's a simple way to memorize some of the important mers (and the resulting polymers). Think of the ethylene mer (below, left) as a capital 'H' or football goal post, with two carbons at the ends of the cross bar and four hydrogens at the ends of the vertical posts. In the following figure we show the development of our "goal post" shorthand notation for polyethylene and polyvinyl chloride (PVC). In the latter case, one hydrogen atom is replaced by one chloride atom. The notation for the rest of the mers/polymers should be self-explanatory. We will revisit these polymers when we consider their recycling.

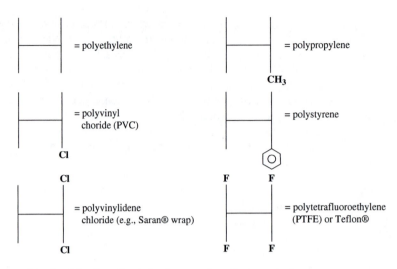

Shorthand "goal post" notation for some important mers/polymers.

To summarize this chapter: the weakness in polymers is the weak van der Waals bonds between adjacent polymer chains. We can strengthen them by three methods:

Crosslinking: using atoms such as oxygen and sulfur which insert bridges between chains and thus inhibit their sliding over each other.

Stiffening of chains: by adding large side groups, to inhibit bonds from rotating and also to roughen the chains to make it more difficult for them to move past each other.

Crystallization: packs the chains very close together over long distances thus increasing the bond strength between them and therefore strengthening them.

In many polymeric materials two of these three methods are used in combination. One with which you are familiar is Dacron® (polyethylene terephthalate or PET—no need to remember this complex name, unless you want to impress somebody!), which combines large atom units in the chain with crystallinity to create a very strong material.

Polymer chemists have become very clever at producing new polymers with combinations of these strengthening characteristics, and also at inventing some new ones. A way of producing a polymer which is both strong and flexible is considered in our case study on high impact polystyrene (Chapter 16) where we shall be introduced to copolymers, in which two different polymers, one stiff and the other elastic, are arranged in the same chain. The possibilities are infinite and hundreds of new polymers are made each year, most of which are too complex for us to consider. In the next chapter we shall look more closely at polyethylene, which is undoubtedly the most common polymer we encounter every day.

Conclusion

We have seen that polymers like metals and ceramics have weaknesses, which can be overcome by altering their structure. This can involve the atomic structure (sulfur added to rubber) or the 'micro-structure.'

The term microstructure was placed in quotes because it is somewhat difficult to apply the term to polymers in the sense we have applied it to metals and ceramics, which are mostly crystalline. As we have seen, most polymers do not show much crystallinity, and for those that do, it is perhaps the fraction of the material that is crystalline, rather than the crystal size, which is important. For polymers we shall take 'microstructure' to refer to the arrangements and characteristics of the *chains*, rather than to those of the *crystals*. Polymer scientists often call this the chain 'architecture.' Do the chains have large appendages? How are they arranged? How long are they? Etc. All these are factors unique to polymers, and can often be modified by suitable processing. We shall see some examples of this in the next chapter.

15. POLYETHYLENE: THE MOST COMMON POLYMER

We have already noted that the word "polymer" means many parts, or many mers. In polyethylene the mer is ethylene, a gas formed from carbon and hydrogen. You probably won't ever encounter it as a gas, although it is interesting to note that it is used commercially to promote the ripening of tomatoes. We don't find large quantities of ethylene occurring naturally so have to produce it from other raw materials. Before we discuss the ways ethylene, and polyethylene, are produced we shall look at its chemical formula and the formulae of some related compounds called paraffins.

The Paraffins

The word paraffin comes from the Latin word meaning "not very reactive." If somebody mentioned the word "paraffin" to you in a word association game, you would probably say "wax", paraffin wax being a white solid sold in supermarkets as a sealant for jelly. In England "paraffin" denotes what is known in the USA as kerosene, and "liquid paraffin" is a laxative. All these uses describe materials that are mostly mixtures of what are known to a chemist as paraffins.

Earlier in the book we saw that a carbon atom has four outer, or valence, electrons, which can form four covalent bonds with other carbon atoms to produce diamond. Most of what we call Organic Chemistry is related to the countless number of ways a carbon atom can form four bonds with different surrounding atoms. In this chapter we shall only deal with cases in which all these surrounding atoms are hydrogens, compounds called **hydrocarbons**. A very simple way this occurs is when a carbon atom forms covalent bonds with four hydrogen atoms and acquires an octet of electrons by sharing the one electron of each hydrogen. The resulting compound is called **methane** and has the chemical formula CH_4. The methane molecule consists of a central carbon atom with four surrounding hydrogen atoms situated on the corners of a tetrahedron. Methane is a gas at room temperature and is the major component in natural gas. A model of a methane molecule is shown in the following diagram.

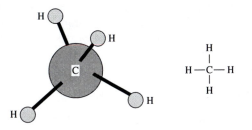

Methane molecule with carbon atoms covalently bonded to four smaller hydrogen atoms on the corners of a tetrahedron. The diagram on the right shows the way the atom arrangement is usually shown for simplicity. When you see such diagrams remember that the atoms are not all in the same plane.

A similar compound called **ethane** is also found in natural gas. Its molecule has two central carbon atoms, each of which shares an electron with the other to form a covalent bond, the remaining three valence electrons on each carbon atom forming covalent bonds with hydrogen atoms to give a molecule with the formula C_2H_6. As suggested earlier, ethane is also a gas.

Propane is a gas you have probably encountered as the fuel used for barbecues and camping gas stoves. It is the next logical extension to the series of compounds started by methane and ethane. At the center of the molecule are a line of three carbon atoms, the middle one of which forms covalent bonds with the adjacent two. If you think about this a little, or look at the diagrams, you will see that this leaves the central carbon atom with two electrons to form covalent bonds, while the outer two carbon atoms are left with three electrons as was the case with the carbon atoms in ethane. These eight electrons form bonds with hydrogen atoms to give a chemical formula C_3H_8.

It should not be difficult to now go to the next possibility. Instead of a line of three carbon atoms we have four. Think of the additional carbon atom being added to the middle of the existing three and forming covalent bonds with the two adjacent atoms. This leaves it with two valence electrons to bond to hydrogen atoms. The resulting compound, a gas called **butane**, has a formula C_4H_{10}. You have probably heard of it as a fuel used in cigarette lighters. The following diagram illustrates molecules of methane, ethane, propane and butane. Don't forget that the four bonds from the carbon atoms point to the corners of a tetrahedron, so that the line of atoms shown is zigzag rather than straight.

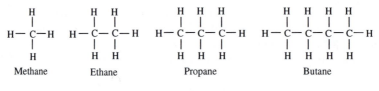

| Methane | Ethane | Propane | Butane |

The first four paraffins.

The four compounds, methane, ethane, propane and butane are the first four members of a series of compounds called paraffins. The next member of the series is obtained by simply adding one carbon and two hydrogen atoms. The general chemical formula is therefore obtained by taking a number (n) of CH_2 units and adding the two hydrogen atoms from the ends, giving C_nH_{2n+2}.

In many lighters you can see through the plastic case and you may have noticed that the butane is a liquid. This is because the butane molecules are under pressure. They have been squeezed together until they bond together. The same occurs in the metal cylinders of propane gas used for barbecues. All gases turn into liquids if the molecules or atoms come close enough together and bonds form between them. This can be accomplished by lowering the temperature, by applying a high pressure, or by a combination of both. What type of bond forms in these circumstances? As already mentioned for the inert gases (Page 33) the bond is usually of the van der Waals type.

Van der Waals Bonds in Paraffins

At this point it may be helpful to remind ourselves how van der Waals bonds form. At any instant in time, the atom or molecule finds that it has more electrons on one side than the other, with the result that the atom or molecule becomes polar. One side of the atom or molecule tends to be negatively charged and the opposite side positively charged, and two such units can therefore attract each other, positive attracting negative. A consequence of this is that the van der Waals bond becomes stronger the larger the number of electrons in the atom or molecule. Why?

Imagine two molecules, one with 100 electrons and another with 200 electrons. If at any instant one in a hundred electrons finds itself on the wrong side of the atom, a dipole is formed. In the molecule with 100 electrons there would be 49 on one side and 51 on the other, a difference of two. In the other molecule the corresponding numbers would be 98 and 102, a difference of four. It is this larger difference in charge, or larger polarity, which produces the stronger bond.

This can be clearly seen for the paraffins by looking at the boiling points of the liquids. Remember that materials (liquids) boil when the heat energy is large enough to break the van der Waals bonds between the atoms or molecules. The stronger the bonds the more energy is needed to break them, thus giving rise to higher boiling points. Here are the boiling points for the paraffins we mentioned above. (Note that since all values are negative, a smaller number is a higher temperature.)

methane	ethane	propane	butane
–161°C	–89°C	–42°C	–1°C

You can see that at room temperature butane doesn't need much encouragement to form a liquid. We don't have to lower its temperature much in order to get it to liquefy, and for the same reasons we also don't have to squeeze it much to accomplish the same thing. As a result it can be kept liquid in a quite thin plastic container. Propane, on the other hand, is more difficult to liquefy, and is usually pressurized inside a metal container.

As you might imagine, as the molecules become larger the boiling points get higher. After butane we have pentane, whose boiling point is 36°C. In other words it is a liquid at normal room temperatures. By the time we get to $C_{20}H_{42}$, a compound called eicosane, the boiling point is over 200°C and the melting point is around 37°C. This means that the bonds are now strong enough to hold the molecules together as a solid, even on the hottest day.

At this stage you may be realizing why polymers are usually solid. The compound just mentioned, eicosane, has a 'chain' of 20 carbon atoms. Polymers have chains of thousands of atoms, and we might therefore reasonably expect the bonds between these chains to be quite strong. We shall come back to this later.

Ethylene

By now you must be wondering where ethylene comes into the scheme of things. It too is a compound of carbon and hydrogen, but it is not a paraffin because it has a different bonding arrangement between the carbon atoms.

When we discussed the combination of two carbon atoms to form ethane, we joined them with one covalent bond, i.e., they shared one pair of electrons. What if they decide to share two pairs of electrons and form two covalent bonds between themselves? They would then each have only two remaining electrons to form covalent bonds with hydrogen atoms, with the result that the molecule consists of two carbon atoms and four hydrogen atoms (C_2H_4). This is ethylene. We say that the molecule consists of two carbon atoms with a **double bond** between them, and two hydrogen atoms bonded to each carbon atom.

Although you may not have encountered ethylene gas, you may have come across **acetylene** gas as used in oxy-acetylene welding. In an acetylene molecule there are also two carbon atoms but they decide to share three pairs of electrons between themselves, forming a **triple bond**, and consequently each carbon only has one electron remaining to bond to a hydrogen atom. Acetylene therefore has the formula C_2H_2. Molecules of ethylene and acetylene are illustrated below.

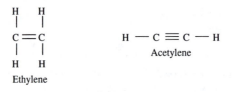

Polyethylene

In the 1930's scientists were curious about the effects of really high pressures on gases. Among the gases investigated was ethylene. The ethylene was placed in a very strong, rigid container and squeezed using pressures over 1000 times greater than atmospheric pressure. This was the equivalent of about ten tons per square inch, or an elephant on tip-toe! When the container was opened a "white waxy solid" was found to have been formed. We now know that the ethylene had polymerized into something similar to what we know as paraffin wax. It turned out that there was accidentally a small amount of oxygen in the ethylene, which was crucial to the reaction. This rather crude experiment led to investigations into how the polymerization process could be controlled to make a useful product—the polyethylene we know today.

The large amounts of polyethylene manufactured nowadays obviously require enormous quantities of ethylene, and we should perhaps be wondering where such quantities can be found, especially since we have already mentioned that we are unlikely to encounter ethylene gas in everyday life. The answer is that the ethylene has to be manufactured. It is either produced from ethane, found in natural gas, or from products of the petroleum refining industry. In both cases the ethylene is produced by a process called **cracking**. For ethane the process is quite simply the splitting (hence the term cracking) of the ethane molecule (C_2H_6) into ethylene (C_2H_4) and hydrogen (H_2). Note that the numbers of atoms balance, something a chemist calls 'balancing the equation'.

The formation of polyethylene from ethylene occurs by a process called **addition polymerization** and involves the use of high pressures, high temperatures, and catalysts. Different pressures, temperatures and catalysts (processing) give different types of materials with different structures and properties. Remember, this is what Materials Science is all about.

This is not the place to enter into a long and detailed discussion of the meaning of the term "catalyst". You have probably heard of it in reference to the catalytic converter on your car, perhaps without really knowing what it is, except that it is something to do with cleaning up the emission gases. A catalyst can simply be thought of as a chemical species, which initiates a chemical reaction, or helps it take place. In the case of polyethylene manufacture the catalyst causes a rupture of one of the two covalent bonds between the two carbon atoms in the ethylene molecule. As a result, each carbon atom in the molecule has an electron that is looking for something with which to form a bond. We call these **unpaired electrons** because they are not satisfied until they have paired up with another electron to form a covalent bond. One of these unpaired electrons becomes satisfied by bonding to the catalyst, while the other one is left hanging, looking for something to react with. What then happens very quickly is that a neighboring ethylene molecule decides to join this reactive unit. One of its double bonds breaks and an unpaired electron on one end pairs up with the unpaired electron on the first molecule to form a covalent bond.

At this point the molecule joining up is itself left with an unpaired electron at the other end and the same thing happens between it and another ethylene molecule. You can see that we have started a process, which can just keep going as more and more ethylene molecules join up, forming a longer and longer chain. In fact the addition of extra ethylene mers occurs so quickly that it takes less than a hundredth of a second to produce a chain of 1000 mers. (Note that each mer contains two carbon atoms and four hydrogen atoms.) This addition polymerization process is illustrated below, where the catalyst is simply designated by the symbol X and * represents a reactive bond. We shall later refer to some specific catalysts used, but their composition is not important for this discussion.

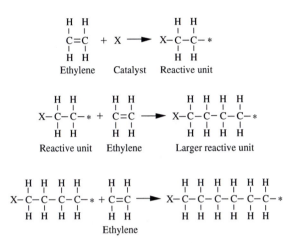

The addition polymerization mechanism for polyethylene.

Of course, if the ends of two chains, each with an unpaired electron come close together, these two electrons can pair up to form a covalent bond and there are no further additions to the chain. As a result, chain growth stops, as shown in the diagram below. Polymer scientists refer to this as termination.

Illustration of how polymerization terminates by the combination of two reactive units.

Chain Branching

During this rapid polymerization process you can well imagine that there are plenty of opportunities for mistakes. In some cases a mer adds to the side of a chain such that a hydrogen atom is replaced by another ethylene mer, which in turn starts the formation of another chain branching off the first. This process of **chain branching** illustrated on the next page, is a very important feature of the resulting polymer's structure and hence affects its properties. Some important parameters are the number of branches which form and their length. These can be controlled by the changing the processing conditions (pressure, temperature, catalyst).

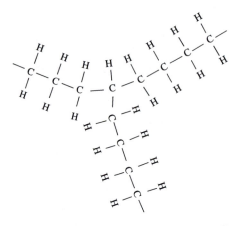

Chain branching in polyethylene. Remember that hydrogen atoms are very small and that the atoms do not all lie in the same plane. They therefore do not interfere with each other as may appear to be the case here.

As an analogy, think of a length of wire. A straight length of wire can be wound onto a spool very efficiently. Adjacent turns of wire lie very close to each other, in fact they tend to close pack in the same way that spherical metal atoms can be considered to pack. If we now put a large number of short branches on our wire, in other words make barbed wire, we find that we can no longer wind the wire as efficiently onto the spool. The reason is **steric hindrance**. The short branches get in each other's way. On the other hand if we attach just a few long branches to the wire, these long wire branches can bend over and lie parallel to the wire to which they are attached. The result is that we can again have a fairly efficient packing of wire on the spool. If you think about it, you will readily see that barbed wire would be ineffective if the spurs (branches) were all two feet long. They would simply bend over under their own weight and you could climb over the fence without difficulty.

The same sort of features are apparent in different types of polyethylene. While the best packing occurs with linear chains, a small amount of long-chain branching still allows the chains to pack very efficiently, whereas short-chain branching does not, especially if there is a lot of it. There are several, related results of this:

- short-chain branching produces a lower density material—if the chains of atoms are closer together there is more weight per volume.
- short-chain branching makes for a lower crystalline content in the material—chains have to be straight and parallel to form polymer crystals.
- short-chain branching produces weaker materials—there is more bonding between straight parallel chains.

These effects are similar to those mentioned in the previous chapter in talking about individual chains. However, when a long branch folds over to lie parallel and close to the parent chain the effect is almost the same as when the two chains are unconnected.

Different Polyethylenes, Their Manufacture, Properties and Uses

There are two major polymerization processes used commercially for the production of polyethylene. One occurs at very high pressures (~20,000 psi) and moderate temperatures (200°C) and uses an oxygen-containing catalyst. This process produces considerable short-chain branching and the resulting product is known as low density polyethylene (LDPE). The second process uses titanium and aluminum chlorides as the catalyst with much lower pressures (~200 psi) and a slightly lower temperature (100 to 175°C). Under these processing conditions high density polyethylene (HDPE), with far fewer short-chain branches, is formed.

HDPE is used extensively for garbage cans, dish pans, pipes, etc. A large plastic can of paint or driveway sealer is likely to have HDPE embossed on the bottom, indicating the type of material from which it is made. These applications take advantage of the much higher strength and stiffness of HDPE.

On the other hand, plastic wrap and plastic bags are often made of LDPE. This material has a lower strength and is more flexible, although it is still a tough material. Don't forget that along the chains of carbon atoms in these large polymer molecules there are still very strong covalent bonds.

The following table gives some property comparisons for these two different polyethylenes. You will readily see that the density difference is really quite small, whereas the property differences are much larger. Incidentally, the theoretical density of a single polyethylene crystal is almost exactly that of water (1.00 gm/cc).

	HDPE	LDPE
Density (gm/cc)	0.96	0.92
Tensile strength (psi)	5,500	3,000
Young's modulus (psi)	180,000	40,000

These data clearly illustrate how the properties of a material can be changed using different processing techniques. Remember that the two materials contain the same atoms and the same polymer chains. Using our classifications of structure we would say that only the microstructure is different, although in this case we are not just concerned with the size, shape and orientation of the crystals, but also the fraction of the material that is crystalline.

Another difference between these two types of polyethylene, which you have certainly seen, is their different transparencies. A polyethylene film made of LDPE, and used for the bags that find many uses in the kitchen, is transluscent. This has the big advantage of allowing you to see what's inside the bag without opening it. On the other hand polyethylene garbage cans are opaque and, if no pigment has been added during manufacture, are white. We shall later come across this same phenomenon in discussing glass ceramics (Page 145), where we shall give it a fuller explanation.

You are probably aware that a large single crystal of sugar is colorless and transparent, while a bowl of the same substance looks white and opaque. The reason for the opacity of the granular sugar is that light is scattered at the boundaries between the crystals. In HDPE the light is scattered whenever it passes from amorphous to crystalline regions, and vice versa, and hence the material looks white. In a LDPE film there is less crystallinity and little light scattering, hence the light passes through and the film appears transparent when very thin. Indeed, all amorphous polymers are usually transparent and colorless. Opacity and color are produced by various pigments and fillers, which are added to the raw material during manufacture of the article.

Another polyethylene product takes advantage of the strong covalent bonds that exist along the chain. Fibers in which these chains are aligned along the fiber length have a high strength and a high Young's modulus, for similar reasons as mentioned for carbon fibers (Page 161). In the latter it is covalently bonded sheets of carbon atoms lying along the fiber whereas here it is linear chains. These polyethylene fibers are 'gel spun', which means they are pulled from a material that is sort of half way between a solid and a liquid. (You've probably seen the term used for some toothpastes, and you know what Jell-o® is.) In this gel the polymer chains do not get as tangled as in a solid, and it is therefore easier to pull them into straight alignments.

Finally, it is important to mention that polyethylene is a thermoplastic material. As mentioned in the previous chapter, this means that the material softens when heated and hardens when cooled. The process can be repeated over and over again without problems. This is because heat energy is sufficient to break some of the weak van der Waals bonds between chains, which are then able to more easily slide over each other. This property allows the material to be easily pressed and stretched into the many polyethylene articles we encounter everyday and is somewhat responsible for their low manufacturing cost. This property also makes polyethylene an ideal candidate for recycling (Page 125). Just keep a look out for the recycling symbols on articles marked HDPE and LDPE. We'll discuss these codes in a later chapter.

Propane Gas   Baby Oil   Paraffin Wax   Polyethylene

We started this chapter by discussing some simple hydrocarbons called paraffins. If you look at the diagrams of the molecules you will see that the progression methane to ethane to propane to butane, etc., is accomplished by adding a unit of CH_2 to the previous molecule. You should have now noticed that CH_2 is simply half an ethylene mer, and that a polyethylene molecule without any branches is therefore simply an enormous paraffin. At room temperature, as the molecules get larger, or chains get longer, the material changes from a gas to a runny liquid to a viscous, oily liquid, to a wax, and eventually to the polymer we know as polyethylene. The composition (atomic structure) has not changed, simply the chain length. This is a structural variable which is not available in ceramics and metals and is a unique feature of polymers.

Indeed, this raises another variable which polymer chemists are able to control: the distribution of chain lengths, or what they usually refer to as the molecular weight distribution. This variable is one we have not considered in our discussion, but it is also very important in determining the properties. Indeed there is yet a third commercial polyethylene product known as ultrahigh molecular weight polyethylene (UHMWPE), in which the processing is optimized to give really long molecular chains. In this material molecular weights greater than a million are common. This corresponds to over 70,000 carbon atoms, or a chain length of around 0.01 mm. The material is commonly used to line the socket of an artificial hip joint, because of its relative inertness in the human body, its low friction and excellent wear characteristics.

Conclusion

Although the details of the processing are complex, you have seen enough to appreciate that, starting with the same atoms (carbon and hydrogen) in the same molecule (ethylene) we are able to produce a wide variety of materials, just by changing the processing (temperature, pressure, catalyst). What started as a rather accidental discovery back in the 1930's has led to a host of different polyethylenes, which we would now probably find difficult to live without. Such has been their effect on our daily lives.

We have now come to the end of a journey that started with a molecule with one carbon atom (methane) and ended with a molecular chain containing tens of thousands. All are related hydrocarbons. Perhaps the next time you use baby oil you will think of it as low molecular weight polyethylene!

16. CASE STUDY: FROM RUBBER TO HIPS TO ABS

No, ABS has nothing to do with having "ripped" abdominal muscles or the antilock brake system on your car, and HIPS has nothing to do with hip joint replacements, but you will probably have these materials on your car and around your house. These are names given to a family of plastics, based on the three basic chemicals that go into them. **A**crylonitrile is the basis of polyacrylonitrile (PA), the acrylic fibers (Dacron®, Orlon®, etc.) you may have in your sweater or blanket. Poly**b**utadiene (PB) is an elastic polymer (**elastomer**) used as a synthetic rubber. And **S**tyrene is the basis of polystyrene (PS), which we have already discussed, used for plastic drinking cups and quite brittle. ABS is simply a complex polymer based on these three constituents. HIPS stands for high impact polystyrene, a somewhat simpler polymer using only PS and PB but with some of the same properties as ABS. But enough of that for now, we need to go back in history.

History

Natural fibers such as wool and cotton are polymers, often quite complex compared to the ones we make in today's chemical industry or the laboratory. Compared to wool, the use of rubber, a naturally occurring polymer, known as an elastomer, is relatively new. It occurs naturally and is collected as the sap, known as latex, from a rubber tree. Over 400 years ago Columbus and other explorers found South American Indians had formed it into a ball, which was used much as a rubber ball is used today for various games. The first practical use was probably when it was found that it could be used to 'rub out' pencil marks, and from this we get the name, 'rubber'. In the early 1800's it was used for waterproof clothing and boots (Wellington boots) but had many disadvantages. Besides its offensive odor, it would freeze and become brittle in winter, and in a hot summer it would flow like a viscous liquid. The wearer literally found his boots around his ankles!

In the 1840's the technique of stopping the flow of rubber by **vulcanization** (cross-linking with sulfur) was discovered, and Thomas Hancock (UK) and Charles Goodyear (USA) were awarded patents for the invention. By 1860 the rubber industry had already reached an annual $5 million in sales. We have already discussed the process of vulcanization in some detail (Page 105) so there is no need to go into it again now.

To put the matter into perspective we need to go back to the periodic table on page 7. You will see there that every element has an atomic weight, which is the weight in grams of 6.02×10^{23} atoms. Carbon has an atomic weight of 12, oxygen 16, hydrogen 1, etc. A benzene molecule (C_6H_6) has a **molecular weight** of $(6 \times 12) + (6 \times 1) = 78$. A polymer chain is one large molecule and therefore has a large molecular weight. In any piece of polymer there are millions of chains of different lengths, and hence different molecular weights. Indeed, one way of changing the properties of a polymer is to change the average length of the polymer chains, or in other words, the average molecular weight. Many polymers have average molecular weights of tens of thousands: for natural rubber it is greater than a million. The atomic structure of the rubber chain is shown below. You can see that the repeat unit (mer) consists of five carbon atoms, four of which are in the chain, and eight hydrogen atoms, giving a weight of 68 for this unit. This means that a chain with a molecular weight of one million (10^6) will contain about 15,000 of these units, meaning a chain of 60,000 carbon atoms. On an atomic scale these chains are very, very long.

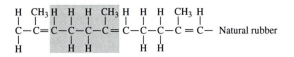

The Properties of Rubber

The long-chain natural rubber molecules are not cross-linked but are considerably entangled, like loose knots in a ball of yarn with which a kitten has been playing. In this state the chains can slowly move over each other and, as long as there is enough time, the rubber can flow. That's why the rubber boots ended up around the wearer's ankles.

You may at some time have played with 'Silly Putty' and found the same phenomenon. If you leave a ball of it on the table, it slowly creeps into a flat pancake. If you drop the ball on the floor it bounces. If it's very cold you can pull it quickly and it breaks in an almost brittle manner. If it's warm and you pull it slowly, it will pull out to very long lengths. The reason for these differences is mainly one of time, and also of temperature. Given enough time, the chain tangles will unravel as the chains flow over each other, and the material 'flows'. If deformation is sudden the chains do not have time to disentangle and the material is resilient. Just think how important this property of rubber is when you next drive over a pot-hole!

Rubber is elastic because of the very long chain molecules it contains. We've already seen how some chains, including rubber, can wiggle about all over the place. Because of a basic scientific principle known as **entropy** (which essentially means 'disorder') the chain does not want to be straight. It prefers the greater disorder of a somewhat tangled state. If we pull a piece of rubber so that the chains straighten, they will automatically return to their original convoluted state when the force is removed. Sometimes the rubber chain is known as an **entropic spring** because of this effect.

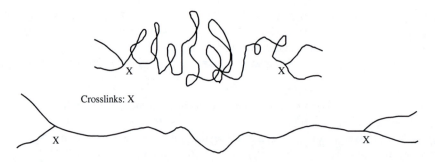

Diagram of how a rubber chain stretches as an entropic spring between crosslinks.

A similar thing happens as temperature is increased—straightened chains (ordered) tend to want to return to the more tangled state (disordered). In fact, this is true of all materials—the tendency to disorder (increase entropy) as temperature increases. You can demonstrate this by melting ice (highly ordered) to form liquid water (less ordered) and eventually boiling it to make steam (highly disordered). The trend is for increased disorder (entropy) with increasing temperature.

What is unique about entropic springs like rubber is their tendency to decrease in length with increasing temperature. Most materials do just the opposite; they increase in length with increasing temperature, a property referred to as thermal expansion. Fortunately for us, entropic springs get shorter as they heat up. This property is used to advantage in the rubber v-belts (named for their "v" cross-sections) used in automobile engines; they get shorter, and therefore tighter, as the engine heats up, which is a decidedly good thing. Otherwise, these belts would lengthen and stop working just when our engines got up to speed!

Vulcanization must be just enough to stop the chains from flowing past each other, as they do in the natural state, but not too much so that they are locked up and the spring is gone. If we lock the chains together completely, we form the hard brittle solid called ebonite.

The synthetic rubbers, including polybutadiene, which has the following very simple formula, have a similar resiliency to natural rubber.

$$
\begin{array}{c}
\text{H H H H H H H H H H H} \\
\text{| | | | | | | | | | |} \\
-\text{C}-\text{C}=\text{C}-\text{C}-\text{C}-\text{C}=\text{C}-\text{C}-\text{C}-\text{C}=\text{C}- \quad \text{Polybutadiene} \\
\text{| | | | |} \\
\text{H H H H H}
\end{array}
$$

Notice that there are no bulky side groups on the chain. The atomic structure is what you get when you replace the CH_3 group on the natural rubber chain with a hydrogen atom.

Polystyrene

We have already seen in the previous chapter how the benzene rings on this polymer chain produce enough steric hindrance to make the chains, and hence the material, very inflexible at room temperature. Not only is it rigid, but it is also very brittle.

With metals and ceramics, we discussed atoms getting enough energy so that they can move around. In polymers heating often results in the motion of whole chains. The thermal energy overcomes the weak van der Waals bonds between chains so they can slide over each other more easily. In addition it is enough to get the bonds rotating, making the chains more flexible. Because of this, polystyrene becomes soft above 100°C. The temperature at which this change from a brittle solid to a ductile one is called the **glass transition temperature**. Below this temperature large chain motion is frozen and the material is brittle and breaks like a glass. Above this temperature the polymer chains are very flexible and are moving around making the material ductile. All thermoplastic and elastomeric polymers have a glass transition temperature and hence exhibit this behavior. Fortunately for us the glass transition temperature for rubber is rather low. You wouldn't want your tires to be brittle in winter, especially when the pot-holes develop.

Taking Advantage of Both Materials—High Impact Polystyrene

Polystyrene and rubber are, as we have seen, quite different materials. The former is tough and hard, but brittle. The latter is resilient but not really strong. Is there any way of taking advantage of both properties so that the polystyrene will withstand impacts? The answer is 'yes' and is found in high impact polystyrene or HIPS.

What if we were to make a mixture of the two polymers, such as by placing small particles of the butadiene rubber within the polystyrene? We can do this using various mixing techniques to produce what we call a **blend**. Unfortunately this produces very little improvement, and the reason is easy to see from the diagram on this page. The crack is prevented from going straight through the polystyrene and has to negotiate a path around the butadiene particles. It stays between the polystyrene chains and, because it goes around the rubber particles, it takes a longer path. The longer path means that more bonds have to be broken and more energy is needed to break the material. Unfortunately the difference is not great and there is little improvement.

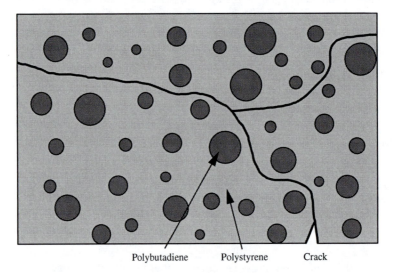

Polybutadiene   Polystyrene   Crack

A crack passing through a polystyrene-polybutadiene blend.

Polymer chemists have developed an answer to this problem by designing two types of **copolymers**: block copolymers and graft copolymers.

A copolymer (co—meaning together) is a combination of two or more different monomers *in one chain*. We have so far talked of polymers with chains made by joining thousands of the same repeat unit (or **mer**), but there is nothing to stop a clever polymer chemist from making a chain with different mers at different places in the chain. Just imagine taking two or three different gold and silver chains, cutting them into different lengths and then joining them randomly to form a new chain. That is what we do with polymers to form a copolymer. In the situation just described we would have effectively produced a **block copolymer**, which has just one chain with segments or blocks of different polymers along its length.

mer A   mer B

Diagram of a block polymer. The chain consists of A mers and B mers.

A graft copolymer takes advantage of the fact that we can, for example, remove a small hydrogen atom attachment from the chain and replace it with another carbon atom, which starts a new chain. In other words we have branching, or we have grafted a new, and in this case a different, chain onto the original one. In the case of HIPS we have a chain structure something like that shown below, a main polystyrene chain with polybutadiene branches.

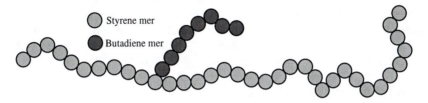

Diagram of a styrene-butadiene graft copolymer. The main polystyrene chain has butadiene branches.

In HIPS we still have polybutadiene (PB) rubber regions in a polystyrene (PS) matrix, but now we have graft copolymer bonding between the two regions. The graft copolymer acts to join the two components in a much stronger manner because the grafted rubber chain prefers to be in the rubber while the polystyrene chain wants to be in the polystyrene matrix. We can think of the main PS chains of these graft copolymers lying in the matrix, wrapping themselves around the PB particles, with the PB branches sticking like tentacles into these particles. We have essentially joined the two different phases (PB and PS) together with what you can think of as rubbery linkages.

Any crack which now tries to pass around these PB particles, as illustrated on the previous page, has to negotiate the network of rubbery chains connecting the matrix to the polybutadiene. The result is an amazing increase in the toughness of the material. Any crack is sort of trapped around the polybutadiene particles and spreads in all directions producing crazing (a fine network of local cracks) of the polystyrene in this area. In fact a strong blow to the material can produce an almost foam-like structure around the PB particles. In so doing there must be a tremendous increase in the number of broken bonds, which absorbs the impact energy and hence the main crack does not propagate throughout, but gets held up. The energy is used instead to produce these crazes.

With HIPS copolymer we have made a material with the rigidity and surface gloss of a glassy polystyrene, but with some of the resiliency of rubber, a material we call a **high impact polymer**. You will probably find it in the dashboard of your car, in the lining of your refrigerator, in computer and telephone housings, etc. In fact any place where we need a really tough material.

ABS Plastics

Those clever polymer scientists have not stopped with just combining polystyrene and polybutadiene. They have produced a whole family of high impact polymers based on polystyrene/polybutadiene, but with an additional ingredient, polyacrylonitrile. These materials use the same principles discussed above, but the additional ingredient allows a wide range of different materials to be produced.

There may be acrylonitrile mers included in either or both of the rubber and polystyrene chains. Things get very complex and there is no need for us to be concerned with the details. We can simply note that adding acrylonitrile to the rubber chain makes it stiffer, and adding it to the polystyrene chain will change the glass transition temperature. Hence we can design an ABS material with desired properties. Keep your eyes open for mention of ABS or acrylonitrile/butadiene/styrene polymers.

Conclusion

This study has introduced you to some of the many ways we can manipulate polymer chains. If you imagine buying a variety of metal chains, different metals, different link sizes, different patterns, you could join them together in a wide variety of ways. The same is true of polymers, which is why there seems to be a never ending discovery of new ones. By suitable processing, which is far too complex to explain here, the polymer chemist can make a most amazing array of materials, most of which will probably never be commercialized. Those that are commercialized, however, will certainly have significant impact on our future way of living.

17. POLYMER RECYCLING

How Well (Poorly?) We are Doing

According to the American Plastics Council, in the early 2000s the USA was recycling only 1 out of 5 polymer products overall. The fraction recycled was significantly higher for pop bottle containers (made from PET, see below), approximately 35%. High density polyethylene or HDPE (unpigmented) was being recycled at approximately 28%, but only 19% for pigmented HDPE. But the numbers for other polymers were dismally small in comparison—approximately 4% for polypropylene, 1% for polystyrene, and a half percent or less for polyvinyl chloride (PVC) and low density polyethylene (LDPE). These numbers are gradually improving, but polymer recycling is hardly a success story.

Challenges to Polymer Recycling

There are many reasons why polymers are difficult to recycle. The first has to do with *mer-incompatibility*. Each type of polymer has its own unique polymer backbone, which requires different processing conditions (e.g., the softening or glass transition temperatures will be different) and imparts different properties. It makes sense that one cannot expect to recycle polyethylene (PE) and polypropylene and combine them readily into a useful product.

A second reason why polymers are difficult to recycle has to do with *polymer-incompatibility*. Even when made from the identical mer, polymers can have different average chain lengths (molecular weights) and properties. They can also differ in the lengths of side-chains, as in the case of LDPE vs. HDPE. As described previously, this can lead to dramatic changes in physical properties. And, as we shall see, engineers in the U.S. give different recycling code numbers to LDPE (4) vs. HDPE (2).

You are probably familiar with recycling codes on polymer products in the U.S., especially containers (beverage, shampoo, food products, etc.). Look at the bottom of such products the next time you take a shower or raid the refrigerator. You should see the triangular recycling symbol with a number inside. Except for number 1, PET, which stands for polyethylene terephthalate, whose mer is:

The mer of polyethylene terephthalate (PET).

The other mers/polymers should be quite familiar to you. You encountered most of them when we introduced the "goal post" notation of the various mers on page 108. The recycling codes are as follows:

Polymer Recycling Codes

- 1 = polyethylene terephthalate (PET)

- 2 = high density polyethylene (HDPE)

- 3 = polyvinylchloride (PVC)

- 4 = low density polyethylene (LDPE)

- 5 = polypropylene (PP)

- 6 = polystyrene (PS)

- 7 = other

A third problem has to do with *processability*. Recycled thermoplastics can be softened and melted by heating, after which they can be reprocessed, much as they were in the first place. But thermosetting resins do not soften/melt upon heating, so thermal reprocessing is not possible. And elastomers, such as rubber, have an even more serious problem. Do you remember the sulfur used to cross-link their chains? That sulfur is released upon heating, which you have probably experienced in that noxious "burned rubber" odor. As a result, elastomers are a challenge to recycle.

Alternatives to Recycling

We mentioned previously that polymers are manufactured from petroleum. As such, they contain quite a bit of energy. For example, most polymers have 50–100% of the energy of the equivalent weight of petroleum. This means that they can be recycled and burned as fuels in thermal power plants. Japan, a resource-poor nation, has been at the forefront of polymer incineration/energy production in their high-tech power stations. There is a problem, however. Polyvinyl chloride must be excluded at all cost, since it produces toxic dioxins when incinerated.

So How Can We Increase Recycling?

The bottom line in polymer recycling has to do with financial incentives/disincentives. Right now it is far less expensive to landfill with waste polymers and make new ones than it is to recycle them. Two 'wild cards' can change the situation, however. The first is the price of petroleum. Should this rise dramatically, it will become economically more feasible to recycle a larger fraction of our polymer waste stream than to make new polymers. The other has to do with the cost of landfilling. Should this rise dramatically, it will also become economically more feasible to recycle than to bury our waste polymers. Of course, governments (federal, state, local) can also get involved by providing incentives to recycle (e.g., required deposits/refunds for returned containers) and disincentives to throw polymers in the trash (e.g., fees/taxes on solid waste). With landfill sites increasing in scarcity (and cost), it is only a matter of time until we all become more adept at polymer recycling.

At the same time, a great deal of research is currently aimed at biodegradable polymers, so they degrade/decompose in days or weeks in our landfills rather then in years, decades, or centuries. (What will our age be known as a thousand years from now, when archaeologists study our landfills and garbage dumps?) But the problems for biodegradable polymers are immense. How long do we want things to survive? If the plastic ring arrangement around your six-pack of soda collapses when you pick it up because it has been sitting in the sun for a couple of weeks, you would not be very happy. This is but one example of the problems current research is trying to solve.

QUESTIONS: Chapters 14–17

1. We call a mixture of different polymers a _____.
   (a) homopolymer   (b) copolymer   (c) branch polymer   (d) block polymer   (e) blend

2. Which of the following is not true about the great majority of polymers?
   (a) electrical insulators   (b) thermal insulators   (c) easily bent into shape
   (d) composed of chains of carbon atoms   (e) all of these are true.

3. What important plastic material uses graft copolymers?
   (a) Lexan   (b) Plexiglas   (c) polycarbonate   (d) ABS   (e) polystyrene

4. Crystalline polymers are stronger and denser than amorphous ones because _____.
   (a) there is greater van der Waals bonding between their chains   (b) their chains are stacked closer together
   (c) their chains tend to be longer   (d) all of these   (e) none of these

5. High density polyethylene (HDPE) is less flexible than low density polyethylene (LDPE) because it is
   (a) less crystalline   (b) more crystalline   (c) crosslinked   (d) less defective
   (e) none of the above

6. Vulcanization uses _____ to make rubber stronger. The element used is _____.
   (a) chain stiffening, Li   (b) chain crosslinking, Nb   (c) chain crystallization, Li
   (d) graft copolymerization, S   (e) none of these is correct

7. Polymers in the glassy state are
   (a) crystalline   (b) ductile   (c) brittle   (d) linear   (e) none of these is correct

8. A polymer made of two mers A and B with the chain below is called a _____.
   A-A-A-B-B-A-A-B-A-A-A-B-B-B-A-A-B-A-A-A-A-A
   (a) chain copolymer   (b) block copolymer   (c) graft copolymer   (d) alternating copolymer

9. Polystyrene is a polymer which has a benzene ring attached to the carbon chain in place of every fourth H atom in polyethylene. The stiffer of these two polymers is _____. The stiffening is caused by _____.
   (a) polystyrene, crosslinking   (b) polyethylene, work hardening   (c) polystyrene, chain stiffening
   (d) polyethylene, chain refining   (e) polystyrene, crystallization

10. The two types of bonds in polymers are
    (a) covalent, secondary   (b) ionic, secondary   (c) metallic, secondary   (d) covalent, ionic
    (e) ionic, metallic

11-12. A rubber chain is known as a/an __11__ because it automatically returns to a/an __12__ state when the force is removed after being stretched.
    11. (a) crosslinked spring   (b) graft copolymer   (c) branched copolymer
        (d) copolymer spring   (e) entropic spring
    12. (a) convoluted   (b) amorphous   (c) crosslinked   (d) crystalline   (e) aligned

13–26. Polymers are based on chains of carbon atoms held together by ___13___ bonds. This gives the chains high strength, but the weakness in polymers which gives them flexibility is ___14___. Below a certain temperature, called the ___15___ temperature, polymers become brittle. For polystyrene, often encountered as styrofoam, it is ___16___. The simplest and most common polymer is polyethylene, in which each carbon atom in the chain is attached to two hydrogen atoms. In polystyrene one of every four hydrogen atoms is replaced with a ___17___. This makes the chain stiffer because of ___18___. Some important materials are made using a mixture of polymers called a(n) ___19___. HIPS is a more complex polymer which includes chains called a ___20___ which join ___21___ inclusions to a polystyrene matrix. In ___21___ car tires the material is stiffened by ___22___ the chains using ___23___ atoms and also by adding ___24___. Some ___22___ also occurs when ___21___ is exposed to air and ___25___ for long times because ___26___ atoms can do the same thing as does ___23___. In addition the ___24___ helps by keeping the ___25___ out.

13. (a) hydrogen   (b) ionic   (c) covalent   (d) metallic   (e) both b & c
14. (a) dislocations   (b) crosslinks   (c) bonds missing electrons   (d) secondary bonds
    (e) surface defects
15. (a) critical   (b) recrystallization   (c) glass transition   (d) solidification   (e) annealing
16. (a) well above 100°C   (b) around room temperature   (c) below 0°C   (d) over 1000°C
    (e) about 100°C
17. (a) fluorine atom   (b) chlorine atom   (c) benzene ring   (d) sulfur atom   (e) none of these
18. (a) steric hindrance   (b) crosslinking   (c) grain refining   (d) work hardening
    (e) crystallization
19. (a) alloy   (b) copolymer   (c) bipolymer   (d) amalgam   (e) blend
20. (a) blend   (b) block copolymer   (c) bipolymer   (d) graft copolymer
    (e) bridging polymer
21. (a) rubber   (b) acrylic   (c) carbide   (d) interstitial   (e) carbon
22. (a) crystallizing   (b) hardening   (c) crosslinking   (d) lengthening   (e) reducing
23. (a) carbon   (b) sulfur   (c) oxygen   (d) lithium   (e) phosphorus
24. (a) dislocations   (b) precipitates   (c) impurities of any sort   (d) carbon black
    (e) nothing extra is added
25. (a) acids   (b) sunlight   (c) pollution   (d) heavy use   (e) oil
26. (a) carbon   (b) sulfur   (c) oxygen   (d) nitrogen   (e) hydrogen

27. One of the reasons polymers are flexible is that _____.
    (a) they have strong C-C bonds   (b) H atoms are attached to C atoms   (c) they have a 3D structure
    (d) they are crosslinked   (e) covalent bonds can rotate

28–34. ABS plastics are based on polybutadiene [PB]/polystyrene [PS] ___28___ copolymers. The polyacrylonitrile [PA] is simply added to obtain a range of materials with slightly different properties. PS is a stiff, strong polymer because of ___29___ whereas PB is ___30___. The material consists of PS which contains some PB. The PB/PS copolymer serves the purpose of ___31___. The resultant material is known as a high ___32___ polymer. When used alone, PS is very ___33___ at room temperature because ___34___.

28. (a) graft   (b) alternating   (c) block   (d) reciprocating   (e) condensed
29. (a) high crystallinity   (b) bulky side groups   (c) crosslinking   (d) larger atoms
    (e) stronger bonds between C atoms
30. (a) lighter   (b) elastic   (c) crystalline   (d) biodegradable   (e) glassy
31. (a) increasing flexibility   (b) joining the PB and PS together   (c) pinning dislocations
    (d) thermal conduction   (e) making longer chains
32. (a) intensity   (b) impact   (c) density   (d) conductivity   (e) rigidity
33. (a) elastic   (b) conductive   (c) transparent   (d) brittle   (e) flaky
34. (a) it has flexible chains   (b) it has free electrons
    (c) light energies are greater than the band gap energy
    (d) it is below the glass transition temperature   (e) it contains weak bonds

35–44. The simplest and most common polymer has only __35__ atoms on a carbon chain, __36__ __35__ atoms to each carbon atom, and is called __37__. A strong __37__ fiber can be made by aligning these chains so that they are __38__ each other. This can be accomplished by a process called __39__. We can also make strong and more rigid __37__ by __40__ the polymer. This increases the __41__ between chains. Sometimes we add side branches of the same polymer chain to the main chain. If these side branches are __42__ and many, their addition has the same effect as placing large side groups on the chain. This is called __43__. This type of __37__, referred to as __44__, is used for garbage bags where flexibility is needed.

35. (a) hydrogen   (b) oxygen   (c) fluorine   (d) nitrogen   (e) both a and b
36. (a) one   (b) two   (c) a varying number of both   (d) four
37. (a) polypropylene   (b) PVC   (c) polystyrene   (d) polyethylene   (e) polycarbonate
38. (a) parallel to   (b) perpendicular to   (c) across   (d) outside   (e) at an angle to
39. (a) pulling   (b) extrusion   (c) gel spinning   (d) weaving   (e) stretching
40. (a) annealing   (b) crystallizing   (c) extruding
    (d) increasing the number of hydrogen atoms on each carbon atom of   (e) both a and d
41. (a) attraction   (b) repulsion   (c) distance   (d) both b and c   (e) both a and c
42. (a) as long as the original chain   (b) long   (c) short   (d) straight
    (e) both b and d
43. (a) steric hindrance   (b) interference   (c) immobilization   (d) deactivation
    (e) crosslinking
44. (a) ABS   (b) LDPE   (c) HDPE   (d) SBS   (e) PVDC

45. Overall, what fraction of polymers are recycled in the U.S.?
    (a) 20%   (b) 35%   (c) 50%   (d) 70%   (e) 90%

46. What are the recycling codes for low-density polyethylene and PET?
    (a) 1,4   (b) 4,2   (c) 7,5   (d) 4,1   (e) 3,6

47. Which of the following is not a reason why it is difficult to recycle polymers?
    (a) poor processability   (b) chain entanglement   (c) mer-incompatibility
    (d) polymer-incompatibility   (e) none of the above

18. HOW HEAT AFFECTS MATERIALS

In the last few chapters we have examined some of the basic properties of metals and polymers, together with some specific examples of recent developments in these areas. Now we shall turn our attention to ceramics, which are typically oxides, carbides, nitrides and borides. To most people ceramics mean the traditional clay-based materials such as found in plates, cups and saucers, cooking ware, etc. We have also mentioned glass as being a ceramic based on silicon oxide. We usually consider such items as being fragile. Stores remind us of this even before we buy, with their "If you break it, you've bought it" signs. Almost everybody has broken a plate or glass at some time and is well aware that they rarely bounce. Before we approach ways in which we can make strong ceramics there is another subject we need to introduce: the effect of heat on materials. At this stage we shall not confine our attention to ceramics.

There are many possible ways in which materials react to heat. We know that if heated enough they glow and become red and then white hot. If they are magnetic they lose that property. Most polymers cannot be heated very much before they begin to decompose or combust. We have also seen that the atoms move around more and that there are more vacancies created, etc. However, for our purposes, there are only two properties to consider. These are known by the scientific terms, thermal conduction and thermal expansion.

Thermal Conduction

Just as materials show different efficiencies at conducting electricity, they also have different heat conducting properties. Our everyday experience tells us that the best conductors are metals. The reason for this is quite simple. The heat is carried through the metal by the movement of electrons. One electron can carry very little heat but there are so many free electrons in a metal (they are the 'glue' which holds the atoms together) and they travel so quickly that they are very efficient heat carriers. Effectively what happens is that each electron picks up some thermal energy from the heat source, runs down to the cold region, where it leaves the heat, and then runs back for more. Obviously, the electrons cannot just stay in the cold region or else they would all end up there and it would acquire a large negative charge, which would push back any other electrons that tried to bring more heat (remember that like charges repel each other). There is therefore a balanced flow with as many coming as going, something we call **dynamic equilibrium** in scientific jargon. A metal seat feels cold because the electrons in the metal quickly take on the heat from your body, carry it away and come back for more! Obviously, this does not happen with wood.

Because heat in metals is transported by electrons, we would expect anything which interferes with the electron motion to reduce the heat conduction. Perhaps the most familiar effect is the result of adding impurities to a metal. A cast iron pot, rather old-fashioned nowadays, is a good conductor of heat and is still used for cooking by some people. The modern stainless steel pans are much nicer to look at but do not conduct the heat nearly as well. This is why they usually have a bottom cladding of copper or aluminum to distribute the heat. If you use a cheap, thin stainless pan with no bottom cladding for cooking, the ring marks from the burner are clearly visible inside the bottom afterwards. The stainless steel does not distribute the heat sideways. The reason for this is that the carbon, nickel and chromium impurities which are added to iron to make stainless steel, get in the way of the free flowing electrons and hence reduce the heat flow. When discussing point defects (Pages 60–63), we saw that they cause distortions to the regular arrangements of atoms in the crystal, and these interrupt the clear straight paths the electrons would otherwise have through the material.

Other materials also conduct heat, although not nearly as well. This is because they have no free electrons. The heat causes the atoms to vibrate, as we have already seen. In ceramics, which have strong ionic and covalent bonds, the movement of one atom causes the adjacent atoms to move as well. Just think of beads threaded on a string. When we make one move up and down (oscillate) the adjacent ones also move and a wave is set up in the string. Such a wave motion of atoms in a crystal is called a **phonon**. You may have a coiled cord on your telephone and sometimes, when talking with the cord extended, you pluck the cord with your finger. A wave travels down the cord and sometimes is reflected back from the other end. You may have seen the same effect when playing with a Slinky. This is very much like the way a phonon travels through a material. The term phonon arises because the wave travels at the speed of sound (nothing to do with the telephone, really!). The heat energy transported by such waves, or phonons, travels much more slowly through the material than do electrons, hence the conduction is not as efficient.

In materials such as polymers, where atoms are linked by very weak bonds, the movement of one atom may produce motion of adjacent atoms in the same chain, but produces little or no motion of atoms in adjacent chains. Heat conduction is therefore even more difficult than in ceramics and only occurs moderately efficiently when an atom is forced to vibrate so much by the heat that it bumps into an adjacent atom and thus transfers some of its heat energy to that atom. The process obviously proceeds very slowly and inefficiently.

To summarize, metallic bonds produce the best heat conductors because of rapid electron motion. Covalent and ionic bonds produce worse conduction by atom waves (phonons) being set up in the material. Weak secondary bonds (van der Waals and hydrogen) produce the worst thermal conductors because they cannot conduct heat until the atoms knock into each other. The three following diagrams illustrate these methods of heat transfer.

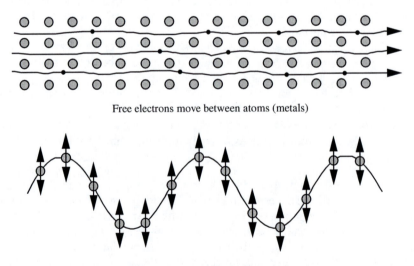

Free electrons move between atoms (metals)

Atom waves or phonons (ceramics)

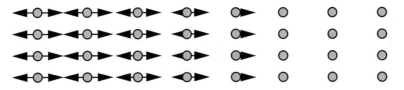

Atom vibrations and knock-on (polymers)

Illustrations of the three ways heat can be carried through a solid material.

It should be stressed that all three mechanisms (free electron motion, atom waves/phonons, and atom vibrations) are possible in metals; it is just that the electronic mechanism dominates. Similarly, both phonons and atom/ion vibrations are possible in ceramics. In unusual cases, phonons can be quite effective conductors of heat. For example, diamond has an anomalously large thermal conductivity rivaling that of copper. It does this by means of phonons, without the help of electrons.

The absolute worst conductor of heat (best insulator) is a vacuum, or failing that, still air. We use the former in vacuum flasks to keep things hot or cold and the second when we insulate houses or design warm winter clothing. Both fiberglass house insulation and down-filled jackets use trapped air to insulate against heat loss.

A modern application of this principle is the thermal protection system of the Space Shuttle. Of course one requirement of such a material is that it does not melt at the temperatures we need to insulate against. If this were to happen, the air pockets would be lost and the insulation would fail. The material used for the space shuttle tiles is composed of a felt-like mat of fibers made of silicon dioxide (quartz). The silica is not of itself a good conductor, but the important fact is that it maintains its rigidity at high temperatures and continues to hold the insulating, trapped, still atmosphere, which is very thin at the altitudes encountered in space. Obviously any polymer material would melt or decompose under those conditions.

Photograph of a space shuttle tile.

Thermal Expansion

The expansion of materials when they are heated is something we are all probably familiar with. We put expansion joints in railroad lines, bridges, sidewalks, etc., to allow them to expand without buckling in hot weather. You have probably noticed the gaps which are left to allow for this.

The fact that materials expand tells us that when they are heated not only do the atoms vibrate, but they also move further apart. The amount they move depends to a large extent on the strength of the bonds. We might naturally expect weak bonds to allow atoms to move further apart for a given heat input than do strong bonds, and to a good approximation this is the case.

Polymers usually expand more than metals, which expand more than ceramics. A graphite crystal expands a lot perpendicular to the planes (van der Waals bonds) but very little parallel to the planes (covalent bonds).

A simple thermostat can be made using two metals with different thermal expansions, joined in what we call a bimetallic strip. When heated, the one with the larger expansion forces the other to bend over as shown. Remember that the inside of a curve is always shorter than the outer, so the strip bends over in the direction of the metal with the smaller expansion. If this strip is part of an electrical circuit and the room temperature is high enough, the strip bends away from an electrical contact, breaking the circuit and turning the heat off. As the room cools, the strip straightens up and makes contact, turning the heat on again.

In today's world we can make thermostats by taking advantage of other properties of materials, but the bimetallic strip remains a cheap means of temperature regulation for household use.

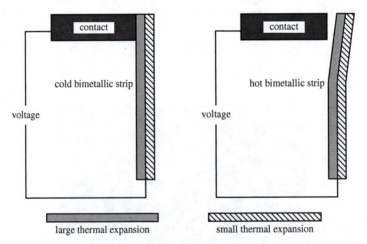

A simple thermostat using thermal expansion of a bimetallic strip.

A similar device is used in garage door openers. When you activate the opener, not only does electricity flow to the motor, but also through a small heating coil around a bimetallic strip. This causes it to bend and make a contact which connects the electric power to the light bulb, thus turning it on. When the door has been raised, the power is disconnected and the bimetallic strip begins to cool. After a couple of minutes it has cooled sufficiently to return to its original position, breaking the contact and the light goes out.

The two thermal phenomena we have discussed are very important as we talk about ceramics. These are strongly bonded solids and as a consequence they tend to have low thermal expansions and very poor thermal conductivity. The poor thermal conductivity leads to what engineers refer to as poor thermal shock resistance. You may have had an experience of a hot ceramic object cracking when placed in contact with a cold surface or, better yet, a cold liquid (e.g., water). Here's what happens. Imagine a hot ceramic object being suddenly immersed in cold water. Just like the bimetallic strip, the outer layers of the ceramic want to contract, but are prevented from doing so by the still hot interior. As we will show in the next two chapters, this places the surfaces in tension, i.e., any cracks on the surface of the ceramic will be forced open. This is not a good situation for a brittle material, and thermal cracking occurs. This also explains why ceramics are more susceptible to thermal shock on rapid cooling (surface cracks placed in tension) rather than rapid heating (surface cracks placed in compression). In contrast, most metals are not susceptible to thermal shock. Their high thermal conductivity prevents the development of thermal stresses by eliminating large thermal differences between the surface and the interior.

Our discussion of thermal stresses is a good introduction to our next topic: the "Achilles heel" of ceramics, namely cracks.

19. CERAMICS: DO THEY HAVE TO BE BRITTLE?

Why are Ceramics Usually Brittle?

We have now seen why metals are usually ductile, how we can make them stronger and stiffer, and why a few metals such as zinc are quite brittle; now we turn our attention to ceramics. If we drop a china mug and a pewter tankard we know that we can expect. The tankard will survive with maybe a dent, but we expect the mug to break into a hundred pieces. Not only will it break, but it will break catastrophically.

The reason for the big difference lies in the types of bonds that are involved. In metals, we have nondirectional, rather fluid, metallic bonds, while in ceramics we either have strong, directed covalent bonds, or ionic bonds between positive and negative charges, which are quite closely packed and hence are quite immobile and have fixed positions.

Because of the existence of directed, rigid, covalent bonds, it is very difficult to move dislocations in these materials. Also, the ions in ionic ceramics make movement of planes very difficult, even using dislocations, because in the process of moving planes of ions over each other, it is usually necessary to move positive ions over positive ions and negative ions over other negative ions. As you know, like charges repel each other, so that there is a great resistance to this movement.

The bonds are quite strong and there is not really an easy way to deform the material. When a ceramic or a glass breaks it usually does so catastrophically. The reason for this is easy to see once we realize what the basic weaknesses are in ceramics or glasses. The answer to the problem is not dislocations, but surface imperfections or flaws in the form of small cracks or scratches. Such surface cracks are the "Achilles heel" of ceramics.

When a person wants to cut a piece of glass, a diamond file is first used to put a surface flaw (scratch) on the material, and the glass can then be easily broken. The break, or fracture, follows the scratch. The glass has not really been 'cut', but has been broken in a controlled manner by taking advantage of the fact that glasses and ceramics break at surface flaws. While you can see the scribe mark a glass cutter puts onto a piece of glass, the surface cracks and scratches in ceramics do not have to be visible to be important, and often aren't.

Take the simple model shown below. The material is carrying a load that is shared by, let's say, a thousand atoms. Each atom takes one thousandth of the load and transfers it to the next atom through the bonds which connect them, shown as vertical dashed lines. So long as the bonds are strong enough the material does not break because when the material breaks, the bonds between the atoms are what give way. The load is transferred through the material until we reach the crack, which is shown as being four atoms deep. Now it becomes necessary for the load to be redistributed so that it can be carried by four fewer atoms, but it is not shared equally by the remaining 996 bonds. The remaining bonds don't just all carry 1000/996 of what they were previously carrying. The ones at the crack tip end up carrying proportionately more than their fair share.

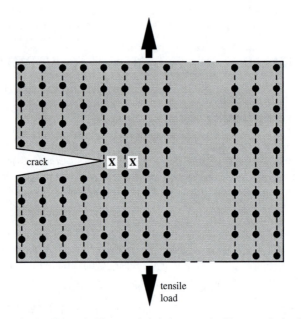

Illustration of what happens at the tip of a crack. The sample is being stretched by a tensile load, but four bonds are broken and cannot carry any load. The two bonds marked X are longer than the others (more strain) because they are carrying more load. They will therefore be the first to break.

In some cases this extra load becomes more than the bonds between the atoms at the crack tip can bear and therefore the bond between them breaks. This places more load on the adjacent atom, which is already somewhat overloaded, and its bond breaks also. The crack grows very rapidly (catastrophically!) and in a very short time the whole material has broken. This is precisely what happens when you drop a ceramic object or hit a ball through a glass window.

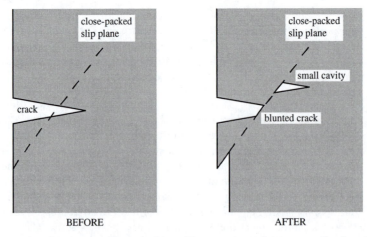

Illustration of how a surface flaw in a metal becomes blunted by movement of atoms on a slip plane. Blunt cracks are not as important as are sharp cracks.

Your experience has shown you that ceramics and glasses break suddenly, what we call **catastrophic failure**, while metals usually stretch before they break. The reason for this sudden failure is what is described above. We say that the surface cracks and scratches are **stress concentrators**; they concentrate the load on the atoms, or rather the bonds, at the crack tip.

Before we move on we should ask why cracks are not so important in metals. We have mentioned several times that for most metals there are many different atom planes that are close packed and can slide over each other via dislocations. Because of this, a surface crack or scratch in a metal is usually very quickly blunted as shown in the previous diagram. Slip of planes in ceramics is very difficult, so cracks grow rather than get blunted.

How then can we strengthen ceramic materials? As with dislocations there are two possibilities: we either eliminate the cracks or stop them from propagating (growing). There are several ways of tackling the problem but we shall mention only a few.

Fibers

One method to eliminate (or greatly reduce) surface cracks in ceramics is to make them into fibers, much as we did with metals (whiskers). This is possible (but costly) for crystalline ceramics, but is much easier with glasses, which can be readily pulled (sometimes called "spinning") from the molten state. It is routinely found that the finer the fiber, the stronger the fiber. In fact, the strengths obtained with the finest fibers approach what theorists predict for pristine, flaw-free glass surfaces. That is, until the surfaces come into contact with just about anything—other surfaces, human contact, even dust particles—which scratch the surface and reduce the strength accordingly. If fibers can be protected by coating them or by imbedding them in a protective matrix (e.g., fiber-reinforced composites), they can retain their superior strengths.

Flame Polishing

Another approach can be employed to remove or at least reduce the cracks on the surface of glasses. Remember that glasses are formed from a molten viscous liquid state. Small cracks form in the surface when the glass cools in the same way that a dried rain puddle leaves a cracked, or crazed, surface. One way of getting rid of them is to remelt the surface layer. We call this **flame polishing**. A flame is passed over the cracked surface and remelts just the few layers of surface atoms. These then solidify with many fewer cracks than they had before.

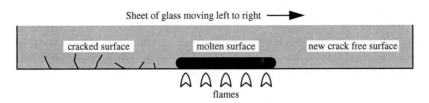

Diagram of the flame polishing process.

Compression

If we can't get rid of cracks, one way to live with them is to put the surface into compression, thereby forcing them shut. This can be done by only using the material in a situation where it sees loads that compress it. The concrete foundations of tall and heavy buildings are fine examples of this. Alternatively one can surround the ceramic material with something that puts the surface (and the cracks) into compression.

Some ceramic bearings are surrounded by a metal band, which is placed over them while the metal is very hot. The band starts out being smaller than the ceramic part but expands on heating so that it can be slipped over the part in the same way that metal rims used to be fitted to pioneer wagon wheels. When the band cools it shrinks and compresses the ceramic, which can then survive knocks much better. The metal band hugs the ceramic very tightly and the compression forces the cracks to close. This is the reason why ceramics are usually stronger when compressed than when pulled: compression closes cracks.

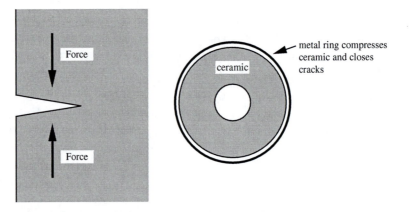

Use of compressive force to close surface cracks in a ceramic.

In glasses we can adopt a rather unusual approach. We use a type of atom gun to fire large atoms (ions) into the surface (see the figure on the next page), a process referred to as **ion-implantation**. These atoms need a lot of space and therefore elbow their way in, pushing surrounding atoms apart. Of course, one of the ways they can get this space is to force any surface cracks and scratches to close. What this does is to effectively make the surface atoms see a compressive force. In this case the compression is exerted within the surface of the material by the large atoms rather than by an external load.

Safety glass in the side windows of automobiles is also manufactured with a compressive surface layer to close cracks. This is created by "tempering" the glass—either chemically or thermally. Chemical tempering involves ion-exchange. The glass is temporarily placed in a chemical bath whereby smaller surface ions are replaced by bigger surface ions, leading to a surface in compression, much as with ion-implantation. Thermal tempering is discussed further in the following chapter.

Here's a life-saving bit of information. You cannot punch or kick your way to safety through safety glass. This presents a potentially deadly situation should you ever find your automobile submerged in water, with the electrical window-lowering controls inactive. But stop and think for a minute about

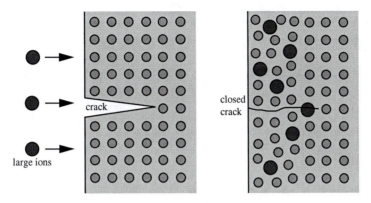

Ion implantation of large ions (left) closes crack (right).

residual stresses and stress concentrators. In the interior of safety glass is a tensile residual stress (to balance the compressive stresses at the surfaces). Once a crack reaches the interior, the window will shatter. In fact, the amount of residual stress is designed to reduce the window to pebble-sized, harmless shards. You may have seen these at the site of an automobile accident. So how to get the crack through to the interior? Use a stress-concentrator. Safety hammers are now sold with pointy ends to concentrate stress. In fact, they also come with built-in sharp pins (to pierce and deflate the deployed airbag) and razor blades (to cut lap and shoulder belts).

Smaller Grain Size

If we have to live with surface cracks, can we somehow limit their size/length in crystalline ceramics? One way to do this is by reducing the grain size. Remember that we also did this in metals, but in that case the boundary stopped the dislocations from moving between grains, whereas here it stops the *crack* from propagating from grain to grain. In other words, the surface crack size will be largely determined by the grain size. The smaller we make the crystals, the smaller the surface cracks and the stronger the ceramic. The grain boundary effectively does for a ceramic what a slip plane does for a metal: they both blunt cracks. A good everyday example of this effect is Corning Ware®, a glass ceramic. We shall consider it in a case study in the following chapter.

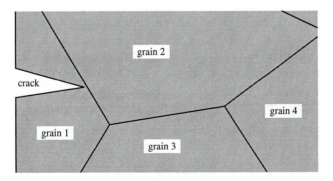

Grain boundary stops crack from propagating.

Nanophase Ceramics

Research has shown that the possibility exists for making ductile ceramics by making the grain size very, very small—smaller than we have ever previously considered. Such ceramics have grain sizes on the order of tens of nanometers. This is 100 to 1000 times smaller than for conventional ceramics. Instead of brittle fracture, **nanophase** ceramics deform by grains sliding over one another, imparting ductile rather than brittle character. The nano-realm is discussed further in the chapter on Nanomaterials.

Conclusion

To summarize: the weaknesses in ceramics and glasses are surface defects, cracks and scratches. To strengthen the material we have several options:

eliminate surface defects: make fibers, or flame polish a glass to remelt the surface to heal cracks, etc.

close surface defects: apply external compressive load; implant large atoms in the surface.

limit surface crack length: make crystals smaller; cracks stopped by boundaries.

To close on a practical note, we can often prolong the useful life of glass objects by stopping them from getting scratched. Reusable beverage bottles are often sprayed with a very thin plastic layer when they come off the production line. This stops the hard glass surfaces from rubbing against each other, which would cause surface scratches and make them more liable to break.

Nowadays we use windshields in our autos made of laminated glass. This is made using two layers of ordinary glass bonded together with a sheet of transparent plastic. This flexible plastic layer holds the glass together so tightly that it will crack but not shatter.

20. CASE STUDY: GLASS-CERAMICS FOR COOKWARE

Background

In our discussion of ceramics and glass we have seen that their major weakness is due to surface cracks or flaws, which concentrate stress. These defects are usually too small to be noticed but are there nonetheless.

You have perhaps broken a drinking glass by pouring boiling water into it. Why does it break? The answer lies in the presence of these surface flaws. The glass starts out being all at the same temperature, but pouring boiling water into it immediately increases the temperature *inside* the glass. Unfortunately ceramics, of which glass is an example, do not conduct heat very well. Thus for the moment the inside of the glass is hot and expanding while the outside surface is still cold. The situation, which exists for this very short time, is exactly that which we discussed in the case of the bimetallic strip. One side has expanded more than the other. In this case it is because of different temperatures rather than different materials, but the effect is the same. One side expands and pulls the other with it. As a result there is a tensile stress on the outside of the glass and the cracks are pulled open. There is now increased stress on the bonds between atoms at the crack tip and eventually the glass breaks. We have given a sort of slow-motion description of the process—it all happens so suddenly. But what we have described can be captured with high speed cameras. And it is, in fact, what happens.

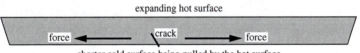

Illustration of how a surface crack is opened by an expanding opposing surface.

Something similar will happen if you take a ceramic pot from the freezer and place it on a hot burner on the stove. Whenever we have a hot expanding surface close to a cold one, the hot surface pulls on the colder surface and tends to open surface cracks so that the material can break.

Corning Ware® is a relatively new material, which can withstand such rapid temperature changes without breaking. It is what is known as a glass-ceramic, a material that has undergone special processing, which turns glass into extremely small crystals. In our discussion of the mechanical strength of ceramics and glass we saw that there are several ways of strengthening the material: flame polishing, compressing the surface, surface ion implantation and making the grains or crystallites smaller. It is this last approach that is used in glass-ceramics. We shall now see how it can be done.

How to Make a Glass with Small Crystals

We know that surface cracks in glasses and ceramics are stress concentrators. The atoms near the crack tip have extra forces on their bonds which can therefore be broken if the force exceeds their strength. The force they were carrying is then transferred to the bonds between the adjacent atoms, etc.

The result is a catastrophic failure. In ceramics we can toughen the material by making the crystallites or grains smaller; the grain boundaries blunt the crack tip and hinder its propagation. But glasses are amorphous, there are no crystallites, no grain boundaries, and the crack cannot be stopped. Glass therefore breaks in the way we are all accustomed to.

What if we could somehow cause small crystallites to form in a glass? There would then be a mechanism for the inhibition of crack propagation. This is what happened accidentally in the discovery of what we now know as glass-ceramics.

It was the overheating of a furnace during the manufacture of another special type of glass in 1957 that led to the discovery of glass-ceramics. This accident produced a scientific breakthrough, which has affected us all. We perhaps know these materials best as Corning Ware®.

The secret of the manufacture of glass-ceramics is getting the crystals to form, or **nucleate**. In normal circumstances there are no crystals formed when glass is cooled, however this can be changed by seeding the glass with tiny crystals of an impurity, which provide surfaces on which the SiO_2 tetrahedra in the glass can crystallize. We may have done something similar in home or high school chemistry experiments. By suspending a crystal of sugar on a thin cotton thread in a concentrated sugar solution we can get the crystal to grow over a period of time, because it acts as a nucleus on which the sugar molecules can arrange themselves. We sometimes call this process **seeding**, in the same sense that we refer to cloud-seeding to try to get raindrops to form in a cloud. The nucleating agent used in glass is titanium oxide. It is added as very, very fine particles. You can appreciate how small they must be when you know that in the glass there can be as many as a trillion (10^{12}) nuclei in a cubic millimeter (a cube with an edge length of 1 mm). This may seem like a lot of nuclei, but it works out to about one nucleus for every hundred million atoms!

The glass (not-yet ceramic!) container or pan is first made as a regular glass object. Because of this it can either be blown or formed in a mold, and then ground and polished to produce, for example, a flat bottom. At this point it appears to be a clear glass-like object. The advantage of this is that the required shape and size can be precisely produced at a low cost. There then follows a special, carefully controlled heat treatment to produce the required **devitrification** (transition from the glassy state: vitreous = glassy). The details of this process are beyond the scope of this discussion. The important thing to understand is that the very small TiO_2 crystals are just what are required to nucleate small crystals of SiO_2.

These small SiO_2 crystals are less than one micrometer (one thousandth of a millimeter) across and are quite free of any porosity. Careful seeding and control of the heat treatment can result in as much as 99% of the glass being converted to small crystals. The remaining glass occupies the spaces between the crystals, cementing them together and producing a solid, non-porous material.

The following photograph shows two halves of a Corning Ware® casserole dish. One half is before devitrification and the other after. You should be able to see two differences after the devitrifying heat treatment: (a) the container is now white and opaque, and (b) is slightly smaller than the original. The reasons for these differences are very interesting:

(a)   A crystal is an ordered arrangement of atoms, and when things are put in order they take up less room. A neatly stacked pile of bricks takes up less space than when just tipped onto the floor from a wheelbarrow, for example. This accounts for the shrinkage during the devitrifying heat treatment - ordered crystals are formed from disordered (amorphous) glass.

(b)   As a result of the numerous small crystals and their associated boundaries, light is no longer able to pass straight through the material, but is scattered at the boundaries so that the material appears white and opaque, the same way that salt and sugar appear white (even though individual crystallites are transparent).

The crystals in glass-ceramics are so small and are so strongly cemented together that no surface flaw or crack can easily pass through the many boundaries that confront it. In addition these materials have a very low thermal expansion so that the hot side of a piece of material does not try to extend the cold side by very much, i.e. it exerts a smaller stress than would be the case if the thermal expansion were large. As a result of this combination of high strength and low thermal expansion, glass-ceramics have what we call a high **thermal shock resistance**. We can take the cookware straight from the oven to a cold countertop without crack or fracture. Remember that these two factors, a small thermal expansion producing less pull, and a high strength, both help to give us the properties of Corning Ware® with which we are familiar.

Photograph of Corning Ware® after (left) and before (right) devitrification. Note that the while the edges at the bottom are aligned, the edges at the top are not. The devitrified half is smaller than the original.

Glass-Ceramics and Light

Another glass ceramic, which you may have seen is called Visions Ware®. This material looks like a glass in that it is transparent, with a reddish tint, although there is a version called 'cranberry' that is much redder. It is also a crystalline material with a very fine microstructure, so why is it not also white and opaque? You may remember that we earlier discussed polyethylene (PE) and said that low density PE was usually clear, but crystalline high density PE was white and opaque (Page 117). We left an explanation until this point because it relates to the nature of light.

Light is what we know as an electromagnetic wave. We shall briefly describe what is meant by 'electromagnetic' later, but for now we shall focus on its wave nature. Most people think of waves as related to water. If you drop a pebble into a pond, a wave radiates from the point where it is dropped.

The following diagram illustrates a simple wave. The distance between the crests or troughs of the wave is called the wavelength, usually denoted λ.

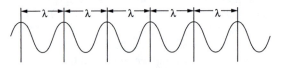

Diagram of a wave, illustrating what is meant by wavelength, λ.

When a light wave strikes a crystal it is scattered. Just think of it as reflection from the surface of the crystal. When the crystals are larger than the light wavelength, the light has no chance of avoiding this scattering, but when the crystals are smaller than the wavelength, there is a chance that the light can simply go around the crystals, as illustrated below.

In Visions Ware® the crystals are even smaller than those in Corning Ware® and the light is able to go around them without being scattered. In other words, the light can pass straight through the material. Another thing about white light, which you probably know is that it consists of a range of colors. This is commonly seen in the colors of the rainbow (red, orange, yellow, green, blue, indigo, violet). Each color has its own characteristic wavelength, with red having the longest and violet the shortest.

The following diagrams illustrate the possibility that a red wave could go around a crystal while a blue one could not. In other words the blue is scattered while the red is not. This is what happens to make the sunset look red. When the sun is setting, the light has to come further to reach us. Over this distance the blue light is scattered, or reflected sideways, by atmospheric dust, while the red light comes directly to our eyes with little interruption. Our eyes therefore see more red light than blue, and the sunset is red. In Visions Ware® the same thing happens. Red light passes through the material with little or no interruption, while blue is scattered. Our Visions Ware® pan therefore has a reddish tinge because more of the red portion of the visible light spectrum reaches our eyes uninterrupted than does the blue, some of which is lost due to scattering. Cranberry Visions® has its much redder color because of intentionally added impurities. We shall discuss how impurities produce color in Chapter 25.

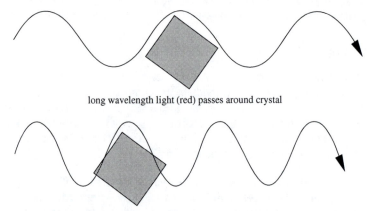

long wavelength light (red) passes around crystal

short wavelength light (blue) is scattered by crystal

Illustration of how red light can pass through a material without being scattered while blue light is scattered. Some red light passes through uninterrupted and the material appears reddish.

Corelle® and Tempered Glass

Another really strong material is the glassy material called Corelle® which is a sort of opalescent glass. In discussing the bimetallic strip and the breaking of a drinking glass when filled with boiling water, we had two layers of material with one pulling on the other. What if we could arrange for this pulling to be compressive rather than tensile? Any surface flaws would then be closed, and the material made stronger.

The way this is accomplished is quite simple, although the processing required to accomplish it required considerable research. We make a three-layer sandwich of two different glasses such that, on cooling, the one in the middle shrinks much more than the one forming the outer layers. In addition to having these quite different thermal expansions, or in this case contractions, the two glasses must adhere very strongly together.

When the three layers are shaped in the viscous molten state they have essentially the same dimensions. When they cool the inner layer contracts more than the outer layers and tries to pull them with it. The result is a compressive force in the outer layers as illustrated in the following diagram. Any surface flaws that develop during the processing are therefore pulled together and closed.

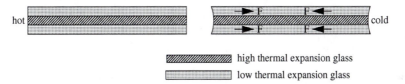

Three layer glass with inner layer contracting more and pulling surface layers into contraction.

Force-balance must be maintained, however, and this requires that the interior glass layer be in tension. Corelle dishes are very strong and tend not to break when dropped. But many of us have had the unfortunate experience of what happens when we knock them just right, or a crack somehow reaches that tensile layer. The dish fractures catastrophically into tiny slivers of glass. This is due to all that "stored elastic strain energy" (the balancing of stresses between surface and interior) being released all at once.

Photograph of the broken surface of Corelle® showing the sandwich structure.

This same principle is used to make tempered glass. The glass used in windshields nowadays is always laminated with a central layer of tough plastic. However, the side windows are made of tempered glass by a process known as **thermal tempering**. We discussed chemical tempering in the last chapter. Thermally tempered glass is all made of the same glass, but a simple trick is used to produce the layering effect we have just discussed.

The sheet of glass is heated so that it is soft all the way through and the top and bottom surfaces are then cooled very quickly with a blast of cold air. These outer surfaces therefore contract and become hard. When they do this, the inside is still quite soft because heat does not travel quickly in these materials, i.e., the inside has not had time to solidify. It therefore flows and adjusts to the smaller dimensions of the outside.

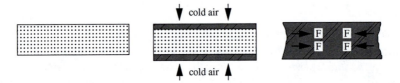

The production of tempered glass produces compressive forces on the surface by the delayed contraction of the inside.

The soft inside glass then cools and solidifies. But it also contracts, and in so doing pulls on the outer layers, which cooled first. As a result, these outer layers are pulled into compression, which as we have already seen, strengthens the material because it closes any cracks or scratches on the surface.

This type of glass is sometimes called **safety glass** and is also often used in household sliding glass doors.

Conclusion

We have seen in this chapter how the careful choice of materials and the ways they are processed can allow us to overcome the limitations imposed by surface flaws on ceramics. These are materials that many of us use regularly. They are not expensive, but are very high-tech, allowing us to enjoy some of the advances made in materials in recent years.

21. CAN CERAMICS BE TOUGH? THE ZIRCONIA STORY

Until now we have largely addressed the question of making ceramics *stronger*, by eliminating/reducing surface cracks (e.g., by making fibers or polishing the surfaces of larger ceramics) or putting their surfaces into compression to close cracks (e.g., by ion implantation/chemical tempering, or making compression-tension-compression sandwich structures, i.e., by thermal tempering and layering as in Corelle®). And we have addressed how to limit surface cracks by very small crystals, as in glass-ceramics. But can we also make ceramics *tough*?

Toughness is not the same as strength. Strength has to do with how large a stress is needed to get a surface crack growing in a ceramic. Once it begins to grow, it usually propagates through the ceramic, leading to catastrophic failure. Toughness has to do with how much energy it takes to move the crack, once formed. Your own experience tells you that metals and plastics are inherently tough. For instance, cut a "crack" in a sandwich bag and use tension to "propagate" the crack. It takes a lot of energy, owing to the plastic deformation taking place at the crack tip. Metals are similarly tough to fracture, which you know from trying to bend and break a paper clip in half.

Actually, we have already seen one instance of ceramic toughening. In fine-grained ceramics, including glass-ceramics, not only does the grain size limit the size of surface cracks (making them stronger), but as cracks propagate, the presence of grain boundaries opposes crack motion. For example, if cracks follow the grain boundaries instead of going through grains, the crack will be constantly changing direction and taking a circuitous path. Both contribute to increased absorption of fracture energy. Therefore, the toughness increases.

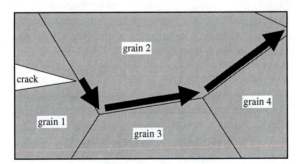

Diagram showing the circuitous path of a crack that chooses to follow the grain boundaries in a crystalline ceramic.

Another way to toughen a ceramic is by putting fibers in the way of moving cracks. The following diagram shows the many ways that fibers can interact with a moving crack. Fibers can "bridge" a crack and help to hold it closed (**crack bridging**). The fiber-matrix interface can undergo **debonding** ahead of a crack, absorbing energy. This can lead to what is known as **crack-blunting**, i.e., the crack tip is no longer sharp, but blunt, and therefore less susceptible to propagate further. Finally, fibers must actually be pulled out of the matrix behind the moving crack, at least until they break. Believe it or not, the friction associated with this sliding (and the energy absorbed), called **pullout friction**, is actually the most effective factor contributing to the increased toughness of fiber-reinforced ceramics. We will talk further about such composites in the next chapter.

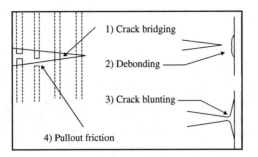

How fibers can interact with a moving crack.

The Zirconia Story

There is yet another way to toughen ceramics, so much so that the resulting material is referred to as "ceramic steel." One of the authors possesses a billiard ball-sized sample of this material, which can be bounced on concrete over and over again (and has been, by thousands of students!). Not only does it fail to fracture, but its surfaces remain visibly unmarred. (The same cannot be said of the concrete, with visible and permanent divots from each impact.)

So what kind of "magic" has been worked to turn an otherwise brittle material into a tough projectile? To tell the story, we need to introduce a **phase diagram**. The following phase diagram is for the water-sugar system. The vertical axis is temperature and the horizontal axis is the amount of sugar. To the left of the sloping line we have a single phase consisting of sugar (the solute) dissolved in water (the solvent). Materials scientists speak of **solutionizing** the material in question. The line represents the "solubility limit," namely how much sugar can be dissolved in water at a given temperature. It slopes to the right, because at higher temperatures more sugar can be dissolved than at lower temperatures. You know this from firsthand experience with hot vs. iced tea. Sugar dissolves much more readily in boiling than near-freezing water.

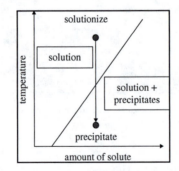

The phase diagram for either water-sugar or zirconia-yttria.

What happens when we exceed the solubility limit? We begin to have a second phase forming, in the form of "precipitates." We mentioned the making of "rock candy" in a prior chapter. This involves saturating the water solution with sugar under boiling conditions, followed by cooling the solution to room temperature. A string with "seed crystals" or nuclei of sugar allows for large sugar crystals to grow.

In the case of "ceramic steel" the solvent is zirconia (ZrO_2) and the solute is yttria (Y_2O_3). Quite a bit of solute can be solutionized at high temperature. Upon cooling below the solubility limit, precipitates want to form. Materials engineers have mastered how to achieve a uniform distribution of tiny precipitates throughout the matrix rather than one or more big crystals, as with rock candy. It is how these tiny precipitates behave that determines the "ceramic steel" behavior of zirconia.

Whereas the matrix phase (the solution) of zirconia is in one crystalline form, namely a cubic crystal structure (not unlike the cubic close-packed structure of metals), the tiny precipitates are in a different crystalline form, called "tetragonal." You don't need to know this structure. But it is highly unstable—it desperately wants to transform to yet another form, called "monoclinic." Again, you don't need to know this structure. But here are some things to know to help you understand the toughening mechanism:

- The precipitates are prevented from transforming by the surrounding matrix, which "clamps" them and keeps them in the untransformed state. This is called a "metastable" situation.
- Once allowed to transform, they do so with a large increase in volume, on the order of 3%.
- The tensile stresses ahead of an approaching crack are sufficient to "trigger" the transformation of precipitates.

The following diagrams illustrate the toughening mechanism in "ceramic steel." An approaching crack "triggers" the transformation of precipitates ahead of it, resulting in their sudden expansion. As the crack moves, it leaves transformed particles (and increased volume) in its **transformation zone** or "wake." The increased volume behind the crack front produces a closing force on the crack. The further it moves, the greater the number of transformed particles behind it and the greater the closing force. Eventually, the crack is so constrained that it stops moving altogether.

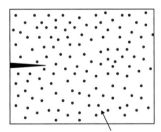

Initial particles "clamped"

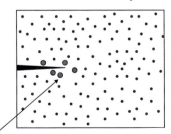

Stress field at crack tip triggers the transformation!

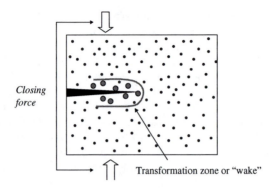

Progress of a crack in transformation-toughened zirconia.

The result is a ceramic that is no longer brittle in nature. We may not be able to eliminate cracks altogether, but we can live with them. By engineering the microstructure (e.g., by small crystals, fibers, transforming precipitates) we can make cracks pay high prices for their propagation. Toughened zirconia is a real triumph of microstructural engineering, leading to exceptional properties. And that's what materials science and engineering is all about.

QUESTIONS: Chapters 18–21

1. The high strength of Corning-Ware® is due to _____ .
   (a) a flame polished surface   (b) precipitation hardening   (c) vitrification   (d) cross-linking
   (e) none of these

2. Choose the false option or choose (e). For ceramics _____ .
   (a) the bonds can carry load   (b) cracks act as stress-concentrators
   (c) compressive forces can close cracks   (d) cracks cannot be blunted by grain boundaries
   (e) all these are true

3. Windshields of cars are made of _____ .
   (a) polycarbonate   (b) compressed glass   (c) tempered glass   (d) laminated glass
   (e) none of these

4. In metals, heat is conducted by _____ while in ceramics it is conducted by _____ .
   (a) protons, electrons   (b) electrons, phonons   (c) phonons, atom knock-on   (d) phonons, electrons
   (e) none of these

5. _____ usually expand less than _____ when heated.
   (a) ceramics, polymers   (b) metals, ceramics   (c) polymers, ceramics   (d) polymers, metals
   (e) none of these options is correct

6. Impurities _____ the conductivity of metals.
   (a) reduce   (b) increase   (c) do not alter   (d) have nothing to do with

7. In general, for a covalently bonded material, the thermal expansion would be _____ and the thermal conductivity would be _____ than for a metallic material.
   (a) higher, lower   (b) higher, higher   (c) lower, lower   (d) higher, lower   (e) none of these

8. In the making of a glass ceramic all the following are involved except _____.
   (a) devitrification   (b) nucleation   (c) seeding   (d) crystallization   (e) all these are correct

9. When a metal gets a crack in it the crack usually _____ .
   (a) causes the metal to fail catastrophically   (b) gets blunted through the slip of planes
   (c) is filled by mobile atoms near the crack tip   (d) stops on its own   (e) none of these

10. Which of the following is a reason why dislocations don't move through ceramics?
    (a) directed covalent bonds   (b) small grains   (c) movement of like charges over one another
    (d) both a and b   (e) both a and c

11. What is the average grain size in glass?
    (a) 0.01 microns   (b) 0.5 microns   (c) 5 microns   (d) 10 microns   (e) none of these

12. Sintering is a process by which _____ .
    (a) atoms are moved toward the middle of a grain   (b) surface cracks are removed
    (c) the surface of a material is placed under compression   (d) impurities are removed from a material
    (e) ceramic particles are joined at temperatures lower than their melting points

13. Which type of bonds in a material would most likely yield the largest thermal expansion?
    (a) covalent   (b) metallic   (c) van der Waals   (d) ionic
    (e) bond type does not affect thermal expansion

14. Sodium ions in glass are bonded to oxygen atoms by _____ bonds.
    (a) covalent   (b) hydrogen   (c) van der Waals   (d) ionic   (e) metallic

15. All of the following are true of glass ceramics except _____ .
    (a) very small grains   (b) low porosity   (c) high strength   (d) high thermal expansion
    (e) high thermal shock resistance

16–25. At absolute zero temperature, the atoms in a material are stationary and in fixed positions. When the material is heated from this temperature, the atoms move __16__ . As a consequence the material __17__ . If only one end of a rod of material is heated, some of the heat energy travels to the other end. The way the energy travels depends on the material, in particular on __18__ . In metals the energy is carried by __19__ ; in ceramics by __20__ ; and in polymers by __21__ . The best insulating materials are __22__ , but they are not useful at high temperatures such as you would find in your furnace because they __23__ . We can greatly improve the insulating properties by incorporating some __24__ into the material. Space shuttle tiles are good insulators which use this principle. The material they are made from is __25__ .

    16. (a) further apart   (b) more rapidly   (c) to form vacancies   (d) from a fixed position
        (e) all of these
    17. (a) becomes amorphous   (b) expands   (c) bends   (d) shrinks   (e) decomposes
    18. (a) its crystal structure   (b) the types of atoms   (c) the bonding   (d) its microstructure
        (e) its dimensions
    19. (a) phonons   (b) photons   (c) free electrons   (d) atom collisions   (e) protons
    20. (a) phonons   (b) photons   (c) electrons   (d) atom collisions   (e) electron holes
    21. (a) phonons   (b) electron holes   (c) electrons   (d) atom collisions   (e) protons
    22. (a) ceramics   (b) semiconductors   (c) polymers   (d) glasses   (e) metals
    23. (a) become brittle   (b) decompose   (c) are flammable   (d) become conductive
        (e) all four are true
    24. (a) precipitates   (b) air pockets   (c) point defects   (d) larger atoms   (e) fibers
    25. (a) silicon   (b) silica   (c) titanium   (d) a silicate   (e) silicone

26. Which of the following is the worst conductor of heat?
    (a) air   (b) fiberglass insulation   (c) an iron pot   (d) a stainless steel pot   (e) a vacuum

27–36. Ceramics are usually materials in which a metal has combined with __27__ using __28__ bonds. Unlike metals they cannot permanently deform, something we know as __29__ deformation, because __30__ find it very difficult to move as a result of the __31__ . While metals are usually formed by starting from a molten material, ceramics are formed by __32__ powders. In metals it is sometimes possible to process a material to produce smaller crystals, such as in __33__ , but in ceramics smaller crystals are usually obtained by starting with a(n) __34__ powder. Smaller crystals help make both ceramics and metals stronger. In metals they __35__ , while in ceramics they __36__ .

    27. (a) boron   (b) carbon   (c) nitrogen   (d) oxygen   (e) any of these
    28. (a) metallic   (b) ionic   (c) covalent   (d) both a and b   (e) both b and c
    29. (a) plastic   (b) polymeric   (c) relaxed   (d) elastic   (e) cooperative
    30. (a) vacancies   (b) ions   (c) dislocations   (d) cracks   (e) electrons
    31. (a) bonding   (b) precipitates   (c) grain boundaries   (d) bulky side groups
        (e) both a and b
    32. (a) sintering   (b) annealing   (c) combining   (d) recrystallizing
        (e) quenching
    33. (a) stainless steel   (b) HSLA steels   (c) aluminum-lithium alloys   (d) cast iron
        (e) superalloys
    34. (a) purer   (b) equiaxed   (c) finer   (d) coarser   (e) acicular
    35. (a) induce precipitate formation   (b) inhibit dislocation motion
        (c) hinder crack propagation   (d) cause grain growth   (e) a combination of a and b
    36. (a) induce precipitate formation   (b) inhibit dislocation motion
        (c) hinder crack propagation   (d) cause grain growth   (e) a combination of a and b

37–44 Ceramics are usually brittle because of the presence of ___37___ . When a stress is applied to a ceramic, it tends to ___38___ at the tips of these defects, which means that the bonds at these points are closer to ___39___ . The less deep these defects, the less the stress is ___38___ d, because there are fewer broken bonds in the defect which are not carrying their share of the load. When you 'cut' glass you don't really cut it, but place a sharp scratch on the surface where it will ___39___ when you try to bend it. The glass on the outside of the bend gets longer, or in other words has a larger ___40___ , and sees a ___41___ stress, while that on the inside sees a ___42___ stress. The thicker the glass, the ___43___ the increase in length of the outer surface, and the ___43___ the ___40___ and stress. Fracture always starts on the ___44___ of the curve.

37. (a) surface cracks and scratches   (b) dislocations   (c) point defects
    (d) precipitates   (e) forces
38. (a) infiltrate   (b) initiate   (c) propagate   (d) concentrate   (e) saturate
39. (a) multiplying   (b) fracture   (c) becoming covalent
    (d) releasing their electrons   (e) slipping
40. (a) modulus   (b) strain   (c) reactivity   (d) stress   (e) both a and b
41. (a) compressive   (b) shear   (c) tensile   (d) bend   (e) isotropic
42. (a) compressive   (b) shear   (c) tensile   (d) bend   (e) isotropic
43. (a) less   (b) smaller   (c) greater   (d) faster   (e) slower
44. (a) bottom   (b) center   (c) end   (d) inside   (e) outside

45. Which is not a method of closing cracks on the surfaces of ceramics?
    (a) ion implantation   (b) chemical tempering   (c) adding fibers   (d) thermal tempering
    (e) none of the above

46. Which of the following is a method to eliminate or limit the size of surface cracks in ceramics?
    (a) adding fibers   (b) flame polishing   (c) reducing the grain size   (d) b and c
    (e) none of the above

47. Which of the following is a process of toughening in fiber-reinforced composites?
    (a) crack-bridging   (b) crack-blunting   (c) debonding   (d) pullout friction
    (e) all of the above

48. The region of increased volume in transformation-toughened zirconia in front and behind crack tips is called:
    (a) the wake   (b) the slip zone   (c) the transformation zone   (d) the tetragonal matrix
    (e) a and c

22. COMPOSITE MATERIALS—GETTING THE BEST OF TWO (OR MORE) WORLDS

Background

Most materials scientists would admit that composite materials, or 'composites' as we usually call them, are one of today's really important materials developments. Not that such materials are novel. The Biblical account of the captivity of the Israelites in Egypt (Exodus chapter 5) refers to their having to gather their own straw to make bricks. Obviously the purpose of the straw was to increase strength. Nowadays we do not use straw in bricks because we have a better knowledge than they did of how to process the matrix phases to cement them together more strongly. The use of straw to strengthen bricks was a problem-solving solution that we have rediscovered in recent years in the form of composite materials. In fact there is now some interesting research being performed on using straw and other natural filamentous material for reinforcing matrices instead of the more exotic ceramic, glass or man-made polymer fibers.

What do we mean by a **composite** material? Some fifty years ago we might have answered this question by saying that it was a material made by mixing two other materials that did not chemically react to form a new compound. These two materials simply coexisted in the same solid, which probably exhibited some properties of both of them. Some of the materials we have discussed already fall into this category because they contain mixtures of two or more different materials. Aluminum-lithium alloys have a solid solution matrix surrounding Al_3Li precipitates. HIPS and ABS plastics have polystyrene and polybutadiene regions. Glass ceramics consist of small crystals embedded in a glassy matrix. Corelle® ware consists of layers of two different glasses.

Today when we talk about composites we usually mean materials in which very strong **fibers** of one material are embedded in another material, called the **matrix**, which completely surrounds them and holds them together. Sometimes the fibers and the matrix are made of different materials, while in others, as is the case with carbon-carbon composites, the two components are made of the same material. Most of these composite materials are very lightweight and have a high strength and a high stiffness. It is these three characteristics that make them very attractive for aerospace applications.

We have already mentioned carbon-reinforced composites (Page 24), which are used for aircraft manufacture. These are often made of carbon fibers in an epoxy matrix (something like you can buy at the hardware store in two tubes, which, when mixed and allowed to cure, form a strong bond for cementing articles together). You may have a tennis or squash racket with a frame made from the same material. For years we have made some household articles, liquid storage tanks, car bodies, etc., from fiberglass, a composite consisting of glass fibers in a polymer (probably polyester) matrix. Today we have special polymer fibers (even polyethylene fibers as mentioned on page 117), ceramic fibers, boron fibers, etc., all of which are being used to make composites.

Wood is an excellent example of a natural composite, containing cellulose fibers in a lignin matrix. It illustrates one of the basic problems with fiber reinforced materials, that of anisotropy. A piece of wood has the cellulose fibers going along what we call the grain. We can break a piece of wood much easier along the grain than across the grain. You don't find a karate expert breaking a plank of wood across the grain with a chop of his or her hand! When broken along the grain the fracture surface is quite smooth because we are producing a fracture between fibers, few, if any, of which are broken in the process. When broken across the grain the fracture surface is very rough because the break has to occur across the fibers themselves.

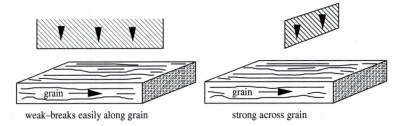

weak–breaks easily along grain   strong across grain

A piece of wood is easier to break along the grain than across the grain.

We shall now look at some of these new strong fibers before coming back to the composites they are used to manufacture. We shall pay particular attention to carbon (graphite) fibers because they are relatively easy to understand, and are those which you are perhaps most likely to encounter. In the following chapter we shall consider the details of carbon/carbon composites and their manufacture for aerospace applications. Some of these materials can be very expensive, but we have already seen that the economics of air travel can justify using some very expensive materials.

Strong Fibers

Modern composites are usually considered to be strong but lightweight. In fact this combination is so important that we often classify materials using a quantity called **specific strength**, which is the strength divided by the density. We shall not be concerned with the units of this quantity because we are really only interested in the relative values, e.g., material A has a value 70% greater than material B. You will see that in the table given later we divide psi by gm/cc, which is mixing systems of units in a way that scientists abhor, but it does give us correct *relative* values. In other words we want to know the percent difference in weight that can be carried by the same weights of different materials, because in many instances (e.g., aircraft) we want to keep the weight as low as possible. We saw when discussing strength (Page 71) that a material can always carry twice the load if we make it twice as thick. Of course this also makes it twice as heavy. If we can replace the material with another which has half the density, but two thirds of the strength, we could achieve a 25% weight saving. The following example will help to explain this.

Example

A rod of material A, with a 2 × 1 rectangular cross section, weighs 10 pounds and can carry 300 pounds (150 psi). If we want it to carry 600 pounds we have to double the area of the rod to 2 × 2, and it now weighs 20 pounds.

The same sized rod of material B weighs 5 pounds (half the density of A) and can carry 200 pounds (100 psi or two thirds the strength of A). If we want it to carry 600 pounds, which is three times its current capacity, we must triple the area of the rod to 2 × 3 , and it now weighs 15 pounds (three times its original weight).

By replacing material A with material B we have reduced the weight from 20 pounds to 15 pounds, a weight saving of 25%.

If we look at the relative specific strengths (strength divided by weight) we obtain the following values:

A : 150 psi/10 pounds = 15
B : 100 psi/5 pounds = 20

The specific strength for A is 25% less than for B and indicates the possible weight saving in going from A to B.

When we look at materials from the standpoint of specific strength, we find that the ceramics, silicon nitride, silicon carbide, and aluminum oxide, boron, graphite, and some of the strong polymers do considerably better than the strongest steel. A table in the following chapter, which compares carbon composites with steel, will give you an idea of how important this can be.

We have already seen (Chapter 19) that the limiting factor in the strength of ceramic materials is the presence of small surface cracks or scratches. Our experiments show us that the smaller the piece of material we use, the less the chance of having one of these surface flaws large enough to cause the material to break. This is why we use very fine fibers. In fact it appears that fibers may always be the strongest form of any material.

Another aspect of very thin fibers, which is worth mentioning, is that they can be more easily bent without breaking than can thick fibers of the same material. If you bend a piece of material you always end up with a longer outside edge and a shorter inside edge. The thicker the piece, the longer this outer edge. As we now know, this stretch, or strain, is produced by a stress. The greater the strain, the greater the stress. It follows that there is more stress in a bent thick fiber than in a thin one bent the same amount, and therefore the thinner the fiber, the more it can be bent without breaking.

We earlier mentioned metal whiskers (Page 78) as having strengths close to the theoretically predicted values because they contain no dislocations. By dividing the material up into such small pieces we reduce the effects of cracks and other defects, and where there happens to be a crack in a fiber in a composite, it cannot find a continuous path through the material to cause fracture because it very soon encounters the less brittle matrix and other unbroken fibers.

Manufacturing Fibers and Composites

We can manufacture glass and alumina fibers by melting the material and drawing out a fiber—just like pulling taffy. We have already mentioned (Page 117) strong and stiff polyethylene fibers produced by gel spinning. Silicon carbide fibers are made from a polymer in which some carbon atoms are replaced by silicon atoms (remember that they both have the similar electron structures with four electrons in their outer shells, so they can often substitute for each other easily) or they can be made by the deposition of silicon carbide on a carbon fiber using chemical vapor deposition (CVD). Carbon fibers are made either from a polyacrylonitrile (PAN) fiber, the acrylic fibers used in clothing, or from pitch. We shall discuss this in chapter 23.

In manufacturing composites from strong fibers there are many criteria that must be met by the matrix material. First, the fiber and the matrix must not react. You cannot just pour a molten metal around carbon fibers because you often end up with a carbide, and the fibers have disappeared. This is because there has been a chemical reaction between the metal and the polymer or carbon fibers. Second, the matrix must be somewhat soft so that it does not damage the fiber. If it scratches the fiber we have lost the main advantage of using fibers. Third, it must adhere well to the fiber so that the fiber does not get pulled out of the matrix when a force is placed on it. In some respects the matrix must hug the fiber just as wet ground holds a wooden stake. You may be able to move the stake, but it is very difficult to pull it out of the ground.

Sometimes the matrix can be melted and poured around the fibers without damage. In some cases the matrix is deposited between the fibers using a CVD process. In others a powder of the matrix can be mixed with the fibers and then sintered together. There are obviously many different processing techniques that can be tried, each with its own limitations. We shall discuss the use of liquid pitch for producing the matrix in carbon/carbon composites in the case study in the next chapter.

Some Current Application of Composite Materials

The use of straw to make bricks, which we mentioned earlier, is an illustration of the use of fibers to reinforce ceramics that tend to break easily because of cracks. The fibers bridge the cracks and carry the load so that the crack does not propagate. This is similar to the effect of the graft copolymer chains in HIPS and ABS plastics. We have used this principle to reinforce cement using asbestos and both glass and carbon fibers, and on a much larger scale with steel reinforcing rods.

An automobile tire is a composite material consisting of an elastomer (itself reinforced with carbon black) as the matrix, which is reinforced with thin steel wires (steel belted radials) or strong polymer fibers, especially the aramid fibers such as Kevlar®.

Commercial applications of composite materials with metal and ceramic matrices are becoming more common. The Toyota automobile company has used ceramic fibers to reinforce parts of aluminum alloy pistons in diesel engines, and aluminum alloy struts reinforced with boron fibers are used in the midsection framework of the US space shuttle. In the future we shall probably see ceramic materials such as silicon nitride or silicon carbide used to reinforce a matrix of the same material, just as we use carbon fibers to reinforce carbon in carbon/carbon composites. These materials would be strong and crack resistant, able to withstand high temperatures, and as such, will be ideal for aircraft engine manufacture.

As is the case for polymers, there are always new composite materials being produced, and research in this particular area of materials science is currently very active. Most recently, carbon nanotubes have been produced with extraordinarily high strengths. These are already making their way into commercial products, e.g., tennis racquets. A later chapter treats these and other emerging nanomaterials.

23. CASE STUDY: CARBON/CARBON COMPOSITES

If you place a piece of fabric, whether of natural or man-made fibers, onto a hot coal or a hot burner on your stove, you will see it shrink, shrivel and turn black. What you are witnessing is the **carbonization** of the material. Any other atoms on the polymer chain such as hydrogen, oxygen and nitrogen are driven off by the heat, and a mass of carbon is left behind. Of course, if there is a supply of air to the material the carbon will eventually burn and form carbon dioxide gas, but it is the carbonization which we are interested in.

In most cases the carbon left behind when the other elements have been driven off is amorphous. There are no graphite crystals produced. However, we discovered about fifty years ago that if we use a single acrylic fiber and heat it while pulling on it to stop it shrinking and shriveling, we can produce a carbon fiber that contains regions of the planes which make up the graphite crystal (Page 12). What's even more important is that these planes lie parallel to the fiber length. The importance of this fact is that this places the strong covalent bonds between the carbon atoms along the fiber length. When we try to stretch this fiber we are pulling on these strong bonds. Further heating at temperatures above 2000°C, in an inert atmosphere to prevent oxidation, causes these little pieces of planes to join up so that we have quite large graphite planes along the fiber length. It is this alignment that makes these fibers both strong and stiff.

More recently we have discovered ways of doing the same thing starting from the black viscous liquid left after gasoline has been removed from crude oil, something we call petroleum pitch. The pitch is what we call a **thermoplastic** material, which means that heat makes it plastic. At room temperature it is a hard brittle solid, but at higher temperatures it becomes a viscous liquid, which can be pulled out into a fiber in the same way that we can pull taffy. Remember that we saw something similar when we talked about the glass transition temperature for polymers (Page 121). This pitch contains many large molecules consisting of several benzene rings (Page 106) linked together, and if you think about it you will see that after removing the hydrogen atoms, these hexagonal molecules can easily link together to form small graphite planes of carbon atoms.

The hot liquid pitch is placed in a container with a small hole in the bottom through which it is pulled to form a thin fiber, a process known as **spinning**, the term used for the production of wool and cotton fiber from the raw material. When this is done the large molecules slip through the hole in the edge-on orientation (sideways), as shown in the following diagram, simply because this is the easiest way through. We then heat the fibers to drive off the other atoms (hydrogen, nitrogen, oxygen, etc.) and are left with hexagons of carbon atoms lying parallel to the fiber length, just as we had in the method starting with acrylic fibers. Further heating at high temperatures (above 2000°C) then causes these little planes to join up and produce a strong, stiff fiber.

Carbon fibers are strong and stiff because they contain the 'chicken-wire' layers of carbon atoms, which are held together by very strong covalent bonds, and these planes lie parallel to the fiber length. When you pull on a fiber you are trying to stretch and break these bonds, which are the strongest bonds known.

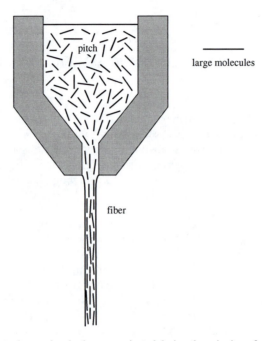

large molecules

Illustration of how hydrocarbon molecules become oriented during the spinning of a pitch-based carbon fiber.

Using different manufacturing techniques (processing) we can make a large variety of fibers with different properties and microstructures. Depending upon the type of pitch used and the dimension of the hole through which the fiber is spun, we can produce fibers with the graphite layers wrapped around the fiber in concentric rings, while in others the layers can radiate from the center of the fiber like spokes on a wheel. In all cases the important point is that the layers lie parallel to the fiber length. The following diagrams show the types of graphite plane orientations you would see when looking at the ends of the fiber, which is about a hundredth of a millimeter in diameter. We can also produce fibers with different strengths by changing the temperature to which they are eventually heated, and the time we keep them at that temperature.

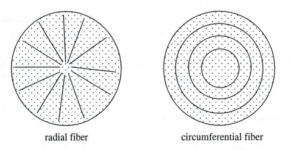

radial fiber   circumferential fiber

Two different types of carbon fiber showing how the layers are arranged along the fiber

Carbon fibers are also very stiff (high Young's modulus), another consequence of the strong, stiff covalent bonds in the graphite layers. As we mentioned earlier (Page 73), stiffness is often the property that is of paramount importance. Many lightweight new materials may be very strong, but they cannot be used for such things as aircraft structures because they are not stiff enough. Here again we are interested in how much stiffness we can get for a certain weight of material, so we also define a **specific modulus**, which is the Young's modulus divided by the density. Carbon fibers are used in many sporting goods on account of their stiffness rather than their strength.

The following table gives the strengths (UTS) and Young's moduli (stiffnesses) of medium strength carbon fibers and compares them with the values given for the high strength low alloy (HSLA) steels on page 100, and with those of typical carbon/carbon composites made with all the fibers parallel in one dimension (1D) and with fibers lying in three dimensions (3D). The table also shows the densities and the relative specific strengths and specific moduli of the materials. The advantage of carbon fibers and their composites are obvious. They give us higher strength and greater stiffness for less weight.

Material	Carbon Fibers	3D C/C Composite	1D C/C Composite	HSLA Steel
Density (A) (gm/cc)	1.8	1.8	1.8	7.8
Tensile strength (B) (10^3 psi)	300	25	95	80
Specific strength* (B/A) $\times 10^{-4}$	16.6	1.4	5.2	1.0
Young's modulus (C) (10^6 psi)	35	10	18	30
Specific modulus* (C/A) $\times 10^{-6}$	19.4	5.6	10.0	3.8

* *We are only concerned with the relative values of these quantities and no units are given. For example, a 1D carbon/ carbon composite has 5.2 times the specific strength of the HSLA steel and over two and a half times (10/3.8) the specific stiffness.*

You will notice from the above table that 1D composites seem better than 3D. This is because in 1D material all the fibers are in the same direction, as they are in wood. Because the force is pulling in that direction, all the fibers are sharing the load and are being stretched, and the strength and modulus shown are measured along this direction. These materials show a large anisotropy. In the 3D material only a third of the fibers are parallel to the direction of the force and so are bearing the load. Each fiber therefore sees three times the stress and stretches more. The 3D composite is therefore not as stiff as is the 1D composite, but is more isotropic. In 1D all the fibers are bearing the load, whereas in 3D only a third do so.

When carbon fibers first became available commercially in the 1970's they cost up to $500 a pound. Today reasonable quality fibers can be obtained for $10–20 a pound, although they can cost several times this amount for special grades. Don't forget that you get a lot of fibers in a pound because of their low density. The following photograph shows carbon fibers alongside a human hair and a fiber

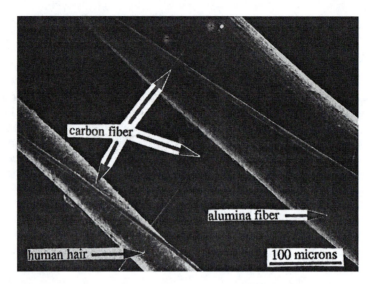

Photograph of three carbon fibers together with a human hair and an alumina (Al_2O_3) fiber.

of alumina (Al_2O_3) to give you an idea of the size. Typical carbon fibers have a diameter of 10 microns (one hundredth of a millimeter).

The Matrix

While fibers of any material may be strong and stiff, their uses in this form are rather limited. They can obviously be braided and twisted into a string or rope, but in order to obtain a rigid material which we can use for structural applications, for example aircraft wing struts, tennis racquet frames, golf club shafts, etc., we have to place the fibers in a matrix.

As mentioned in the previous chapter, the matrix we use has to satisfy the following criteria. It must be somewhat soft so that it does not scratch the fibers, which usually means that it will either be a metal or a polymer. It must also adhere well to the fiber surface so that the fiber is not easily pulled out of the matrix, and it must blunt any cracks that pass through a fiber and then try to cross the matrix. It is this last criterion which gives rise to one of the really valuable properties of fiber composites: they do not fail just on account of one fiber breaking.

For our carbon fibers we use a matrix of either polymer or carbon. It is very difficult to reinforce metals with carbon fibers because if we try to pour molten metal around the fibers, there will be a chemical reaction to produce a metal carbide, and the thin carbon fibers are soon lost.

For the matrix we often use an epoxy resin, which sets hard when cured. We can easily coat the fibers with this material and fill the spaces between them, in a process called impregnation. This bonds them together to form a solid body. This material is called a **carbon fiber reinforced plastic** (CFRP) and is the type of carbon fiber composite you will often find in sporting goods. Carbon fiber manufacturers produce a tape of fibers that are already coated and held together with the uncured epoxy, something called prepreg tape. It is then common to have a form or model of the required finished article made and then wind this tape around it to obtain the required shape. After curing, we now have a solid body of the desired CFRP part. For sporting goods the carbon fibers used do not need to be the strongest available and the product can often be produced without much of a price increase over those made from more conventional materials.

Such CFRP composites are not of use at high temperatures because the polymer matrix decomposes and the material ceases to be what it was designed to be. At this point we can probably see how we can form a carbon matrix, because when the polymer matrix decomposes into its constituent elements (hydrogen, oxygen, and possibly nitrogen) it leaves behind the carbon, just as we saw when talking about carbon fiber manufacture. In fact by heating a carbon fiber reinforced plastic we produce a crude **carbon/carbon composite** (carbon fibers in a carbon matrix).

Carbon/carbon composites have the great advantage of not only being able to withstand very high temperatures, they also retain almost all their strength up to temperatures as high as 2500°C. Their one major drawback is that they burn if allowed to come into contact with any oxidizing atmosphere at temperatures above around 500°C.

We mentioned that heating a carbon/epoxy composite would produce a *crude* carbon/carbon composite. This is because the epoxy does not leave behind much carbon, or to use the technical jargon, it does not have a 'high carbon yield'. When we make carbon/carbon composites for practical use we need to find something we can use to fill the space between (impregnate) the fibers, which gives a high carbon yield. Sometimes we use a polymeric resin, but the more likely candidate for this purpose is the same type of pitch from which we also make the fibers. This pitch impregnant can give carbon yields greater than 60%.

The principles of manufacture are quite simple, but the process is very time consuming and expensive. The fibers are first arranged in the manner required and hot pitch is forced between them by high pressures. The resulting material is then placed in a furnace and heated very slowly (baked) to release the other elements (oxygen, hydrogen, etc.) from the pitch in their gaseous form. This must be done very slowly so that the escaping gases do not all come out in one big blast and blow the part to pieces.

After baking, the part is placed in a higher temperature furnace (as hot as 3000°C) in the absence of oxygen and heated so that the small graphite layers in the carbon produced by the pitch join up in the same way we mentioned in making the fibers themselves. We now have a strong carbon matrix holding the carbon fibers together.

Unfortunately, the carbon matrix produced contains many pores through which the gases escaped. We only have a fraction of the pitch left behind, and have therefore only filled maybe a half (depending on the carbon yield) of the original space between the fibers. We now get rid of some of this remaining space, or porosity, by repeating the whole cycle of impregnation, baking, and heating at high temperature. Each time we repeat the cycle, we further reduce the porosity of the article we are making by a half, so that after four impregnations we have a sixteenth of the porosity remaining. For some special aerospace applications the cycle is repeated around ten times, each cycle giving diminishing returns.

The whole process of as many as ten impregnations can take a few months and consumes a tremendous amount of energy. It is not cheap to heat materials to 3000°C, let alone do it ten times. The energy costs are tremendous. You can now perhaps see why some of these special carbon/carbon composite materials cost thousands of dollars per pound.

An alternative, and also expensive, way of creating the matrix is to flow a gas such as methane through the woven fibers at high temperature. The heat cracks (decomposes) the methane into hydrogen, which escapes, and carbon which is deposited (chemical vapor deposition again) between the fibers.

The photograph below shows a typical carbon/carbon composite. You can see the individual fibers and distinguish them from the carbon matrix. In some cases the matrix has not adhered well to the fibers, while in others there is apparently a good bond between them. This illustrates some of the problems we encounter in making this advanced material.

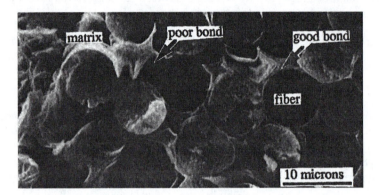

Photograph of a carbon/carbon composite showing fibers and matrix. Examples of good and poor bonds between fiber and matrix are pointed out.

The Composite

While we have now seen something of the processing which goes into the manufacture of one fiber-reinforced composite material, we have to still consider the arrangement of the fibers within the article we are making. As mentioned earlier with reference to wood (Page 158), the fibers only give strength in the direction along their length. Engineers perform very complex calculations to see where and in what direction the stresses in a part will be, and then attempt to manufacture the composite part with the fibers arranged in the directions where strength is needed.

Note that this implies we cannot just make a block of composite and cut off a piece from which to make our part. We can do this with a billet of steel because the material has isotropic properties. The presence of fibers in a composite automatically makes the material anisotropic.

If all the fibers are arranged parallel to each other, we only have strength in one direction, just like a piece of wood. To obtain strength in two dimensions we can place layers of fibers in different directions, as we do in a piece of plywood. With fibers there is also the possibility of weaving them into two-dimensional mats for incorporation into the composite. For three-dimensional strength there are special machines which weave or braid the fibers into a three dimensional form for impregnation. You can see that there are numerous ways in which the fibers can be arranged, and for some special applications the only way these arrangements can be achieved is by having skilled personnel weave and lay the fibers into the required arrangement by hand. Here again, there are tremendous costs involved.

The following diagrams illustrate some of the weave patterns that have been used for fiber composite manufacture. We should note that there is no reason why we cannot use short lengths of chopped fiber to make the composite, but these do not allow us to weave and arrange the fibers in the ways that are possible using continuous lengths.

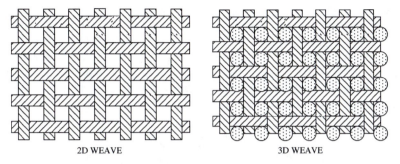

2D WEAVE   3D WEAVE

Weave patterns for fibers used in carbon/carbon composites.

We have mentioned several times the great cost of some of these materials and you may be wondering how these can be justified. An illustration will help you see why we are sometimes willing to pay hundreds of thousands of dollars for a pound of lightweight, strong composite. A telecommunications satellite contains electronics for several message-carrying channels, and each channel can be rented for several millions of dollars a year. If you could provide the manufacturer with a new material, which would save enough weight in the casing and rocket construction to allow the installation of an extra communication channel, just imagine how much you could charge for this material! Carbon/carbon composites are also used as heat shields for space vehicles for reentry into the earth's atmosphere, being the only material that can really stand up to the extreme conditions encountered during this event. This shield protects hundreds of millions of dollars worth of equipment, so what value can we place on it? The fact is that there are some applications for materials in today's world for which we are quite willing to pay very large sums of money. Some carbon/carbon composites may cost several thousands of dollars for one pound, but in some applications they are worth it.

Currently carbon/carbon composites are being used for aircraft brakes (originally used in the supersonic Concorde where it is claimed they produced a weight saving of over half a ton), as heat shields for space vehicles, and for rocket nozzles. Some progress has also been made in taking advantage of carbon's biocompatibility (it shows almost no adverse interactions with body tissue) in developing carbon/carbon plates for joining broken bones, and carbon/carbon prostheses for hip joints, etc. We can tailor our composite so that it has almost the same stiffness and density as bone, which is an added advantage over the traditional metal prostheses. These are other aspects are considered further in chapter 34.

CFRP materials are currently being used in aircraft frames and even for the frames of the seats, where they not only have a weight advantage (dramatically reduced fuel consumption) but can also be made thinner, enabling operators to pack in more passengers. (Not an advantage for us consumers!)

Why does a Composite Work?

To understand how composites give us the advantages that they do, we will consider a very simple situation; one where the fibers are all aligned in the same direction as shown in the next figure.

If we pull on this material both the fibers and the matrix will stretch by the same amount so long as there is good adhesion between them. Otherwise the fibers will pull out of the matrix. We can therefore say that the strains in the fibers and the matrix are the same.

Now remember that the fiber is normally much stronger and stiffer than the matrix, and stiffness is given by stress/strain (Page 73). If the fiber has a higher stiffness but the same strain as the matrix, this means that it has the higher stress, i.e., the fibers are carrying almost all the load. Because of this high load on the fibers, some of the cracked fibers will break, but for the whole piece to break the crack has to pass through the matrix, which is usually plastic and almost rubbery compared to the fiber. The matrix therefore does not break, and as a consequence the load that was carried by the broken fiber has to be borne by another part of the composite.

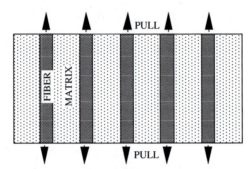

When a composite is stressed the matrix and fibers have equal strains.

Once a fiber in the matrix is broken any force will now try to pull the fiber from the matrix, and the result is what we call a shearing force (Page 69) along the boundary between the broken fiber and the matrix. You can think of it as a type of friction between the fiber and the matrix. As long as the fiber stays in the matrix the load is carried by this frictional force through the matrix and returns to the fiber on the other side of the break. In other words the broken fiber ends are prevented from separating by the adhering matrix; shear forces occur in the matrix and the force gradually returns to be carried by the fiber. At a short distance from the break the fiber is carrying as much load as it did previously.

A good analogy to this shearing force holding the broken fiber in the matrix, is found in trying to remove the stake we put in the ground to support a tree or plant. Moist earth is somewhat plastic like the matrix in a composite. The rigid stake, wood or metal, is like the broken fiber. Trying to pull the stake out of the ground is like trying to pull the fiber from the matrix; it is held tight by the frictional shear forces between it and the soil. You can try a simple experiment to demonstrate this by holding a finger of one hand tightly in the other hand. There is a certain amount of 'give', but you cannot easily pull the finger out unless you relax your grip.

Another contribution to the strength of a composite is the fact that there are individual fibers in the material, and even though they may all break at some point along their length, as discussed above, these breaks will all be at different points along the material's length. If the fiber fractures were all lined up, it would, of course, make it very easy for a crack to pass right through the material and failure would occur, but this is not going to happen where hundreds of thousands of fibers are concerned. This is why fibrous materials, such as wood, are so difficult to break across the grain. Not only do we have to break the fibers, we also have to pull them out of the matrix, which is why we need good adhesion between them and the matrix. In the following photograph of a broken carbon/carbon composite you can see some fibers pulled out of the matrix as well as some broken ends.

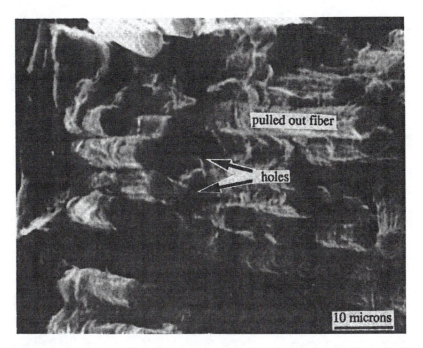

Fractured carbon/carbon composite. The black holes are where fibers have been pulled out. The visible fibers have been pulled out of the matrix of the other half, and in some cases you can see small pieces of matrix adhering to them.

Conclusion

Carbon/carbon composite materials have become very important light-weight materials used in aerospace. Unfortunately they are very expensive and burn in air when hot. There is much current research being performed aimed at preventing this oxidation, but at present there is no perfect solution. For our everyday purposes, the use of carbon fibers in a polymer matrix produces adequate materials, and there are now many examples of their use in sporting goods, racing automobiles and aircraft.

QUESTIONS: Chapters 22–23

1–5. For some applications such as an internal strut of an airplane wing we are more concerned with the strength and stiffness we get for a pound of material rather than the strength and stiffness themselves. We call the ratio of the strength to the weight, or rather the density, the __1__. A 10" long rod of material A with a square cross section of 2" × 2" breaks under a tensile load of 8,000 pounds. Its ultimate tensile strength is therefore __2__. This material has a density of 20 pounds per cubic foot. Material B has an ultimate tensile strength of 5,000 psi and a density of 50 pounds per cubic foot. The material with the higher __1__ is therefore __3__. If the rod of material A was 10.5" long when it broke its strain at that time was __4__. Materials with the highest __1__ values are usually __5__.

    1. (a) absolute strength   (b) tensile strength   (c) specific strength   (d) shear strength
       (e) bend strength
    2. (a) 2000 pounds   (b) 2,000 psi   (c) 800 psi   (d) 4000 psi   (e) 4000 pounds
    3. (a) A   (b) B   (c) they are both the same   (d) there is not enough information to say
    4. (a) 0.05   (b) 5   (c) 5%   (d) both a & c are correct   (e) both b & c are correct
    5. (a) elastomers   (b) metals   (c) composites   (d) minerals   (e) plastics

6–12. Composites have always occurred in nature. Wood consists of __6__ fibers in a lignin __7__. It breaks easily along the grain (along the direction of the fibers) because the break occurs only in the __7__. In this case the break is smooth. When broken across the grain, the break is rough. This is because __8__. Composites are very strong because, not only are the fibers strong and difficult to break, they also __9__. Unfortunately wood has a large UTS (ultimate tensile strength) in only one direction, the grain direction. In order to make a material which is strong in two directions we make plywood. But now the UTS measured along the sheet decreases because __10__. Man-made composites using carbon fibers are used in sporting goods where they have a polymer __7__, but for the high temperatures in rocket nozzles a __11__ __7__ must be used. In many cases, conventional materials such as steel are stronger but __12__.

    6. (a) polyethylene   (b) carbon   (c) lignin   (d) cellulose   (e) polyester
    7. (a) solution   (b) mixture   (c) concentration   (d) matrix   (e) gel
    8. (a) fibers are broken   (b) fibers do not all break in the same plane   (c) some fibers do not break
       (d) both a and b   (e) both b and c
    9. (a) have a high Young's modulus   (b) are very elastic
       (c) have to be pulled out of the surrounding material   (d) are usually polymers   (e) both a and d
   10. (a) the glue between the plies makes it weak   (b) only half the fibers give the strength
       (c) fibers are weakened by processing   (d) both b & c   (e) strength does not decrease
   11. (a) titanium   (b) aluminum   (c) boron   (d) carbon   (e) none of these
   12. (a) are less flexible   (b) are stiffer   (c) are much heavier   (d) have no durability

13–22. The carbon and polymer fibers used in the commonly available composite materials today have a high strength because they have __13__. These fibers are held in a matrix which serves to support them. The matrix must __14__ and in addition must __15__. Carbon/carbon composites are made from carbon fibers which are strong because __16__. The fibers are made from pitch by using a __17__ process. At room temperature pitch is a brittle solid because it __18__, but at higher temperatures it becomes a viscous liquid. The fibers are arranged in the required manner and then the softened pitch is allowed to flow around them to form the matrix. It is also easy to surround the carbon fibers with a(n) __19__ matrix. We might like to make this composite using a metal matrix such as by allowing molten aluminum to flow round the fibers, but we cannot because __20__. An aluminum matrix would allow us to overcome a major problem with carbon/carbon and carbon/ __19__ composites, which is that they __21__. The major reason why carbon/carbon composites can cost thousands of dollars per pound is the vast amount of __22__ used in their manufacture.

   13. (a) covalent bonds parallel to the fiber length   (b) light atoms   (c) an ion-implanted surface
       (d) very small crystals   (e) a small cross sectional area
   14. (a) not react with the fibers   (b) not damage the fibers   (c) not be brittle   (d) a & b
       (e) all three, a, b & c, are correct.

15. (a) allow the fibers to slide easily in the matrix   (b) form a strong bond with the fibers
    (c) keep the atmosphere away from the fibers   (d) both a and b   (e) both b and c
16. (a) they contain carbon atoms   (b) they contain few impurities
    (c) the graphite planes are aligned perpendicular to the fiber length
    (d) the graphite planes are aligned parallel to the fiber length   (e) carbon is inherently strong.
17. (a) CVD   (b) refining   (c) quenching   (d) spinning   (e) rolling
18. (a) has surface cracks   (b) is below its glass transition temperature   (c) contains impurity atoms
    (d) has large grains   (e) is strongly crosslinked
19. (a) ceramic   (b) polymer   (c) silica   (d) nanophase   (e) amorphous
20. (a) the aluminum is not strong enough   (b) aluminum is difficult to melt
    (c) aluminum has too many dislocations to be very strong   (d) molten aluminum reacts with carbon
    (e) aluminum is expensive
21. (a) are too soft   (b) are too expensive   (c) are brittle   (d) burn or decompose at high temperatures
22. (a) man hours (labor)   (b) energy   (c) time   (d) pitch   (e) machining

24. ELECTRONS IN MATERIALS

We have already seen (Page 25) that the electrons in an atom are arranged in shells that fill from the inside out. Before we develop a model for electrons in solid materials we must remind ourselves of the following:

(1)   There are $2n^2$ electrons in each shell, where n is the number of the shell. There are therefore 2 electrons in the first shell, 8 in the second shell, 18 in the third, etc.

(2)   Atoms link up with bonds to get 8 electrons in the outer shell, (like the inert gases).

The reason the electrons arrange themselves in this way is simply a matter of energy. Whatever electrons and atoms do in a material is often in an attempt to lower their energy as much as they can.

If you take a weight tied to a piece if twine and twirl it around in a circle, the weight has energy. If you lengthen the twine and want the weight to make a circuit in the same time as previously, you have to give it more energy because it has to move faster. The bigger the radius of the orbit, the more energy the weight will have. The same is true of electrons orbiting a nucleus, except that only certain orbits, and hence certain energies, are allowed. This is a result of the quantum theory, which is something quite outside our normal experience. Our cars have a certain number of gears, and when we shift from one gear to another we make a different range of speeds available. We can accelerate and decelerate without difficulty within any range. The electron in an orbit around the nucleus of the atom has a fixed speed (energy), and when it shifts to a larger orbit (outer shell) it has a higher speed, but there are no speeds in between. There is a quantum leap from one orbit to the other. We cannot imagine driving a car under such conditions. You would make, for example, a quantum leap from 10 m.p.h. to 25 m.p.h. when changing from first to second gear.

This idea of fixed energies gives rise to the idea of an energy ladder for the electrons moving around the nucleus of an atom. If an electron is to move to an outer shell it needs an increase in energy, just as you need energy to climb one rung on a ladder, or one step on a staircase. In an atom, the difference between the energies of adjacent steps becomes lower the higher up the ladder you go. Eventually the electron gets to the top of the ladder and is now no longer in a fixed orbit around the atom but is free to leave the atom, i.e., the atom is now a cation.

The shell structure we have already mentioned (Page 25) tells us that there are more electrons in a shell as we go away from the nucleus of the atom. We incorporate this into our ladder model by saying that there is more space for electrons on our energy ladder the higher up the ladder we go. The lowest step can accommodate only two electrons, the next one eight electrons, etc. In fact things are a little more complicated than this because each step or level has some little steps within it, which we can call sub-steps or sub-levels. A truer picture is therefore the step diagram shown below. The second step has two sub-levels, holding 2 and 6 electrons, the third step has three sub-levels, which can hold 2, 6, 10.... electrons, etc. We usually refer to the main levels by the number of the shell, and, for historical reasons, we give the sub-levels the letters s, p, d, and f. This gives rise to the model shown.

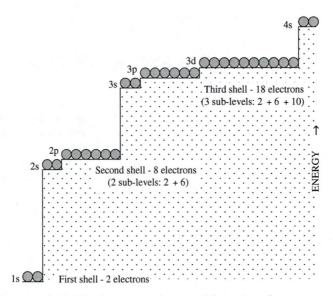

The energy 'ladder' for electrons moving around the nucleus of an atom.

There are three important points we must make about this diagram before we continue. First, the height of the step between 1s and 2s is perhaps a thousand times greater than the step between 2s and 2p. In other words the vertical scale is very distorted. We have to do this in order to get the diagram on the page. Second, it is impossible for an electron to have any energy other than those corresponding to the position of a step. Movements between steps are possible, but they involve quantum leaps as far as energy changes are concerned. The electrons do not accelerate or decelerate their energy changes abruptly. Third, the positions of the steps are different for each atom, with step heights getting larger the higher the atomic number. An electron dropping from 2s to 1s in copper (atomic # 29) will therefore lose more energy than an electron doing the same thing in aluminum (atomic # 13).

You may be wondering how we know about this energy ladder and such things as sub-levels, and the answer is not difficult to understand. We simply look at the energies electrons lose when they fall to a lower level. Before we can discuss this we need some background concerning the units used to measure the energy of an electron.

The Electron Volt

Perhaps the energy unit you are most familiar with is the **calorie** (the amount of energy needed to increase the temperature of a gram (1 cm³) of water by 1°C). There are 1,000 of these calories in a food calorie (it should really be called a kilocalorie), which is the calorie unit used on cereal boxes, etc. These units are much too big to be a convenient measure of the energy of an electron. You are well aware that the more massive a moving article, the more energy it has. Better to be hit by a fast tennis ball than by a truck with the same velocity! Because the electron has such a small mass we need a new unit, and the one we chose is called the **electron volt**, denoted by the symbol, **eV**. It is the energy an electron picks up when it moves between a potential (voltage) difference of 1 volt. For example, a regular C cell battery for a flashlight produces a voltage of 1.5 volts. An electron moving from the negative pole to the positive pole of the battery would pick up an energy of 1.5 eV. There are 2.6×10^{19} eV in one **calorie**, so one of these food calories is equal to 2.6×10^{22} eV.

From this it should be clear that the electron volt is an exceptionally small amount of energy, but that should not surprise us, after all the electron is a very small particle. Even when traveling through a copper wire (electric current) at a fast speed, one electron has little energy.

The Atomic Energy Ladder

As already stated, the energy ladder is an illustration of a scientific principle known as the quantization of energy. The electrons can only have certain energies, corresponding to the steps on the ladder. There is no possible energy between the steps. Another consequence of the quantum theory is that if an electron needs 2 eV to reach the next step and we provide it with energy in packets, or quanta, of only 1.5 eV, the electron is never able to make the jump to the next step.

If you throw a ball up a staircase it can land on the stair immediately below its highest point but it cannot reach the next stair until you increase its energy to get it that much higher. There is no intermediate energy level on which it can rest. Then the ball will reduce its energy by falling down the stairs and it will lose energy in discrete amounts. It may drop down two stairs, then three, then one, etc.

If we wish to move an electron to a higher step on its energy ladder, we have to provide it with energy. We can do this using heat, an electrical voltage, light, x-rays, etc. Sometimes we can even do it by hitting a piece of material very hard. The electron will only stay there if there is no lower level to which it can fall. If there is room on a lower level the electron will lower its energy by tumbling down to this level, sometimes stopping briefly at an intermediate level or even by starting a cascade in which several electrons each move down one level rather than one electron moving down two or three levels. The electron usually stays on the higher step for a very short period of time, often too short to be noticed, before falling to its original level.

When it falls back to a lower level the electron loses energy, and the question we have to answer is: how does this energy appear? What state is it in? How do we recognize it? If we drop a clay pot on the floor it loses energy. Where does the energy go? Some will undoubtedly go into breaking bonds in the material (it shatters). Some will be noticed as sound. Another part of the energy causes the floor to vibrate, although probably not enough for us to notice. In other words, the energy is given off in at least three different forms. When an electron falls from one level to another it loses its energy in only one way, the emission of **radiation**, which may be in the form of visible light rays, x-rays, ultraviolet rays, etc. The energies of these radiations correspond to the differences between the energies of the different steps. It is from this emission of radiation that we gather much of our knowledge about the electron energy ladder in atoms. We shall confine our immediate discussion to the emission of visible light, but you should remember that the same principles apply to the production of x-rays, ultraviolet and infrared rays. Indeed these are essentially the same things, the only difference being in their energy. While visible light rays do not harm our eyes, we know that one reason for wearing sunglasses is to protect from ultraviolet light (higher energy), and eyesight can be lost by staring into a beam of x-rays (even higher energy). The three radiations differ only in their energy, higher energies doing more damage.

Light Emission From Atoms

If you dip a piece of fabric or paper into a salt (NaCl) solution and then place it in the hot flame of a bunsen burner, you will see the flame produce a bright yellow light. The heat of the flame causes the sodium chloride to vaporize to sodium and chlorine atoms, and also has enough energy to cause the outer electrons in the sodium atoms (atomic number 11, 2 + 8 + 1), which sit on the 3s step, to jump to higher steps on their energy ladder. These electrons immediately come tumbling back down to their original step. It turns out that when they pass from the 3p step to the 3s step they lose 2.1 eV in energy, and this is the energy of yellow light. The step model for this process is shown below. Note that light is **emitted** from the sodium **atoms** in the vapor.

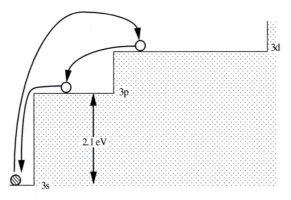

Energy ladder for a sodium atom's outer 3s electron. If it is given an energy quantum large enough to raise it to a higher level it will return to its original level, possibly as shown. The drop from the 3p to the 3s results in an energy loss of 2.1 eV, which is the energy of yellow light.

Before we leave this diagram, notice that we have provided the electron on the 3s level with enough energy to go above the 3d level, but there is no step there, so it settles on the 3d level and then jumps back to the 3s, usually via the 3p. In other words it behaves like we do, sometimes going up and down stairs two at a time and sometimes one. Notice also that it is the jump between the 3p and 3s levels which produces the yellow light. The jump from the 3d to the 3p level involves a smaller amount of energy and does not produce visible light.

As you know, white light consists of a number of colors, each of which has a different wavelength and a different energy. We call this the visible spectrum. You may have already learned to remember the colors of the rainbow by the abbreviation ROYGBIV (red, orange, yellow, green, blue, indigo, violet). These different colors of the visible light spectrum have different energies:

red...violet

1.7 eV....................................3.1 eV

whereas yellow is intermediate, around 2.1 eV.

A simple way of testing a substance to find out the different metals it contains is to take a platinum wire, dip it into hydrochloric acid, then into a powder of the material, and then place it in the hot flame of a bunsen burner. The metals react with the hydrochloric acid to produce chlorides, which vaporize and emit light in a similar way to that which we have already mentioned for sodium. The outer electrons in the metal atoms are moved to higher levels by the heat of the bunsen burner, and then different colors are emitted by the different atoms depending on the energies lost by their electrons as they fall back to their original energy levels in the atom. Lithium emits a deep red, calcium an orange-red, and potassium a violet color.

In a sodium vapor lamp, used extensively for street lighting, a high voltage does the same thing to the sodium atoms, but because the sodium is a solid at room temperature, it first has to be heated to produce the vapor. That's why these lamps have quite a long warm up time before the light is emitted. Remember that the light is emitted by the sodium vapor, as is indicated by the name. The resulting color is a ghastly yellow-orange. These may not be aesthetically pleasing, but they are three times as efficient as the next competitor for lighting the streets of our cities. They therefore save lots of energy and taxpayer money. The mercury vapor lamp works on the same principle, except that the color is bluish because it involves electron jumps between different steps on a different energy ladder, i.e., that of mercury atoms.

You can now see how we can obtain information about the energy ladder for electrons in atoms. We simply look at the energies of the radiation they emit when their electrons jump down from one step to another.

Unfortunately the model we have developed so far only applies to isolated atoms. When we put many atoms together to make a solid, the electrons interact to form bonds and the situation becomes more complicated, but in some respects it becomes simpler. We must therefore now turn our attention to electrons in solids.

The Band Energy Diagram

If we put N atoms together, we obviously need space on the energy ladder for N times the number of electrons. The material does this by creating N times the number of levels on the energy ladder. The complexity involved is obvious when we note that in a solid of any reasonable size there are at least 10^{22} atoms! How can we manage a model, which now needs ten billion trillion times the number of energy levels?

The result is that we now have a model for which we cannot draw the individual steps, because there are so many of them. In fact, it is like having a ramp of energies. However we must remember that this ramp consists of small discrete steps with only a certain number of electrons allowed on each step. The energy difference between adjacent steps on this ramp is very, very small, being only around 10^{-23} eV (about 10^{-45} food calories). Very small indeed! The model we draw is therefore as shown below.

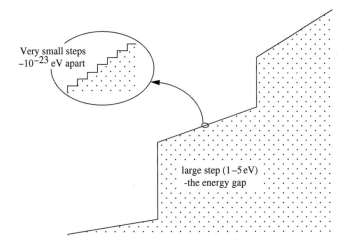

Very small steps
-10^{-23} eV apart

large step (1–5 eV)
-the energy gap

Energy ladder (ramps) for electrons in a solid.

We call these energy ramps **bands** of energy because there exits a range (band) of energies within which the electrons can essentially have any value - differences of 10^{-23} eV are so small as to be negligible. Remember, however, that these bands contain millions of millions of discrete energies, which we call energy levels. The large jumps between bands we call **band gaps**.

The diagram we usually draw to represent this model is the view you would have of the above ladder if you looked at it from the front rather than from the side, and is called a **band energy diagram**. We draw only the upper two bands: the last one to have any electrons on its levels and the next empty band.

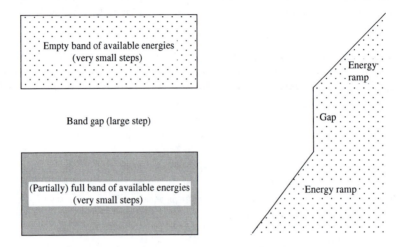

Front (left) and side (right) diagrams of available energies (bands) in a solid material.
Note that the lower band may have all or only some of its steps full of electrons.

There are three basic types of energy band diagrams: those for metals (conductors), semiconductors and insulators.

Referring to the above diagram with only two energy bands, **conductors** have no electrons sitting on the levels in the upper band, and a lower band with only the lower levels of the band occupied with electrons. This means that these electrons can move to higher energy levels when they are given very small amounts of energy, even as small as 10^{-23} eV. There is then a gap, followed by another band of available energies.

Semiconductors have a lower band of energies with electrons filling all the steps within the band. There is then a gap (usually less than 2 eV) before the next band. The electrons in semiconductors therefore need at least 1–2 eV in order to move to the next available energy step.

Insulators have essentially the same band arrangement as semi-conductors, but the band gap is much larger. Large energy quanta (usually over 5 eV) are needed to lift an electron to a higher energy level in these materials. We shall soon see that this is very unlikely using electrical voltage, although we can calculate the voltage necessary to do so.

Remember that the electrons in these materials need energy quanta equal to, or greater than, the energies mentioned in order to change what they are doing. This includes moving to produce an electrical current. The three different possibilities are illustrated in the following diagrams.

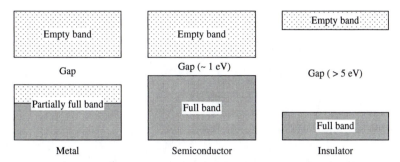

Band energy diagrams for three major classes of electrical materials.

Notice that materials do not oblige us by having gaps that are either small (~ 1 eV) or large (> 5 eV). Instead, there is a wide range of all possible band gap energies in all the materials at our disposal. Our division at 2 eV is purely arbitrary.

In silicon, the most common semiconductor, the band gap energy is 1.1 eV. In germanium the gap is 0.7 eV, and in diamond it is nearly 6 eV. These all have the same atom arrangement (crystal structure). Diamond is an insulator, whereas silicon and germanium are semiconductors.

What Energy Quanta are We Concerned With?

We must now consider what these different band energy diagrams mean in terms of what we can and cannot do with electrons in solids. Once again we go to that branch of physics called quantum theory. It is somewhat frightening to undergraduate physics majors because of its mathematical complexity. However the results we need are really simple and quite understandable. As mentioned earlier, energy comes in packets called quanta. For example, red light comes in quanta of 1.7 eV. If a material has all the levels in the lower energy band filled and there is a band gap of 2 eV, we can shine red light on the material all day and an electron will never be able to jump the gap up to the next step on the energy ladder. The electron cannot increase its energy at all and no electricity can flow. The energy packets are discrete and are absorbed singly. They do not add together.

The major types of energy we shall be concerned with are electrical, heat (thermal) and light. We shall now consider the energy quanta associated with them.

Electrical Energy. Here the quantity which determines the energy is the "**voltage gradient**" which is defined as voltage divided by distance. In terms of energy quanta, a voltage gradient of one million (10^6) volts per cm is worth about 2 eV. For example, if we have a 5 cm thick sheet of a material and we connect the household line voltage (120 volts) across it, there is a voltage gradient across the material of 120 volts/5 cm = 24 volts per cm. In this case the energy quantum is (by taking a simple ratio) around $(24/10^6) \times 2$ eV $= 4.8 \times 10^{-5}$ eV.

If the band gap energy of a material is 2.5 eV, and a voltage of a million volts were placed across an 8 mm thick piece of this material, the voltage gradient would be 1.25 million volts per cm. Since we get around 2 eV per million volts per cm, a voltage gradient of 1.25 million volts per cm would give an energy quantum of $2 \times 1.25 = 2.5$ eV, just enough to shift electrons across the gap. The material will therefore now conduct electricity. This phenomenon is known as **breakdown**. All insulators will breakdown, i.e., lose their insulating property, if enough voltage is placed across them.

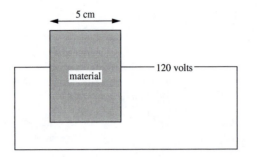

Illustration of a voltage gradient of 24 volts per cm across a material.

Thermal Energy. This form of energy is unusual in that at any temperature (except absolute zero) there is a range of energy quanta available, so that we cannot give an exact value. At a temperature T in Kelvin (°Celsius + 273) the **average** energy quantum is $T \times 0.86 \times 10^{-4}$ eV. Therefore, at room temperature (~300K) the average thermal energy quantum is $300 \times 0.86 \times 10^{-4} = 0.026$ eV. At 2000°C the mean thermal energy quantum is about 0.2 eV. However, one must remember that these values are average values, and that there are always some quanta in thermal energy that are much larger than this. This is quite different from light quanta, where each color has a fixed energy.

Light Energy. We have already seen that visible light has energy quanta (called **photons**) with energies from 1.7 to 3.1 eV. Ultraviolet light has energy packets of higher energy and infrared light has lower energy. X-rays are physically identical to light waves but they have much higher energies and are not seen by the human eye.

It is worthwhile considering the above statements in a slightly different way. We have already seen that very large voltage gradients are needed to increase the energy of (move) electrons in a material with a band gap of 2.5 eV. To accomplish this with heat we have seen that at 2000°C the *average* quantum is 0.2 eV, but there will be a few quanta as large as 2.5 eV, meaning that there will be a few electrons that can increase their energy. However, by just shining blue light (2.7 eV) on the material, there will be plenty of energy quanta large enough to enable many electrons to increase their energy.

If we were asked to rank the energies of these three phenomena in light of our everyday experience, we would almost certainly place them in reverse order. We are more afraid of electricity than heat and light. The reason for this is that we are large bodies, and the quantum theory does not apply to us as it does to small electrons. We respond to the total energy rather than to the size of the individual energy quanta.

Electrical Conduction

We can now better understand the band energy diagrams for the three different materials. Electrical conduction is the movement of electrons under the influence of a voltage. In a metal the electrons are free and are moving about all over the place, with just as many going in any direction as in the opposite direction, so that there is no net electron flow. In order to produce a net flow, which we call current, we have to increase the speed, and hence the energy, of some of the electrons. If we apply a voltage of 120 volts across a 25 meter (2500 cm) length of copper wire, a situation which may be typical of an average house, the voltage gradient is

$$\frac{120 \text{ volts}}{2500 \text{ cm}} = 0.048 \text{ volts/cm}$$

which gives an energy quantum of around 10^{-7} eV. However, this is more than enough to lift the electrons to higher levels within the band of energies, (remember the levels in the band are about 10^{-23} eV apart) and hence the electrons can accept the energy, increase their velocity, and thus produce an electric current, i.e., the material conducts. Remember that it is only the electrons in unfilled bands, which can accept such small energy quanta and hence produce an electric current.

In a regular flashlight we may only use a 1.5 volt cell, and the wire may be around 10 cm long. This gives a voltage gradient of 0.15 volts/cm, which is even larger than we calculated for household wiring.

For both insulators and semiconductors, there are no energy levels for the electrons to go to except for those across the gap. Normal voltage gradients are not enough to provide this energy (1–2 eV) so the electrons cannot go to higher energy levels, cannot increase their velocity, and therefore no current is produced. The materials are therefore not good conductors. In order to conduct electricity, the electrons have to first be moved to a higher band, which contains no electrons. Once they are in this now partially filled band, they can accept the small energy quanta provided by the voltage and produce the net electron flow, which we call an electric current. Shining visible light (1.7 – 3.1 eV) on silicon (gap energy 1.1 eV) moves many electrons over the gap. These can now further increase their energy using the small quanta provided by a battery, and an electric current will be produced.

Another way of looking at the energy gap is to think of it as the energy required to make an electron free. In metals they are already free; in other materials they need a certain amount of energy (an energy quantum) to strip them from the covalent or ionic bonding state in which they exist. For example, electrons in diamond are held very tightly in strong covalent bonds. Silicon has the same crystal structure and is also covalently bonded, but the bonds are not as strong. It is therefore easier to strip electrons from the bonds in silicon than it is in diamond. This corresponds to a smaller energy gap in silicon (1.1 eV) than in diamond (~6 eV). Once the electrons have crossed the energy gap in a semiconductor or insulator, they are free to conduct electricity. Any small electrical voltage is enough to increase their energy by the 10^{-23} eV necessary to go to the next level.

We now have a simple picture of the electrons and their energies in solid materials. This will enable us to understand a wide variety of phenomena. In closing this section we may note that any solid can be made to conduct electricity if the electrons are given enough energy to cross the energy gap. This energy can come from any of the sources we have mentioned. In fact any material will conduct electricity if heated to a high enough temperature (assuming it doesn't melt or decompose first), or is exposed to high energy x-rays, or is exposed to light, as long as the light quanta have an energy greater than the band gap energy. These external influences lift the electrons over the gap and then the voltage can give them energy to go to higher levels in their new band. They are therefore able to take on the electrical energy, i.e., conduct electricity.

But there are other ramifications of the energy band diagrams we have just discussed, namely how the various materials (or rather their electrons) interact with light. This is the subject of the next chapter.

25. ELECTRON INTERACTIONS WITH LIGHT

or

SOME CAUSES OF COLOR

In our discussion of the energy band diagrams we mentioned that the energy gaps between bands are usually a few electron volts. We also know that visible light quanta have energies of a few electron volts, in the range 1.7 to 3.1 eV. Ultraviolet light has larger energies and infrared light has smaller energies. The fact that these energies are about the same as the band gap energies gives rise to some very interesting phenomena, which are of great importance to us in our everyday lives. Without them we would not have fluorescent lights, television tubes, and some of the valuable colored gems we use in jewelry.

Before we start to explore some of these phenomena we should mention that there are many different reasons for the coloration of materials. We will only explore one or two of these. Most materials are colored by very complex mechanisms, which are difficult to understand at this level. For example most dyes used in clothing are organic, with very complicated molecules giving rise to the color. We will only consider the color of opaque metals and some transparent gemstones and will conclude by considering colors emitted from fluorescent lamps and TV screens.

What produces the color? The natural sunlight is what we often call 'white' light. It contains all the colors of the rainbow (ROYGBIV); indeed the rainbow is simply caused by raindrops splitting the sunlight into its component colors. When this light hits a material it is either transmitted (passes through) or is reflected. During these two processes some of the spectral colors may be selectively absorbed or scattered by the material, so that the light which is either transmitted or reflected to our eyes is missing these colors. Instead of being white, it has a color that depends on the colors lost. We have already mentioned an example of this in discussing Visions Ware® (Page 146). Because we shall be talking about energy band diagrams we shall usually refer to the energies of the light quanta. Remember that each color has its own energy.

In the following discussion we must be careful to distinguish light that we see after it has passed through a material (**transmitted** light), as is the case with many gemstones, and light that is **emitted** by the material. Reflection is, as we shall see, really a part of this latter category. We shall be careful to point out which of these two is happening to produce the color.

One problem that arises in discussing color is that of understanding how colors mix, and what happens if some colors are missing. Many people think of mixing paint. You go to the store, select your color from a chart of a thousand shades, and watch the assistant mix the color. Unfortunately thinking in terms of paint can lead us to some wrong conclusions. You can probably well appreciate that if you were to mix cans of red, orange, yellow, green, blue, indigo and violet paint, you would not end up with white. The result would be something awful. That is because the mixing of paints involves combinations of pigments that individually *subtract* certain wavelengths from transmitted light, leading to the various colors. By combining them, just about all wavelengths will be equally subtracted. On the other hand, a mixture of these same colors in emitted light produces white light; in this case the different wavelengths *add* rather than subtract.

A good way to look at the problem is to realize that this mixture of light colors does produce white. Let's take a specific example, using the letters ROYGBIV to denote the colors of the rainbow. If something happens to block out every color reaching our eyes except the red, we see only red. It's simple. Now imagine that your eyes see ROY, the result will be an orange color. Up to this point it seems that the mixing of paint would give a similar answer. Now add green. How does the color change? Our paint mix would start to become rather muddy (owing to color subtraction), whereas our light must be getting closer to white. The progression as we add the remaining spectral colors to our light beam will be R   RO   ROY   ROYG   ROYGB   ROYGBI   ROYGBIV, which means going from red   reddish orange   orange   yellowish orange   yellow   pale yellow   white. Starting at the other end of the spectrum with only violet and then adding indigo and blue, etc., the colors must progressively change from violet to white. A consequence of this is that if just the yellow is missing we see a pale blue, whereas if just the violet is missing we see a pale yellow. The following discussion will be much simpler if you can appreciate what we have just said.

The Color of Metals

We have already seen that light quanta have energies of 1.7 eV (red) to 3.1 eV (violet). In metals there are electrons in an unfilled band, which can often take on all these energies by jumping to higher levels in the band, and they do so. The light is therefore unable to get through without being absorbed by the electrons and the metal is opaque. The electrons go to steps higher in the band but stay there for a very short time. They tumble back down the steps giving out, or emitting, light and this is what gives metals their characteristic white or silvery luster. We talk of the light being **reflected**, but what is happening is that the light energy is being absorbed and then re-emitted. The light does not really reflect as a ball bounces off a wall. A better analog is a baseball being caught by a fielder, who immediately throws it to second base in an attempt to get the double-play. The ball is released almost as soon as it is caught. The same is true of electrons in metals and light. The electrons absorb (catch) the light and almost immediately (so quickly that we don't even notice the delay) re-emit it. What is absorbed is emitted, as the electrons are constantly increasing and decreasing their energy.

In all the following diagrams we shall denote quantum jumps, which occur with arrows, while those which cannot occur do not have arrows.

In a large number of metals there is at least a 3.1 eV space at the top of the band of electron energies. As a result all the light energy quanta (all colors) are absorbed by the electrons and re-emitted equally, with the consequence that the '**reflected**' light is white. The metals therefore appear silvery. Aluminum, titanium, chromium, iron, silver and nickel are all like this. In other metals there is not as much space at the top of the energy band for the electrons to move to, so that while the red light may be easily absorbed, the blue light passes further into the material and gets lost by other processes outside the scope of this discussion. As a consequence the absorbed light that is **re-emitted** is mostly in the red, orange and yellow part of the spectrum. This is true of copper and gold.

This process of absorption and remission takes place in a very thin layer at the surface of the metal. It is very difficult to make metal foils thin enough to see through them, because the light absorption by the electrons in the material is very, very efficient. One metal, which can be made this thin is gold. When beaten to form the gold leaf used for decoration it is very, very thin (1000Å=100 nm, or one ten thousandth of a

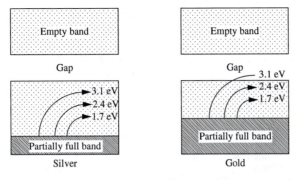

Absorption and re-emission of light in silver and gold. In silver there is enough space in the band of energies for all light energies to be absorbed. When the electrons fall back they therefore emit all colors and the metal is white (silvery). In gold the higher light energies cannot be absorbed. Only the red and yellow end of the spectrum is absorbed and re-emitted and the metal is yellow (gold) colored.

millimeter) and you can see through it if you hold it against a strong light. Even thinner gold layers are routinely deposited on insulating surfaces to keep them from charging up when examined by the beam of electrons employed in an electron microscope. For example, gold layers on the order of nanometers thick can be deposited on glass microscope slides. When you reflect white light off the surface of gold leaf or the gold-coated microscope slide, it appears gold in color (absorbed/re-emitted or reflected light). On the other hand if you look at light through the leaf or gold-coated slide, it appears bluish green (transmitted light). Why this color change? The answer is simple. The yellow light you usually see from gold is 'reflected'. The other colors of the spectrum pass deeper into the metal and, if it is thin enough, they can escape from the other side. We therefore have the two complementary colors, yellow and bluish green; together they would approximately make white light. (Complementary colors are those, which together would make white light.)

The Color of Pure Insulators

A good insulator has a band gap energy of at least 5 eV which is greater than the energies of all visible light quanta. The electrons fill the lower energy band in the material and cannot take on any energy unless it is enough to cause the electrons to cross the gap. They therefore cannot absorb any of the light quanta, so they pass through without any interruption. Because of this, the material is colorless

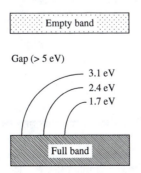

Visible light is unable to move electrons in a good insulator and is transmitted with no absorption. The material is colorless and transparent.

and transparent. The light simply passes through without any absorption because the electrons cannot accept any of its energies. Most good insulators are transparent if they are pure.

We must emphasize this matter of purity because, as we have seen, impurities are common in most materials, and it is these impurity atoms that are usually responsible for the color and opacity of the material.

The Color of Semiconductors

You should now be able to see that a piece of silicon, which has a band gap energy of only 1.1 eV, will behave like most metals. All visible light energies (1.7–3.1 eV) can be used to make electrons jump across the energy gap. When they tumble back down the energy ladder they emit light of all energies and as a consequence a bare piece of silicon has a metallic luster and looks very much like a metal. The color is **re-emitted** (reflected).

There are also some materials, which have band gap energies between 1.7 and 3.1 eV. Let us consider the case of a cadmium sulfide, a material with a band gap of 2.6 eV. Light with energies less than this (red, orange, yellow, green and some blue) will pass straight through because it can do nothing to the electrons in the material. Light with energies greater than 2.6 eV (mostly violet) will be absorbed, or used by the electrons to reach levels in the next band. We therefore see the materials as an orange-yellow because this is the combined color of the light that passes through. In this case the color is **transmitted**.

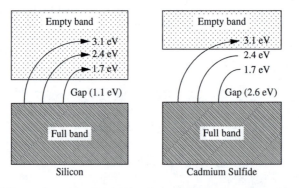

In silicon (left) all light energies can be absorbed by electrons just as they are in a silvery metal. Silicon therefore has a silvery luster and is opaque. In cadmium sulfide (right) only the blue/violet light can be absorbed by the electrons and the red/yellow part of the spectrum is transmitted. The material is therefore a yellow-orange color.

This mechanism of producing color is very limited. If you think about it, it must always be the low energies that are passed through uninterrupted (not enough energy to push the electrons across the gap) while it is the high energies that are absorbed. With this process there is no way to produce a blue material because it is always the high energy light (blue) which is absorbed and the low energy light (red and yellow) which is allowed through to produce the color. Remember that the color we see in such cases is **transmitted**. We shall see that to make things blue we need impurities.

Insulators Colored by Impurities—Gemstones

When we add impurities (point defects) to a material they add some steps of their own to the energy ladder, and these steps lie inside the gap. This has the effect of making it easier for electrons to cross the gap. For our purposes, we can divide impurities into two types, those that have more electrons than the atom they replace and those that have fewer. Those that have more are called **donor** impurities because they donate an extra electron or two to the system. Those that have fewer electrons are called **acceptor** impurities because they have room to accept electrons from neighboring atoms. Both types of impurity create extra steps in the gap in the energy ladder. With donor impurities the extra electrons sit on these steps; with acceptor impurities these new levels are empty and can accept electrons from lower levels.

The following band energy diagrams illustrate what can happen in these solids. It is now possible for the jumps shown to correspond to the absorption of red light, while there is no possible jump corresponding to blue light. We can therefore get a blue color because red is absorbed and blue is **transmitted**.

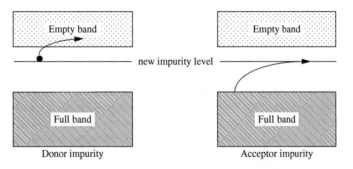

Illustration of new possible absorptions as a result of impurities.

These two types of impurity allow some different jumps to occur, such as those shown in the previous diagram. Some energies can therefore be absorbed which could not be absorbed previously. If these new absorptions are in the range of visible light energies, some color of the light spectrum which was previously transmitted is now lost to absorption in the material. Thus a previously transparent colorless material becomes a transparent colored material.

There are two examples of this with which you are probably familiar. In powder form pure aluminum oxide is white and is used as a fine, abrasive polishing material because of its hardness. A single crystal is colorless and transparent with no particular interest. If we add small amounts of titanium the material becomes a blue sapphire, while small amounts of chromium turn it into a red ruby. In both cases some light is absorbed by electrons using the new levels as steps in the energy ladder. With titanium, red is absorbed and the blue passes through while with chromium the reverse is true.

We already mentioned (Page 13) that adding boron (an acceptor impurity because it has one fewer electron than carbon) to diamond turns the diamond blue, while adding nitrogen (a donor impurity because it has one more electron than carbon) turns it yellow. These colors are also produced by the above mechanism. The following diagrams illustrate what happens.

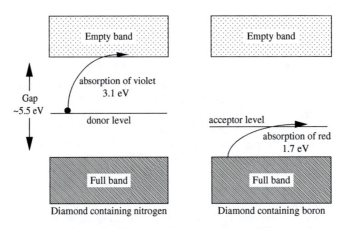

Nitrogen with one more electron than carbon is a donor impurity in diamond. Its extra electron can be freed with blue light, so some blue is absorbed and the diamond transmits a yellow color. Boron has one fewer electron than carbon. A carbon electron can be moved to the impurity level using red light, so some red is absorbed and the diamond transmits a blue color.

The presence of a little nitrogen turns the diamond yellow. A nitrogen atom has one more electron than a carbon atom and this electron sits on the impurity level. An energy quantum of around 3.1 eV is needed to move this electron, so some of the violet/blue end of the spectrum is absorbed. The light passing through the diamond is therefore missing some of the blue end of the spectrum and appears yellow. A little boron, which has one fewer electron than carbon, provides an energy step to which one of the carbon's electrons can jump using a quantum of only 1.7 eV (red). Some red light is therefore absorbed and the transmitted light is bluish. In both cases the color is due to **transmitted** light.

The amount of impurity needed to produce these colors is quite small. Replacing one carbon atom in 100,000 with a nitrogen atom produces a yellow diamond, while replacing one in 1,000,000 (a million) with a boron atom produces an attractive blue color. Natural blue diamonds are rare and therefore quite expensive. The Hope diamond at the Smithsonian Institution in Washington D.C. is perhaps the best known example.

Diamond can also be found with different colors. In some cases we have no idea what causes this coloration. For example, there are some very pretty, and valuable, pink diamonds whose color is not understood.

Fluorescence and Phosphorescence

There is one further aspect of this interaction of light with materials that we use on a daily basis. It is concerned with the phenomena of **fluorescence** and **phosphorescence**, which together are known as **luminescence**. In both phenomena light is **emitted** from a material.

We have already seen how impurities in insulators introduce extra energy levels in the gap. There is another way we can use these levels. Ultraviolet (UV) light has greater energies than those of visible light (i.e., greater than 3.1 eV) and these energies can be greater than the band gap energy. If we shine UV light on an insulator containing impurities, the UV can lift electrons over the gap to the next band. Once again the electrons don't stay there but tumble back down to the band where they came from. But just as a ball thrown up a staircase will bounce down from step to step, the electron can opt to return to its original level by means of the intervening impurity level(s). In this way the large quantum of UV light is released in smaller quanta, and one or more of these could be visible light in the range 1.7–3.1 eV. The material can therefore **emit** visible light. Because the impurities activate this phenomenon of luminescence, they are called **activators**.

The following diagram illustrates how this happens. The material shown has a band gap of around 4.5 eV, so an ultraviolet photon of greater energy can move an electron and is absorbed. The electron returns to its original energy by jumping from one impurity step to another. The diagram shows two impurity levels with an energy difference of 2.1 eV between them. When an electron moves between these two levels, a photon of 2.1 eV (yellow light) is **emitted**.

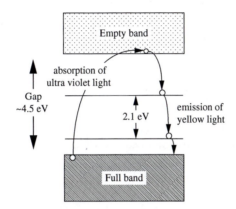

Band energy diagram for an insulator showing how UV light can be absorbed and yellow light emitted.

You can see an excellent display of this phenomenon (luminescence) in most mineral museums. The dull gray rocks are transformed into a wide variety of brilliant colors when illuminated with ultraviolet light.

With **fluorescence** the emitted light only occurs while the UV light is being shined on the material. This is because the electrons are moving up and down the energy ladder so rapidly that we cannot notice any time delay.

You have all heard of, and used, fluorescent lights. They are a relatively new invention, having been invented in the 1930's and brought into more general use in the 1940's. These are tubes, which contain mercury and are coated inside with some materials which fluoresce, such as cadmium phosphates, zinc silicate, and magnesium tungstate, the color depending on the impurity used as the activator. The electricity acts on the mercury vapor in the tube, just as in a mercury vapor lamp, causing it to emit the yellow/green light we usually associate with mercury vapor lamps, but it also emits quite a lot of ultraviolet light. This UV light is absorbed by the coating inside the tube, which in turn then emits light.

We can have white tubes, pink tubes, special grow-light tubes for plants, etc., the colors emitted depending on the impurities in the fluorescent materials coating the inside of the tube.

Phosphorescence occurs when these extra impurity levels are what we can describe as 'sticky'. The electrons stay on an impurity level and take their time returning to the original level. Light is therefore emitted over a much longer period of time and continues for maybe a few seconds or even minutes after the UV light source has been turned off. You can sometimes notice this as an afterglow on your TV screen after it has been turned off, if the room is dark. This phenomenon is known as phosphorescence and is characterized by a noticeable decay of the emitted light after the UV light is switched off. With some minerals you can still see light being emitted twenty minutes after the UV light has been turned off.

In old-fashioned color TV sets the inside of the tube was coated with phosphorescent materials, which were given energy by striking them with an electron beam. They then emitted light of the colors corresponding to the differences in the energy levels in their energy ladders. Look carefully at a TV picture, and you will see that it is made up of small dots or short stripes, of three colors, blue, green and red. Each color corresponds to the dots of different phosphor materials used to coat the screen.

Color TV pictures improved steadily over time because of new phosphorescent materials that were discovered. For example, element number 63 in the period table is europium (Eu), which is used as the activator (impurity) in yttrium vanadate (YVO_4) to give brilliant reds. Perhaps this is the only place you will ever come across europium in your life. It is a rare element, but it has a place in our everyday lives. For the blue we often use zinc sulfide with a silver activator, and for the green, zinc silicate with a manganese activator.

Of course, "vacuum tube" TV sets are becoming a thing of the past, owing to the advent of flat-panel, high-definition screens. But this has not eliminated the need for "phosphors" (phosphorescent materials). These are still found in the individual "pixels" of so-called "plasma" televisions. Inside these tiny cells, inert gases (xenon or neon) get ionized—an electrical voltage is used to turn them into mixtures of energetic ions and electrons. The resulting plasma then bombards the phosphor in that pixel with ultraviolet light. Depending upon the phosphor used in that pixel—red, blue or green—that color of light gets emitted.

QUESTIONS: Chapters 24–25

1. Which of the following form of energy cause fluoresence?
   (a) red light   (b) blue light   (c) violet light   (d) infrared radiation   (e) ultraviolet radiation

2. Fluorescence can occur in which of the following materials?
   (a) semiconductors   (b) conductors   (c) pure insulators   (d) insulators with impurities
   (e) fluorescence can occur in all of these materials

3. A yellow diamond gets its color because _____.
   (a) blue light is absorbed   (b) yellow light is absorbed   (c) yellow light is reflected
   (d) yellow light is emitted   (e) none of these

4. The phenomenon when light emission occurs after UV light is removed from a material is called _____.
   (a) phosphorescence   (b) fluorescence   (c) activation   (d) luminescence   (e) none of these

5. A very thin sheet of gold transmits _____ light.
   (a) red   (b) yellow   (c) white   (d) orange   (e) blue-green

6. The acronym used for remembering the colors in white light is _____.
   (a) ROYBGIV   (b) VIBYGOR   (c) VIGBYOR   (d) BIVGYOR   (e) none of these

7. Pure materials with a band gap greater than 5 eV are _____.
   (a) black   (b) white   (c) violet   (d) colorless   (e) pink

8. An acceptor level in a diamond exists such that yellow light is absorbed. What color is the diamond?
   (a) blue   (b) black   (c) colorless   (d) red   (e) yellow

9. The energy quanta for visible light are called _____.
   (a) phonons   (b) radiation   (c) rads   (d) electron volts   (e) photons

10. The energy of yellow light is _____ eV.
    (a) 1.7   (b) 3.1   (c) 2.4   (d) 2.1   (e) 2.7

11. The highest average energy quantum is found in _____.
    (a) visible light   (b) heat at room temperature   (c) electrical energy   (d) infrared light
    (e) ultraviolet light

12. Materials with a band gap energy less than 1.5 eV are _____.
    (a) red   (b) lustrous   (c) opaque   (d) both a and c   (e) both b and c

13–21. When sodium chloride is heated in a flame it vaporizes and the electrons in the sodium atom are given energy. The outermost electron is lifted up from the 3s step and on its return from the 3p step it loses 2.1eV. As a result __13__ light is __14__. A diamond can also be given a slight __13__ color by adding nitrogen. The nitrogen is a/an __15__ impurity, and its extra electron can be freed by a quantum of __16__ light. As a result the __16__ light is __17__ and the diamond is __13__.
A material which gives out light for a few minutes after being exposed to _____18_____ is called a/an __19__ material. This phenomenon is caused by impurities in the material which are called __20__, and is used in TV picture tubes. The color which is __14__ depends on __21__.

    13. (a) red   (b) yellow   (c) fluorescent   (d) blue   (e) orange
    14. (a) transmitted   (b) absorbed   (c) emitted   (d) reflected   (e) removed
    15. (a) acceptor   (b) donor   (c) activator   (d) substitutional   (e) both b and d
    16. (a) red   (b) yellow   (c) green   (d) violet   (e) orange
    17. (a) transmitted   (b) absorbed   (c) emitted   (d) reflected   (e) amplified
    18. (a) red light   (b) ultraviolet light   (c) infrared light   (d) heat

19. (a) fluorescent   (b) incandescent   (c) evanescent   (d) phosphorescent   (e) photonescent
20. (a) activators   (b) relaxors   (c) modifiers   (d) intensifiers   (e) acceptors
21. (a) the type of impurity   (b) the energy band gap of the material   (c) the maker of the TV
    (d) both a and b   (e) both a and c

22–32.   A diamond is solid __22__. Because it is a solid there are now bands of possible energy for the electrons. Between the top two bands there is a large energy step of around __23__, which is greater than the energy of any color of visible light. As a result no electrons can use visible __24__ to jump to the next band and the diamond is __25__; there is no __26__ of light. In some diamonds boron atoms are present as __27__ impurities. These boron atoms have one less electron than the __22__ atom and are therefore __28__ atoms which produce an extra energy level called a(n) __28__ level. An electron from the full band can jump to this level using the energy of __29__ light which is around __30__ eV. As a result the __29__ light is absorbed and the diamond appears __31__. This __31__ color is the color of the __32__ light.

22. (a) boron   (b) silicon   (c) silicon oxide   (d) carbon   (e) silicon carbide
23. (a) 6 eV   (b) 1000 eV   (c) 100 eV   (d) 0.02 eV   (e) 10 eV
24. (a) photons   (b) phonons   (c) protons   (d) positrons   (e) photorons
25. (a) transparent   (b) lustrous   (c) colorless   (d) both a and b   (e) a and c
26. (a) absorption   (b) transmission   (c) reflection   (d) refraction   (e) none of these
27. (a) extrinsic   (b) interstitial   (c) substitutional   (d) both a and b   (e) both a and c
28. (a) colorator   (b) acceptor   (c) receptor   (d) activator   (e) donor
29. (a) red   (b) yellow   (c) blue   (d) green   (e) orange
30. (a) 3   (b) 1.7   (c) 2.1   (d) 2.7   (e) 5.4
31. (a) yellow   (b) orange   (c) blue   (d) pink   (e) colorless
32. (a) absorbed   (b) transmitted   (c) reflected   (d) refracted   (e) emitted

26. ELECTRONS IN SEMICONDUCTORS

Background

The ability of a material to conduct electricity, which is measured by the quantity known as the electrical conductivity, is perhaps the most variable property that materials have. On the low end we have materials which can insulate from very high voltage gradients (so-called 'insulators'), letting no electrons through, and at the high end we have superconductors, materials in which electrons will keep on traveling without impediment. We have already briefly discussed (Page 178) the reasons why materials exhibit quite different electrical conductivities. In this chapter we shall discuss some of the unique properties of silicon, the most commonly used semiconductor, which make it quite useful for a variety of electronic components.

As we saw earlier, metals are conductors because their electrons can take on the energies offered by even as small a voltage source as a 1.5 volt battery. There are energies on the energy ladder to which they can go when they absorb this energy. As a result of this increased energy they can set up a net flow of electrons in the material so that an electrical current flows. We usually refer to them as free electrons. In semiconductors there are no such available energies and something else is needed to lift the electrons up the large step we know as the energy gap between bands.

In the previous chapter we saw that light energies are large enough to do this in many materials, especially in semiconductors, where such events cause the material to have a luster and look somewhat metallic (Page 186). Because of this you never see a bare piece of silicon in your calculator or radio if you open it up. It is encapsulated in something that not only protects it, but also keeps the light out. The silicon 'chips' in electronics have had their conductivity tailored for the purpose they are to be used for, and letting light in will simply turn all these components into good conductors. We would then have short circuits all over the place!

We also know that heat produces an average energy quantum of 0.026 eV (in future we shall round it up to 0.03 eV) at room temperature (Page 180). There are some quanta that are larger than this value, and at any temperature there may be some of these thermal energy quanta that are also large enough to lift electrons across the energy gap. This will be especially true if we increase the temperature to several hundred degrees Celsius.

In a good insulator light does not have enough energy to lift the electrons over the energy gap, and it therefore remains an insulator when exposed to light and is colorless and transparent. However there are other sources of energy quanta, which are certainly large enough to make electrons jump across the gap. Ultra violet light may have enough energy, and x-rays will certainly produce the required jump. As mentioned earlier (Page 181), we can make any material conduct electricity if we expose it to x-rays, or heat it to a high enough temperature.

Tailoring the Properties of Silicon

The silicon we use in our semiconductors is usually not pure, but it contains specific impurities in well determined quantities. First of all we make ultrapure silicon (Page 63) after which we add impurities in carefully measured and controlled amounts. We have seen in our discussion of color (Page 187) that impurities add new energy steps in the gap between the energy bands, and therefore, in order to be able to control things, we want to start with a pure material, which will have none of these extra energy steps, and then add a chosen impurity to produce a step where we want it.

Let's start by assuming that we are going to add an impurity, which has one more electron than silicon. This impurity is what we call a **donor** impurity. It replaces (as a substitutional impurity) a silicon atom in the crystal structure and has one more electron than is necessary to form covalent bonds with the surrounding four silicon atoms. If we can find such an impurity, which gives a new donor energy level close to the empty energy band, a thermal energy quantum may be able to give the extra electron sufficient energy to jump into the empty band. We now have a conducting free electron.

Every impurity atom we add contributes one free electron, so the larger the amount of impurity atoms the greater the number of free electrons and the greater the conductivity. In this way we can control the conductivity of the material. At room temperature we would need a donor level about 0.03 eV below the empty band, as shown in the following energy band diagram.

Similarly, we may add an atom (**acceptor** impurity), which has one fewer electron than the silicon and provides an acceptor level about 0.03 eV above the full energy band, as shown in the following diagram. An electron from the full band can then jump to this new level using the thermal energy quantum, leaving a space in the previously full band. Electrons in this band can now move around using this space, much in the same way that atoms can move around in crystals using atom vacancies. We call this space an **electron hole**. We shall discuss the electron hole in more detail later.

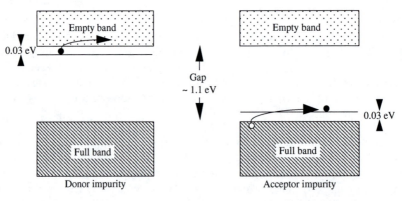

Diagrams showing the impurity energy levels needed in silicon in order that
average thermal energy quanta at room temperature can move electrons.

The impurities that produce the energy levels we desire must have electrons whose energies are very similar to those of the electrons in silicon. It makes good sense that these should be the elements that are adjacent to silicon in the periodic table (Page 7). Let's look at it. Here is the section of the table of the elements that is relevant.

B	C	N
Al	Si	P
Ga	Ge	As
3 outer electrons	4 outer electrons	5 outer electrons

It turns out that boron, aluminum and gallium all give acceptor impurity levels about 0.05 eV above the full energy band, and nitrogen, phosphorus and arsenic all give donor impurity levels about 0.04 eV below the empty energy band. In other words, just about what we were looking for.

N- and P-Type Silicon

If we add phosphorus to silicon, we are adding an element, which is almost the same size and has just one extra electron. It sits in the silicon lattice as shown in the following diagram.

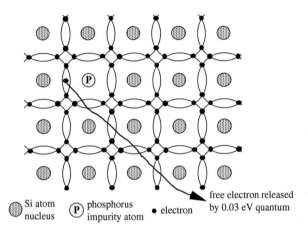

Diagram of the electron structure of n-type silicon. It takes only 0.03 eV to release the extra electron from the phosphorus atom. It is then a free electron.

Note that this is a simple two-dimensional representation of the three-dimensional crystal structure of silicon. In the diagram, the four surrounding silicon atoms are shown in a plane whereas in reality they are situated on the corners of a tetrahedron. Four of the five outer electrons of the phosphorus are used to form covalent bonds, just as the silicon atom would. The extra (fifth) electron hangs around the phosphorus atom because this atom has a larger positive charge on its nucleus than does a silicon atom and therefore has a slightly larger attraction for this extra electron. (Remember that the individual atom is neutral because the number of positive charges on the nucleus is equal to the number of negatively charged electrons that orbit around it.) However a thermal energy quantum gives this electron enough energy to pull itself away from the attraction of the phosphorus and become a free electron. This is the true physical picture of what is happening inside the material. From the energy ladder, or band energy diagram we have used, which is simply a model for the possible energies of the electrons in the material, the thermal energy quantum is enough to lift the electron up to the empty energy band. The impurity atom has **donated** this extra electron to the crystal.

If we put an aluminum atom in place of a silicon atom we have one electron too few to complete the covalent bonds with the surrounding four silicon atoms and the resulting situation is illustrated on the next page.

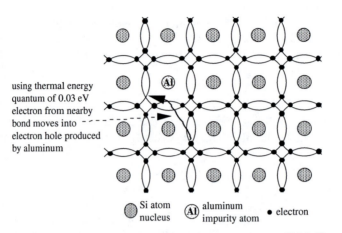

using thermal energy quantum of 0.03 eV electron from nearby bond moves into electron hole produced by aluminum

Si atom nucleus   Al aluminum impurity atom   • electron

Diagram of the electron structure of p-type silicon. Using a thermal energy quantum of 0.03 eV, an electron from one of a nearby silicon's covalent bonds can move into the electron hole provided by the aluminum impurity atom.

One of the bonds of the silicon atoms to the aluminum is now missing an electron, which can be thought of as something like an electron vacancy. It is just like a missing atom in a crystal in some respects, but it is a missing electron in a bond. Similarly, just as a missing atom (vacancy) allows atoms to move around by jumping into the vacancy, the missing electron allows electrons to move around by moving into this electron vacancy. Naturally we have a term for this electron vacancy. We call it an **electron hole,** or often just a 'hole'. Be careful to note the scientific jargon. A hole is a missing electron in a bond; a vacancy is a missing atom in a crystal.

The energy provided by a thermal energy quantum gives a nearby electron enough energy to jump into this hole, leaving another hole where it came from. An electron from the next atom can then move into this new hole, etc. In other words, the aluminum atom in the above diagram **accepts** an electron from an adjacent silicon atom and the chain of electron motion is started. Here again we have just described what is really going on in the material. In terms of our energy ladder model an electron moves from the full band into the acceptor level leaving a **hole** in the band. An electron on a lower step in that band can then use electrical energy to move into the hole. Remember that for electrons to move they must be in an unfilled band. In this case there is only one electron missing from the band, but it is enough to allow some movement. However, the more impurity atoms there are, the more holes there are for electron movement.

Before going any further we should repeat something we mentioned earlier. A **hole** is a missing electron in a bond. It allows electrons to move by going from one bond to a hole in an adjacent bond. In the same way a **vacancy** allows atoms to move by moving from one atom position in the crystal structure to an adjacent vacant atom position. In other words, it is not just one electron that is moving, but it is the cooperative motion of a large number of electrons, all shuffling over to the next bond that produces the net electron flow.

Where this vacancy-movement picture breaks down is that, in fact, the resulting holes do not really belong to a given atom or bond at all, but to the crystal at large. In the same way that donated electrons (donor doping) are "free electrons" able to migrate through the crystal at will (or in response to a voltage), the holes resulting from acceptor doping are "free holes" similarly able to migrate through the crystal at will.

So in summary, silicon doped with an impurity having an extra electron (i.e., five valence electrons) is called an **n**-type semiconductor. The impurity do**n**ates an extra electron to the crystal. Silicon doped with an impurity having one less electron is called a **p**-type semiconductor. The impurity acce**p**ts an electron from an adjacent silicon atom, thereby producing an extra electron hole in the crystal. [Note that P (phosphorus) creates an n-type material; things can get very confusing!]

We should note in conclusion that at high temperatures, thermal energy quanta are large enough to give the electrons sufficient energy to jump across the whole gap. Also at very low temperatures the thermal energy quanta will not be sufficient even to move electrons as we have just described. This sets limits on the temperatures at which we can use these silicon semiconductor devices. Remember that at high enough temperatures all materials become conductors.

In the next chapter we discuss various semiconductor devices relying on the motion and interaction of electrons and electron holes. These devices have revolutionized our lives since the development of the transistor in 1947.

27. SEMICONDUCTOR DEVICES

Have you ever wondered how devices like solar cells and transistors work? Now that we have a working knowledge of how n-type and p-type semiconductors are obtained, we can begin to put these together into useful devices. As we will see, the action takes place largely at the **"junctions"** between the two kinds of semiconductors.

Semiconductor Diodes

The following diagram represents an interface between a p-type semiconductor on the left and an n-type semiconductor on the right. Nothing much happens because the circuit connected to the device has its switch in the open position.

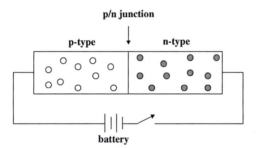

A semiconductor p–n junction with no current flowing.

Now let's close the switch and see what happens. As shown in the following diagram, electrons begin to flow to the right and into the n-type semiconductor; electrons must therefore flow in the semiconductor from right to left toward the p/n junction. At the same time, the opposite (positive) terminal of the battery repels electron holes, which therefore flow from the left to the right, i.e., toward the junction. At the junction electrons from the right can jump into holes approaching from the left. They recombine in the "recombination zone," allowing current to flow through the device. This condition is referred to as "forward bias."

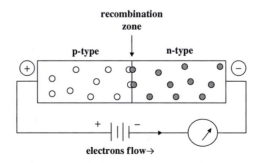

A semiconductor p–n junction under forward bias.

But now consider what happens when we reverse the polarity of the battery, with the negative terminal on the left and the positive terminal on the right. This time the electrons in the n-type semiconductor on the right are attracted away from the junction. Similarly, the electron holes in the p-type semiconductor on the left are attracted away from the junction. Since there is no transfer of charge at the interface, the two types of carriers simply build up at the ends and little or no current flows through the device. This condition is what is referred to as "reverse bias."

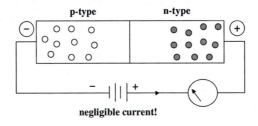

A semiconductor p–n junction under reverse bias.

The device we have just constructed is called a semiconductor **diode**. You may not know it, but you use diodes all the time. They are essential components in the AC-to-DC converters for everything from laptop computers to digital music players to digital cameras, etc. These are sometimes referred to as "wall warts," which is a pretty accurate description for the small boxes we plug into AC outlets on our walls. Inside those boxes are the all-important diodes that convert "alternating current" (AC), which comes out of the wall (and would actually harm semiconductor-based devices like transistors!) into the "direct current" (DC) that our devices really need a process known as **rectification**, AC-to-DC converters are often referred to as battery-eliminators. By only allowing current to flow in one direction (forward bias), a diode cuts off any current in the opposite direction (reverse bias). In this way, an AC voltage, which cycles in both directions (forward and reverse) is transformed into a DC voltage (forward direction only). Of course, other components smooth out the resulting bumpy DC voltage, so it behaves like a battery in output.

Light-Emitting Diodes and Lasers

There is another type of semiconductor junction you have probably used, but did not know it was a semiconductor junction. Let's again consider forward bias across a junction between two semiconductors, as shown on the next page. This time we have included the band diagrams for the two materials—p-type on the left and n-type on the right. If we chose the right combination of semiconductors, the recombination of electrons and holes in the recombination zone can lead to the production of light. The light energy produced is precisely the drop in energy from the n-type side to the p-type side, i.e., essentially the "band gap" of the semiconductor employed. The resulting device is called a semiconductor **light-emitting diode** (it is a diode after all!) or LED.

Now, as we learned previously, silicon has a band gap of around 1.1 eV, which is smaller than the visible spectrum (1.7–3.1 eV). What we need are semiconductors with band gaps in the visible range. Two examples are gallium arsenide (GaAs), with a red emission (2.0 eV) and gallium nitride (GaN), with a blue emission (2.9 eV). You have probably seen red and blue light emitting diodes on the dashboard of your automobile, or on your digital music system, or even on your key chain.

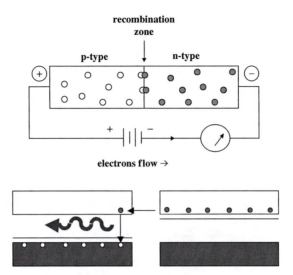

Schematic and band diagram of a light-emitting diode.

You may have also used a **laser** pointer to make a computer presentation in one of your classes. Or perhaps your professor uses one during lecture. The heart of a laser pointer is a semiconductor laser. This differs only slightly from a semiconductor light-emitting diode. In a semiconductor laser, light is produced just as we described—under forward bias, electrons and holes migrate to the p-n junction and recombine, with the production of band-gap energy light. But whereas this light is "diffuse" in an LED (goes in all directions), the light in a semiconductor laser is contained in a narrow chamber, bouncing back and forth between two mirror-smooth ends of the laser. As the light bounces back and forth, it gets in resonance with the light being emitted from other electron-hole pairs recombining. Resonance means that all the peaks and troughs of their waveforms line up; they get "in step." The resulting beam is described as "coherent" and eventually gets strong enough to emerge from the laser as a powerful, narrow beam of monochromatic (a single wavelength or color) light.

You may not realize it, but there are semiconductor lasers in your CD and DVD players, and also in the CD/DVD drives of computers. First, semiconductor lasers can be used to write digital information in the surface of laser disks, by producing "pits" or otherwise altered "dots" along surface tracks on the disks. These correspond to the "1s" (pits) and "0s" (no pits) of digital information. (This process is often referred to as "burning.") Later, when you want to listen to music, or watch a movie, or retrieve a computer file, another laser beam is used to bounce off the same tracks. Then a detector (yet another semiconductor device, beyond the scope of this book) reads the "1s" and "0s" and reconverts the stored information back into music, or video, or information.

Solar Cells

The operation of a **solar cell** is not far removed from the semiconductor diode-based devices described above. In fact, one can think of a solar cell as a light-emitting diode operating in reverse, as shown on the following page. Whereas an LED involves using an applied voltage to send electrons and holes toward the junction, where they combine to produce visible light, a solar cell involves the reverse process. First, light is captured at the p-n junction, with the consequent production of **electron-hole pairs**. These pairs are then separated, the electrons moving to the right (in the n-type semiconductor) and the holes moving to the left (in the p-type semiconductor). As a result, a voltage and current are produced, which can do useful work.

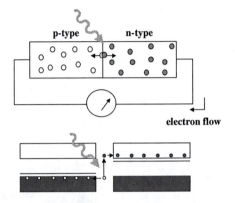

Schematic and band diagram of a solar cell.

It may not be immediately obvious why the electrons and holes from the electron-hole pairs should move away from each other at all, but rather simply move back to the p-n junction and annihilate one another. The following diagram will explain what happens. At the boundary where the two types of semiconductor meet, and before any light shines on the cell, some of the free electrons from the n-type side cross over and fill the holes just across the junction on the p-type side. As a result, there is a thin layer on either side of the physical junction where there are no electrons in the n-type material and no holes in the p-type material.

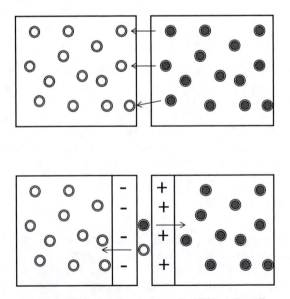

Diagrams illustrating the working of a silicon solar cell.

Now we need to remember that before all this, both original pieces of semiconductor (n-type and p-type) were electrically neutral. In the n-type material, the extra electrons balance the *higher* positive charge on the nucleus of the donor dopant atoms (e.g., phosphorus) whereas in the p-type material the extra holes balance the *lower* positive charge on the nucleus of the acceptor dopant atoms (e.g. aluminum). When the two semiconductors make contact, the electrons which come from the n-type side leave behind a layer that is *positively* charged, and the holes that are eliminated in the adjacent p-type side (by electrons jumping into them) leave this layer negatively charged. This causes what we refer to as an electrostatic field across the junction. It is this field which sends electrons to the right and holes to the left whenever light produces an electron-hole pair at the junction in a solar cell, resulting in an electrical current.

The following diagram shows the cross-section of a solar cell. A very thin n-type layer is on the side that faces the sun and the light that hits it penetrates far enough so that some electron-hole pairs are produced. One reason that early solar cells were very inefficient had to do with light being reflected from the top surface. In order to slove this problem, we place a very thin anti-reflection coating on the top surface. You may have encountered anti-reflection coatings on your eye glasses. This coating is transparent and very thin so there is no loss of light as it passes through. If you look closely at the solar cell in your pocket calculator, you will notice that it appears dull and non-reflective, whereas silicon itself is very shiny and reflective, like a metal (Page 186). To collect the current we place metal contacts on both the top and bottom surfaces of the semiconductor sheet. The contact on the back of the cell can be a simple (opaque) metal, but that on the front surface has to allow the light through. For this reason, it is usually in the form of a very thin metal grid, which you may not notice unless you look closely.

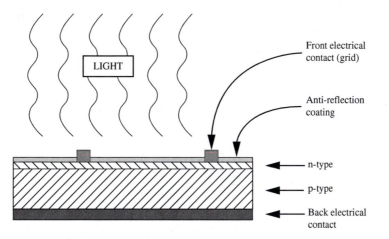

Diagram of cross-section of a solar cell.

Solar cells can be found in many places, from digital watches to electronic calculators. They are often seen along highways to charge batteries that power remote telephone installations or traffic signals. In sunny climates, solar panels are increasingly found in rooftop installations. (Semiconductor-based solar panels, which produce electricity, should not be confused with "passive solar" panels, wherein a fluid picks up heat from the sun and is circulated through the house for heating purposes.) As fossil fuels become increasingly more rare and expensive, we will be forced to turn to so-called "renewable" energy sources. By renewable, we are referring to energy derived from the sun, which each year provides over 1000 times more energy than we can extract in the form of coal and oil (fossil fuels).

What are the prospects for solar cells?

Today only a very small percentage of all power generated by man-made devices comes from solar energy. The main reasons for this are high cost and low efficiency. In the electronics industry we are looking for miniaturization to make our silicon semiconductor parts smaller and smaller. Small pieces of silicon are all we really need for this purpose. However, for the production of large quantities of power using silicon solar cells we want bigger and bigger pieces of silicon in order to intercept more light, produce more electron-hole pairs, and produce a larger current. Ideally these large cells should be single crystals. Polycrystalline silicon contains many grain boundaries, which hinder the flow of electrons and also make many opportunities for the free electrons to jump back into the holes they came from. Naturally, large single crystals are difficult to make and are very expensive. In addition to the high cost, solar cells are relatively inefficient. Although laboratory solar cells have achieved better than 30% efficiency, silicon-based commercial modules are much less efficient, on the order of 10%.

To make large amounts of electric power we must certainly try to improve the efficiency of a cell, but there is no escaping the fact that for commercial power production we require large cell areas. A plant generating a million watts would today occupy about 15 square miles (a rectangular area 5 miles by 3 miles, for example). This seems a large area, but just imagine how much of the earth's surface we disturb to mine coal and dispose of the waste! The solar power station would be clean and quiet with no moving parts requiring service and no need for fuel delivery, etc.

There are some other major problems that we should mention. One is the lack of sunshine in some parts of the world and its unpredictability in others. Where there is little sunshine, the economics of using these solar cells are extremely unattractive. Even in those areas of the world where sunshine is almost guaranteed, solar power is expensive, costing 2 to 3 times that of fossil fuels (oil and coal), even though costs have fallen considerably in the last decade. Another problem is that solar cells produce direct current (DC) and this would need to be converted to alternating current (AC) before being supplied to our homes to operate the appliances we now own. This again costs money and results in loss of power. In the end, environmental issues may drive the move to "renewable" energy sources, since no "greenhouse" gases are produced.

Field-Effect Transistors

To bring this semiconductor junction-based device chapter to a close, let's consider how a **field-effect transistor** works. The following diagram will help. We now have three components and two junctions. At both ends we have p-type regions on the surface of a semiconductor. In between we have an n-type region. Deposited on top are three electrodes. The one on the left is called the "source," since it is the positive electrode and source of holes. The one on the right is called the "drain," since it is the negative electrode and the eventual destination of all our holes. The middle electrode is called the "gate," and that is a pretty good description of what it does. Without any "bias" or voltage on the gate, there is little current from source-to-drain, as shown. The holes pile up at the p-n junction on the left, but nothing happens, because the circuit is "open" (the gate is not connected to the source).

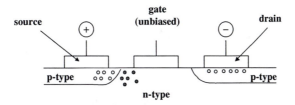

A field-effect transistor with its gate unbiased.

Now consider what happens when the gate is biased negatively. To understand the following diagram, you need to appreciate that even though we have donor-doped the middle region, there are always minority carriers (holes) around. Their population may be infinitesimally small compared to the majority (electron) population, but they are still there. What happens under negative bias is that the majority electrons are repelled and the very few minority holes get attracted to the gate, forming a narrow channel of high hole conductivity from source-to-drain, as shown.

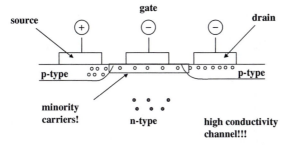

A field-effect transistor with its gate biased negative.

And this is precisely how a transistor functions. A very small change of field applied to the gate results in enormous swings in the source-to-drain current. To put this in terms you can relate to, your digital music player produces signals far too weak for your ear to hear. What we need is a process called "signal amplification." So a power-FET (field-effect transistor) is employed. The weak input signal is applied to the gate. Small swings in this field amount to whopping changes in the source-to-drain currents, which go through the headset or earpieces on/in our ears. Even more powerful FET-based amplifiers can be used to drive room-sized or even coliseum-sized speakers at concerts.

Summary

All these things—rectification, light-emission, lasers, solar cells, and field-effect transistors—arise from semiconductor-based technology and p-n junctions, which you can now understand.

28. CHANGING THE CONDUCTIVITY OF MATERIALS

We have so far talked about the conduction of electricity in materials as being caused by the motion of electrons. These electrons can be thought of as things that carry charge. In scientific jargon we call them **charge carriers**. The more carriers there are, the better the material conducts electricity. In some respects this is a matter of common sense. The more trucks we have, the faster we can shift a large load. There is, of course, another factor involved in our analogy, and that is the speed at which the trucks move. Continuing the analogy, it is not only the speed shown on the speedometer, which is important, but how direct is the route taken. Driving from Pittsburgh to Philadelphia at 65 m.p.h. will get us there in under five hours, but not if we have to go via Buffalo! If we were to take the latter route, our effective speed would be halved.

What we are concerned with in the movement of electrons in a material is this effective speed, something we call the **electron mobility**. In practice the current that flows depends not only on the number of electrons that are available and their speed, but also the ease with which they travel. If there are obstacles to their motion in the material, the electrons have to take a roundabout route and their mobility, and hence the conductivity decreases.

In every conductor and semiconductor, there is a basic speed at which electrons can travel. In silicon this is over two thousand miles per hour. We are used to using copper wire for conducting electricity in houses. Laboratory measurements tell us that each copper atom only provides approximately one electron for conduction. Other metals may provide more electrons, but have a lower conductivity because the electrons do not travel as quickly in the atom arrangement of that metal.

In addition to this basic speed, the mobility depends on the number of obstacles to the electron's motion. A pure metal is almost always crystalline (Page 53). In this ordered atomic arrangement there are nice clear paths between the atoms on which the electrons can move. Anything that disrupts this order will interrupt the electron flow and decrease its mobility, thus lowering the conductivity.

Conductivity in Metals

There are several ways in which we can decrease the mobility of electrons in a metal, all of which involve slightly moving the atoms out of their normal ordered positions. The electrons then bump into these displaced atoms as they pass through the material and are scattered from their straight paths. The voltage is still pushing the electrons in the same direction, but they are forced to take a roundabout path through the material. Here are the most common ways we affect the electrical conduction of a metal:

1. **Heating** the material causes the atoms in the solid to vibrate (see diagram on Page 51) and this makes the electron's path through the crystal more difficult. The atoms move into the clear paths and deflect the electrons as they attempt to move through the crystal. For this reason, metals become worse conductors when they are heated and better conductors when cooled.

2. **Bending and deforming** a metal produces dislocations. We've seen (Page 56) that these dislocations introduce distortions in their neighborhood and these too disturb electron motion. The effect is not great, but the conductivity drops slightly when we work harden a metal.

3. **Impurity atoms** also produce distortions in their surroundings (Page 62). This is a very effective way of reducing electrical conductivity. This is why the copper used for the first transatlantic telegraph cable had only ten percent of the conductivity of pure copper.

4. **Smaller crystals** can be produced by different processing methods (see for example the HSLA steels—Chapter 13). This introduces many more grain boundaries into the metal and these too disrupt the electron flow and thus reduce conductivity. The crystal on the other side of the boundary has a different orientation and the straight electron path in one crystal does not line up with that of the second (see figure on Page 96).

Of these four methods, the greatest effect is produced by impurity atoms, and these are easily added to the metal when it is molten. We already mentioned some of these effects in talking about thermal conductivity (Page 131). Remember that in metals the electrons are responsible for carrying both heat and electricity, so we can expect a decrease in thermal conduction to be accompanied by a decrease in electrical conduction.

The concept is amazingly simple. Electricity is carried by electrons, and the fewer obstructions to their movement in the crystals the better the conductivity. One would therefore expect conductivity in amorphous metals to be very poor, and it is.

Another way of looking at this property of metals is the converse. If we want good conductivity we want a pure material with large crystals. Some wires manufactured for connecting hi-fi components claim to have this feature, thus producing lower distortion to the sound. Some people claim to be able to hear the difference, although many people are skeptical. While the claim for better sound may or may not be true, the claims about conductivity should be valid. It is also worth noting that the connectors at the ends of these wires are often gold plated. This metal does not react with the oxygen in the air so there is no poorly conducting oxide layer on the surface.

Conductivity in Semiconductors

Everything we have said above concerning electron mobility in metals is also true in semiconductors. However, in silicon and other semiconductors we have seen that we can change the number of charge carriers. Impurities may donate free electrons or provide electron holes, which allow electron motion. Heating a semiconductor can also increase the number of electrons and electron holes able to carry the current by providing enough energy to release electrons from the bonds (or jump the energy gap). In most cases this increase in the number of available electrons to carry the electrical charge overwhelms the lower mobility, which also occurs because of the impurity atom deflecting carriers (by itself or by displacing the surrounding atoms) and also by increased atom vibrations, just as in metals. The overall effect is that the conductivity of semiconductors usually increases when they are heated or have impurities added to them.

In computers and some other electronic devices the speed at which they can operate is limited by the speed at which electrons or holes can move through the electronic components. Increased speed of operation therefore needs increased electron mobility. Although, as discussed above, there are some ways we can make sure the electron's mobility is a maximum, it is ultimately determined by the material itself. Electrons and holes simply have different mobilities in different materials.

Research has discovered a material in which the electron and hole mobilities are increased over those in silicon. It is gallium arsenide (GaAs). If you look at the part of the periodic table shown earlier

(Page 194), you will see that gallium and arsenic appear each side of germanium. Gallium has three outer electrons and arsenic has five. They form a compound that is identical in crystal structure to diamond and silicon except that the atoms are alternately arranged, one gallium, one arsenic, etc. They pool their electrons (five and three) to give the eight electrons typical of the four covalent bonds around a silicon atom. The result is a compound with the same properties as silicon except that the electrons travel faster. This technology has been employed in radar detectors (look out for GaAs in advertisements) and may eventually produce much faster computers.

In the future, the fastest computers will use light beams rather than electrons, because nothing travels faster than light. Although there have been some exciting recent developments in this area, the development of optical computers is still many years away.

Another limitation of semiconductors is temperature. At high temperatures the thermal energy quanta become large enough to free electrons from the covalent bonds in which they normally exist (Page 197). The material then becomes a conductor. For a high temperature semiconductor we need a material with a larger energy gap. Such a material is diamond (carbon). Notice that it is immediately above silicon in the periodic table and has the same crystal structure. In the last few years there has been much research on the production of diamond films for electronic components. The diamond is produced by causing a carbon-containing gas such as methane (CH_4—a hydrocarbon) to decompose under special circumstances (CVD again!) so that it forms diamond rather than soot. In the future, diamond and other large gap "semiconductors" will see application in high temperature/high power electronics.

Ultimately, it would be wonderful to reduce all barriers to electron flow to zero, such that there was no limit to the mobility. This sounds like a pipe dream, but this really happens in what are referred to as "**superconductors**." The physics are difficult to understand, but at low enough temperatures certain materials go through a phase transition to a state where electrons can pair up. These so-called "Cooper pairs" set up the lattice of the superconductor such that one electron paves the way for the other. In other words, the electrons can move without any interaction with the lattice. Without any deflection or scattering, a "zero resistance" state can be obtained.

This means that if we apply a voltage to set an electron moving in a loop of wire, it will continue to circle the loop until we do something to make it stop. The temperature at which the electrical resistance of the material suddenly drops to zero is called the **critical temperature** or T_c.

The effect was first discovered in 1911 by a Swedish physicist, H. Onnes, who found that the electrical resistance of mercury suddenly dropped to zero at $-269°C$ (very, very cold). In the following 75 years scientists sought for materials that would be superconductors at higher temperatures but improvements (increases in the critical temperature) were very slow. In 1986 the record critical temperature was still only $-250°C$ for a niobium-germanium compound.

In 1986, came news of a major breakthrough. Scientists working at IBM laboratories in Zurich, Switzerland, discovered that superconductivity was shown by a special type of ceramic at temperatures higher than had previously been possible. Not that the temperatures were high relative to our everyday experience; they were still only $-237°C$. This relatively high critical temperature surprised most scientists because ceramics are usually thought of as insulators. The material was a copper oxide containing some lanthanum and strontium. Some later juggling with the **atomic structure** and combining copper oxide with yttrium and barium produced further increases in the critical temperature to $-183°C$ so that there are now materials for which the T_c is above the temperature of boiling liquid nitrogen ($-196°C$).

This is significant because it allows us to cool the conductor using a rather (comparatively) cheap liquid, liquid nitrogen, which costs about the same as milk.

There are two major problems with these new ceramic superconductors, which we should mention. First, we know that ceramics are usually brittle. Making wires that we can bend like metal wires is obviously a problem. We have already mentioned (Page 141) a way of possibly overcoming this problem by making the crystallites very small (so-called nanophase materials). Another way of overcoming the problem is to make the superconductor in the form of a powder and then pack it into a silver tube. The silver is ductile so the whole may be drawn down into a fine wire. The second problem is that, even below the critical temperature, these materials can lose their superconducting ability if we pass too much current through them. There is a **critical current** above which they revert to their "normal" behavior even below T_c.

Nevertheless, laboratory experiments have shown that some of these ceramic superconductors can carry currents of over 100,000 amps per square centimeter. The significance of this is best seen by stating that a copper wire can carry about 500 amps per square centimeter. Ceramic superconductor wires are now poised for applications ranging from magnetic resonance imaging or MRI—hospitals rely on a version of these with superconducting metal wire-wound magnets for non-invasive tissue/organ imaging—to high power transmission cables over limited spans.

QUESTIONS: Chapters 26–28

1. If an electron needs 2 eV of energy to reach the next energy level it can be attained by giving it _____.
   (a) 2 quanta (packets) of 1 eV   (b) one quantum of 2 eV   (c) one quantum of 3 eV   (d) both b and c
   (e) any of these

2. Which of the following would increase the conductivity of a semiconductor?
   (a) addition of impurities   (b) removal of impurities   (c) heating the material   (d) both a and c
   (e) both b and c

3. All of the following are true of a rectifier except _____.
   (a) an n-type material borders a p-type material   (b) conductivity can occur in both directions
   (c) donor electrons from the n-type material jump into electron holes in the p-type material
   (d) a rectifier has a net neutral charge   (e) all of these are true

4. When we add donor dopant atoms to silicon we change the _____ structure.
   (a) atomic   (b) electronic   (c) crystal   (d) both a and b   (e) both a and c

5. Which of the following is true for both p-type and n-type pieces of silicon?
   (a) conduction occurs through electron hole motion   (b) materials have a net neutral charge
   (c) nitrogen or phosphorous could be used as dopant impurities   (d) both b and c   (e) none of these is true

6. If we add a donor impurity to silicon at room temperature we will produce a(n) _____ .
   (a) vacancy   (b) free electron   (c) electron hole   (d) rectifier   (e) both a and c

7. In order to have a metal with good electrical conduction we want the electrons to have as clear a path through the material as possible. Which of the following is (are) therefore undesirable in a good conductor?
   (a) dislocations   (b) precipitates   (c) impurities   (d) both a and b   (e) all of these

8. Which one of the following has a lower electron energy band which is not completely full of electrons?
   (a) silicon   (b) germanium   (c) gold   (d) diamond   (e) silicon carbide

9. Which one of the following has the largest gap in its energy diagram?
   (a) silicon   (b) germanium   (c) gallium arsenide   (d) diamond   (e) they are all nearly identical

10. In a piece of doped silicon, the donor impurity level is _____ the empty band while the acceptor level is _____ the full band.
    (a) close to, close to   (b) close to, far from   (c) far from, close to   (d) far from, far from
    (e) none of these is correct

11. Gallium arsenide is a _____.
    (a) superconductor   (b) metal   (c) insulator   (d) semiconductor   (e) polymer

12–18. __12__ conduct electricity better as they are cooled because the __13__ increases as the atoms vibrate less and cause less interference with the conduction. As it is being cooled, the __14__ of the metal drops to zero at a certain temperature. At this point, the metal has become a superconductor. Surprisingly, the best superconductors are __15__. If they are to be used as superconductors, __15__ must be made __16__ enough to be made into wires. The way this may be accomplished is by making __15__ with ultrafine grains. These materials are called __17__ materials. Unfortunately, no materials have been discovered which exhibit superconducting properties at __18__.
    12. (a) polymers   (b) semiconductors   (c) glasses   (d) metals   (e) all materials
    13. (a) impurity content   (b) number of vacancies   (c) electron mobility   (d) phonon activity
        (e) electron speed
    14. (a) conductivity   (b) strength   (c) thermal expansion   (d) ductility   (e) resistivity
    15. (a) polymers   (b) ceramics   (c) metals   (d) semiconductors   (e) composites
    16. (a) brittle   (b) strong   (c) ductile   (d) stiff   (e) pure

17. (a) composite   (b) alloy   (c) nanophase   (d) oxide   (e) intermetallic
18. (a) room temperature   (b) low voltages   (c) low light conditions   (d) both a and b
    (e) all of these

19–28. A rectifier uses two different types of ___19___ in the form of a p-n junction. In the p-type material the electrons move ___20___ while in the n-type material they move ___21___. Motion is usually faster in the ___22___ type material. Electrons can only move from the ___23___ type to the ___24___ type because if they try to move in the opposite direction they move away from the ___25___ and ___26___. One way of making faster computers is to make electrons move faster. This happens in a material called ___27___. The fastest computers would use ___28___ to carry the signals rather than electrons.

19. (a) plastic   (b) gallium   (c) alloy   (d) activator   (e) silicon
20. (a) from hole to hole   (b) randomly   (c) freely   (d) at the speed of light
    (e) from nucleus to nucleus
21. (a) from hole to hole   (b) randomly   (c) freely   (d) at the speed of light
    (e) from nucleus to nucleus
22. (a) n   (b) p   (c) normal   (d) junction   (e) none of these
23. (a) n   (b) p   (c) normal   (d) junction   (e) none of these
24. (a) n   (b) p   (c) normal   (d) junction   (e) none of these
25. (a) n-type end   (b) p-type end   (c) impurity atoms   (d) anti-reflective coating
    (e) junction
26. (a) there are no electrons to join up with   (b) there are precipitates in the way   (c) they are scattered
    (d) there are no holes to drop into   (e) they don't fit
27. (a) gallium   (b) germanium   (c) niobium carbide   (d) gallium arsenide   (e) none of these
28. (a) light   (b) heat   (c) neurons   (d) protons   (e) none of these

29–43. Silicon is the most common element in the earth's crust. A silicon atom has ___29___ valence electrons and forms four ___30___ bonds to surrounding atoms which sit on the corners of a ___31___. These units are joined together to form a(n) ___32___ crystal. It takes about ___33___ of energy to free an electron from a ___30___ bond in silicon. This can be easily accomplished by a quantum from ___34___, and when silicon is exposed to ___34___ it is a(n) ___35___, because the silicon now contains ___36___. The atomic number of silicon is 14, which tells us that an atom of silicon contains 14 ___37___ s. When a phosphorus atom, which has an atomic number 15, is added to silicon it is a(n) ___38___ impurity, and because it has an extra ___37___ the silicon ___39___. However, the extra electron provided by the phosphorus can be freed by an energy quantum of ___40___ which can be provided by ___41___. We call silicon which has been doped with phosphorus a(n) ___42___ semiconductor. At really high temperatures silicon-based electronics fail to operate properly because ___43___.

29. (a) 14   (b) 6   (c) 0   (d) 2   (e) 4
30. (a) ionic   (b) covalent   (c) weak   (d) directed   (e) both b and d
31. (a) cube   (b) square   (c) tetragon   (d) tetrahedron   (e) rectangle
32. (a) HCP   (b) FCC   (c) BCC   (d) CCP   (e) both b and d
33. (a) 0.03 eV   (b) 5 eV   (c) 10-23 eV   (d) 1.1 eV   (e) you cannot free an electron in Si
34. (a) thermal energy at room temperature   (b) visible light   (c) normal (120V) electrical voltages
    (d) microwaves   (e) none of these
35. (a) superconductor   (b) electrical insulator   (c) electrical conductor   (d) resistor
    (e) rectifier
36. (a) vacancies   (b) free electrons   (c) electron holes   (d) both a and b   (e) both b and c
37. (a) positron   (b) neutron   (c) electron   (d) proton   (e) both c and d
38. (a) existential   (b) substitutional   (c) interstitial   (d) residential   (e) combinational
39. (a) remains electrically neutral   (b) becomes positively charged   (c) becomes negatively charged
    (d) becomes very reactive   (e) none of these
40. (a) 0.03 eV   (b) 5 eV   (c) 10-23 eV   (d) 1.1 eV   (e) you still cannot free an electron
41. (a) thermal energy at room temperature   (b) visible light   (c) microwaves
    (d) normal (120V) electrical voltages   (e) none of these
42. (a) regular   (b) irregular   (c) p-type   (d) n-type   (e) there is no special name for it
43. (a) electrons find it more difficult to move   (b) impurity atoms evaporate
    (c) electrons begin to be freed from Si-Si bonds   (d) atoms vibrate too much
    (e) atoms form ionic bonds

44. All of the following are true concerning solar cells except _____.
    (a) high cost   (b) low efficiency   (c) large, single crystals of silicon are difficult to produce
    (d) solar cells only produce DC current   (e) silicon is extremely rare

45–57. Solar cells convert light energy into __45__ energy. They basically consist of a thick p-type layer of __46__ with a thin n-type layer on the surface. In the n-type __46__ __47__ energy quanta give electrons on the __48__ level enough energy to jump up to the empty band. At the boundary between the n- and p-type layers some of the electrons from the n-type layer cross over and __49__. The result of this is that there is a thin volume at the boundary where there is/are __50__. This causes a(n) __51__ across the junction because there is a net __52__ charge in the n-type region near the boundary and a net __53__ charge in the p-type region near the boundary. Since __46__ has a band gap of approximately __54__ eV, __55__ light which penetrates the thin n-type layer will produce __56__. The electrons move under the influence of the __51__ thus producing an __57__.

45. (a) thermal   (b) electrical   (c) radioactive   (d) ultraviolet   (e) free
46. (a) silicon   (b) carbon   (c) germanium   (d) phosphorus   (e) nitrogen
47. (a) electrical   (b) free   (c) radioactive   (d) thermal   (e) all of these
48. (a) interstitial   (b) acceptor   (c) donor   (d) valence   (e) full
49. (a) become free electrons   (b) conduct electricity   (c) fill vacancies
    (d) become substitutional impurities   (e) fill electron holes
50. (a) no free electrons   (b) no electron holes   (c) free electrons   (d) both a and b
    (e) both b & c
51. (a) voltage gradient   (b) electrostatic field   (c) magnetic field   (d) electic current
    (e) heat sink
52. (a) positive   (b) negative   (c) neutral
53. (a) positive   (b) negative   (c) neutral
54. (a) 0.03   (b) 1.1   (c) 1.7   (d) 3.1   (e) 7.0
55. (a) red   (b) yellow   (c) green   (d) blue   (e) all of these
56. (a) donor electrons   (b) vacancies   (c) electron-hole pairs   (d) both a and b   (e) all of these
57. (a) voltage gradient   (b) electrostatic field   (c) magnetic field   (d) electic current
    (e) heat sink

58. Which of the following semi-conductor devices does not involve a p-n junction:
    (a) field-effect transistor   (b) solar cell   (c) light-emitting diode   (d) rectifying diode
    (e) none of the above.

Given the choices:
    a. Solar cell
    b. Light-emitting diode
    c. Rectifying diode
    d. Laser diode

59. Which of the above devices involves the conversion of electricity into light?

60. Which of the above devices involves the conversion of light into electricity?

61. Which of the above devices converts AC electricity into DC electricity?

29. THE OPTICAL BEHAVIOR OF MATERIALS

Some fifty years ago, we hardly gave much thought to optical materials. Glass had been used for centuries to make vessels, ornaments and window panes, and more recently we had used them as lenses in cameras, eye glasses, microscopes and other optical instruments, but that was about all. Today we are well aware of the widespread use of optical fibers for telephone and information communications. We may also be aware of optical fibers being used in medical instruments, automobiles, etc. The development of optical fibers used for these applications has required a much greater understanding of the properties of glass and the discovery of ways to produce special high-purity glass materials. We shall therefore devote some time to exploring the science behind this material's development in today's world. We shall specifically consider the manufacture and working of optical fibers for telephone transmission in the following case study. First we need to consider the basis of their operation.

Background

If you were asked what x-rays, gamma rays, light, microwaves, and radio and TV waves had in common you would probably say "nothing". You would be wrong because they are all basically the same thing. They are simply different parts of what we call the **electromagnetic spectrum**. Just as yellow is part of the spectrum of visible light, so is light part of an even larger spectrum. We have already seen (Page 176) that visible light stretches from the low energy red light (1.7 eV) to the high energy blue violet light (3.1 eV). What distinguishes this range of energies is simply that it is what our eyes are able to see. Below these energies are the infrared rays (down to 0.01 eV), microwaves (10^{-4} eV) and radio and TV waves (10^{-8} eV). Above are the ultraviolet rays (up to 100 eV), x-rays (10,000 eV) and gamma rays (10^6 eV). In other words our eyes are only able to see a very small part of this electromagnetic spectrum. (Note that we shouldn't say that they are not sensitive to other parts of the spectrum. Because of their high energies a direct beam of x-rays will destroy your eyes. We are sensitive to them but we just don't see them.) You may never have thought that the microwaves that cook your food and the x-rays that allow doctors to see inside your body are really the same thing as light, but they are. The only difference is the size of the energy quantum associated with them.

What is an Electromagnetic Wave?

What do we mean by an **electromagnetic wave**? The answer is very complex but for our purposes we can simply say that as the wave passes through materials it produces magnetic and electrical disturbances. When you drop a pebble in a still pond you can see the waves spread out as concentric circles from where the pebble hit the water. This is a mechanical disturbance. The pebble hitting the water caused the water molecules to move in this way. We have also talked about a phonon wave (Page 132) where atoms are caused to vibrate by heat. The electromagnetic wave produces small oscillating magnetic and electric forces in the material, and because electrons have a charge and are very lightweight, they are the particles in the material which are most influenced by this wave. You will of course remember that an electric field is what causes electrons to move.

When light enters a transparent material it loses some energy by moving the electrons, or rather the electric and magnetic fields cause them to oscillate. The light therefore slows down. You can imagine the electrons in the material as something the light wave has to push through. You can walk through air with little difficulty. If you try walking under water (with suitable equipment of course!) you find that you cannot go as quickly. Now if you did the same experiment with molasses your progress would be even slower. The same thing happens in materials. The more electrons the light has to push through, the slower it travels.

We often use the phrase "the speed of light"; indeed we may have heard that nothing moves faster than the speed of light. Most people are unaware that light changes its speed when it moves from one material to another. It is this change in its speed that causes light to bend when passing from one material to another. Its velocities in the two media are different.

When a beam of light hits a transparent material some of it is reflected from the surface. We mentioned earlier (Page 203) that we can put a coating on the surface to reduce this reflection, but in normal circumstances a significant amount is reflected. The remainder of the light enters the material and starts to make its way through, albeit at a slower speed and in a different direction. As it passes through the material it may lose some of its intensity by absorption, very often acquiring a color, because some colors (energies) are absorbed more than others (Pages 184–188). Eventually the light passes out of the material as what we call transmitted light. The following diagram illustrates these different phenomena.

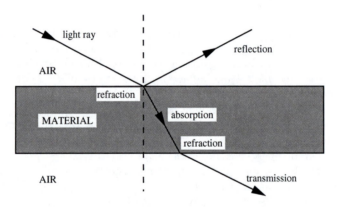

The various interactions of light with materials.

We have already talked about the way light interacts with some materials to produce color (Chapter 25). Some light can be absorbed by the electrons in the solid, lifting them to higher levels on the energy ladder. We have also seen that absorption is often due to impurities in the material. We usually think of window glass as clear, but if we try to look at it through an edge we find it impossible to see anything but a blue-green color. This color is caused by iron impurity in the sand from which the glass is made. It takes only a very small amount of impurity to produce this kind of absorption, in fact it is extremely difficult to eliminate.

As we said earlier, light is a wave and can be simply represented as shown below. The distance between identical points on the wave is the wavelength, . On the following diagram we have drawn vertical lines through the crests of the wave and we shall now use these lines, which are perpendicular to the direction of the wave motion, to represent the wave rather than draw the waves. When such a wave enters a material along a path perpendicular to the surface, as shown in the diagram on the following page, the speed changes but not the angle. The slower wave is shown below by lines which are closer together.

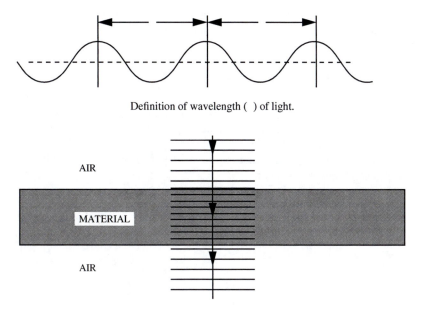

Definition of wavelength ( ) of light.

Light entering a material perpendicular to the surface slows down but is not bent (refracted).

When the light wave is at an oblique angle to the surface, as shown in the following diagram, one end of the wave enters the material before the other so that one end slows down while the other end is still going fast. This is exactly what happens when a marching band turns a corner. One end of the line slows down and the whole line rotates. Note that the light wave bends so that it is closer to the perpendicular to the surface. When it emerges at the bottom face it is bent in the opposite direction so that it is now parallel to the original wave.

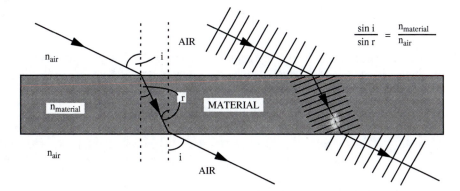

$$\frac{\sin i}{\sin r} = \frac{n_{material}}{n_{air}}$$

Light entering a material at an oblique angle is bent when it enters the material because it is slowed down by the higher electron density. See later text for definition of refractive index, n.

This bending of light is what we call **refraction**. Note that the light ray leaving the material is parallel to the original ray, but is displaced from it. This is what makes things appear to be where they really aren't, for instance if we are looking at an object on the bottom of a pool of water. The amount by which the light is bent, or slowed down, is characterized by a property known as the refractive index (n) of the material which is given by:

$$\text{refractive index (n)} = \frac{\text{velocity of light in a vacuum}}{\text{velocity of light in the material}}$$

This quantity is always greater than one, because light always travels fastest in a vacuum, and its speed is related to the number of electrons in the material, or more exactly the number of electrons in a certain volume of material, something we call the **electron density**. In general, the larger the atoms in the material, the more electrons there are, and the larger the electron density and the refractive index. Some typical values of refractive index are:

air	1.0003
hot air	1.0001
ice	1.33
silica glass	1.45
lead glass	1.65
diamond	2.42

By definition the refractive index of a vacuum is one.

We can also assign a mathematical formula to the refractive index, as shown in the previous figure.

$$\frac{\sin i}{\sin r} = \frac{n_{material}}{n_{air}}$$

Because the refractive index of air is approximately one, we can write $\sin i / \sin r = n_{material}$, which can be rewritten as $\sin i = n_{material} \cdot \sin r$.

The maximum value of the sine of any angle is 1 (angle = 90°) so the maximum value of sin i is 1, when the angle i is equal to 90°, which we know is equal to $n_{material} \cdot \sin r$. When this happens, the emitted beam is traveling parallel to the boundary between the material and the air and

$$\sin r = \frac{1}{n_{material}}$$

This formula tells us the maximum value r can have for there to be a value of i, i.e. for the light to pass through the boundary. The angle r simply cannot be any greater than this value if the light is to escape from the material.

Some of you are not mathematical so don't worry if the previous two paragraphs are not readily understandable. We shall consider the result we are aiming at a little differently later.

What happens if the angle r is greater than this **critical angle**? The fact is that the beam is reflected back into the material by the boundary. We call this effect **total internal reflection**. All three words are important. It is reflection that happens inside the material as the light ray is trying to leave, and it is 100% (**total**). We earlier mentioned that some partial reflection occurs at the surface when light enters a material. However the reflection we are talking about here is 100% (**total**). It is this fact, which becomes very important in designing optical fibers. We shall mention the partial reflection of the light at the top surface at the end of this section.

Let us look at this situation in another way. When the light goes into the less dense material (air) it is bent away from the perpendicular to the boundary as shown in the following diagram. As we increase the angle r, the angle i also increases. Four different situations (1–4) are shown. For ray 3 the emerging beam is just grazing the surface. Now if we increase the angle further (beam 4) the beam cannot emerge from the material and is totally reflected inside the material. The angle for beam 3 is the **critical angle**. Any light rays approaching the boundary with angles greater than this angle (measured from the perpendicular to the surface as shown) will be totally internally reflected. Notice that in this case the angles between the surface and both the reflected and incident rays are equal.

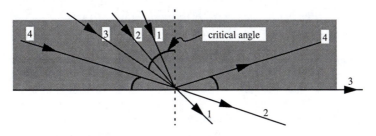

Illustration of what is meant by the critical angle.

For light going from silica glass (n = 1.45) into air (n = 1.0) this critical angle is just over 43°. When going from ice to air the critical angle is 48°. Notice that for total internal reflection to occur the light must be traveling in the material with the higher refractive index (slower speed) and be trying to enter a material with a lower refractive index (higher speed). In this general case the critical angle is given by

$$\sin r = \frac{n_{material1}}{n_{material2}}$$

The most common optical material is simple silica glass (SiO_2). By choosing impurities that do not add extra levels within the band gap, thereby avoiding the absorption of visible light, we can change the refractive index of the glass without affecting the color. These impurities will change the number of electrons in the material, i.e., they will change the electron density, and hence the refractive index. In the table on page 218 we refered to lead glass, which is more commonly known as lead crystal, or simply "crystal." It is not crystalline (it has no crystal structure) but is an amorphous glass whose refractive index has been increased by additions of lead. This increases the bending of the light and also increases the reflection of light from the surface of the glass. Its refractive index is nowhere near that of diamond but it is significantly larger than that of regular silica glass.

Improvements in camera lenses have resulted from the formulation of new glasses, but the major development in glass affecting us has to do with optical fiber communication. Because of the phenomenon of total internal reflection, a light beam can be sent down an optical fiber with almost no absorption and will continue to pass down the fiber for large distances as long as it never meets the surface at an angle smaller than the critical angle. You must remember that we always measure the angle from the perpendicular to the surface. The material around the fiber must have a smaller refractive index than the fiber. It too can be glass.

In a typical fiber arrangement, shown in the following figure, the core is made of a glass with a high refractive index (say 1.6) and is surrounded by a glass with lower refractive index (say 1.55). This gives a critical angle of around 75° so that the light will stay in the fiber so long as it never hits the surface at an angle greater than 15°. We shall discuss how we ensure this condition is satisfied in the next chapter.

Cladding glass: n = 1.55

less than 15°

Core glass: n = 1.6

Illustration of total internal reflection in an optical fiber.

*Note carefully that the angle drawn on the figure is **not** the critical angle. You have to be careful whether you are measuring angles from the surface, or from the perpendicular to the surface. Remember that the critical angle is defined as the angle from the perpendicular.*

The development of suitable glasses with almost zero absorption for optical fibers was a major research problem. Some details of these materials and their advantages will be given in the case study in the following chapter.

Notice that the glass fiber is surrounded with another glass. Before leaving the subject we should mention why this cladding is necessary. We have said that the light never escapes from the fiber unless it hits the surface at an angle to the normal less than the critical angle. The core glass (fiber) is surrounded by a cladding glass to protect the fiber from scratching. A scratch would allow the light to escape as shown below. Indeed if you can see the light passing down the fiber it is because it is escaping through surface imperfections. It may be difficult to imagine that if a bare optical fiber cable carrying all sorts of light signals, even high power laser light, were suspended across a totally dark room, you could sit in that room and see nothing. To see the light, some has to escape and reach your eyes. The major point about optical fibers is that they are designed to not allow any light to escape, not even the slightest amount.

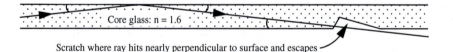

Core glass: n = 1.6

Scratch where ray hits nearly perpendicular to surface and escapes

A scratch on the surface of a fiber can allow the light to escape.

There is one illustration of this phenomenon of total internal reflection with which we are all familiar. When driving along a straight road in hot weather we often see what appears to be a pool of water in the distance, something we call a mirage. The black road becomes very hot from the sun's rays and the air layer immediately above the surface is heated by the road so that its refractive index is decreased. Sunlight coming onto the road therefore passes from a higher to a lower refractive index, and total internal reflection is possible. Using the values given in the table on Page 218 we can calculate the critical angle to be around 89°. If we look down the road a long way this angle is exceeded. Near to us the reflection angle is much lower. If our eye is four feet above the road surface the mirage will be seen about 75 to 100 yards in the distance and of course it always stays that far away.

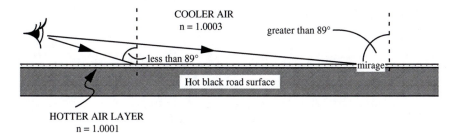

Production of a mirage in the distance on a hot road.

Reflection of Light From the Surface of a Transparent Material

While this subject is not really relevant to our discussion, we have mentioned it, and should perhaps explain it a little more. If a transparent material has a refractive index n, the amount of light (R) reflected from its surface as the light enters it is given by the following formula:

$$R = \frac{(n-1)^2}{(n+1)^2} \times 100\%$$

Using this formula and the values for refractive index given on page 218 you can calculate the amounts of light reflected from the surfaces of these materials. You will find that only 2% is reflected from ice, while 6% is reflected from lead glass ('crystal') and over 17% from diamond. It is this high reflection combined with strong refraction that makes diamond an attractive, and hence valuable gemstone.

30. CASE STUDY: OPTICAL FIBERS FOR TELECOMMUNICATIONS

Background

Advertising has done its best to convince us of the superiority of optical fibers for the transmission of telephone conversations. The first transatlantic fiber optic telephone cable began operation in late 1988 and with it has come increased clarity and the loss of other people's conversations audible in the background. Let's try to understand something of the way this new materials development uses some of the scientific principles we have already considered and puts them into practice.

First we should explain that any sound can be put into a digital code. The way this is done need not concern us here, but it is a technique that is used in all digital recording. During recording, the sound is sampled many times in a second and at each time the signal picked up is translated into a number that is expressed in a binary form. This simply means that the number uses only the digits 0 and 1, rather than the ten digits we normally use for counting. This binary number can then be expressed as a series of pulses transmitted very rapidly at fixed intervals, maybe a ten thousandth of a second apart. If a pulse is transmitted we have the digit 1, and if no pulse is transmitted we have the digit 0. On a compact disc these digitally coded sounds are in the form of very small pits on the surface. In a CD player a very finely focused beam of light from a laser hits the surface and is reflected from these pits. The pattern of pits is thus translated into a pattern of reflected light pulses, which are then somehow converted back to reproduce the original sound. The details of these translation mechanisms are not of importance here. We are here interested in how the sound of our voice can be transmitted thousands of miles through an optical fiber after it has been turned into a series of light pulses.

What is a Typical Optical Fiber Like?

We have already seen (Page 220) that our optical fiber must satisfy two important criteria. First it must contain the light, i.e., it must be designed to produce total internal reflection and have no defects at the surface to let the light out. Second it must allow the light to pass through large distances without significant loss of intensity, i.e., there must be almost no absorption of the light in the glass. Sometimes this light loss is called **attenuation**. We therefore say that the glass must have a low attenuation factor.

A typical optical fiber has three components as shown in the following diagram. First there is an inner core of glass with a relatively high refractive index. This is the fiber along which the light travels. This fiber is surrounded by a sheath of glass with a lower refractive index. This arrangement satisfies the criterion that light traveling in the core is in the higher refractive index material, while the outer glass layer ensures a smooth surface and serves to protect the surface of the core from scratches and other surface imperfections. An outer polymer coating adds strength and protects the whole fiber from damage. The entire three-layer unit has a diameter of about a quarter of a millimeter (250 microns).

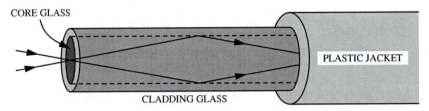

Diagram illustrating the three layers in an optical fiber.

You will see from the next diagram that the light ray must enter the fiber within a certain acceptance angle. Light rays that enter the fiber at greater angles will strike the surface of the fiber at an angle that allows them to cross the boundary between the two glass layers and thus exit the fiber.

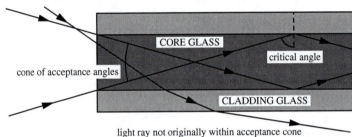

Illustration of how a light ray entering the fiber at an angle outside the acceptance cone leaves the core when it reaches the cladding glass.

How do we Make a Fiber?

Our earlier discussions of the interactions of light with materials have shown that impurities can produce light absorption (Page 187). A pane of window glass appears very clear when in the window, but try looking through it from the edge! You will be lucky to see anything even through a piece an inch thick. The reason for this is the impurities in the glass. The silica sand from which glass is made contains some iron, not much, but enough to cause considerable light adsorption and give the glass a blue-green color. The secret to producing an optical fiber that will allow light to be sent over long distances with very little absorption is therefore to get the impurities out. However this is easier said than done.

Solids are notoriously difficult to purify (Page 63) and getting the iron and other metallic impurities out of silica sand is no exception. To get what we need we take a rather roundabout way. Compounds of metals and the halides (chlorine, bromine and iodine) often have very low melting and boiling points (we mentioned this on Pages 64 and 176) and these temperatures differ according to the compound. Thus, if we react our impure sand with chlorine to produce iron chloride and silicon chloride we have two different compounds, which have different boiling points. If we now heat this mixture, the iron chloride will boil at a different temperature than the silicon chloride and we can collect and condense the vapors separately. This process is the same we mentioned in the production of pure chromium (Page 64) except that here we are using chlorine rather than iodine, and is essentially the same as used in the distillation of whiskey and other alcoholic spirits. In the same way, in any cooking with wine or spirits there is almost no alcohol in the finished sauce, etc., because the alcohol evaporates at a lower temperature than the water.

To make the super-pure glass required for optical fibers, we therefore first change the silicon oxide into silicon chloride, purify it as a gas and then change it back into the oxide by reacting it with oxygen. With this background we can understand one of the common manufacturing methods for optical fibers. Note that the cladding glass is not responsible for the light transmission so its purity is not critical. It simply serves to provide a smooth defect-free surface for the fiber that is carrying the light.

The manufacturing technique involves a process known as chemical vapor deposition (CVD, Page 64). A mixture of the ultrapure silicon chloride ($SiCl_4$) vapor and oxygen (O_2) is heated to a temperature where they react to form chlorine and silicon oxide (SiO_2), the basic component of glass. Of course this chlorine can be collected and used to form more $SiCl_4$ by reaction with more of the impure sand, so it is recycled and not released into the atmosphere.

A tube of regular silica glass is held in a piece of equipment similar to a lathe so that it can be rotated. Around the tube there is a furnace, or oxygen-hydrogen torch, which encircles the tube and slowly moves back and forth along its length (see Page 226). The pure $SiCl_4$ and O_2 flow into the tube and react to form SiO_2 where the tube is being heated by the flame, and the particles of silica glass which are formed are deposited on the tube walls. The rotating tube and the moving furnace all help to give a coating of uniform thickness in the tube.

At this stage you may be asking how the deposited glass has a higher refractive index than the silica tube in which it is formed. The answer is quite simple. Remember that the refractive index is a measure of the slowing of the light's speed in the material. The higher the refractive index of a material, the more it slows the motion of the light as it passes through. This slowing is caused by the electrons in the material. The more electrons it has to pass through, the slower the light travels.

We can make the light move more slowly, i.e., increase the refractive index, by replacing some of the silicon atoms with atoms having more electrons, i.e., with a higher atomic number. However we must ensure that these impurity atoms do not cause any absorption of the light we wish to transmit. A suitable impurity atom is germanium, which you may remember has the same number of *outer* electrons as does silicon, but has a *total* of eighteen more electrons (32 versus 14). Remember that it is also a semiconductor and has the same crystal structure as silicon. This large increase in the number of electrons produces a significant increase in the refractive index when only a small amount of this germanium impurity is added.

Now the question is how we can add small amounts of ultra pure germanium to our glass. The answer is again quite simple. We produce pure germanium chloride ($GeCl_4$) in the same way that we produce the pure silicon chloride and mix a small amount into the gas stream of $SiCl_4$ and O_2. This is sometimes called the **dopant** for the glass, just as we refer to impurities in semiconductors as dopants. Notice that in both cases the word refers to impurities we have *intentionally* added to change the atomic structure of the material and hence its properties.

As the furnace moves up and down the tube it not only causes more glass droplets to be deposited on the tube walls, but the heat also sinters, or fuses, the deposited particles of glass together so that they form a solid mass.

The next stage of the process is to increase the temperature so that the glass softens, and the tube collapses to form a solid rod consisting of a core of higher refractive index glass and a surrounding sheath (the original silica glass tube) of lower refractive index glass. The rod is then placed in a high temperature furnace where it is softened and drawn out into a thin fiber in much the same way as one pulls taffy (see Page 227). A thin protective plastic layer is then placed on the surface to complete the manufacturing process.

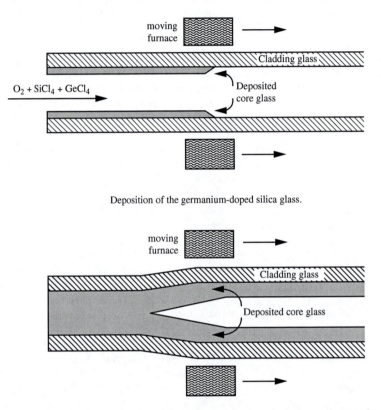

Deposition of the germanium-doped silica glass.

Furnace made hotter to soften the glass so that the original tube and the deposited glass collapse to form a solid body, which can be drawn into a fiber.

The breakthrough in optical fiber manufacture has been the development of methods for producing pure glass. In 1970 only 1% of the light entering a one kilometer length of the best available optical fiber was transmitted to the other end. Today that figure is better than 95%. Quite a difference! The following diagram illustrates the dramatic improvements in transmission in optical fibers from 1968 to 1980. The tremendous increase in the early 1970's was due to the manufacturing techniques we have outlined above.

Of course even these improvements do not allow light in an optical fiber to cross the Atlantic Ocean unaided. This means that the transatlantic cable has to have light amplifiers built in at intervals along its length. There are also problems with splicing, or joining, such fine glass fibers. However these subjects are beyond this discussion.

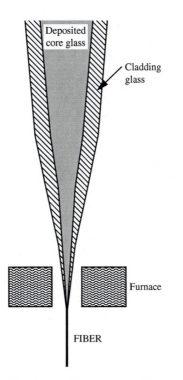

Glass being pulled to produce fiber.

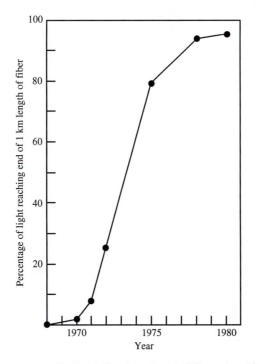

Improvement of transmission through optical fibers since 1968.

You may be thinking that this method of producing the core glass for a fiber goes to unnecessary extremes to get rid of impurities. It is most important to realize that even very small amounts of impurity produce significant absorption. Using the criterion which we mentioned in the previous paragraph, the following concentrations of impurity atoms (given as the numbers of atoms per *billion*) would only allow 1% of the light to reach the end of a one kilometer length of fiber: cobalt, 2; iron, 20; copper, 50.

Just think how much purer than this we need the glass to be in order to be able to get 95% of the light through this 1km length!

Fibers used for telephonic transmission have a core diameter of only about 10 microns, a thousandth of a centimeter. Why do we make the fibers so thin? There are two important answers. The first is that when we bend a fiber, the outside stretches and therefore sees a tensile stress. The thicker the fiber, the greater the stress and the greater the chance of fracture. Thin fibers are therefore more flexible. The second is that, if the fiber is thin, there is less chance of the light hitting the fiber wall at an angle less than the critical angle, and therefore escaping. The following diagram show a light ray entering three fibers of different thicknesses at the same angle, and the paths that these rays take through the fibers. In the thick fiber the light ray makes only one reflection in the fiber and hits the fiber wall at a smaller angle (measured from the perpendicular to the surface) than any angle of incidence in the medium thickness fiber. In the thinnest fiber the angles of incidence are the largest. As a result of these two factors really thin fibers can be bent more and have less change of losing the light than do thicker fibers.

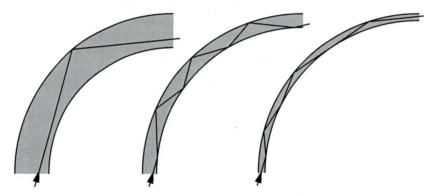

Three parallel light rays entering different thickness optical fibers. In the thinnest fiber there is less change of the angle of incidence being smaller than the critical angle.

The Advantages of Optical Fibers

What are some of the advantages of optical fibers over copper wires for telephone transmission? The two major ones are clarity of signal and the ability to carry many conversations in one fiber at the same time. In addition there are factors of weight and volume. Optical fibers are obviously much thinner than a copper wire and they have a much lower density. This means that the Atlantic Ocean could be crossed with two shiploads of optical fiber as opposed to five of copper wire, which would not be able to carry as nearly as many conversations.

When an electrical current travels along a copper wire it produces a magnetic field outside and around the wire. This magnetic field in turn causes a small current to flow in an adjacent wire, which is in the influence of this magnetic field. A signal is **induced** into the second wire, which duplicates the signal in the first wire although at a much lower intensity. This is why one often heard a second conversation on the same line when making a telephone call. For obvious reasons the phenomenon is known as **crosstalk**. One conversation has crossed over to an adjacent line. With light waves in an optical fiber there is no such phenomenon. With total internal reflection, light does not in any way cross over to an adjacent fiber, with the consequence of a better and clearer signal.

Another benefit related to the absence of crosstalk is the security of conversations carried on optical fibers. Telephone lines are tapped using the same phenomenon as that causing crosstalk. A small coil of wire placed around the wire carrying the conversation will pick up the conversation because an identical signal is induced in the coil. With an optical fiber the only way to tap the light is to break into the fiber and allow some light to escape, a loss that would immediately be detected. We should, however, note that the optical fibers only connect the main transmitting and receiving stations, and that connections between them and our homes and businesses are still primarily by copper wires. It will only be when the total connection is by fiber optics that we can be certain that nobody is listening.

To understand the second major advantage of being able to carry many more conversations, one has to remember that the audio signal is transmitted along the optical fiber by a series of pulses (light flashes). These pulses need only be around a ten thousandth of a second (10^{-4} sec) apart. You may think that this means the pulses are very close together. True, but when you think that each pulse need only be around 10^{-8} seconds in duration (a ten thousandth of the time between pulses) it means that a thousand other pulses could easily be placed between two adjacent pulses from one conversation, and these thousand other pulses could each come from a different conversation. This slotting together of pulses from many different conversations can easily be accomplished nowadays with the electronics at our disposal. Such techniques allow over 10.000 simultaneous voice conversations to be carried over a single optical fiber. This technique of passing many signals down one fiber is known as **multiplexing**. An illustration of how this is done (not to scale) is given in the next diagram.

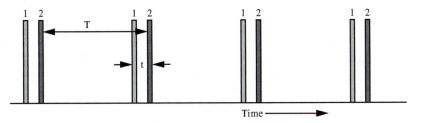

Illustration of how two different conversations (1 & 2) can be transmitted at the same time.
Note that the time T is really over ten thousand times greater than the time t.

The first transatlantic fiber optic cable (many fibers), which is about the diameter of a garden hose, was capable of handling 40,000 simultaneous conversations, more than twice the combined number possible using the three previously existing copper cables. At that time each fiber could carry around 600 simultaneous conversations. Today's more advanced technology allows one fiber to carry 30,000 simultaneous conversations. There are now several transatlantic fiber optic links and a large fraction of the capacity is unused! It is perhaps even more remarkable to note that the first transatlantic cable was completed in 1956 and could handle only 52 simultaneous calls! The last 50 years have brought tremendous changes. This quantum leap is due to the new materials technology of optical fibers.

Some other advantages of sound transmission by optical fibers are the lack of electrical interference and the absence of corrosion effects. Recent data also show that the maintenance costs of a fiber optic network are about a fraction of those for conventional wires.

Other Uses

The use of optical fibers to carry light from one place to another with very little loss in intensity is finding so many applications in our daily lives that it is impossible to catalog all of them.

The illumination of the switches and dials in an automobile can now come from one bulb in an 'easy-to-reach' location rather than from many small bulbs in awkward locations behind the dashboard. The light is carried to the instruments by optical fibers.

Fiber optics are increasingly used in medicine, for example. Endoscopes for seeing inside the body use a bundle of optical fibers to carry the light to the area/organ to be examined, while another bundle of fibers fitted with a lens is used to see what is happening. There now exist fiber optic laser scalpels for non-invasive surgery with light beams.

Another example involves remote illumination. By means of fiber optic bundles, sunlight can be conducted into windowless rooms at considerable distance.

Another growing application is in the area of sensing. The index of refraction (and speed of light) in an optical fiber is quite sensitive to the state of strain, and also to temperature. There are now optical fiber sensors that can quite sensitively detect strain, temperature, pressure and other parameters, without requiring electrical power for operation.

Optical fibers already play an important role in the internet backbone including undersea optical fiber cables, but "fiber to the curb" or "fiber to the home" may soon become available, beginning with urban areas. (Rural areas will continue to use satellite or wireless internet connections.) At present, so-called "broadband" internet connections are handled by copper wires (over conventional phone lines) or by cable television lines. These "information conduits" have "bandwidth" limits, referring to the amount of information that can pass through them at a given time. The "bandwidths' of optical fibers are much larger, owing to multiplexing, as described on Page 229. As a result, fiber optic-based telecommunications offer the promise of blazingly fast upload and ownload rates, compared to current experience.

Examples could be multiplied but those given are sufficient to illustrate the importance of this new materials technology. Remember that the major developments have taken place in the last few decades. Optical fibers are truly an example of the importance of new materials in today's world.

QUESTIONS: Chapters 29–30

1. Which of the following electromagnetic waves has an energy of approximately 10 eV?
   (a) blue light   (b) gamma rays   (c) infrared rays   (d) ultraviolet rays   (e) microwaves

2. Light will travel the slowest in _____.
   (a) air   (b) ice   (c) glass   (d) diamond   (e) a vacuum

3. The core glass in an optical fiber is formed by _____.
   (a) melting   (b) zone refining   (c) annealing   (d) sintering   (e) chemical vapor deposition

4. Which of the following is not true of the core glass of an optical fiber?
   (a) no cracks   (b) higher electron density than the cladding glass   (c) must be thin
   (d) no unwanted impurities   (e) all of these are true

5. The distance between two identical points on a wave is called the _____.
   (a) wavelength   (b) frequency   (c) energy   (d) speed of light   (e) none of these

6. Light loss that occurs through absorption is sometimes called _____.
   (a) refraction   (b) attenuation   (c) multiplexing   (d) crosstalk   (e) total internal reflection

7. When we make optical fibers we must make sure that the fiber is free of unwanted impurities and microscopic surface scratches. These correspond to processing the fiber to control the _____ structure (impurities) and the _____ structure (scratches).
   (a) crystal, micro   (b) atomic, micro   (c) crystal, macro   (d) electron, crystal
   (e) atomic, crystal

8. Which of the following is not true of light?
   (a) it is an electromagnetic wave   (b) the wavelength of light is different in different media
   (c) the velocity of light is the same in different media   (d) light incident on a material may be reflected and refracted
   (e) nothing can travel faster than light

9–11. The bending of light when it enters a material is called __9__. It is dependent on the __10__ in the material. The ratio of the speed of light in a vacuum to the speed of light in a material is called the __11__.
   9. (a) reflection   (b) attenuation   (c) refraction   (d) reverberation   (e) the critical angle
   10. (a) electron density   (b) electron mobility   (c) number of neutrons   (d) electron hole density
        (e) type of electrons
   11. (a) transmission coefficient   (b) velocity gradient   (c) reflective index   (d) attenuation constant
        (e) refractive index

12–26. In the manufacture of pure optical fibers, impure sand (silicon oxide) is reacted with __12i__ and the resulting mix-ture of __12ii__ s is separated by a process of __13__. The required glass is then made by a process called __14__. In this process, a mixture of __15__ vapor and __16__ gas is heated to form __17__ and __12i__. In order to increase the refractive index of this glass, we add some __18__ __12ii__ vapor to the gas stream. The refractive index of the glass produced with this dopant is higher because __18__ has __19__ electrons than silicon. We use __18__ as the dopant because it is a __20__ impurity in glass and has __21__ valence electrons. It is therefore neither an acceptor nor a donor. As a result we can increase the refractive index of the glass but it will still not __22__ any light. An optical fiber carries signals by means of __23__ and as many as a few hundred telephone conversations can be car-ried by one fiber at the same time using a technique called __24__. A kilometer length of the best optical fiber loses about __25__ % of the light when it passes from one end to the other, but very little light would be __26__ over distances of hundreds of kilometers.

   12. (a) nitrogen, nitride   (b) iodine, iodide   (c) chlorine, chloride   (d) fluorine, fluoride
        (e) oxygen, oxide
   13. (a) distillation   (b) zone refining   (c) decimation   (d) doping   (e) annealing
   14. (a) internal reflection   (b) zone refining   (c) chemical vapor deposition   (d) melting
        (e) vitrification

15. (a) $NbCl_4$ (b) SiO_2 (c) $SiCl_4$ (d) TiO_2 (e) NaCl
16. (a) nitrogen   (b) chlorine   (c) hydrogen   (d) oxygen   (e) carbon dioxide
17. (a) TiO_2 (b) GeO_2 (c) SiO_2 (d) NbO_2 (e) none of these
18. (a) niobium   (b) titanium   (c) silicon   (d) lithium   (e) germanium
19. (a) a larger number of   (b) a smaller number of   (c) twice the number of   (d) larger
     (e) slower
20. (a) refractive   (b) interstitial   (c) precipitate   (d) large   (e) substitutional
21. (a) 8   (b) 4   (c) 10   (d) 18   (e) 0
22. (a) transmit   (b) absorb   (c) diffract   (d) reflect   (e) refract
23. (a) electrons   (b) phonons   (c) neurons   (d) light pulses   (e) protons
24. (a) crosstalking   (b) multiplexing   (c) concentrating   (d) superpositioning
     (e) complexing
25. (a) 10   (b) 0.2   (c) 20   (d) 4   (e) 0.01
26. (a) transmitted   (b) reflected   (c) absorbed   (d) refracted   (e) emitted

27–29. A mirage is an illustration of the phenomenon of the __27__ of light. For this to occur, light must be traveling in the material with the __28__ refractive index and the angle of refraction must be __29__ the critical angle.

27. (a) refraction   (b) total internal reflection   (c) total internal absorption   (d) total transmission
     (e) attenuation
28. (a) higher   (b) lower   (c) much greater   (d) weaker   (e) much smaller
29. (a) equal to   (b) smaller than   (c) half as much as   (d) greater than

31. MAGNETIC MATERIALS

There is no doubt that magnetic materials play a vital role in our everyday activities in today's world, even though we may be unaware of their presence. At some time we have probably all played with magnets, or toys containing them, but if we were asked today to name a place where we could find them, we would probably mention the little magnets we use to hold notes to the refrigerator door. If we take a simple magnet and walk around trying to pick things up with it, we are unsuccessful most of the time. We recognize very few materials as magnetic and the vast majority of those are based on iron. What makes iron or any other material a magnet? Or more generally, why are most materials not magnets? The answer to these questions can get very complex; indeed the magnetic behavior of materials is perhaps the most difficult to understand. We shall find a simple answer provided we are willing to accept two simple statements on faith. But, to be honest, we have to do that all the time.

Background

If we wish to magnetize a bar of iron we do so by placing it in a strong magnetic field. Usually we do this in the following way. We make a coil of wire and pass a direct current through it. The result of this is that the coil behaves like a magnet. If we slowly push our iron bar into the coil and take it out, as illustrated below, we find that it has been magnetized. The magnetic field of the coil has somehow magnetized the iron. Why is this?

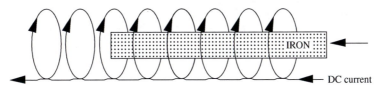

A piece of iron may be made magnetic (magnetized) by slowly pushing it into a coil through which
a direct electric current is flowing, and then withdrawing it.

The first thing that we have to accept is that *electrons going round in circles produce a magnetic field*. This is certainly true of the coil of wire shown in the diagram, where the radius of the circles is the radius of the coil. It may seem quite a large change in scale, but electrons go round in circles when they orbit the nucleus of an atom and when they do this they also produce a small magnetic field. This is our first clue. We should therefore expect each individual atom to act like a little magnet. Physics tells us that in such a case the strength of the magnetic field is proportional to the area of the circle. Obviously this is very small for electrons orbiting an atomic nucleus.

Because magnets can attract and repel each other we might expect atoms to show some reaction to a magnetic field. In fact, if we take individual atoms and place them in a magnetic field, we can easily show that they are moved by that field just as small weak magnets would be. The only exceptions are the inert gases. Apart from the inert gases, every individual atom acts like a little magnet. Notice carefully that we are here talking about individual atoms, and for this the atoms must be separated as in a vapor, but this is often not difficult to accomplish. We are not really interested in the magnetic behavior of atomic gases, but they do give us the next clue that we need.

What is it that makes the inert gases different in their magnetic behavior, i.e., why, of all the atoms, do they not behave like little magnets? We have already seen that they are characterized by having eight electrons in their outer shell. These eight electrons have orbits around the nucleus such that for every electron going one way there is another going the opposite way, and the opposite directions produce magnets which are opposed to each other and therefore cancel each other out. This canceling of magnets is basically what leads to most materials being non-magnetic and it occurs at so many different structural levels. Here it occurs at the level of the electron structure. This leads us to the second fact we have to accept: *there are some atoms, including those with the electron structure of the inert gases, which do not behave as if they are little magnets*. In fact, any atom with only full sub-shells of electrons behaves the same way.

Now we have the necessary basic information to understand why most solids are not magnetic, because we have already seen that when atoms bond together they usually do so by sharing or exchanging electrons so that they both end up with the electron structure of the inert gases, i.e., eight electrons in their outer shell. This is why most solid materials are not magnetic. For example we saw that common salt (NaCl) consists of sodium and chlorine ions which each have an inert gas electron structure.

Now that we have seen why most solids are not magnets, we need to ask why it is that some materials manage to have atoms which do produce a magnetic field? For this we shall consider metal magnets and ceramic magnets separately.

Metal magnets

At this point, we need to look once more at the periodic table provided at the beginning of the book (Page 7). Across the middle of this table you will see the following elements:

Scandium	Titanium	Vanadium	Chromium	Manganese	Iron	Cobalt	Nickel	Copper	Zinc
Sc	Ti	V	Cr	Mn	Fe	Co	Ni	Cu	Zn

These elements are called the **transition metals,** and their major feature is that they contain electrons in their 4s level while the 3d level is only partly full. This is because the fourth electron shell begins to fill before the third shell has its full complement of 18 electrons ($2n^2$). In other words the energy ladder we drew earlier (Page 174) is a little more complex than we imagined. The 4s level shown in the diagram should be slightly below the 3d level, i.e. between the 3p and 3d levels. Don't let these details overwhelm you, just grasp the important fact that many of these transition metals have a 3d level which is only partly full while having electrons on the 4s level. When these atoms form bonds with themselves, or with other atoms, they usually use the electrons in the fourth shell for the bonding and leave the third shell unfilled. This is enough to make the atom a small magnet, because it is left with an unfilled electron shell.

This raises yet another question. If this is true for these transition metals, why are they not all magnetic? It **is** true that the atoms in these circumstances each act like a small magnet but, just as we have seen that the electrons in an atom can produce magnetic fields which cancel each other, so the individual atom magnets can be arranged to cancel each other. In some elements (e.g. titanium) each atom points its magnet in a random direction. As a consequence there is no resultant, or net, magnetic field. We call such materials **paramagnets**. In other elements (e.g. chromium) the individual atom magnets arrange themselves so that they alternate in pointing in opposite directions. Again there is no resultant magnetic field. Such materials are called **antiferromagnets**. The following illustrations may help you to visualize this. The arrows on the atoms are pointing in the directions of their atomic magnetic fields. In both these cases the magnetic cancellation occurs on the atomic level.

Within this group of transition metals there are only three which, in the solid form, arrange their individual atom magnets to all point in the same direction. These are iron, cobalt and nickel. We call these three elements **ferromagnets** (ferro = iron) and they are the only common metals that we consider to be magnetic. In some magnets we use combinations (alloys) of these elements to obtain a desired property.

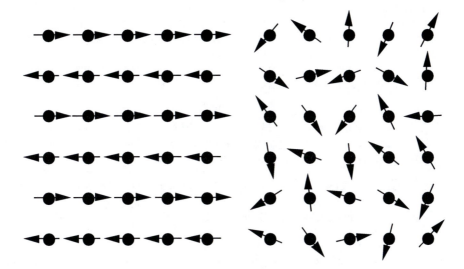

On the left the atom magnets are systematically arranged to oppose each other, something called antiferromagnetism (e.g., chromium). On the right the atom magnets are randomly oriented to produce an effect called paramagnetism (e.g., titanium).

It is not possible for us to explain why the atoms arrange their individual atom magnets in the way that they do. We must simply note that the alignments are spontaneous and we cannot manufacture the materials so that they arrange their atom magnets in any other way. For example, we know that the chromium atom produces a stronger magnet than the iron atom, but we can't use chromium as a magnet because the atoms insist in pointing their individual atom magnets in alternating opposite directions so that they cancel each other. The material is antiferromagnetic.

There is one final point to consider. If the iron atoms in a crystal spontaneously arrange their atom magnets to point in the same direction, why are not all pieces of iron magnetic? To explain this, we must consider both the atomic structure and the microstructure. Locally, all the atom magnets are aligned (atomic structure). This order persists within microstructural regions called **magnetic domains**. In each domain the atoms point their magnets in the same direction but atoms in adjacent domains point their magnets in opposite or different directions, so that they cancel each other. A typical illustration is given on the next page, where the arrows again show the directions in which the individual atoms point their magnets in each of the four domains.

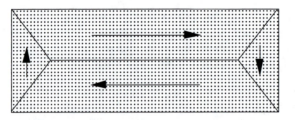

In an iron single crystal there are regions called domains in which the atoms point their magnets in the same direction, but different domains point in different directions so that the magnets cancel.

Note that this diagram shows a single crystal, and a single crystal can contain many different domains. The atoms are arranged in a continuous ordered array throughout this piece of material, and there are no grain boundaries. The only difference between the domains is that the atoms point their magnets in different directions in different domains. This is simply the natural state of the material. Here we have cancellation on a microstructural level. Domains are a new feature of microstructure that we have previously not encountered. They are unique to materials, like ferromagnets, which undergo such ordering of their individual atom magnets.

Note that we have now seen three ways in which magnets cancel each other. In single atoms, the fields of the individual electrons may cancel. In titanium and chromium, for example, the individual atom magnets cancel, either by pointing in random or opposite directions, a situation that we cannot change. In the ferromagnets, magnetic domains can cancel one another, a situation that we shall now see can be changed.

When we place a piece of iron in a coil of wire, the magnetic field in the coil forces the individual atom magnets to turn to point in the same direction as the applied magnetic field of the coil. The way they do this is rather interesting because it tells us much about the way we can influence the magnetic behavior of materials.

In the above diagram we have shown four domains (not grains or crystallites), and just as grains are separated by grain boundaries, so are domains separated by domain boundaries or walls. However the domain boundary is a thin *volume* of material in which the individual atom magnets gradually change direction. The following diagrams illustrate what we are talking about, where the arrows represent the magnets of the individual atoms.

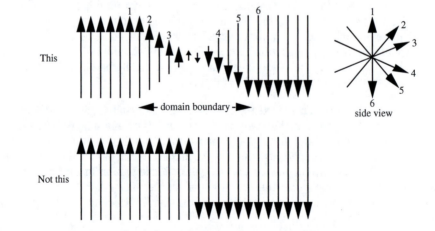

Atom magnets near a domain boundaries are changing direction gradually as shown in the upper diagram rather than suddenly as shown in the lower diagram.

When we place a piece of iron in our coil in order to magnetize it, the domain walls in the material move and this movement is accomplished by rotating the atom magnets in the wall a small amount. In some respects it's just like turning a screw; the wall moves forward as the magnets rotate.

Now think what this does. It allows us to change the direction of an atom magnet a little at a time rather than completely reverse it in one go. There is some similarity here with the dislocation, which we discussed earlier (Page 55). The dislocation makes it easier for planes of atoms to slide over each other by moving a row at a time, while domain boundaries allow atom magnets to rotate more easily by doing this a little at a time. As the domain boundary moves, we end up with more atoms pointing their magnets in the direction of the magnetic field acting on them. After the material has been magnetized, any supply of energy, such as heat or a sudden jolt, e.g. dropping the bar on a concrete floor, may cause the domain boundaries to return to their original positions and the net magnetism of the material to be lost. The following diagrams illustrate what happens when a domain boundary moves in a crystal. We must note that the domain boundary, which in the previous diagram is shown as only 10 atoms wide, is in fact about 300 atoms across. This means that the boundary has a width of close to 100 nm.

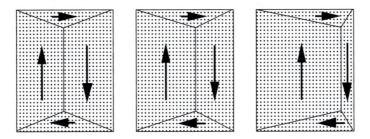

Material being magnetized in a vertical-up direction.

Using Domain Boundaries

Now we come to the interesting way in which the materials scientist can influence the properties of magnetic materials by way of these domain boundaries. There are some instances when we want to be able to quickly change the direction of magnetization of a material. For example in an electrical transformer, the alternating current changes direction 60 times per second, which means that the magnetic field produced in the coils of the transformer also changes direction this frequently. We also need the magnets in the transformer to be able to change their direction in pace with this current change, which means that we want the domain walls to move very easily, because, as we have seen, they are what allow the atom magnets to change direction. On the other hand there are instances when we want our material to stay magnetized in a given direction and not be easily changed. An important example of this is on magnetic hard disks in our computers and some digital music players. When we record information in the form of a magnetic signal on the hard drive, we don't want this information to disappear when we turn off the computer, or if the temperature gets too high.

It turns out that we can stop, or hinder, the motion of domain boundaries by putting small precipitates in the magnetic material. If we do this, it becomes more difficult to move the domain boundaries when we magnetize the material, so we need much stronger magnets to do this, but conversely it is more difficult to move the boundaries back to their original positions, i.e., to demagnetize the material. Putting precipitates in the material helps produce a **permanent magnet**, one which does not readily revert to the unmagnetized state. Now in the case of a metal, you also know what other effect precipitates have: they stop dislocations moving, making the material harder (Page 80). The two effects are inseparable, and we therefore often call such materials **hard magnets**. This can really be taken to have two meanings. The materials are mechanically hard, and they are also hard (difficult) to demagnetize.

Of course, if we now want a material for a transformer we need a material without precipitates so that there are no obstructions to domain boundary motion. This is why you may see such material referred to as **soft iron**; it is mechanically soft because there are no precipitates to pin dislocations. Materials which are easily magnetized, and demagnetized are called **soft magnets**.

There is one other way of making permanent magnets, which we must discuss. We have already mentioned that the domain boundary has a width of around 100 nm. If we now make our magnet using smaller and smaller crystals, we reach a point where the boundary occupies almost the whole crystal. Each crystal wants to divide itself into domains, as already illustrated, but the walls are now beginning to take up too much room. Just think how wasteful it would be to build a house using building blocks ten feet thick! We would end up with rooms that were so small as to be practically useless. We therefore use thinner walls. In a magnetic material the domain boundaries, or walls, are quite thick on an atomic scale (over 300 atoms across) and there is no way of reducing this thickness. As soon as the crystal becomes so small that a domain boundary would occupy a large fraction of its volume, the crystal gives up the notion of dividing into several domains and assumes the form of just one domain per crystal. In each small crystal, all the atom magnets now point in the same direction. This means that there is now no easy way for the atom magnets to change their direction and they become small permanent magnets. We call these materials **single domain magnets**.

This is the technique used on magnetic recording tape and computer discs. The following photograph, taken using a scanning electron microscope, shows the particles on a disc. They are small, with a width of about two tenths of a micron (200 nm), so that each particle is only large enough to contain one domain. In some other magnets, we manage to process them so that we have a microstructure something like the aluminum-lithium alloys we discussed earlier (Chapter 11). In this case there are very fine precipitates of magnetic metal surrounded by non-magnetic metal. The magnetic particles are so small that they are single domains. In order to get a really strong magnet, and to make sure that these domains don't all point their magnets in different directions, we solidify the material inside a strong magnetic field. This forces the atom magnets in all single domain particles to line up in the same direction when they crystallize, so we obtain a material which is both a strong and a permanent magnet.

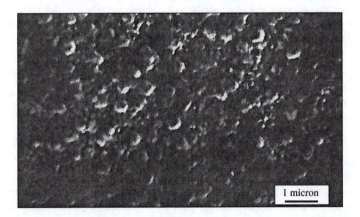

Photograph of small magnetic particles on a computer disc. Each particle is a single magnetic domain.

It is interesting to note that when we make metal particles as small as this, they are also too small to contain dislocations. If we make thin metal **whiskers** (Page 78) and measure their strength, we find that they are about a thousand times stronger than normal metals. This confirms our earlier statements that it is the dislocations that weaken the metal. Unfortunately metal whiskers are too small to be of much use to us.

Amorphous Metal Magnets

We have already seen that amorphous metals are very difficult to make (Page 53) but they are also of great importance for magnetic materials. Of course the atoms have to be magnetic to start with, which limits us to iron, nickel and a few others. To simplify matters we shall only consider a piece of amorphous iron. Under normal circumstances the metal is crystalline. At room temperature the iron crystals are body centered cubic, and for a reason very difficult to understand, the atom magnets insist on pointing in directions parallel to the crystal cube edges. They just don't like pointing in other directions, a phenomenon we call **magnetic anisotropy**. However if we want to reverse the magnetization direction, which is done via domain boundary motion, we have to turn the atom magnets so that at some time they point in directions they don't want to point.

Atom magnet lies parallel to cube edge (1), but in order to reverse direction (5) must pass through directions 2 and 4, which it does not like to do.

In the above diagram we show an atom magnet pointing parallel to an edge of a cubic crystal (1). As the domain boundary comes up to this atom it tries to turn the direction of the magnet to point in the opposite direction (5). Notice that the atom is not moving, only the direction of its little magnet. In order to reverse direction, the atom magnet has to be made to point in directions (2 and 4), which it doesn't like. It takes energy to move the magnet through these directions. Turning the atom magnet is like moving a ball over a wavy surface, as shown in the accompanying diagram. Energy is required to push the ball over the humps just as it is required to move the atoms magnets around. It is this magnetic anisotropy, which makes it difficult to move the domain boundary and hence magnetize the material in a different direction.

We mentioned earlier that a transformer contains a magnet in which the atom magnets reverse direction every time the current direction changes (60 times per second). Each time this happens energy is used, and this energy comes from the power we are transmitting, i.e., we have an energy loss. Now think what happens if we replace this magnet with an amorphous magnetic metal. In this material the atoms are randomly arranged. There are no cubic crystals and no cube edges to align the atom magnets, so the atom magnets don't mind which direction they point in. They can point as easily in any direction and very little energy is required to change this direction, i.e., they are truly soft magnets. As a consequence there is not the energy loss that is found with crystalline metal magnets.

It is estimated that by using amorphous metals in the transformers used in power transmission in the U.S.A., we would save energy to the value of well over $1 billion a year! These amorphous metal magnets are now being produced commercially and are being used in new installations. It is, of course, not economical to replace all existing installations with the new material, but it is gradually making an impact in today's world.

Remember what we said about amorphous metals earlier (Page 54). They can only be produced in very thin sheets, so we have to make our magnets by laminating these sheets in the same way we build up a thick piece of plywood. Also, because they have no atomic order, there are no straight paths for electron motion and electron mobility is low, making for a high electrical resistance. It turns out that this is an added advantage, because not only does the alternating current in the transformer produce a rapidly changing magnetic field, it also shunts the electrons back and forth in the metal magnet, producing heat. The random atom arrangement in an amorphous metal inhibits this electron motion and therefore reduces this effect.

There is one final curiosity about these new amorphous magnets. Because the atoms are randomly arranged, there are no planes of atoms to slip over each other, and of course there are no dislocations, so the materials are quite hard and brittle. However, they are soft magnets. This combination of mechanical hardness and magnetic softness is quite unique, because in crystalline materials anything we do to stop domain boundaries moving also stops dislocations moving. We therefore usually produce mechanical hardness and magnetic hardness at the same time. This is not the case here.

Ceramic Magnets

Not only can the transition metals themselves be magnetic, but so can some of their compounds. They also have the domain structure we have just discussed and exhibit many of the properties of metal magnets. However there are some really important differences.

Perhaps the earliest known, naturally occurring, magnetic material is known as lodestone, which is an iron oxide (Fe_3O_4). The iron atoms give up electrons so that the four oxygens each have the extra two, which they need to have their outer shells of eight. These eight electrons are obtained by two of the three iron atoms each losing three electrons and the third losing two electrons. In both cases, the iron atom (ion) is left with an unfilled outer electron shell, which does not contain eight electrons and is therefore a magnet. In the crystalline solid the three iron atoms arrange their magnets in the following manner.

$$Fe^{3+} \qquad\qquad Fe^{3+} \qquad\qquad Fe^{2+}$$

Two of the three atom magnets cancel each other and the third iron ion ($Fe2+$) produces a net magnetic field. Notice that the oxygen ions are not magnetic—they have a full outer shell of eight electrons. Therefore in each molecule (Fe_3O_4) there is no magnetic field from the oxygens, two of the irons are little magnets that cancel each other, leaving only one iron ion to produce the magnetic field. In a piece of magnetized iron, **all** the atoms contribute so the metal magnet is much stronger than the ceramic magnet.

What then is the importance of these ceramic oxide magnets if they are not as strong as metallic magnets? One answer to this question lies in the fact that ceramics are electrical insulators.

When we were talking about the advantages of using amorphous metals in transformers we mentioned that we lose energy for two reasons; as the individual atom magnets rotate, and as the free electrons are shunted back and forth in the material. Ceramics have no free electrons, so there is therefore no energy loss produced by the second of these two effects. In circumstances where the magnetic field is changing direction extremely rapidly we therefore use ceramic magnets.

One application of ceramic magnets is in the vacuum tube of an old-fashioned television set or computer monitor. A magnet at the back of the tube causes an electron beam to scan across the screen, which is dotted with different phosphors (Page 190). This electron beam is scanned very rapidly, 525 lines every sixtieth of a second. Using a ceramic magnet in this situation causes a much lower energy loss than would be the case for metal magnets. It also makes the TV set considerably lighter in weight. Of course flat panel displays are now replacing vacuum tube displays, for both TVs and computers.

Ceramic magnets also have the advantage of being brittle and can be ground to very fine powders without loss of their magnetic properties. They are also corrosion resistant. They do not rust! Iron metal powder rusts very quickly, especially on hot, humid summer days. Because of these properties, ceramic magnet powders can be easily mixed into plastics to produce the material used for the door seal on your refrigerator and for some advertisements attached to car doors, etc. You will also find particles of ceramic magnet in the little decorative magnets you use to attach notes or bottle openers to the refrigerator door. This resistance to corrosion is why most old-fashioned recording tapes are made using ceramic magnets. We could easily grind them to single domain size and there was no need to protect them from the atmosphere.

The early recording tapes used iron oxide for this same reason, then came chromium oxide (CrO_2) tapes. Remember that we earlier said that a chromium atom is a stronger magnet than an iron atom, but that chromium was, unfortunately, antiferromagnetic. In the oxide we can take advantage of this stronger magnet. Metal recording tapes were a much later development because the problems of corrosion and making very small, single domain, particles had to be overcome. Their advantage was that metals are stronger magnets because, as we mentioned earlier, all their atoms could contribute to the magnetic field rather than some of them, as in the case of oxide magnets.

Of course, the days of recording tape are numbered. Nowadays, most recording is onto magnetic discs (hard drives) in everything from iPods to camcorders to DVRs (digital video recorders), which have replaced the once ubiquitous VCRs (video cassette recorders).

Conclusion

We encounter magnetic materials in many places during our everyday lives and they have grown very much in importance during the last 20–30 years. Unfortunately, there are not many materials in which this occurs.

Magnetic materials are an excellent example of the way structure affects properties. Remember that all magnets depend on the electrons orbiting the atomic nucleus. A magnet must contain atoms which have less than eight electrons in their outer electron shell (**electron structure**), and these little atom magnets must be arranged in the solid so that they do not cancel each other. We have also seen that the atoms in crystalline metals point their atom magnets along certain directions in the **crystal structure**, and that if we make the crystals very small (**microstructure**), we produce permanent single domain magnets. And of course, we are probably aware that if we want to produce a really strong magnetic field we place the two ends (north and south poles) of the metal magnet close together by bending the rod into a horseshoe shape (**macrostructure**).

We can also change the properties of magnets by replacing some atoms with others (**atomic structure**). This is especially true of ceramic magnets, but a discussion of these effects is outside the scope of this text.

QUESTIONS: Chapter 31

1–10. Magnets are important components of all electric motors, automobiles, tape recorders and computer memory storage devices. We can classify magnets as metallic or ceramic, although there are two different types of metallic magnets: crystalline and amorphous. Amorphous iron has the advantages that it can be magnetized easily in any direction and __1__ because __2__, but it has the disadvantage(s) that __3__. Ceramic oxide magnets have the advantage(s) of __4__ but compared to metal magnets have the disadvantages of __5__. A metal magnet contains crystals which are subdivided into __6__ s and can be considered as either hard or soft, depending on how easily it gains and loses its magnetization. For an audio tape and magnetic storage devices we need __7__ magnets because __8__. This is accomplished by using single __6__ magnets. The early magnetic tapes were made using ceramic oxide particles because the inherent __9__ of ceramics made it easy to obtain single __6__ magnets. This is an example of the __10__ structure of the material.

 1. (a) is stiff   (b) is more shiny   (c) has a high electrical resistance   (d) both a and c
    (e) both b and c
 2. (a) the atoms don't have 8 electrons in the outer shall   (b) there is no crystal structure
    (c) it is always thin   (d) its crystals point in all directions
    (e) it has more free electrons because the electrons are not used in bonding
 3. (a) it is always in thin sheets   (b) it is brittle   (c) it rusts   (d) both b and c
    (e) all of these
 4. (a) being easy to grind into powders   (b) not corroding   (c) a high electrical resistance
    (d) both b and c   (e) all of these
 5. (a) rigidity   (b) lower magnetic strength   (c) brittleness   (d) low luster   (e) both b and c
 6. (a) precipitate   (b) domain   (c) grain   (d) microcrystal   (e) crystallite
 7. (a) soft   (b) amorphous   (c) hard   (d) either b or c   (e) any of the these
 8. (a) they do not rust   (b) they are easy to magnetize   (c) they hold sound easier
    (d) they are cheaper   (e) they are difficult to magnetize and demagnetize
 9. (a) rigidity   (b) lower magnetic strength   (c) brittleness   (d) low luster   (e) strength
10. (a) electron   (b) atomic   (c) micro   (d) macro   (e) crystal

11–20. Magnetism is produced by electrons moving in circular orbits. This can be demonstrated by passing an electrical current through a __11__. In a magnetic material it is the motion of the electrons __12__ which produces the magnetism. Metal magnets are usually __13__ than ceramic magnets but have the disadvantage(s) that they __14__. Recording tape uses very small magnetic particles because __15__. Ceramic magnets are used in __16__. Amorphous iron is a very important magnetic material which can be used to advantage in __17__. It is produced by cooling molten iron at a rate of a __18__. Unfortunately, it is only available in the form of __19__ pieces and it is quite __20__.

11. (a) rectifier   (b) light bulb   (c) coil of wire   (d) ceramic   (e) battery
12. (a) freely between the atoms   (b) around the atom nuclei   (c) from bond to bond
    (d) from one energy level to another   (e) none of these
13. (a) magnetically weaker   (b) magnetically stronger   (c) more amorphous   (d) larger
    (e) lighter
14. (a) oxidize (rust)   (b) cannot easily be ground to a fine powder   (c) do not transmit light
    (d) both a and b   (e) they have no disadvantages
15. (a) they do not rust as easily   (b) they allow the tape to be flexible   (c) they are cheaper
    (d) it is difficult to change the magnetization of such very small particles   (e) both b and d
16. (a) refrigerator door seals   (b) magnetic note holders   (c) VCR recording heads   (d) TV sets
    (e) all of these
17. (a) rectifiers   (b) activators   (c) transistors   (d) transformers   (e) both c and d
18. (a) million degrees per minute   (b) thousand degrees per second   (c) million degrees per second
    (d) billion degrees per second   (e) these cooling rates are all too slow
19. (a) small   (b) thin   (c) large   (d) thick   (e) powdered
20. (a) expensive   (b) brittle   (c) ductile   (d) both a and b   (e) both a and c

21–24. There are some ceramic magnets and they are very important in today's world. One/some of their advantages is/are that they __21__. As a result they can withstand the repeated passage of a recording tape in a VCR for years, and can also be mixed with a plastic for use as __22__. Ceramic magnets do not rust because they __23__. The big advantage of metal magnets is that they are __24__.

21. (a) resist abrasion   (b) can be ground to a fine powder because of their brittleness   (c) are lightweight
     (d) both a and b   (e) all of these

22. (a) magnets holding notes to refrigerator doors   (b) recording heads for cassette players and VCR's
     (c) refrigerator door seals   (d) both a and b   (e) both a and c

23. (a) have ionic bonds   (b) are very strong   (c) are oxidized   (d) are based on metals
     (e) both b and c

24. (a) less likely to oxidize   (b) stronger magnets (more attraction)   (c) free of dislocations
     (d) both a and b   (e) both b and c

32. NANOMATERIALS

Background

It is important to separate fact from fiction when it comes to **nanotechnology**. According to the popular media, nanotechnology will soon deliver everything from genetic engineering to injectable "nanobots," inserted into the body to repair diseased or damaged tissue. And what if these nanobots become self-replicating and even sentient—the stuff of science fiction? We find out later in this chapter why such nanobots are highly unlikely.

The reality of nanotechnology is far less "fantastic." There are many examples of ways **nanomaterials** are being used to advantage in products that affect our lives. For example, tennis racquets are being made with carbon nanotubes to improve their mechanical properties. Stain-repellent fabrics are being made with hydrophobic (water-repelling) nanoparticles, making use of their unique chemical properties. And skin creams are being produced with ultraviolet-absorbing nanoparticles for UV-protection, taking advantage of their unique optical properties. New applications are emerging on a regular basis.

But the real potential for nanomaterials is still on the horizon. As early as 1959, in a now famous lecture entitled, "There's Plenty of Room at the Bottom," Nobel laureate Richard Feynman envisaged being able to write all the volumes of Encyclopaedia Britannica on the head of a pin. This would require patterning on the scale of tens of nanometers. Such "nano-writing" is now possible, as we will see. Actually, we store larger amounts of information on pin head-sized spaces in the current generation integrated circuits or "chips." But the reign of **Moore's Law**, where the memory capacity of IC chips has doubled approximately every 18 months since 1970, may soon come to an end. In this chapter and the case study to follow, we'll find out why and how further miniaturization of electronic devices will require the development of reliable **nanoelectronics**.

How Small is a Nanometer?

In the 1966 movie, "Fantastic Voyage," a medical team was miniaturized and injected into the body of an ailing scientist to repair damaged tissue. Let's follow the lead of "Fantastic Voyage" and take a journey into a human hand. If you look at the palm of your hand, it is something like 10 centimeters across. The lines in my palm are spaced approximately 1 centimeter apart. Under a microscope, you would see skin cracks spaced on the order of 1 millimeter apart, and approximately one-tenth of a millimeter wide. This is about the thickness of human hair (50–100 micrometers, or 0.05–0.1 millimeter). But we have a long way to go, size-wise, to reach nanometer scale.

Again under the microscope, the diameter of a white blood cell is approximately 10 micrometers, and its cell membrane is around 1 micrometer thick, as illustrated in the following diagram. To "see" any smaller, we need to use electron microscopes instead of light microscopes. Also shown in the following illustration, DNA strands are at least 0.1 micrometers long (or 100 nanometers) and can be much longer. The famous double helix is on the order of 2 nanometers wide. At the finest scale there are individual atoms in DNA molecules. These are typically one-tenth of a nanometer in size.

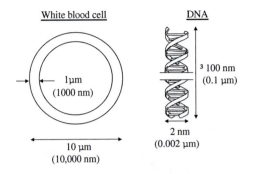

The dimensions of a white blood cell and strand of DNA demonstrate the relative size of a nanometer.

So a nanometer-sized object is quite small. For the purpose of comparison, if we enlarged it to the size of a penny held in your palm, your foot would be large enough to extend from Miami to Seattle!

Everything Is Different at the Bottom!

Until now, the properties of the materials considered have not been size-or shape-dependent. For example, the properties of a cube of gold are the same whether it is a meter on a side or a micrometer on a side—the gold will have the same color and the same electrical conductivity. Furthermore, both cubes of gold will melt at the same temperature—you can look this up in a handbook as 1064°C. And it doesn't matter whether the gold is in the shape of a cube or a sphere, or some other shape. Properties are shape-independent.

Everything changes, however, in the nanorealm! For example, small nanoparticles of gold can melt as low as 300°C. And the color of gold changes from opaque yellow in micrometer or larger crystals, to transparent blue or crimson red in the 30–500 nm range, to transparent red in the 3–30 nanometer range. Below 3 nanometers, gold appears transparent orange in color, and these particles are no longer metallic! But there is more to the strange behavior in the nanorealm. 100 nanometer diameter silver spheres are pale blue in color, whereas triangular prisms of silver the same size are crimson. So the optical properties change with shape as well as size. Incidentally, one of the earliest uses of nanoparticles was in stained glass. Gold nanoparticles impart a rich crimson color to glass, whereas silver nanoparticles give a bright yellow color. Of course, medieval artisans did not know they were forming nanoparticles when they added gold or silver to their glasses.

Why do properties change so dramatically with size in the nanometer range? One reason has to do with something called the surface-to-volume ratio. Consider a cube of gold one centimeter on a side. There are approximately 10^{23} atoms per cubic centimeter in gold. (You may recall Avogadro's number, or 6.02×10^{23} atoms per mole. There is something like a tenth of a mole of atoms in a cubic centimeter of gold.) But how many atoms are on the surface of our cube? A shortcut is to take the two-thirds power of the number of atoms per cm³ or approximately 10^{15} per cubic centimeter. Since there are six faces of area 1 cm² (1 cm by 1 cm), we have something like 6×10^{15} atoms on the surface. This gives a surface-to-volume ratio of 6×10^{15} divided by 10^{23}, or 6×10^{-8}. In other words, only six atoms out of every 100 million atoms are on the surface. The surface will have very little influence on the properties.

Bulk Cube

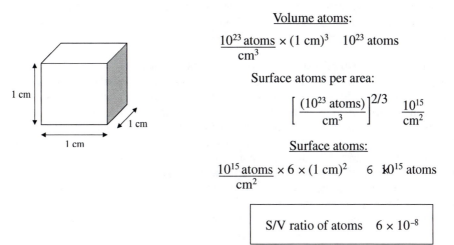

Volume atoms:

$$\frac{10^{23} \text{ atoms}}{\text{cm}^3} \times (1 \text{ cm})^3 \quad 10^{23} \text{ atoms}$$

Surface atoms per area:

$$\left[\frac{(10^{23} \text{ atoms})}{\text{cm}^3}\right]^{2/3} \quad \frac{10^{15}}{\text{cm}^2}$$

Surface atoms:

$$\frac{10^{15} \text{ atoms}}{\text{cm}^2} \times 6 \times (1 \text{ cm})^2 \quad 6 \ \times 10^{15} \text{ atoms}$$

$$\boxed{\text{S/V ratio of atoms} \quad 6 \times 10^{-8}}$$

On the other hand, consider a cube 1 nanometer on a side. A nanometer is 10^{-7} of a centimeter, so our nanocube is 10^{-21} cubic centimeters in volume. Multiplying this value by 10^{23} atoms per cubic centimeter gives us 100 atoms in this small cube. How many atoms are on the surface? Each face will be 10^{-14} cm^2 (10^{-7} cm squared) and there are 6 faces. Using the 10^{15} atom per cm^2 figure (above) we arrive at approximately 60 atoms. Now 60 of the atoms are on the surface, or 60% of the atoms in our nanocube!

Nano Cube

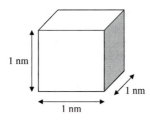

Volume atoms:

$$\frac{10^{23} \text{ atoms}}{\text{cm}^3} \times (10^{-7} \text{ cm})^3 \quad 100 \text{ atoms}$$

Surface atoms per area:

$$\left[\frac{(10^{23} \text{ atoms})}{\text{cm}^3}\right]^{2/3} \quad \frac{10^{15}}{\text{cm}^2}$$

Surface atoms:

$$\frac{10^{15} \text{ atoms}}{\text{cm}^2} \times 6 \times (10^{-7} \text{ cm})^2 \quad 6 \ 0 \text{atoms}$$

$$\boxed{\text{S/V ratio of atoms} \quad 0 6.}$$

This proves that nanocrystals have much higher surface-to-volume ratios than larger crystals, but they also have much higher energies. This has to do with bonding. In the interior of a crystal, atoms are bonded to other atoms in all directions, but on the surface the bonds facing outward are "unsatisfied," meaning that they don't have other atoms to bond to. As a result, surfaces have higher energies. The same is true of nanoparticles, which are almost "all surface," so to speak. This explains why nanocrystals melt at temperatures far lower than their bulk melting points. Nanocrystals are also much more reactive, which is used to advantage in chemical **catalysis**. For example, large gold crystals are chemically inert, whereas nanocrystalline gold particles are capable of catalyzing (promoting, speeding up) many chemical reactions.

Surface forces also increase as size decreases into the nanometer range. One such force is **adhesion**, which describes the "stickiness" of a surface. With so many unsatisfied bonds, nanoparticles tend to be very "sticky." Another surface property is surface "tension," which describes the tendency of water to form beads (to minimize its surface energy by decreasing its surface area) or to rise against gravity in a small diameter "capillary" tube. Such forces are referred to as **capillary forces**, and can be quite strong at the nanoscale. For example, an insect like an ant can pick up objects several times its mass, but cannot escape from a drop of water. The capillary forces are just too strong. Now we know why functioning nanobots for the human body are highly unlikely. Surface forces such as adhesion and capillary action are just too strong at the nanoscale. A nanotool like tweezers might be made to close on a nano-object, but getting it to open again might be difficult or even impossible. A more recent Nobel laureate, Richard E. Smalley, concluded, "Such a nanobot will never become more than a futurist's dream."

How Do You Make Nanoscale Materials?

As with all materials, there are two approaches—so-called "top-down" approaches and "bottom-up" approaches. In top-down approaches we remove material much like a sculptor chisels material away from a block of marble to produce his sculpture. Bottom-up approaches are more like working with Lego® to build up a comparable sculpture.

As described in the Semiconductor Device chapter, **photolithography** is a means of top-down patterning. A light-sensitive polymer or **photoresist** is coated on the surface of silicon and then exposed to light through a "mask." These regions of the photoresist can then be etched away, exposing the underlying semiconductor surface for further treatments such n-type or p-type doping in selected areas by ion implantation. The problem with light is that its wavelength is on the order of 0.5 micrometers. (Visible light is 0.4 to 0.7 microns, or 400 to 700 nanometers.) Of course, ultraviolet light can be used, but the "minimum feature size" will still be limited to on the order of 0.05 micrometer (50 nm). How can we make smaller features?

Two "top-down" methods are **nano-imprint lithography** and **nanosphere lithography**. In nano-imprint lithography, a special mold is made with features as small as 40 nm. One way to "carve" such a mold is with a carefully guided electron beam. Think of this mold as being like a stamp from a child's stamp set. As shown in the diagram below, this mold can be pressed against photoresist layers on a suitably prepared surface to emboss or "punch out" resist-free areas for subsequent lithography, just as in conventional photolithography. The mold can be moved from spot to spot to build up a much larger pattern, just as with a stamp in a stamp set.

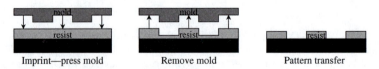

Imprint—press mold   Remove mold   Pattern transfer

Nano-imprint lithography uses a mold that can be "stamped" across a photoresist. To complete pattern transfer, the remaining resist is etched away with a beam of reactive ions.

Nanosphere lithography takes advantage of the ability to produce small spheres of various materials in the 100 nanometer range, and to make them of identical size. These can then be deposited on surfaces in close-packed layers, not unlike the close-packed planes in CCP and HCP crystal structures. But the spheres are only temporary. They serve as a template through which the real "nano" material gets deposited from above. The key here is that the interstice size (the holes between the spheres) is much smaller than the spheres themselves. Once a small quantity of material is deposited in the interstices, the spheres are dissolved away, leaving the interstice pattern behind. The diagram below illustrates the process. With 100 nanometer spheres, it is possible to get nano-dots in the 10 nanometer range.

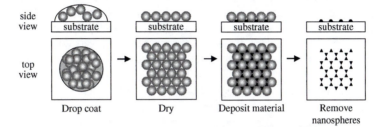

Nanosphere lithography uses the interstices between close-packed nanospheres to deposit material. The nanospheres can be dissolved away or lifted off to produce the desired pattern.

The other way to pattern nanomaterials is from the bottom up, much the way that nature builds materials. The key to many "bottom-up" approaches is molecular **self-assembly**. This refers to the tendency of molecules to self-assemble into nanometer-scale layers or clusters, largely due to secondary bonds (e.g., hydrogen and van der Waals), which we have discussed previously. Certain techniques make use of delivering "inks" containing such molecules to selected areas of a surface in the desired pattern. One such technique uses a mold, just like in nano-imprint lithography, only this time the mold is "inked" with molecule-containing ink. This is really like the child's stamp and ink set. As it is pressed against a surface, it leaves behind its pattern of ink marks. The process is referred to as microcontact printing. It is easy to imagine going from a "stamp" to a "paint roller" to accomplish mass fabrication of nanostructured layers.

Another "molecular ink" technique takes advantage of the ability to produce very sharp tips. Such tips are routinely used in the **atomic force microscope (AFM)** as shown below. An AFM measures attractive or repulsive forces between the tip and the surface of a sample. The tip is located on the end of a leaf spring or cantilever. As the tip is moved back and forth across the surface of a specimen, the cantilever records nano-deflections of the tip (in response to small changes in surface height). These tips can also be used much like quill pen tips in what is called dip-pen nanolithography, which is illustrated below. When dipped in molecule-containing ink and then carefully moved across a surface of a substrate, they can "write" nanofeatures in ink as thin as 50 nanometers.

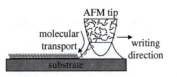

Dip-pen nanolithography uses a very sharp tip to deposit "molecular ink" onto a substrate. The sharp tip is often used in atomic force microscopy (AFM).

Sufficiently fine lines can now be written to literally fulfill Richard Feynman's vision of writing the Encyclopaedia Britannica on the head of a pin! In both microcontact printing and dip-pen nanolithography, subsequent processing steps such as heating are required to complete the molecular self-assembly process.

Are still finer features possible? Can we manipulate individual atoms? The **scanning tunneling microscope (STM)** also makes use of a very sharp tip and highly precise x-y-z positioning of that tip above a surface. It can be brought so close to the surface of a material that **quantum mechanical tunneling** takes place. You don't need to know the complicated physics behind tunneling, but with such tunneling the current becomes very sensitive to distance. In fact, the STM is sensitive to height differences of 0.1 nanometer on the surface of a material. By moving the tip back and forth across a surface, the STM is capable of resolving individual rows of atoms. That's the "microscope" mode, but voltage pulses can also be applied to blast "lines" or groups of atoms off the surface of specially prepared monolayers (single layers). For example, hydrogen monolayers can be laid down on silicon surfaces, and then blasted away in controlled patterns. The unsatisfied bonds along such rows or at such sites are then quite attractive for the selective deposition of yet other molecules. In this way lines or dots of molecules can be deposited in predefined nano-patterns.

What Can You Do with Nanotechnology?

It would be impossible to cover all of the current, emerging and potential applications of nanotechnology. Furthermore, this field is moving so quickly that any specific application might be obsolete by the time you get to read this chapter. But we can at least consider some of the fields in which nanotechnology will have major impact. The following table lists some key areas, including the properties being exploited and some example applications. Some of these have been around for a long time (e.g., catalysis), others are just now emerging (e.g., sensors), and still others have yet to be fully developed (e.g., **spintronics**).

Examples of Nanotechnology

Area	Properties	Example Applications
Nanochemical	chemically active surfaces	catalysis, propulsion
Nano-optical	color, absorption	UV skin protection, chemical sensors
NEMS	mechanical, electrical	accelerometers, sensors
Nanomagnetism	spin, giant magnetoresistance	spintronics, hard disks
Nanoelectronics	tunneling, junctions	nano-transistors, computer processors

It should be stressed that the unique properties of nanomaterials enable each of the current and pending applications. For example, high surface area/reactivity underlies the use of nanoparticles in catalysis, thereby speeding up technologically important chemical reactions. The unusual color vs. size/shape relationships of nanoparticles can be used in chemical sensing. As a chemical species to be sensed interacts with nanoparticles, adsorption on their surfaces and/or aggregation of particles can lead to readily detectable color changes. The field of **MEMS** or **micro-electro-mechanical systems** is the integration of mechanical elements, sensors, actuators and electronics on silicon substrates by micro-fabrication methods. Similarly, **NEMS**, or **nano-electro-mechanical systems** will be the integration of nano-sized elements (sensors, actuators, electronics) via nanofabrication. An example of a NEMS sensor might be a cantilever (a nanoscale "leaf spring"), which can bend as a chemical species to be sensed is adsorbed on it, resulting in a change in electrical signal. Yet another area of interest is nano-magnetism. Scientists are learning how information can be stored in the spins of electrons (as opposed to its storage as charge) and also how really thin nanolayers can exhibit big changes in resistance with changes in magnetic field, so-called **giant magnetoresistance or GMR**. This exciting new area is referred to as "spintronics," i.e., spin-based electronics. The last area of nanoelectronics deals with how we might perpetuate Moore's law, stuffing more and more transistors into smaller and smaller spaces. This exciting area is more fully addressed in the following case study.

We would be remiss not to mention some potentially deleterious aspects of nanotechnology. For instance, there are growing concerns about nanoparticles entering our water supplies. Given thier small size, nanoparticles are extremely difficult to remove, e.g., they are far too small for conventional filtration. Recent animal studies have demonstrated that nano-fibers (e.g., carbon nanotubes) can be carcinogenic. As with any new technology, we need to proceed in a responsible way, if we are to realize the benefits of nanotechnology and mitigate any risks.

33. CASE STUDY: NANOELECTRONICS

One of the most talked-about aspects of the microelectronic revolution is **Moore's Law**, the fact that the number of transistors on a single integrated circuit (IC) "chip" has roughly doubled every 18 months over the past few decades (referred to as an "exponential" increase). This translates into increasingly fast and powerful personal computers, with the only downside being their equally fast obsolescence. But the end—of Moore's Law and faster/more powerful computers—may be in sight, unless we can find a way to pack still more transistors into smaller spaces on the ICs of the future. In this chapter we consider the limits to conventional micro (micron-scale) electronics and why nano (nano-scale) electronics may save the day by perpetuating Moore's Law into the future. In the words of Gordon Moore, "No Exponential is forever … but we can delay 'forever'."

The Limits to Microelectronics

We can translate the number of transistors on an integrated circuit into their spacing or "minimum feature size." This actually refers to the "gate length" of an individual transistor (see the Semiconductor Device chapter), but the spacing of transistors is closely related. Obviously, the more transistors per area on a chip the closer their spacing and the smaller their individual size. The following figure shows minimum feature size in integrated circuits vs. year of manufacture. Back in the 1960s, early IC elements were in the 10–100 micrometer range, or similar to the diameter of a human hair. As shown in the graph below, by the 1980s, feature size had been reduced to approximately 1 micrometer.

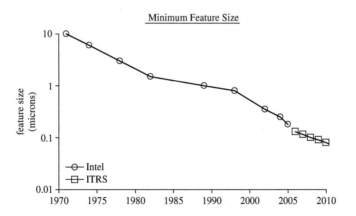

The decreasing minimum feature size of transistor components is shown for both Intel products and data reported by the International Technology Roadmap for Semiconductors (ITRS).

For comparison purposes, a white blood cell is approximately 10 micrometers in diameter with a wall thickness of 1 micrometer. By 2005, minimum feature size had been reduced an additional order of magnitude to 0.1 micrometer, or approximately the size of the AIDS virus. This is an absolutely amazing accomplishment.

But there are major problems with the downsizing of microelectronics. The first problem has to do with fabrication. We are nearing the capability limits of conventional **photolithography**, the process used to make ICs. In this process, light is used to weaken the bonds in a polymer **photoresist** layer placed on top of silicon. By exposing the photoresist to light through a mask, the exposed regions can then be removed by a solvent, leaving behind the unexposed regions in the exact pattern of the mask (see Chapter 27). Doping of the exposed silicon can then be accomplished by techniques such as **ion implantation**, whereas the remaining photoresist regions do not allow for implantation. In this way, n- and p-type areas can be selectively made on the IC surface in precisely the pattern dictated by the mask. The limitation has to do with the wavelength of light, from 0.4 to 0.7 micrometers, which governs the minimum feature size possible with photolithography. There are various strategies, including the use of ultraviolet light for photolithography, capable of getting the minimum feature size down below 0.1 micrometers or 100 nanometers—we are currently at the level of 50 nm—but not much further.

The other problem has to do with power losses or **dissipation**. As described in Chapter 27, field effect transistors depend upon a thin insulator layer placed between the "gate" electrode and the underlying silicon. As this gets thinner and thinner, **quantum mechanical tunneling** becomes possible. This produces unwanted leakage current and power dissipation. We are fast approaching the point where power losses due to leakage will match those due to the normal operation of the IC, and heat management is already a major issue in IC operation. One gets a good feel for heat dissipation by operating a laptop computer on his or her lap.

Nanoelectronics to the Rescue

Nano-transistors will be required to go much smaller than 50 nm, and to overcome the tunneling/leakage problem associated with the further downscaling of microelectronics. There are many possible strategies for the realization of nanoelectronics, but we will focus on two—carbon nanotube-based **nanoelectronics**, and **molecular electronics**.

Carbon nanotubes (Page 15) can be thought of as layers of the graphite crystal structure rolled up into hollow tubes. In spite of the fact that carbon nanotubes were known about for decades, they received much more attention since the report by S. Iijima in 1991. An example of a "single-walled nanotube" or SWCNT is shown in the on Page 15. By adjusting the "twist" of the rolling process, one arrives at tubes with very different properties, e.g., semiconducting vs. conducting. The following figure shows a semiconducting SWCNT placed between two electrodes but adjacent to a third "gate" electrode

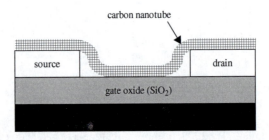

Diagram of a nanotube field-effect transistor (FET) with a semiconducting carbon nanotube placed between a source and drain electrode; the electric field on the lower gate electrode governs current transport through the nanotube.

in a field effect transistor configuration. Small changes in electric field applied to the "gate" leads to large swings in the current along the axis of the nanotube, hence a nanotube transistor.

In addition, leakage between the nanotube and the gate can be quite small, reducing dissipation losses. The challenge is how to reliably and reproducibly manufacture and place literally billions of such nanotubes (per chip) into standard IC configurations.

The second approach involves what is referred to as **molecular electronics**. The field of molecular electronics seeks to use individual molecules to perform functions in electronic circuitry now performed by semiconductor junction devices. For example, asymmetric molecules can be placed between electrodes spaced nanometers apart, leading to differences in forward vs. reverse current. It is ironic that the process of molecular conduction takes advantage of the same quantum mechanical tunneling we wish to avoid in conventional microelectronics.

When John Bardeen, Walter Brattain and William Schockley demonstrated the first transistor at IBM in 1947, no one could have imagined the impact that microelectronics would have on our lives. Similarly, scientists have recently demonstrated carbon nanotube-based transistors and a variety of single molecule electronic devices. It remains to be seen how nanoelectronics will shape life in the 21st century.

34. BIOMATERIALS

You probably know someone with **biomaterials** in their body. Common examples of biomaterial devices are joint replacements, heart valves, and intraocular lenses (corneal implants for cataract surgery). You may even have biomaterials in your mouth in the form of metal fillings or ceramic onlays. This chapter considers a brief history of biomaterials, some of their unique requirements, and current and emerging applications.

Biomaterials have been around since antiquity. Sutures for closing up large wounds have been employed for millennia. The ancient Egyptians used linen sutures whereas catgut was favored during the Middle Ages in Europe. Dental implants were developed in several early civilizations. For example, around 600 A.D. the Mayans were fabricating teeth from the nacre or "mother of pearl" in sea shells and were able to achieve what is now referred to as "bone integration." **Dental amalgams** have been around for more than 150 years. When roughly equal amounts of liquid mercury and a powdered mixture of several metals (silver, tin and copper) are mixed, a hard and stable filling/sealant for dental "caries" (cavities) results. In spite of concern over us carrying mercury around in our mouths, there seems to be little evidence linking any health risks with the proper application of such amalgams (American Dental Association).

The major developments, however, in biomedical materials have been since World War II, including hip and knee prostheses, dental implants for artificial teeth, "stents" (expandable tubes of metallic mesh) for opening blocked arteries, replacement heart valves, and intraocular lenses for cataract surgery. The highly publicized (and litigated) use of polymers known as silicones for breast reconstruction (following mastectomy) or augmentation illustrates some of the unique challenges associated with using biomaterials in the human body. On the other hand, the lives of a million patients worldwide depend upon the use of other biomaterials. These patients suffer from kidney failure and rely on hemodialysis to filter their blood, typically three times a week. Polymer films such as polymethyl methacrylate (PMMA) serve as the membranes in dialysis machines. Without such treatments, life expectancy is less than a month. Although we are a long way from the "bionic" man, there are many applications of biomaterials in the human body, some of which are shown in the following illustration.

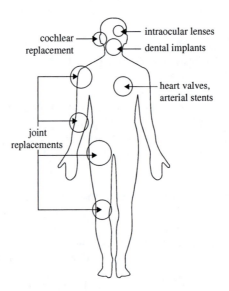

Illustration of biomaterials in the body.

A frequently cited definition of a biomaterial is "a nonviable (non-living) material used in a medical device, intended to interact with biological systems." With the advent of "tissue engineering," whereby living cells are used to aid tissue formation or regeneration, and biotechnology applications extending far beyond medicine, biomaterials should be defined more broadly as "materials designed to interact with biological systems."

But is "biomaterials" worthy of being considered a separate subdiscipline within materials science and engineering? On the basis of materials currently employed in the human body, the answer might seem to be "no." The following table lists a wide range of biomedical applications, and the types of materials involved. These clearly span the gamut of traditional materials, from titanium-based metals in joint replacements to "hydroxylapatite" ceramics[*] in "bony defect repair" to polymers in bone cement and intraocular lenses. If we add the silicon-based micro-circuits employed in pacemakers, all the major classes of materials are represented in the list.

What makes biomaterials distinct is their "interaction" with biological systems. The biomaterials scientist/engineer is concerned with all the issues addressed thus far in this book: processing-microstructure relationships and microstructure-property relationships. For example, in load-bearing applications such as implants or joint replacements, mechanical strength and toughness are of paramount importance. But he or she will be equally concerned with property-performance relationships, especially related to the all-important issue of biocompatibility.

---

[*] Hydroxylapatite is a crystalline calcium phosphate ceramic that is especially compatible with human bone tissue.

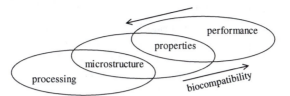

The processing-microstructure-properties-performance continuum for biomaterials.

Biocompatibility has to do with maintaining designed function over time in the biological system, e.g., the human body. This requires that there be no adverse influence of the body on the implanted biomaterials, for example due to corrosion. But more importantly, there must be no adverse impact of biomaterials on the surrounding tissues. Examples of "good" responses include resistance to blood clotting, resistance to bacterial colonization, and normal, uncomplicated healing. Examples of "bad" responses include immunological reactions (the body rejecting the implanted material), inflammation, and even tissue damage.

This means that the field of biomaterials, by definition, is an interdisciplinary enterprise at the intersection of materials science/engineering, biology, and medicine. The biomaterials scientist/engineer must know, or at least appreciate, these other fields, and will usually collaborate on teams with biologists and physicians.

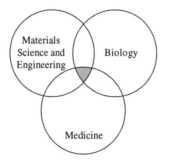

Biomaterials science and engineering.

Furthermore, the field of biomaterials is in a state of constant evolution. Three generations of biomaterials science and technology have been identified. The first generation, beginning in the 1950s, was concerned primarily with "bioinertness", i.e., the biocompatibility of materials in the human body. The second generation began in the 1980s. To the concept of bioinertness was added the concept of "bioactivity." For example, resorbable materials were developed to aid with controlled drug delivery and release, and also to facilitate bone bonding. **Resorbable materials** are temporary; they accomplish their function (drug release, bone bonding) and then are resorbed by the body.

We are now in the third generation of biomaterials (since 2000), which focuses on **tissue engineering**, in addition to bioinertness and bioactivity. In tissue engineering, biomaterials serve as temporary (resorbable) or permanent "scaffolds" on which or into which cellular growth occurs leading to tissue formation or regeneration. For example, implantable porous metal or ceramic scaffolds can now be fabricated into which living bone tissue can grow and become fully integrated. One recent ramification of this third generation of biomaterials is the heated public debate over stem cell research. Embryonic stem cells are particularly flexible in being guided (by proper scaffolding) into forming specific and even "designed" tissues/structures. It remains to be seen how this and future generations of biomaterials will help to improve the quality of human life.

Examples of Biomaterials in the Human Body

Applications	Types of Materials Employed
Joint replacements	Titanium, Ti-Al-V alloy, stainless steel, polyethylene
Bony defect repairs	Hydroxylapatite
Bone cement	Polymethyl methacrylate (PMMA)
Dental implants	Titanium, Ti-Al-V alloy, stainless steel, polyethylene
Heart valves	Stainless steel, carbon
Stents (for occluded arteries)	Stainless steel, Ni-Ti alloy (Nitinol)
Intraoccular lenses	Polymethyl methacrylate (PMMA), silicone rubber, hydrogel
Cochlear (inner ear) replacement	Platinum electrodes

QUESTIONS: Chapters 32–34

1. Which of the following changes does <u>not</u> happen to materials at the nanometer scale?
   (a) the color changes   (b) the melting point increases   (c) the surface-to-volume ratio increases
   (d) all of these occur   (e) none of these occur

2. Surface atoms exhibit higher energy than bulk atoms because of _____ .
   (a) altered bonding   (b) their greater numbers   (c) smaller size
   (d) the shape of the particle   (e) none of these

3. As a particle becomes smaller in size, its surface-to-volume ratio _____ .
   (a) decreases   (b) increases   (c) stays the same
   (d) depends on the shape of the particle   (e) has nothing to do with particle size

4. Which force(s) become dominant at the nanoscale?
   (a) capillary   (b) gravitational   (c) adhesive   (d) b and c
   (e) a and c

5. Nano imprint lithography uses a(n) _____ to carve out a mold used for creating nanoscale patterns.
   (a) ion beam   (b) laser beam   (c) ultraviolet beam   (d) electron beam
   (e) none of these

6. With nanosphere lithography, _____-sized spheres create dots that are around _____ in size.
   (a) 100 nm, 10 nm   (b) 1 μm, 1 μm   (c) 10 nm, 1 μm   (d) 1mm, 100 nm
   (e) 10 nm, 100 nm

7. Which of the following microscopy techniques can be used to manipulate nanoparticles by dip-pen lithography?
   (a) SEM   (b) STM   (c) STEM   (d) AFM   (e) none of these

8. What is the limiting factor for the size of transistors made today using photolithography?
   (a) the wavelength of light used for etching
   (b) the intensity of light used for etching
   (c) the materials used for making masks
   (d) the chemical solvents used to remove the photoresist
   (e) all of the above

9. Quantum mechanical tunneling causes which of the following problems in today's integrated circuits?
   (a) dissipation   (b) short-circuiting   (c) current leakage   (d) a and c   (e) none of the above

10. What is varied in SWNT's to produce semi-conducting properties?
    (a) length   (b) diameter   (c) twist   (d) radius   (e) composition

11–16. Like photolithography, nano-imprint lithography is a ___11___ approach to creating nanoscale materials. Because photolithography is constrained by the ___12___ of visible or ultraviolet light used, nano-imprint lithography uses electron beams with ___13___ wavelengths to etch finer structures for the mold. This mold can then be pressed into a resist substrate in multiple layers to create 3-D nanostructures. For ___14___ procedures like dip-pen lithography, a(n) ___15___ tip can be used to precisely drop and arrange nanoparticles in a desired pattern. The particles are suspended in a "molecular ink" and deposited on a substrate by carefully ___16___ the tip across the surface.

    11. (a) bottom-up   (b) top-down   (c) simultaneous   (d) piece-by-piece
    12. (a) intensity   (b) polarization   (c) wavelength   (d) brightness   (e) speed
    13. (a) longer   (b) wider   (c) slower   (d) shorter   (e) faster
    14. (a) bottom-up   (b) top-down   (c) simultaneous   (d) piece-by-piece
    15. (a) STM   (b) SEM   (c) STEM   (d) AFM   (e) HRTEM
    16. (a) dotting   (b) etching   (c) scanning (d) scraping

17. Which metal is not a major constitutent of dental amalgams?
    (a) copper   (b) iron   (c) mercury   (d) tin   (e) silver

18. Which of the following is a "good" biocompatibility reaction?
    (a) inflammation   (b) tissue damage   (c) uncomplicated healing   (d) immunological reactions
    (e) none of the above

19. Which of the following is not a property of resorbable biomaterials?
    (a) temporary   (b) resorbed by the body   (c) can serve as scaffolds
    (d) can deliver controlled drug release   (e) none of the above

SUMMARY QUESTIONS

1–3. The processing of a material can involve __1__ . By changing these manufacturing stages one can significantly change the __2__ which in turn changes the __3__ .

1. (a) annealing   (b) heating   (c) quenching   (d) rolling   (e) all of these

2. (a) structure   (b) size   (c) density   (d) properties   (e) both b and c

3. (a) structure   (b) properties   (c) shape   (d) melting point   (e) color

4–7. Throughout the book we have encountered some elements which are probably new to us. What applications (materials) did we mention which used the following elements?

4. cobalt   5. gallium   6. europium   7. niobium
(a) HSLA steels   (b) magnets   (c) TV screen phosphors   (d) optical fibers
(e) high efficiency solar cells

8. Select the true statement from the following:
(a) all polymers are ductile at room temperature
(b) the core glass of an optical fiber is pure SiO_2
(c) tempered glass contains very small crystals
(d) impurities are important in determining the color of a phosphor dot on a TV tube
(e) a broken fiber cannot be tolerated in a composite

9. Select the incorrect statement from the following:
(a) some metals are non-magnetic
(b) most metals are ductile
(c) no metals are liquid at room temperature
(d) metals contain ions but do not have ionic bonds
(e) metals are lustrous because they contain free electrons

10. Which of the following is not one of the ways to strengthen polymers or ceramics?
(a) flame polishing   (b) precipitation hardening   (c) compressive loading   (d) vulcanization
(e) crystallization

11–14. What application do you identify with the following materials?

11. cordierite   12. gallium arsenide   13. polyacetylene   14. chromium oxide
(a) magnetic recording tape
(b) a catalytic converter
(c) a conducting polymer
(d) optical fibers
(e) high speed electronics

15–24. Getting impurities out of a material is a challenge for the materials scientist. We discussed how chromium could be purified by first reacting the chromium (and all its impurities) with __15i__ to produce __15ii__ s. The resulting mixture of __15ii__ s is then purified using a process called __16__ . Purified chromium __15ii__ is then decomposed by passing it through a very hot furnace where pure chromium is produced by a process called __17__ . We also saw how the __18__ of carbon-carbon composites can be formed from the __17__ of carbon from __19__ .In optical fibers the core glass is also produced using __17__ . A gas mixture of purified __20__ and __21__ passes through a hot tube and glass is formed. To increase the __22__ we add a small amount of purified __23__ to the gas mixture. This adds an impurity to the glass which increases the __22__ but produces no light __24__ .

15. (a) chlorine, chloride   (b) iodine, iodide   (c) sulfur, sulfide   (d) bromine, bromide
(e) oxygen, oxide

16. (a) distillation   (b) vitrification   (c) annealing   (d) chemical vapor deposition
    (e) sintering
17. (a) zone refining   (b) chemical vapor deposition   (c) polycondensation   (d) doping
18. (a) matrix   (b) surface   (c) precipitates   (d) filler   (e) both a and d
19. (a) carbon dioxide   (b) chlorine   (c) acetylene   (d) methane   (e) diamond
20. (a) titanium oxide   (b) geranium chloride   (c) silicon chloride   (d) silicon oxide
21. (a) nitrogen   (b) oxygen   (c) helium   (d) both a and b
22. (a) density   (b) reflectivity   (c) electron density   (d) strength   (e) crack resistance
23. (a) chromium iodide   (b) gallium arsenide   (c) geranium iodide   (d) iron
    (e) germanium chloride
24. (a) reflection   (b) absorption   (c) transmission   (d) emission   (e) refraction

25–26. The electrons in a certain material have a full band of possible energies separated from a completely empty energy band by an energy gap of 7 eV.

25. This material is a(n) _____.
    (a) semiconductor   (b) insulator   (c) electrical conductor   (d) none of these

26. What color is a single crystal of the material?
    (a) red   (b) violet   (c) yellow   (d) colorless   (e) none of these

27–29. An impurity atom is added to the material of questions 25–26 and introduces an energy level 2.1 eV below the empty band. __27__ kick(s) an electron from the full band to the empty band, and when the electron returns to the full band via this impurity level __28__ light is __29__ .

27. (a) microwaves   (b) infrared light   (c) blue light   (d) ultraviolet light
    (e) radio waves
28. (a) red   (b) yellow   (c) violet   (d) orange   (e) green
29. (a) transmitted   (b) reflected   (c) emitted   (d) absorbed   (e) absorbed

30–46. Impurities in materials are very important. As single atoms they can be __30__ and sometimes they occur in large groups called __31__. Regular window glass is opaque and a blue-green color if you try to look through a few inches thickness. This is because of the presence of __32__ impurity which produces some __33__ of light. Glass for optical fibers is pure __34__ which has been doped with __35__. This impurity is chosen because it produces no __33__, and because it is a __36__ impurity with more __37__ it increases the __38__ of the glass. In making Corning Ware we add __39__ impurity to act as nuclei for the formation of __40__. This process of forming __40__ from glass is called __41__. Corning Ware is very strong because of the presence of very small __40__, and does not break when taken straight from the freezer and placed on a hot burner. We call this property __42__. We add the impurity __43__ to rubber to produce __44__. The important impurity in HSLA steels is __45__; the impurity making silicon a p-type semiconductor is __46__.

30. (a) substitutional   (b) interstitial   (c) intrinsic   (d) both a and c   (e) both a and b
31. (a) dislocations   (b) point defects   (c) interstices   (d) precipitates   (e) chains
32. (a) silicon   (b) germanium   (c) iron   (d) carbon   (e) oxygen
33. (a) refraction   (b) transmission   (c) aberration   (d) emission   (e) absorption
34. (a) silicone   (b) silicon oxide   (c) geranium   (d) lead silicate   (e) silicon carbide
35. (a) silicon   (b) germanium   (c) iron   (d) carbon   (e) oxygen
36. (a) substitutional   (b) interstitial   (c) intrinsic   (d) both a and c   (e) both a and b
37. (a) photons   (b) phonons   (c) bonds   (d) neutrons   (e) electrons
38. (a) hardness   (b) refractive index   (c) absorption   (d) internal reflection
    (e) conductivity
39. (a) titanium oxide   (b) aluminum oxide   (c) lead oxide   (d) niobium carbide
    (e) gallium arsenide
40. (a) voids   (b) crystals   (c) precipitates   (d) both a and c   (e) both a and b
41. (a) solidification   (b) hardening   (c) devitrification   (d) deregulation   (e) sintering
42. (a) thermal shock resistance   (b) impact resistance   (c) shear strength
    (d) chemical interness
43. (a) boron   (b) carbon   (c) sulfur   (d) nitrogen   (e) oxygen
44. (a) chain stiffening   (b) crystallization   (c) amorphization   (d) crosslinking
    (e) relaxation

45. (a) germanium   (b) aluminum   (c) niobium   (d) iron   (e) nitrogen

46. (a) germanium   (b) aluminum   (c) niobium   (d) iron   (e) nitrogen

47–56. Metals consist of atoms held together by metallic bonds, whereas ceramics can contain __47__ bonds. Polymers have chains of carbon atoms with __48__ bonds along a chain but __49__ bonds between adjacent chains. In polymers it is the __49__ bonds which are usually thought of as the weakness in the material. Metals can often be strained several percent in tension because of __50__ , whereas polymers often can be strained much more than metals because of __51__ . Ceramics cannot be strained very much because the __50__ cannot move easily. One reason for this is the __52__ bonds which are __53__ . Usually ceramics break catastrophically because of __54__ . Polymers break in a similar manner when they __55__ . It is important to remember that in all materials, fracture involves the breaking of __56__ .

47. (a) covalent   (b) hydrogen   (c) ionic   (d) metallic   (e) both a and c
48. (a) covalent   (b) van der Waals   (c) hydrogen   (d) ionic   (e) metallic
49. (a) covalent   (b) secondary   (c) ionic   (d) metallic   (e) directional
50. (a) grain boundaries   (b) dislocations   (c) precipitates   (d) impurities
    (e) weak bonds
51. (a) chain sliding   (b) chain straightening   (c) steric hindrance   (d) both a and b
    (e) both a and c
52. (a) covalent   (b) van der Waals   (c) hydrogen   (d) ionic   (e) metallic
53. (a) strong   (b) directional   (c) non-directional   (d) rotating   (e) both a and b
54. (a) surface flaws   (b) weak bonds   (c) vacancies   (d) impurities   (e) dislocations
55. (a) contain fluorine   (b) are compressed   (c) are above the glass transition temperature
    (d) are copolymers   (e) none of these
56. (a) grain boundaries   (b) crystals   (c) atoms   (d) bonds   (e) any of these

57–65. Metals are __57__ because they have rather fluid metallic bonds and __58__ motion occurs when metals are stressed, causing deformation. Ceramics deform very little under stress because they either have __59__ bonds or ions which repel each other if moved. Both of these interfere with __58__ motion and as a result, ceramics __60__ under stress. Ceramics can be strengthened by eliminating surface cracks and scratches or keeping them from propagating. One approach used to strengthen glasses is __61__ where the surface is remelted to get rid of small surface cracks. Another method is to cool the surfaces of the hot glass quickly, setting up __62__ stresses at the surface. __63__ ceramics may be strengthened by __64__ . The __65__ in ceramics blunt cracks in the same way that the __65__ in metals stop __58__ motion.

57. (a) brittle   (b) soft   (c) weak   (d) strong   (e) ductile
58. (a) grain boundary   (b) impurity   (c) dislocation   (d) precipitate   (e) bond
59. (a) strong   (b) weak   (c) directional   (d) both a and c   (e) both b and c
60. (a) bend   (b) fail catastrophically   (c) stretch   (d) blunt   (e) slip
61. (a) sintering   (b) hot rolling   (c) flame polishing   (d) tempering
    (e) layering
62. (a) tensile   (b) shear   (c) compressive   (d) yield   (e) no
63. (a) amorphous   (b) dense   (c) light weight   (d) crystalline   (e) layered
64. (a) making the grains larger   (b) stopping dislocation motion   (c) making the grains smaller
    (d) scratching the surface   (e) adding pores
65. (a) grain boundaries   (b) pores   (c) bonds   (d) tensile stresses   (e) both a and c

GLOSSARY

Acceptor impurity: An substitutional impurity in an insulator or a semiconductor which has (usually) one less electron than the atom it replaces. Because of this there are insufficient electrons to form the covalent bonds and an electron hole is produced.

Activated carbon: A granular and highly porous form of carbon used in filtration.

Activators: Special impurities added to materials to introduce mid-band gap states and therefore introduce specific energies (and color) of emission in luminescence.

Adhesion: The molecular attraction exerted between bodies in contact, causing them to "stick" together.

Alloy: A mixture of two or more metals. Mixing usually occurs in the molten state. The solid may contain more than one phase, as in aluminum-lithium alloys, and each phase often contains some of each metal. There is no need for the two atoms each to be arranged in a repeat pattern (see 'Intermetallic compound').

Alloying element: An element added to another to produce an alloy. It is usually the element which is present in the smaller proportion. Example, niobium in HSLA steels.

Amorphous: Having no long-range periodic crystal structure. There may be some short range order, such as the silicon/oxygen tetrahedra in glass, but the order does not extend further than a few atoms. Often considered the opposite of crystalline. In polymers it means that the carbon chains are not arranged in an ordered manner.

Angstrom unit (Å): Small distance measurement, being 10^{-8} cm. An atom is around 2Å across. This unit is gradually being replaced by the nanometer (10^{-9} meters). One nanometer is equal to ten angstrom units.

Anion: An atom which has acquired one or more electrons so that it has a negative charge.

Anisotropy: A characteristic of a material showing quite different properties in different directions. Example, graphite is strong parallel to the planes of carbon atoms but weak in the perpendicular direction. Caused by the crystal structure of the material.

Annealing: Process of heating a material to a high enough temperature for the atoms to move around and thus eliminate defects. Used to soften materials after work hardening or precipitation hardening.

Anode: The positive electrode or terminal of a battery. It attracts anions: negative ions.

Antiferromagnets: Materials such as chromium in which the atoms are magnetic but arrange their individual magnets so that they are aligned in opposite directions and therefore cancel each other.

Atomic force microscope (AFM): A microscope with very high resolution (on the atomic scale) that functions by dragging a small cantilevered tip over a sample and recording the miniscule forces that result from the interaction between the tip and the sample. These forces can then be combined to form an image of the surface of the sample.

Atomic number: The number of electrons and the number of protons in an atom. Equal numbers make the atom electrically neutral. Each element has a unique atomic number.

Atomic structure: Refers to features of the material which are of the size of atoms, e.g. impurity atoms, vacancies, interstitials. When we substitute one atom in the material with another we are also changing the atomic structure, i.e. the atoms which compose the material.

Atomic weight: The weight in grams of 6.02×10^{23} atoms of an element.

Attenuation: Another term for the absorption of light as it passes through a transparent material.

Austenite: The face centered cubic (FCC) form of iron which exists at temperatures above approximately 912° C. It is the form of iron which can dissolve the most carbon. When iron is heated to form austenite it becomes softer because the carbon dissolves. When cooled, the carbon forms precipitates with the alloying elements causing the metal to become harder. (Also called "gamma" phase.)

Band energy diagram: Diagram showing the energy steps in a solid which are so close together that they seem to form continuous bands of possible energies.

Band gap: Large jumps of energy between bands of filled and unfilled energy bands in the band energy diagram of a material.

Bands: The energy "ramps" of narrowly-spaced filled or unfilled energy states in the band energy diagram of a material.

Bend strength: The stress needed to fracture a material in a three-point or four-point bending test.

Benzene ring: A hexagon of six carbon atoms. When it exists as benzene, each carbon atom is covalently bonded to a hydrogen atom. In polystyrene there are only hydrogen atoms on the five carbon atoms which are not directly attached to the polymer chain.

Biocompatibility: The biological compatibility, i.e., long-term stability and maintained function over the course of time, of materials use in biological systems (usually the human body).

Biomaterials: Non-living materials used in a medical or biological device and intended to interact with living systems.

Blend: A mixture of two or more polymers.

Block copolymer: A material in which the polymer chain consists of two or more mers which occur in blocks along the chain.

Body-centered cubic (BCC): A non-close-packed metallic crystal structure, based upon a cubic unit cell with atoms at corners and the body center.

Breakdown: The loss of insulating character when a high enough voltage is placed across an insulator.

Calorie: Unit of energy being the amount of energy required to raise the temperature of one gram of water by 1°C.

Capillary force: Is the force by which one substance draws another (usually liquid) substance into it. This occurs when the adhesive intermolecular forces between a liquid and substance are greater than the cohesive forces/intermolecular forces in the liquid. This causes the liquid to be "sucked up" or "sucked into" the substance.

Carbon black: A purified form of amorphous carbon.

Carbon/carbon composite: A composite of carbon fibers in a carbon matrix.

Carbon fiber reinforced plastic (CFRP): A composite made from carbon fibers in an epoxy resin.

Carbon nanotube: An ordered molecule made from rolling graphene sheets (the same layer in graphite) into seamless tubes.

Carbonization: Process of heating a material, often a polymer, to decompose it and drive off the elements other than carbon, and therefore leave a carbon residue. The heating must be done in the absence of oxygen so that the carbon does not burn.

Casting: Process of melting a material and pouring it into a mold, where is solidifies.

Cast iron: From antiquity, the term for iron containing large amounts of carbon which would be melted and cast into various shapes. Cast irons are still made today.

Catalysis: The acceleration (increase in rate) of a chemical reaction by means of a substance called a catalyst, which is itself not consumed by the overall reaction.

Catastrophic failure: Description of how ceramics (and glasses) tend to shatter.

Cathode: The negative electrode or terminal of a battery. It attracts cations: positive ions.

Cation: An atom which has lost one or more electrons so that it has a net positive charge.

Ceramics: inorganic, non-metallic materials (usually compounds, e.g., of metals and oxygen) that tend to be brittle but refractory (high melting) and poor conductors of heat and electricity.

Ceramist: a materials scientist/engineer who specializes in ceramics.

Charge carrier: An entity which carries the electrical current in a material. The two major types are electrons and electron holes. In some ionically bonded materials the ions may themselves move and thus transfer charge.

Chemical tempering: The process of "stuffing" the surfaces of brittle ceramics with large ions, whether by ion implantation or by ion exchange. A method of closing surface cracks for the purpose of strengthening.

Chemical vapor deposition: Process for producing a solid material from vapors. Sometimes it involves only one compound which decomposes when heated (methane to produce carbon or soot) whereas in other cases it involves the reaction of two or more gases to produce a solid and another gas (silicon chloride and oxygen react to produce solid silicon dioxide and chlorine gas).

Close packing: Arrangement of atoms in which they are packed like balls racked up for a pool game. Usually only used for metals, and solid inert gases, where all the atoms are the same size. Two types exist, cubic close packed (CCP) and hexagonal close packed(HCP).

Composites: Materials made by intentionally mixing two different materials to produce one which is superior to both. Nowadays this term is usually taken to refer to materials made with fibers of one component embedded in a matrix of another.

Composition: The chemical make-up of a material, i.e., the elements it contains.

Compressive strength: The stress needed to fracture a material under compressive loading.

Conductor: A material with its lower energy band being only partly filled. Very small amounts of energy are required to promote electrons to available energy levels, resulting in high conductivity.

Copolymer: A combination of two or more monomers in a polymer chain. Copolymers are classified as "block" (alternating lengths of different monomers along the backbone) or "graft" (with side branches being of different monomers than the backbone).

Covalent bonding: The primary bond type in which electrons are shared between adjacent atoms, leading to highly directional bonding. Since there are no free electrons, low conductivity (electronic, thermal) results.

Crack blunting: Exemplified by sharp cracks becoming blunt when encountering fibers in traversing a fiber-reinforced composite.

Crack bridging: Behind a propagating crack in a fiber-reinforced composite, where unbroken fibers hold the severed sides of the matrix together.

Cracking: The chemical splitting of complex hydrocarbons into simpler molecules.

Critical angle: Angle measured from the perpendicular to the surface at which a light ray in a material can just escape parallel to the outside surface of the material.

Light rays at angles greater than the critical angle suffer total internal reflection.

Critical current: Maximum amount of current which can be passed through a superconductor with it retaining its superconducting property.

Critical temperature: Maximum temperature at which a superconductor is superconducting.

Crosslinking: The forming of bonds or connections between adjacent polymer chains, e.g., by vulcanization. A means of toughening polymers.

Crosstalk: A problem with "twisted pairs" of wires in conventional telephone cables, whereby one pair "induces" currents (and overheard conversations!) in adjacent pairs.

Crystals: Volumes of material in which the atoms are arranged in a discernible repeat pattern in three dimensions. The repeat unit is known as the unit cell.

Crystallite: Term for small, micro-sized, grains or crystals.

Crystallization: The process of forming crystals. A means of strengthening polymers.

Crystal structure: The arrangement pattern of atoms within a unit cell, e.g. the BCC and FCC crystal structures. Materials can have the same atomic structure but different crystal structures (glass and quartz, diamond and graphite).

Cubic close-packed (CCP): One of two close-packed metallic crystal structures, where the basic motif on the close-packed plane is a triangle. Also often referred to as face-centered cubic (FCC), the unit cell is a cube with atoms at corners and also at face centers.

Debonding: Ahead of a propagating crack in a fiber-reinforced composite, where additional cracks open along fiber-matrix interfaces.

Delta prime: The crystal structure of the Al_3Li precipitates in Al-Li alloys.

Density: The mass or weight of a material divided by its volume.

Dental amalgams: Also known as silver fillings, dental amalgams are comprised of a mixture of mercury (45 to 50 percent), and an alloy of silver, tin, and copper.

Devitrification: Process of heating a glassy material to a temperature where the atoms begin to move around and arrange themselves to form crystals.

Diamond: The transparent, colorless, crystalline form of carbon, which is very hard (scratches glass).

Dimensionless quantity: A number obtained by dividing two quantities with the same units, e.g. strain is length divided by length.

Diode: An electrical device consisting of a junction that passes current in only one direction (under forward bias) but not the reverse (reverse bias).

Dipole: Any object having a separation of positive and negative charges.

Dislocation: A linear defect in a material often described as the termination of a partial plane of atoms in the material. It is the defect which allows planes of atoms in metal crystals to slide over each other a thousand times easier than they otherwise would.

Dislocation line: The line at the very edge of an edge dislocation.

Dissipation: The undesirable loss of energy over time, usually in the form of heat.

Domains: Regions where atom magnets are all aligned in the same direction.

Domain boundary: Volume between two magnet domains in which the individual atom magnets gradually change orientation from that of one domain to that of the other.

Donor impurity: A substitutional impurity in an insulator or a semiconductor which has (usually) one more electron that the atom it replaces. Because of this it has enough electrons to form the bonds and then has one left over. It donates this electron to the structure.

Dopant: Intentional impurity added to a material (e.g., a semiconductor or glass).

Doping: Process of intentionally adding impurities to a material (e.g., a semiconductor or glass).

Ductile: Malleable, susceptible to permanent deformation, as are most metals.

Dynamic equilibrium: A balance of flow, with as many objects (e.g., electrons) coming as well as going.

Ebonite: A rigid black solid produced by extensive vulcanization of rubber.

Edge dislocation: The line defect caused by a partial plane of atoms.

Elastic deformation or strain: A change in shape or dimensions of a material which disappears as soon as the force producing it is removed.

Elastomer: A polymer which has elastic properties like rubber.

Electric current: A flow of electricity.

Electromagnetic spectrum: The range of energies covering (with increasing energy)—radio waves, TV waves, microwaves, infrared light, ultraviolet light, and x-rays.

Electromagnetic wave: A wave such as light or x-rays, which has associated magnetic and electric fields. Because of this it causes electrons and other charged particles to move.

Electron density: Parameter which indicates the relative number of electrons in a certain volume of a solid. A higher electron density produces a larger refractive index.

Electron hole: The absence of an electron in the filled lower energy band of a semiconductor. Holes behave just like electrons, moving freely throughout the crystal, but in the opposite direction to electron movement.

Electron-hole pair: Defect produced when an electron is pulled out of its bond to produce a free electron and an electron hole.

Electron mobility: The effective speed of electrons or holes in a material in response to an applied field or voltage.

Electron shells: A simplified model of an atom has electrons in orbits or shells varying in distance and energy from the nucleus.

Electronic structure: The smallest structure level in a material referring to the arrangement and density of electrons, number of free electrons and electron holes, etc.

Electron volt: The energy picked up by an electron when it moves between a potential (voltage) difference of 1 volt.

Electrostatic attraction: Attraction between opposite electrical charges, e.g. an anion and a cation, and an electron and a cation.

Electrostatic field: An influence which exists between negatively and positively charged entities so that charged particles are accelerated from one to the other.

Elements: Any of the more than 100 known substances that cannot be broken down into simpler substances and that singly or in combination make up all matter.

Emitted light: Light that originates from, or is reflected (absorbed and re-emitted) from a material.

Engineering: The sum of all disciplines applying engineering design method of analysis-design-fabrication, in order to improve our quality of life.

Entropy: A physical parameter of a material which describes its disorder. The tendency to increase entropy is responsible for the spring of a polymer rubber chain.

Equiaxed microstructure: Microstructure of a material in which the crystals have approximately the same size in whichever direction you measure.

Extrinsic defects: Defects which come from outside the material, usually in the form of impurities (interstitial or substitutional).

Face centered cubic: Arrangement of atoms, all of the same type, which has them sitting on the corners of a cube with one in the center of each cube face. When the atoms are in contact, as in pure metals, the arrangement is also cubic close-packed (CCP).

Ferrite: 1. The low temperature (BCC) form of iron. (Also called "alpha" phase.)
    2. Name given to ceramic magnets in which some of the ions produce a net magnetic field.

Ferromagnets: Materials in which the individual atoms are magnetic and spontaneously align their magnets in the same direction to produce a magnetic field. Iron (ferro) is the most common example. Nickel and cobalt are others.

Field-effect transistor: The fileld-effect transistor (FET) is a three-terminal (transistor) device that relies on an electric field to control the extent and hence the conductivity of a 'channel' in a semiconductor materials (adjacent to the middle terminal or "gate"). Small change of field at the gate lead to dramatic changes of current through the channel.

Fiber: Thin filaments, often used to strengthen composites.

Firing: Term used to describe the heat-treatment of materials during processing.

Flame polishing: Process of passing a flame over the surface of glass to melt a thin layer of the surface. This gets rid of surface cracks, which do not form again on cooling because of the thinness of the melted layer.

Fluorescence: Property of a material in which it absorbs high energy ultraviolet light and emits visible light. The emission stops as soon as the ultraviolet light is turned off.

Fluxing ions: Impurity elements added to glass to make it melt at lower temperatures.

Free electrons: Electrons not tightly bound to a given atom and free to move.

Fullerenes: A family of cage-like molecules composed of hexagonal rings of atoms, e.g., of carbon, the most famous member being the C-60 molecule.

Giant magnetoresistance: Magnetoresistance is the property of a material describing its change of electrical resistance when an external magnetic field is applied to it. Materials with unusually large magnetoresistances are referred to as being "giant" or GMR materials.

Glass-ceramics: Materials which started as a glass but which have been devitrified so that they now contain very fine crystals cemented together with a little remaining glass.

Glass transition temperature: Temperature above which many polymers are quite plastic or rubbery, but below which they are brittle and will break like glass.

Glassy carbon: A hard brittle material in which graphite-like ribbons are all tangled up.

Graft copolymers: Polymers which have a main chain of one mer and side branches of a different mer.

Grain boundaries: The borders between adjacent grains in a microstructure, where the alignment of atomic planes are different on each side. Grain boundaries are often associated with disorder and have properties that differ from that of the adjacent grains (e.g., diffusion rates, etc.)

Grains: A term used interchangeably with 'crystals' for the individual crystals in a polycrystalline material. Adjacent grains have different orientations and are separated by **grain boundaries**.

Grain refining: Process of treating a metal (e.g., hot rolling in HSLA steels) to produce a very small (fine) grained microstructure.

Graphite: the opaque, black, layered crystalline form of carbon, which is very soft and slippery, but is very strong and stiff and conductive (heat, electrons) in one plane.

Hard magnets: Magnetic materials that tend to be hard mechanically and difficult or "hard" to demagnetize, often owing to the presence of precipitates.

Heat treatment: Term used in metallurgy to describe the various heating and cooling processes the material may be subjected to during its manufacture.

Hexagonal close-packed (HCP): one of two close-packed metallic crystal structures, where the basic motif on the close-packed plane is a hexagon, and resulting unit cell has hexagonal symmetry.

High-impact polymer: A copolymer grafting a rigid polymer to a rubbery polymer, imparting impact resistance as in high impact polystyrene (HIPS).

High-strength low-alloy (HSLA) steels: Steels with low impurity content, having high strength owing to grain refining.

Hydrogen bonding: The secondary bond type involving the electrostatic interaction of polar molecules.

Hydrocarbons: Molecular compounds containing hydrogen and carbon.

Imperfections: Defects in the periodic arrangement of atoms in crystals. These can be zero-dimensional (point defects), one-dimensional (dislocations) or two-dimensional (grain boundaries).

Inert gases: Elements in the rightmost column of the periodic table, which tend not to react with other elements to form compounds.

Insulator: A material with a relatively large band gap (typically > 5 eV) between its filled lower energy band and its higher energy unfilled band. Neither light nor heat can promote electrons to the unfilled bands, hence its insulating character.

Intermetallic compound: A compound of (usually) two metals in which the two atoms are each arranged in a regular repeat manner, see e.g. Al_3Li in aluminum-lithium alloys. (Different from an alloy where one atom may be randomly substituted for another in the crystal.)

Interstice: A small hole which exists between atoms in a crystal. Sometimes it is large enough to accommodate a small impurity atom (usually a non-metal such as carbon or nitrogen).

Interstitial: An impurity atom in an interstice (extrinsic) or sometimes an atom from the material itself which has been displaced into an interstice (intrinsic).

Intrinsic defects: Defects arising within the pure material itself, such as a vacancy (common) or an intrinsic interstitial (rare).

Ion exchange: A process whereby a ceramic or glass is dipped in a solution. Big ions from the solution exchange for smaller ions in the surface of the object, leading to tensile stresses at the surface. A method of closing surface cracks for the purpose of strengthening.

Ion implantation: A process of bombarding the surface of a material with a flux of ions that penetrate the surface and take up residence within the material, usually altering the properties (mechanical, electrical, etc.) close to the surface.

Ionic bonding: The primary bond type in which electrons are transferred from electropositive species (which become cations) to electronegative species (which become anions). Since there are no free electrons, low conductivity (electronic, thermal) results. This type of bonding is also non-directional.

Kiln: Term used by ceramists for furnaces used to heat ceramics during processing.

Laser: A semiconductor laser is similar to a light-emitting diode, except light bounces back and forth between mirrored surfaces, stimulating other light emission to get in resonance, until the light emerges as a highly coherent beam.

Light-emitting diode (LED): A semiconductor diode device that combines electrons from the n-type side and holes from the p-type side to produce visible light.

Long range order: The regularity of atom/molecule positions over long distances, as in crystals.

Luminescence: Collective term for the emission of light by fluorescence and phosphorescence.

Macrostructure: The largest structure level of a material, referring to its overall shape and engineering design.

Magnetic anisotropy: The behavior of crystalline magnetic materials with one or more strongly preferred directions of magnetization, i.e., spins strongly prefer specific crystallographic orientations.

Magnetic domains: Small volumes of a material in which all the individual atom magnets point in the same direction. A single crystal can be divided into many different domains.

Materials engineering: Engineering discipline which seeks to exploit processing-structure and structure-property relationships in order to tailor the properties of materials for specific applications.

Materials science: Scientific discipline which seeks to understand the relationships between the properties of a material and its different structure levels, and then to change properties by modifying the structure through different processing techniques.

Matrix: In a two phase material the matrix is the continuous part of the structure which contains the precipitates (as in Al—Li alloys) or the fibers (composites).

Mer: The unit which repeats to make up the polymer chain.

Metal whiskers: Very thin (1000Å crystals of metal which are not wide enough to allow dislocations to form. They are not more than a few microns long.

Metallic bonding: The primary bond type in metals where the atom cores (also called cations) are held together by a sea of all the valence or free electrons. The free nature of the electrons leads to high conductivity (electronic, thermal). This type of bonding is also non-directional.

Metals: opaque, lustrous materials (typically elements) that tend to be ductile and good conductors of heat and electricity.

Micro-electro-mechanical systems (MEMS): The technology of the very small mechanical devices, capable of converting electrical signals to mechanical changes or vice versa, merging at the nano-scale into nanoelectromechanical systems (NEMS).

Micron: Abbreviated form of the length measurement known as a micrometer (10^{-6} meters). One micron is equal to ten thousand (10^4) angstrom units or one thousand (10^3) nanometers.

Microstructure: Structure level in a material which relates to the size, shape, and orientation of the crystals (grains).

Mixing: Description of various processes used to homogenize composition of a material during processing.

Molecular Electronics: The use of individual molecules to perform functions in electronic circuitry now performed by semiconductor junction devices.

Molecular weight: Value obtained by adding the atomic weights of all the atoms in a molecule. For example, a water molecule (H_2O) has a molecular weight of ($2 \times 1.008 + 15.999$). Polymer chains are considered long molecules and can have molecular weights of tens of thousands up to a million.

Moore's Law: The observation that the number of transistors on a microchip has been increasing exponentially, doubling approximately every eighteen months and quadrupling every three years.

Multiplexing: The ability to pass many conversations or data streams simultaneously down an optical fiber, without interference.

Nano-electro-mechanical systems (NEMS): Nanoelectromechanical systems or NEMS are similar to Microelectromechanical systems (MEMS) but smaller, i.e., on the nanoscale.

Nanoelectronics: The term referring to high-density, patterned electronic devices, e.g., transistors, in "chips," similar to conventional microelectronics, but with devices on the nanoscale in size. Because of the small scale, quantum mechanical effects like tunneling need to be considered.

Nano-imprint lithography: A top-down method of creating nanoscale patterns by using an electron-beam to create a mold with 40 nm sized features. This mold is pressed onto a photoresist like a stamp to transfer the features and etch the pattern on the substrate.

Nanomaterials: Term for all classes of materials with features in at least one dimension being on the nanometer scale. The study of how materials behave when their dimensions are reduced to the nanometer scale. It can also refer to the materials themselves that are used in nanotechnology.

Nanometer: One billionth of a meter (10^{-9}), or about half the width of a DNA molecule.

Nanophase materials: Solid materials which have an exceptionally fine grain structure.

Nanosphere lithography: A top-down method for creating "nano-dots" by depositing the nanomaterial to be so patterned in the small spaces between sub-100 nm close-packed spheres. Once the spheres are dissolved away, the remaining interstitial spaces form a regular array of nanoparticles.

Nanotechnology: The term referring broadly to a field of applied science and technology whose unifying theme is the control of matter on the atomic and molecular scale, normally 1 to 100 nanometers, and the fabrication of devices within that size range.

n-type semiconductor: A semiconductor which has been doped with donor impurity atoms.

Nucleation: The onset of a phase transition in small regions, called nuclei, usually leading to the formation of precipitates.

Paramagnets: Materials such as titanium in which the atoms are magnetic but arrange their individual magnets so that they are aligned in random directions and therefore produce no net magnetic field.

Permanent magnets: Magnets which are not easily returned to the unmagnetized state, either because their domain boundaries are locked in position or because they are composed of single domain magnets.

Phase: A distinguishable portion of matter. The distinction may be because of atomic structure (e.g. aluminum-lithium solid solution and delta prime, Al_3Li) or crystal structure (e.g. FCC and BCC iron) differences. A material may consist of two or more phases.

Phase diagram: A map of conditions where certain phases are stable, usually in terms of temperature versus composition.

Phonon: A cooperative motion of atoms in the form of a wave which moves through a material carrying energy from one place to another. Phonons transport heat in materials which are held together by covalent and/or ionic bonds.

Phosphorescence: Property of a material in which it absorbs high energy ultraviolet light and emits visible light. The emission can be seen to continue for some time after the ultraviolet light has been turned off.

Photolithography: A process of patterning materials (e.g., silicon) by using a light-sensitive polymer, or photoresist, to mask certain regions of the surface and etch away only those places where further processing is desired.

Photon: Term used for an energy quantum of light. Light comes in discrete energy packets (photons) with each a different energy for each color.

Photoresist: A light-sensitive material used in several industrial processes, such as photolithography and photoengraving to form a patterned coating on a surface.

Pile-up: Name given to the crowding of dislocations on a slip plane where they are stopped by a grain boundary.

Plastic: Description of materials that can be permanently deformed or shaped (metals and many polymers).

Plastic deformation or strain: A change in the shape or dimensions of a material which remains after the force which produced it has been removed. It is the result of the movement of a large number of dislocations.

p-n Junction: The interface between n-type and p-type semiconductors, responsible for various diode processes (e.g., rectification, light-emission).

Point defects: Defects in a material which are concerned with the atomic structure, i.e. they are approximately the size of atoms. Vacancies and interstitial atoms are examples.

Polar molecules: Molecules in which there is a non-uniform distribution of electrons, causing one end of the molecule to have a positive charge and the other a negative charge.

Polycrystalline: Term used to describe a crystalline material which is made up of many small grains.

Polymers: long-chain molecules (macromolecules) built up from small units called, "mers," typically consisting of carbon (the backbones of the chain) and hydrogen, i.e., they are "hydrocarbons." They tend to be weaker than metals or ceramics, and are poor conductors of heat and electricity.

Powder metallurgy: Process of producing metal parts by compressing a powder into a mold of the desired part and then sintering.

Precipitate: Small particle of a different phase which is often produced in a material by the motion of atoms during heat treatment.

Precipitation hardening: Process of hardening a material by heat treating it so that a large number of small precipitates are formed, which impede dislocation motion during plastic deformation.

Primary bonds: The three strong bonds: covalent, ionic and metallic.

Processing: Term describing how materials are fabricated, how their microstructures are arrived at, and how they are shaped, including intentional control of composition, and often involving the application of temperature (e.g., furnaces, kilns, etc.) and pressure.

p-type semiconductor: A semiconductor which has been doped with acceptor impurity atoms.

Pullout friction: One of the most effective energy absorption mechanisms in fiber-reinforced composites, where fibers being pulled out of the matrix on either side of a propagating crack rub against the adjacent matrix.

Pyroceram: Special ceramics that can withstand sudden changes in heat (temperature).

Quantum mechanical tunneling: In quantum mechanics, quantum tunneling is the phenomenon by which a particle violates principles of classical mechanics by penetrating or passing through a potential barrier that should ordinarily prevent that process from occurring.

Quenching: Process of cooling a material very quickly with the aim of freezing the movement of atoms so that they stay in the positions they were in before quenching.

Radiation: The emission of electromagnetic energy in the form of visible light, x-rays, ultraviolet rays, etc.

Rapid solidification: Term used for the rapid cooling of a metal from the liquid (molten) to the solid state. Cooling is not quick enough to produce an amorphous metal, but can produce solid solutions with compositions which cannot be achieved with slow cooling methods.

Recrystallization: Process which often occurs inside a metal during annealing, when atoms move around enough to produce new and more perfect crystals than the previous ones which were dislocated and defective.

Rectification: The action of a diode to allow current flow in only one direction (forward) and not the reverse. Used to convert alternating current (AC) into direct current (DC).

Reflected light: Light that is absorbed and re-emitted by the surface of a material.

Refraction: The bending of a light wave as it moves from one medium to another.

Refractive index: Parameter of a material which is the ratio of the velocity of light in a vacuum to its velocity in the material. It determines the amount of bending (refraction) of a light ray when it enters a material.

Resorbable materials: Biomaterials that are temporary, i.e., they accomplish their function (drug release, bone bonding) and then are resorbed by the body.

Safety glass: The tempered (strengthened) glass used in side windows of automobiles.

Scanning tunneling microscope (STM): The STM is based on the concept of quantum mechanical tunneling. When a conducting tip is brought very near to a metallic or semiconducting surface, electrons begin to tunnel through the vacuum between them. The amount of current becomes very sensitive to distance (between the tip and the surface). Variations in current as the probe passes over the surface can be translated into high resolution (atomic-scale) images of the surface.

Science: The sum of all disciplines applying the scientific method of observation-hypothesis-experiment, in order to advance our understanding of the physical universe.

Secondary bonds: The two weaker bonds: van der Waals and hydrogen.

Seeding: The addition of impurity species that promote the formation of nuclei during precipitation or recrystallization.

Self-assembly: Self-assembly is a term used to describe processes in which a disordered system of pre-existing components forms an organized structure or pattern as a consequence of specific, local interactions among the components themselves, without external direction.

Semiconductor: A material with a relatively small band gap (< 2 eV) between its filled lower energy band and its higher energy unfilled band. Both light and heat can promote electrons to the unfilled bands, resulting in some conduction.

Shear strength: The stress needed to fracture a material in a shear (twisting) test.

Short range order: The regularity of atom/molecule positions over short (few atom) distances.

Single domain magnets: Magnets whose grain size is so small that each grain can only exist as a single domain because there is not enough room for domain boundaries.

Sintering: The fusion of ceramic or metal powders into a solid when heated to high temperatures. Occurs because of vacancy motion allowing atoms to move around. Sometimes a high pressure is also applied to push the particles together.

Slip planes: The planes in a crystal which slip over each other by dislocation movement during plastic deformation. They are usually the planes containing the highest atom density, i.e. the planes with the closest atom packing. (Sometimes called 'close-packed planes' even though they may not be close-packed in the strict sense of the word.)

Slip systems: The combination of close-packed planes (slip planes) and close-packed directions on which slip tends to take place.

Soft magnets: Magnetic materials that tend to be soft mechanically and easy to magnetize and demagnetize.

Solar cell: A semiconductor diode-based device, in which absorbed light results in the production of electron-hole pairs at the p-n junction. The resulting electrons and holes are separated and harvested at external electrodes, producing a voltage that can do work.

Solid solution/solubility: An intimate mixture of two or more types of atom in the solid state with no special spatial arrangement between them. Analogous to a liquid solution but in a frozen form.

Solid solution hardening: A means of strengthening/hardening metals by adding impurities that tend to pin dislocations, thereby impeding their motion.

Solubility limit: The maximum amount of a substance that can be dissolved in another substance.

Solutionizing: Heating a two-phase material to a high enough temperature to re-dissolve a second phase particle into solution in the major phase.

Soot: Very impure carbon, having no crystal structure.

Specific modulus: The stiffness or Young's modulus of a material divided by its density.

Specific strength: The strength of a material divided by its density.

Spinning: A means of making polymer fibers by pulling the polymer through a narrow orifice.

Spintronics: An emerging technology, which exploits the quantum spin states of electrons as well as making use of their charge state to store information, e.g., for computer memories.

Steric hindrance: Term used for the situation where a polymer chain cannot move or twist because there are large groups of atoms on it which get in each other's way.

Strain: The fractional change in a dimension of a material. Usually expressed as a percentage of the original length.

Stress: The force or load per unit area on a material.

Stress concentrators: Surface defects such as cracks amplify applied stresses at their tips, leading to premature fracture of materials, especially ceramics.

Structure: The internal architecture of a material, concerning a wide spectrum of sizes, from the structure of the individual atoms, which make up the material to the design and shape of the part being produced. We define five different scales of structure: electron(ic), atom(ic), crystal, micro and macro, in increasing size order.

Substitutional: Refers to an impurity atom taking the place of an atom of the pure material in its crystal structure, i.e. the impurity substitutes for the original atom.

Superalloy: A metal alloy, usually made using nickel or cobalt, which is resistant to high temperatures.

Superconductor: A material showing no electrical resistance.

Talc: A layered silicate mineral that is extremely soft and has a soapy or greasy feel; used as talcum powder.

Tensile strength: The strength of a material under tension.

Tension (or tensile testing): Measuring the response of a material by pulling on it.

Thermal shock resistance: Property of a material which indicates its resistance to cracking and fracture when subjected to large, sudden temperature changes.

Thermal tempering: Blowing cool jets of air on a glass going through its glass transition in order to set up a layered structure, with the interior in tension and the surfaces in compression. A method of closing surface cracks for the purpose of strengthening.

Thermoplastic: A polymer which becomes soft at high temperatures so that it can be plastically deformed.

Thermosetting resins (thermosets): polymers which harden when heated.

Tissue engineering: One use of biomaterials is to serve as temporary (resorbable) or permanent "scaffolds" on which or into which cellular growth occurs leading to tissue formation or regeneration.

Total internal reflection: Phenomenon used in optical fibers in which a light ray is 100% reflected at a boundary between the material it is in and a material with a lower refractive index.

Toughness: Related to the energy required to propagate cracks through a material. Plastic materials have deformation mechanisms that absorb a lot of energy during crack propagation; brittle ceramics do not.

Transformation zone: The region just ahead and behind a propagating crack in toughened zirconia, where the added volume of transformed second-phase particles acts to close the crack, leading to toughening.

Transition Metals: Term referring to the 40 chemical elements in the periodic table ranging from atomic numbers 21 to 30, 39 to 48, 71 to 80, and 103 to 112. They have partially filled d-level electrons, which are important in determining magnetic behavior.

Transmitted light: Light that passes through a material without being absorbed.

Ultimate tensile strength: The maximum stress a material can carry wihtout breaking.

Vacancy: A missing atom or ion in a crystal.

Vacancy motion: Important method for atom motion in a material in which the atom moves into an adjacent vacancy. Material is transported by the cooperative motion of a large number of atoms.

Valence electrons: the outermost electrons of an element, available for bonding.

Van der Waals bonding: The secondary bond type involving the electrostatic interaction of temporary dipoles between otherwise non-polar molecules.

Viscosity: The measure of a material's resistance to flow. Viscous fluids are resistant to flow.

Voltage gradient: Voltage divided by distance.

Von Mises criterion: In order to be ductile, a polycrystalline metal must possess five or more slip systems.

Vulcanization: The use of sulfur to form cross-links between the polymer chains in rubber or similar elastomers.

Whiskers: Small metal crystals, which are about 1000Å (100 nm) in diameter and no more than a few millimeters long. Their small size does not allow dislocations to form in them, hence they are very strong.

Work hardening: A means of strengthening/hardening metals by deforming them, thereby increasing their dislocation density. The additional dislocations get in the way of one another, thereby impeding their motion.

Yield strength: The load required to initiate permanent plastic deformation, usually defined by 0.2 percent (0.002) plastic strain.

Young's modulus: Physical parameter of a material which is a measure of its stiffness. Calculated by dividing stress by strain.

Zone refining: A process in which a molten zone is passed along the length of a bar-shaped specimen, whereby impurities concentrate in the zone and are swept up and toward the ends.

SOLUTIONS TO QUESTIONS

Chapters 1–5

1. a	2. d	3. c	4. b	5. a	6. b	7. c	8. e	9. a	10. d
11. c	12. d	13. a	14. e	15. c	16. d	17. d	18. b	19. b	20. d
21. a	22. b	23. e	24. d	25. d	26. a	27. b	28. d	29. d	30. b
31. b	32. a	33. d	34. c	35. a	36. a	37. a	38. a	39. c	40. c
41. e	42. d	43. e	44. c						

Chapters 6–8

1. e	2. d	3. a	4. a	5. b	6. c	7. c	8. c	9. d	10. d
11. a	12. a	13. a	14. e	15. b	16. d	17. d	18. d	19. a	20. a
21. c	22. b	23. c	24. a	25. c	26. b				

Chapter 9

1. b	2. d	3. c	4. d	5. d	6. b	7. e	8. c	9. c	10. c

11. (a) 100 p. s. i.   (b) 0. 1%   (c) 100,000 p. s. i.   (d) 300 p. s. i.   (e) yes

Chapters 10–13

1. d	2. e	3. b	4. d	5. e	6. b	7. d	8. b	9. d	10. c
11. a	12. a	13. d	14. b	15. a	16. c	17. b	18. d	19. e	20. b
21. c	22. d	23. b	24. c	25. e	26. c	27. a	28. d	29. b	30. c
31. a	32. c	33. e	34. c	35. d	36. a	37. a	38. d		

Chapters 14–17

1. e	2. e	3. d	4. d	5. b	6. e	7. c	8. b	9. c	10. a
11. e	12. a	13. c	14. d	15. c	16. e	17. c	18. a	19. e	20. d

21. a   22. c   23. b   24. d   25. b   26. c   27. e   28. a   29. b   30. b

31. b   32. b   33. d   34. d   35. a   36. b   37. d   38. a   39. c   40. b

41. a   42. c   43. a   44. b   45. a   46. d   47. b

Chapters 18–21

1. e   2. d   3. d   4. b   5. a   6. a   7. c   8. e   9. b   10. e

11. e   12. e   13. c   14. d   15. d   16. e   17. b   18. c   19. c   20. a

21. d   22. c   23. b   24. b   25. b   26. e   27. e   28. e   29. a   30. c

31. a   32. a   33. b   34. c   35. b   36. c   37. a   38. d   39. b   40. b

41. c   42. a   43. c   44. e   45. c   46. d   47. e   48. e

Chapters 22–23

1. c   2. b   3. c   4. d   5. c   6. d   7. d   8. d   9. c   10. b

11. d   12. c   13. a   14. e   15. b   16. d   17. d   18. b   19. b   20. d

21. d   22. b

Chapters 24–25

1. e   2. d   3. a   4. a   5. e   6. e   7. d   8. a   9. e   10. d

11. e   12. e   13. b   14. c   15. b   16. d   17. b   18. b   19. d   20. a

21. d   22. d   23. a   24. a   25. e   26. a   27. e   28. b   29. a   30. b

31. c   32. b

Chapters 26–28

1. d   2. d   3. b   4. d   5. b   6. b   7. e   8. c   9. d   10. a

11. d   12. d   13. c   14. e   15. b   16. c   17. c   18. a   19. e   20. a

21. c   22. a   23. a   24. b   25. e   26. d   27. d   28. a   29. e   30. b

31. d   32. b   33. d   34. b   35. c   36. e   37. e   38. b   39. a   40. a

41. a   42. d   43. c   44. e   45. b   46. a   47. d   48. c   49. e   50. d

51. b	52. a	53. b	54. b	55. e	56. c	57. d	58. e	59. b and d	60. a

61. c

Chapters 29–30

1. d	2. d	3. e	4. e	5. a	6. b	7. b	8. c	9. c	10. a
11. e	12. c	13. a	14. c	15. c	16. d	17. c	18. e	19. a	20. e
21. b	22. b	23. d	24. b	25. d	26. a	27. b	28. a	29. d	

Chapter 31

1. c	2. b	3. e	4. e	5. e	6. b	7. c	8. e	9. c	10. c
11. c	12. b	13. b	14. d	15. e	16. e	17. d	18. c	19. b	20. d
21. e	22. c	23. c	24. b						

Chapter 32–34

1. b	2. a	3. b	4. e	5. d	6. a	7. d	8. a	9. d	10. c
11. b	12. c	13. d	14. a	15. d	16. c	17. b	18. c	19. e	

SUMMARY

1. e	2. a	3. b	4. b	5. e	6. c	7. a	8. d	9. c	10. c
11. b	12. e	13. c	14. a	15. b	16. a	17. b	18. a	19. d	20. c
21. b	22. c	23. e	24. b	25. b	26. d	27. d	28. b	29. c	30. e
31. d	32. c	33. e	34. b	35. b	36. a	37. e	38. b	39. a	40. b
41. c	42. a	4. c	44. d	45. c	46. b	47. e	48. a	49. b	50. b
51. d	52. a	53. e	54. a	55. e	56. d	57. e	58. c	59. d	60. b
61. c	62. c	63. d	64. c	65. a					

INDEX

(numbers in italics refer to glossary entries)

ABS (acrylonitrile, butadiene, styrene), 119, 123, 160
Absorbing energy, 149
Absorption of light, 187, 188, 216
Acceptor impurity, 187, 194, *267*
Acetylene, 113
Activated carbon, 15, *267*
Activators, 189, *267*
AC-to-DC converters, 200
Addition polymerization, 114
Adhesion force, 248
Airbus, 91
Aircraft, 85
Alloying element, 95, *267*
Alloys, 1, 22, 81, 85, 93, *267*
Alpha phase, 97
Alternating current, 204, 262
Alumina, 22, 164, 187
Aluminum, 85, 194, 195
Aluminum-lithium alloys, 8, 85
Amorphous materials, 14, 15, 51, *267*
Amorphous metals, 53, 239
Amorphous silicon, 17
Anion, 30, *267*
Anisotropy, 47, 163, *267*
Annealing, 80, 98, *267*
Anode, *267*
Antiferromagnets, 235, *267*
Arsenic, 195
Asbestos, 160
Asymmetric molecules, 255
Atom knock-on, 132, 133
Atomic force microscope (AFM), 249, *268*
Atomic number, 10, *268*
Atomic structure, 11, 13, 62, 241, *268*
Atomic weight, 10, *268*
Attenuation, 223, 227, *268*
Austenite, 97, *268*
Automobiles, 95, 119

Baby oil, 118
Band diagrams, 200, *268*
Band energy diagram, 177, *268*
Band gap, 178, 200, 201, *268*
Battery-eliminators, 200
Bend strength, 69
Benzene rings, 106, 161, *268*

Bimetallic strip, 134
Bioactivity, 259
Biocompatibility, 259, *268*
Biodegradable polymers, 127
Bioinertness, 259
Biological systems, 258, 259
Biomaterials, 2, 257–260, *268*
Biomedical applications, 257, 258
Blend, 122, *268*
Block copolymer, 122, *268*
Blue emission, 200
Body centered cubic (BCC), 44, 98, *268*
Boeing, 91
Boiling conditions, 150
Bonds, 247
Bone bonding, 259
Bony defect repair, 258
Borides, 22
Boron, 13, 187, 195
Brittleness, 137, 210, 241
Bronze, 1
Bunsen burner, 175
Butane, 112

Cadmium phosphate, 189
Cadmium sulfide, 186
Calorie, 174, *269*
Capillary forces, 248, *269*
Carbides, 22
Carbon blacks, 14, *269*
Carbon fiber reinforced plastics, 164, *269*
Carbon fibers, 15, 29, 161, 162
Carbon nanotube-based nanoelectronics, 254
Carbon yield, 165
Carbon, 10, 161
Carbon/carbon composites, 161, 165, *269*
Carbonization, 161, *269*
Cast iron, 1, *269*
Casting, 93
Catalyst, 114
Catastrophic failure, 137, 138, 149
Cathode, *269*
Cation, 27, 30, *269*
CCP crystal structure, 249
Cement, 160
Ceramic magnets, 23, 240

Ceramic scaffolds, 259
Ceramic steel, 150, 151
Ceramic superconductors, 7, 209
Ceramic toughening, 149
Ceramics, 22, 137, 149, *269*
Cesium chloride, 47, 48
Chain branching, 115, 116
Chain crystallization, 49, 106
Chain stiffening, 105
Charge carriers, 207, *269*
Chemical catalysis, 248
Chemical element, 6, 7
Chemical vapor deposition (CVD), 64, 160, 166, 225, *270*
Chromium, 64, 187
Chromium oxide, 241
Close packed planes, 39, 42
Close packed structures, 30, 39, 47
Close packing, 39, *270*
Close-packed layers, 249
Clusters, 249
Cold rolling, 97
Color, 183, 246
Color TV, 190
Combinatorial synthesis, 7
Compact discs, 223
Complementary colors, 185
Composites, 86, 87, 161, *270*
Compression, 71, 139
Compressive strength, 70, *270*
Computers, 208
Concorde, 167
Conductors, 178, 208, *270*
Cooling, 150, 151
Copolymers, 108, 122, *270*
Copper, 22
Core glass, 224
Corelle, 147
Corning Ware, 8, 18, 52, 141
Covalent bonds, 28, 132, 134, 137, 162, *270*
Crack-blunting, 149, 150, *270*
Crack bridging, 149, 150, *270*
Cracking, 114, *270*
Crack propagation, 149, 152
Cracks, 88, 138–140, 143
Crack triggering, 151
Cristobalite, 17
Critical angle, 219, 224, *270*
Critical current, 210, *270*
Critical temperature, 209, *270*
Crosslinking, 105, 120, *270*
Crosstalk, 229, *271*
Crystal growth, 150
Crystal structure, 11, 17, 18, 39, 46, 93, 241, *271*

Crystalline ceramic, 149
Crystalline polymers, 49, 106
Crystallization, 106, 144, *271*
Crystals, 2, *271*
Cubic close packed (CCP), 40, 87, *271*
Cubic crystal structure, 151

Dacron, 108, 119
Debonding, 149, 150, *271*
Defects, 55
Deformation, 43
Degradable plastics, 127
Delta prime, 88, *271*
Density, 85, *271*
Dental amalgams, 258, *271*
Devitrification, 52, 144, *271*
Diamond, 11, 29, 46, 188, 209, *271*
Dimensionless quantity, 72, *271*
Dipole, 33, *271*
Dip-pen nanolithography, 249
Direct current, 200
Directional bonds, 29, 32
Dislocation pile-up, 78, 97
Dislocations, 55, 77, 96, *271*
Dislocation tangles, 79
Dissipation, 254, *271*
Distillation, 64
Domain boundary, 237, *272*
Domains, 235, 236, *271*
Donor impurity, 187, *272*
Doping, 17, 205, 248, *272*
Drain electrodes, 204
Drug delivery, 259
Drug release, 259
Dynamic equilibrium, 131, *272*

Ebonite, 105
Elastic strain, 60, *272*
Elastomer, 103, 119, *272*
Electric current, 27, *272*
Electrical conduction, 180
Electrical energy, 179
Electromagnetic spectrum, 215, *272*
Electromagnetic wave, 215, *272*
Electron density, 218, *272*
Electron glue, 27
Electron hole, 194, 196, 208, *272*
Electron holes, 199
Electron mobility, 207
Electron population, 205
Electron shells, 25, 26, *272*
Electron structure, 10, 16, 17, 241, *273*
Electron volt, 174
Electron-hole pair, 201, *272*

Electrons, 10, 25, 27, 173, 193
Electron recombination, 200, 201
Electrostatic attraction, 27, 30, *273*
Electrostatic field, *273*
Elements, 6, 7
Embryonic stem cells, 260
Emitted light, 183, 189, *273*
Entropy, 120, *273*
Entropic spring, 120
Epoxy resin, 86, 164
Equiaxed microstructure, 12, 98, *273*
Ethane, 111, 112
Ethylene, 113
Europium, 190
Extrinsic (point) defects, 60, *273*

Face centered cubic (FCC), 46, 88, 97, *273*
Ferrite, 97, *273*
Ferromagnets, 235, *273*
Fiberglass, 133, 157
Fiber-reinforced ceramics, 149
Fibrous structure, 5
Field-effect transistor (FET), 204, 205, 254, 255
Fine-grained ceramics, 149
Flame polishing, 139, *274*
Fluorescence, 188, 189, *274*
Fluorescent lights, 183, 189
Fluxing ions, 52
Forward bias, 199, 200
Fracture energy absorption, 149
Free electrons, 27, 132
Friction, 149
Fullerene, 13, 14

Gallium, 195
Gallium arsenide, 24, 200, 208
Gallium nitride, 200
Gamma phase, 97
Gamma rays, 215
Garage door opener, 134
Gate bias, 204, 205
Gate electrodes, 204, 205, 254, 255
Gate length, 253
Gel spinning, 118
Germanium, 225
Giant magnetoresistance (GMR), 251, *274*
Glass-ceramics, see Corning ware, 143, 149, *274*
Glasses, 18, 219
Glass transition temperature, 121, *274*
Glassy carbon, 15
Gold, 22, 184
Gold cube, 246, 247
Gold nanoparticles, 246, 247
Graft copolymers, 123, *274*

Grain boundaries, 2, 96, 149, 204, *274*
Grain refining, 97, *274*
Grains, 2, 12, 97, *274*
Graphite, 11, 34, 134, 162

Hard magnets, 238
Heat treatment, *274*
Hexagonal close packed (HCP), 40, 249, *274*
Hexagonal symmetry, 32
High density polyethylene (HDPE), 117, 125, 126
High impact polymer, 123, *275*
High strength low alloy steels (HSLA), 8, 95, 163, *275*
Hole conductivity, 205
Hole recombination, 200, 201
Hot rolling, 97
Hydrocarbons, 111
Hydrogen bonds, 31
Hydrogen monolayers, 250
Hydroxylapatite ceramics, 258

IC elements, 253, 254
Ice, 32
Imperfections, 55, *275*
Implantable porous metal, 259
Implants, 258
Impurities, 61, 62, 187, 224, 228
Inert gases, 26, 33, 173, 233
Infrared light, 183
Insulator colors, 185
Insulators, 178, *275*
Integrated circuit, 253
Intermetallic compounds, *275*
Interstices, 44, 61, *275*
Interstitial, 60, 61, *275*
Intrinsic (point) defects, 60, 62, *275*
Ion implantation, 140, 253, 254, *275*
Ionic bonds, 29, 132, 137, *275*
Ions, 30
Iron, 1, 238
Iron oxide, 240

Joint replacements, 258

Kevlar, 160

Laminated glass, 142
Lasers, 200, 201, *276*
Lead glass, 221
Leakage current, 254
Light absorption, 184, 216
Light-emitting diodes, 200, 201, *276*
Light energy, 180
Light-sensitive polymer, 248
Lithium, 176

Long range order, 51
Low alloy, 95
Low density polyethylene (LDPE), 125, 126
Luminescence, 188, *276*
Luster, 21, 184, 186, 193

Macrostructure, 13, 98, 241, *276*
Magnesium, 93
Magnesium tungstate, 189
Magnetic anisotropy, 239, *276*
Magnetic domains, 235, 236, *276*
Magnetism, 21, 233
Manganese, 190
Material processing, 6
Materials engineering, 2, 5–8
Materials properties, 6, 246
Materials science, 2, 5–8, *276*
Materials structure, 6
Matrix, 157, 164, 166, *276*
Mechanical strength, 258
Mer, 107, *276*
Mercury vapor lamp, 177
Metal colors, 184
Metal magnets, 234
Metal whiskers, 78, 239, *276*
Metallic bonds, 27, *276*
Metals, 21
Metastable state, 151
Methane, 111, 112, 209
Microelectronics, 253, 254
Micron, *276*
Microstructure, 2, 12, 13, 63, 89, 98,
    152, 241, *276*
Microstructure-property relationships, 259
Microwaves, 215
Minimum feature size, 248, 253
Mirage, 220, 221
Molecular conduction, 255
Molecular electronics, 254, 255, *277*
Molecular ink technique, 249
Molecular self-assembly, 249
Molecular weight, 119, *277*
Monochromatic light, 201
Monoclinic crystalline form, 151
Moore's law, 253, *277*
Multiplexing, 229, *277*
n-type doping, 248
n-type semiconductor, 199, 201, *277*
n-type silicon, 195
Nano-electro-mechanical systems (NEMS), 250, *277*
Nano-imprint lithography, 248, *277*
Nanomagnetism, 251
Nanomaterials, 2, 245–251, *277*
Nanoparticles, 246, 247, 251

Nanophase materials, *277*
Nanosphere lithography, 248, 249
Nanotechnology, 250, 251
Nano-transistors, 254, 255
Nanotube field-effect transistor, 254, 255
Niobium, 98
Nitrides, 22
Nitrogen, 188, 195, 209
Non-directional bonds, 28, 30, 33
Nucleation, 144

Optical fibers, 215, 223, 224
Orlon, 119

p-n junction, 199–202
p-type doping, 248
p-type semiconductor, 199, 204, *279*
p-type silicon, 196
Pancaked microstructure, 98
Paraffins, 111
Paraffin wax, 118
Paramagnets, 234, *277*
Periodic table, 6, 7, 194
Permanent magnets, 237, *278*
Phase, 88, *278*
Phase diagram, 150
Phonons, 132, *278*
Phosphorescence, 188, 189, *278*
Phosphorus, 195
Photolithography, 248, 254
Photomask, 248
Photons, 180, *278*
Photoresist layers, 248, *278*
Pile-up of dislocations, 78, 83, 96, *278*
Pinning of dislocations, 81, 82, 96
Pitch, 161
Plastic deformation, 60, 149
Plastic strain, 70, *278*
Plexiglas, 106
Point defects, 60, *278*
Polar molecules, 31, *278*
Polyacrylonitrile (PAN), 159
Polybutadiene, 121
Polycarbonate, 23, 106
Polycrystalline structure, 95, *279*
Polyethylene, 34, 48, 49, 103, 111, 114–116, 118
Polyethylene terephthalate (PET), 125, 126
Polymer blends, 122
Polymer incompatibility, 125
Polymer photoresist layer, 254
Polymer recycling, 125–127
Polymers, 26, 132, *279*
Polymethyl methacrylate (PMMA), 106, 257, 260
Polypropylene (PP), 107, 125, 126

Polystyrene (PS), 23, 106, 121, 126
Polytetrafluoroethylene, 107
Polyvinylchloride (PVC), 23, 125, 126
Polyvinylidene chloride, 107, 126
Porous metal, 259
Porous structure, 5
Pounds per square inch (psi), 71
Powder metallurgy, *279*
Power dissipation, 254
Power field-effect transistor (FET), 205
Power losses, 254
Precipitate, *279*
Precipitation hardening, 90, *279*
Primary bonds, 30, *279*
Processability, 126
Processing, 9, *279*
Processing-microstructure relationships, 259
Propane, 112
Property-performance relationships, 259
Pullout friction, 149, 150
Pyroceram, 18 (also see Corning Ware), *279*

Quantum mechanical tunneling, 250, 254, 255
Quartz, 18, 133
Quenching, 51, *279*

Radiation, 175
Rapid solidification, *279*
Recombination zone, 199, 200
Recording tape, 237, 241
Recrystallization, 98
Recycled thermoplastics, 126
Recycling, 125–127
Recycling codes, 125, 126
Red emission, 200
Refining, 63, 97
Reflected light, 184, 216, 221
Refraction, 216, 217
Refractive index, 218, *280*
Renewable energy sources, 204
Resorbable materials, 259
Reverse bias, 200
Rubber, 105, 119
Ruby, 187

Safety glass, 148, *280*
Sapphire, 187
Saran wrap, 107
Satellite, 167
Scanning tunneling microscope, 250, *280*
Scattering, 117, 146
Sea of electrons, 19
Secondary bonds, 31, 34, *280*
Seeding, 144, *280*

Self-assembly, 249, *280*
Semiconducting carbon nanotube, 254
Semiconductor colors, 186
Semiconductor diodes, 199, 200
Semiconductor junction devices, 255
Semiconductors, 23, 178, *280*
Shear, 41
Side groups, 121
Signal amplification, 205
Silicon, 7, 8, 16, 46, 179, 181, 186, 193, 200, 203
     204, 248, 254
Silicon carbide, 12, 159, 160
Silicon chloride, 224
Silicon nitride, 159, 160
Silicon oxide, 17, 18
Silver, 185, 210
Silver nanoparticles, 246
Single domain magnets, 238, *280*
Single-walled carbon nanotube (SWCNT), 254
Sintering, *280*
Slip planes, 42, 70, 77, 95, *280*
Slip systems, 43, *281*
Sodium chloride, 47
Soft iron, 238
Soft magnets, 238, 240, *281*
Solar cells, 201, 204, *281*
Solid solubility, 63
Solid solution, 88, *281*
Solubility limit, 88, 150, *281*
Solutionizing, 150, *281*
Soot, 14
Source electrodes, 204
Source-to-drain current, 204, 205
Space shuttle, 133
Specific modulus, 163, *281*
Specific strength, 158, *281*
Spintronics, 250
Stainless steel, 22, 55
Steels, 21
Stem cells, 260
Steric hindrance, 49, 116, *281*
Stiffness, 73
Strain, 72, 73, *281*
Straw, 160
Strength, 69
Stress, 69, 71, 72, *281*
Stress concentrators, 138
Stress field, 151
Substitutional impurity atom, 62, *282*
Substitutional solid solution, 88
Sulfur, 105
Superalloys, *282*
Superconducting transition temperature, 7
Superconductors, 7, 209, *282*

Surface crack, 149
Surface defects, 142
Surface energy, 248
Surface forces, 248
Surface tension, 248
Surface-to-volume ratio, 246, 247

Teflon, 107
Television, 183
Tempered glass, 147
Tensile load, 69
Tetragonal crystal, 151
Thermal energy, 180
Thermal expansion, 134
Thermal shock resistance, 145, *282*
Thermoplastic, 103, 118, 161, *282*
Thermoset, 103
Thermosetting resins, 126, *282*
Thermostat, 134
Tile, 5
Tires, 14, 160
Tissue engineering, 258, 259
Titanium, 187
Titanium-based metals, 258, 260
Total internal reflection, 218, *282*
Toughening mechanism, 151
Toughness, 149, 258, *282*
Transatlantic telephone cable, 55, 228
Transformation zone, 151, *282*
Transformers, 54, 240
Transistors, 253
Transition metals, 234
Transmitted light, 183

Tunneling, 250, 254, 255
Two-phase mixture, 88

Ultimate tensile strength (UTS), 71, 91, 100, *283*
Ultraviolet light, 183
Unpaired electrons, 114

Vacancy, 60–62, 196, *283*
Vacancy motion, 61, *283*
Valence electrons, 10, 28, *283*
Van der Waals bonds, 33, 134, *283*
Viscous, 51
Visible spectrum, 176, 183
Visions Ware, 146
Voltage gradient, 179
Von Mises criterion, 83, *283*
Vulcanization, 105, 119, 120

Water sugar system, 150
Waves, 132,
Whiskers, 78, *283*
Wood, 157, 158
Work hardening, 79

X-rays, 175, 181

Yield strength (YS), 70, 72, 91, 100, *283*
Young's modulus, 73, 91, 100, *283*

Zinc silicate, 189, 190
Zinc sulfide, 190
Zirconia, 150–152
Zirconia-yttria, 150, 151